Third Edition

The Politics
of
Ethnic
and
Racial
Inequality

A Systematic Comparative Macro-Analysis
from the Colonial Period to the Present

J. Owens Smith

K⊟ KENDALL/HUNT PUBLISHING COMPANY
4050 Westmark Drive   Dubuque, Iowa 52002

Contents

Tables

Preface to the Third Edition

The study of the causes of ethnic and racial inequality in America is a very complex and intriguing enterprise. What I attempted to do at the outset of the first edition was to develop a conceptual framework by which groups' socio-economic behavior can be explained on a systematic basis. Although I have received many positive comments for my effort, I still feel the need to fine tune my original conceptual framework in order to bring clarity and empirical accuracy to this area of inquiry.

The major problem with studying the causes of group inequality is that such a task is politically driven. Accompanying any explanation for the causes of group inequality has the potential for policy implications. These implications have divided writers into proponents and opponents of civil rights. In the process, the art of scientific inquiry is too often ignored by writers on both sides.

This eddition is an attempt to restore the art of systematic analysis to this area of inquiry. I rely heavily on evaluating groups' socioeconomic behavior within the framework of the liberal democratic theory and conducting comparative macro-analyses of groups' behavior. Although I am confident that I have made substantial progress in this area, there is still room for improvement. I just hope that other writers, both proponents and opponents of civil rights, would adhere to the principles of systematic research—that is producing theories supported by data.

Fullerton, California   J. OWENS SMITH
September 10, 2003

Preface to the Second Edition

When I first wrote this book, my primary concern was directed toward developing a conceptual framework by which the cause of racial inequality can be explained on a systematic basis. My objective was very simple. First, I was to develop a conceptual framework that could best explain the cause of group inequality with the maximal degree of certainty. Second, I was to identify and isolate those independent variables that could possibly influence the growth and development of racial groups. Finally, I was to marshal forward evidence to support my theory. A survey of the reviews of my book strongly suggests that I was relatively successful in my efforts.

Since the first publication of this book, two arguments have emerged: the "model minority" and the "deficit model" neither were part of my original analysis. I find them to be renegades to my conceptual framework; therefore, I was compelled to bridle them and bring them within purview of my conceptual framework in order to analyze them for their internal consistency. In order to accomplish this goal, I found it necessary to expand my study to cover not only the cause of racial inequality, but ethnic inequality as well—this is the reason for the name change.

The "deficit model" seems to have three underlying premises. First, it contends that the blame for African Americans' lack of economic growth and development must be placed on the backs of African Americans themselves and not on the failure of the national government to fulfill its duty and obligation to protect their rights to a system of protection that safeguarded their civil rights to acquire property and to pursue a wide range of economic and employment opportunities that were previously closed to them.

An analysis of the Pacific Rim groups and the Hispanics—except for the Puerto Ricans, Japanese, and Chinese—was purposely omitted in the first edition of this book. Many members of these groups immigrated in large numbers after the adoption of affirmative action policy. Their subsequent behavior is consistent with the conceptual framework of this study: that is, groups can overcome the effects of discrimination if the government adopts positive laws to safeguard their rights to acquire and possess property.

To further add conceptual clarity to this area of study, I added chapters 9 and 10 to this second edition. The former chapter addresses the controversy centered around the "deficit model," while the latter examines the politics of the "model minority" argument.

In the first edition, I noted that the major shortcoming of the study of the cause of ethnic and racial inequality was not the lack of data but scientific theories to interpret the existing data. A review of the literature finds this still to be the case. In the first edition, I relied heavily on data that was published before the 1970s. I was seeking data that was unadulterated with or supportive of the "deficit model." I used the same approach in this edition.

J. Owens Smith, 1992

Preface to the First Edition

This is not just another book about race and ethnic relations. It summarizes the results of an eight-year study during which I sought a scientific explanation as to why African Americans have been unable to escape the slums, as did the European immigrants. The term "scientific explanation" is to be understood here as a systematic interpretation of the cause of the growth and development of race and ethnic groups in America.

Ever since this question was raised by the Kerner Commission in 1968, there have been countless articles and books written on the subject. A survey of the literature reveals one common denominator: there is not a paucity of data collected on the subject, but a lack of systematic interpretations of the existing data.

One of the major problems with current approaches to the study of the cause of racial inequality is that they lack a conceptual framework that is capable of explaining the causes with empirical accuracy. These approaches consist of writers starting their mode of analysis by constructing speculative theories and making various assumptions that allegedly explain the cause of group success, and then turning their attention on the failure of African Americans, where they proceed to victimize them for their lack of success.

What is consistently absent from the traditional approaches to this study is the lack of a systematic analysis between public policies and theories of group upward mobility. For example, many writers identify groups' cultural values as the cause of their success, without attempting to show a correlation between values, public policy, and the theory of socialization. It is fruitless to discuss groups' cultural values without examining the role that the agents of socialization played in developing and shaping these values.

Because of a lack of systematic analysis in the literature, I was trapped, like other students, in the realm of speculative research concerning the primary reason why African Americans have been unable to escape the slums in the same way the European groups did. Because such an approach was not systematic, I was committed to a never-ending task of defending my theories and arguments.

It was not until I started searching for empirical evidence to support the theories that purport to explain why white ethnic groups were able to elevate themselves to the middle-class plateau that I was able to grasp a handle of the inherent problems in studying the cause of racial inequality. To my surprise, I found that the evidence to support the most widely used arguments was often too flimsy to fit into a scientific argument and that the theories themselves were, at best, speculative.

Conspicuously absent from the literature is a systematic analysis of the role that the government played in the economic success of white ethnic groups. The historical data overwhelmingly supports the theory that white ethnic groups have been able to escape the slums because the government has consistently offered them a system of protection that safeguarded their civil rights to acquire property and to pursue a wide range of employment and economic opportunities—and it failed to do the same for African Americans. This unequal application of the laws has led to and sustained racial inequality.

To avoid the pitfalls of the traditional approaches to the study of racial inequality, I conducted a systematic comparative macro-analysis of the historical experience and immigration/migration of thirteen race and ethnic groups. I began my mode of analysis by examining the economic and political linkages that groups fashioned between themselves and the American polity from the Colonial Period to 1970. I purposely limited my analysis to 1970 because the effect of the civil rights laws is reflected in the data after this period. Briefly, these laws offered African Americans a system of protection that safeguarded their civil rights to acquire property and to pursue a wide range of economic and employment opportunities that were previously closed to them.

The Southeast Asian groups and the Hispanics—except the Puerto Ricans, Japanese, and Chinese—will be excluded from this discussion because these groups immigrated in large numbers after the implementation of affirmative action policy, which constitutes a system of protection.

In the Introduction chapter, I develop a conceptual framework for group analysis. Chapter 2 consists of an analysis of those ethnic groups that immigrated during the colonial period. Chapter 3 consists of an examination of the first and second waves of immigrants who arrived during the early and midpart of the nineteenth century—that is, the Irish, the Germans, and the Scandinavians. This chapter focuses on the differences and similarities in those economic and political linkages that these groups fashioned with the American polity and the ones they had maintained in their homeland.

Chapter 4 addresses the experience of the late-nineteenth-century immigrants–that is, the Italians and the Jews. I advance the argument in this chapter that the human capital that these groups brought with them had a determinative impact upon their rates of adjustment.

In Chapter 5, I examine the experiences of three racial groups: the British West Indians, the Japanese, and the Puerto Ricans. Here, I demonstrate that both the acquisitions of human capital and a system of protection are the best variables that can explain group success.

In Chapter 6, I examine the chief cause of the lack of economic success among African Americans. My basic units of analysis were those laws that foreclosed the freedom of African Americans to elevate themselves onto the middle-class plateau from the end of the Civil War to the 1970s.

Chapter 7 consists of an assessment of group adjustments and the economic and political linkages that groups have fashioned with the American polity in their early stages of contact.

Chapter 8 examines the role that the government played in assisting European groups in elevating themselves up off the beaches of the culture of poverty onto the middle-class plateau.

Introduction

For the last twenty years, I have been working toward developing a conceptual framework that can best explain the causes of group inequality and upward mobility with the maximal degree of certainty. As I mentioned in my second edition, there is no single issue that is so heavily and emotionally charged as the explanations given for the cause of socioeconomic inequality found among ethnic and racial groups in America. The group that has received the most attention during this period has been African Americans. Writers have raised the following question: Why did African Americans not escape the slums as did other groups? This issue, however, is nothing new. Originally, this issue was centered around racial inequality where it was most frequently referred to as "the race problem" or "the Negro problem"[1] during the twentieth century. W.E.B. Du Bois, an African American sociologist, dedicated his entire career to studying the causes of this problem.[2] Gunnar Myrdal's classical study, entitled *An American Dilemma* (1944), identified the African American problem as a "problem in the heart of the American. It is there that the decisive struggle goes on."[3] He further observed that at the core of the problem "is the moral dilemma of the American—the conflict between his moral valuations on various levels of consciousness and generality." He correctly predicted that American society was moving toward two societies: one African American and one white. In 1968, the Kerner Commission on Civil Disorders documented this prediction.[4]

After the publication of the Kerner Commission report, social scientists started advancing various explanations for the reason for African Americans' failure to escape slums. In formulating their arguments, writers have too often selected dependent variables as their basic unit of analysis. A systematic analysis of these arguments and theories will reveal that they are devoid of any major scientific import. These writers can be divided into two camps: the proponents and opponents of civil rights. Proponents seem to have selected racism (which is a dependent variable) as their basic unit of analysis. Opponents, on the other hand, seem to have selected various self-victimization arguments (which are also dependent variables), in which great efforts have been undertaken to place the blame of African Americans' low socioeconomic status on African Americans.

Among these writers, supporters of the self-victimization theories have been the most prolific in cranking out literature to support their arguments. Starting in the early 1970s, writers such as Ben J. Wattenberg, Richard Scammon, and Nathan Glazer became the forerunners of the voluminous articles and books produced during and after the 1970s. More recent writers in this area were Stephen and Abigail Thernstrom who published a 704-page book that was tantamount to nothing more than a reiteration of the self-victimization argument advanced by the previous writers.[5] Essentially, these writers have attempted to advance the argument that African Americans were making marked progress before the adoption of the civil rights laws. From its extreme manifestation, this argument is antithetical to the liberal democratic theory. America has long abandoned the ideal that individuals or groups can secure adequate socioeconomic advancement by instituting their rights to do so among the good will of men.

In the first edition of this book, I attempted to develop a systematic comparative conceptual framework by which groups' behavior can be evaluated on a systematic basis. My main focus was to offer a scientific explanation as to why African Americans have been unable to escape the slum, as did other groups. Thus far, my theory and explanation have withstood systematic scrutiny. No one has come forward to refute my original explanation. Although my theories offered a breakthrough approach to the understanding of the problems in group mobility, there still is a need for a more coherent theory. The problem that I encountered was a lack of data and funds to support research in this area.

Fortunately, the technological breakthroughs in the media solved numerous problems that I had previously encountered in terms of gathering data. First, there was the invention and the proliferation of the personal computer. The PC has significantly reduced the cost in gathering and processing data. Secondly, there was the invention of the Internet, which former Vice President Albert Gore called the "Super Highway." Information that would normally take months and years to gather can now be downloaded from the Internet in a matter of minutes with my PC without leaving the comfort of my home. Third, there was the development of the public broadcasting system (PBS) which broadcasted numerous historical events that operated to fill the information gap that I could not easily obtain or recognize by reviewing the literature in the library.

For example, there was one PBS documentary that provided me with two pieces of information that helped me immensely in documenting and pinpointing precisely how and when the late nineteenth century immigrants were able to escape the slums: the G.I. Bill of Rights and the Levittown projects.

Out of all the literature this writer reviewed, there was no discussion of the role that the Levittown project played in creating and maintaining slums. On the other hand, this writer was unable to find any discussion in the literature on the impact that the G.I. Bill had in the creation of the suburbs and the promotion of education among the late nineteenth-century immigrant groups. These groups' success have always been interpreted as a result of hard work, strong family values, and the internalization of the Protestant work ethic. As will be demonstrated in Chapters 8 and 9, these arguments are dependent variables. These groups were able to escape the slum as a result of government intervention and various forms of subsidies.

In an attempt to address the pitfalls that plague this area of inquiry, I expanded upon the systematic comparative conceptual framework that I had developed in the previous editions of this book. This expansion can be found in Chapter 1. Here I examined the methodological weakness of the traditional arguments and developed a conceptual framework that is capable of identifying those independent variables that can best explain the cause of group mobility with conceptual clarity and empirical accuracy. Chapters 2 and 3 consist of an attempt to identify those independent variables that can explain group mobility for the colonial and the second wave European immigrants of the late eighteenth and early nineteenth centuries. Chapter 4 examines the experience of the Southern Christian and non-Christian European immigrants. Chapter 5 examines the experiences of the racial minority groups. The focus here is to hold the variable race constant in an attempt to isolate and identify those independent variables that can best explain these groups' mobility in America.

Because the status of African Americans has been the major focus of group inequality, I separated them from the other racial minority groups and discussed their experience in Chapter 6. Here, I attempted to identify those independent variables that operated to constrain African Americans' growth and development from the close of the Civil War up to the 1960s. Chapter 7 is an assessment of the socioeconomic linkages that the European immigrants fashioned with the American polity between the period of 1920 and 1970. Chapter 8 offered a scientific explanation as to how the late nineteenth century European immigrants were able to gain an economic foothold in the American economy. Chapter 9 documents the exact time in history, and the means, as to when and how the late European immigrant groups were able to escape the slums. This chapter refutes the traditional arguments used to explain their success, which were mentioned previously.

Chapter 10 consists of an attempt to isolate the independent variables that can best explain the cause of poverty. This chapter deviates from the regular trend of discussing group mobility, because the cause of poverty dominated the discussion of public policy from the 1960s to the present. An attempt is also made to refute the self-victimization arguments advanced by critics of civil rights during the 1970s and 1990s.

From the 1960s to the 1980s, the critics of civil rights pushed the self-victimization arguments. In an attempt to support their argument, they shifted focus from self-victimization to emphasis on the relative success of the Asian population as evidence that race within itself does not constrain group mobility. They started arguing that the Asians were the "model minorities" and that they were able to excel socioeconomically despite their race. They attempted to explain their success within the framework of the traditional arguments, as mentioned. Chapter 11 is an attempt to refute these arguments by identifying those independent variables that can best explain these groups' success.

Chapter 12 discusses the methodological problems that occur as a result of the government lumping all Hispanic groups together. Chapters 13 and14 discuss the experiences of the Spanish-speaking populations. These groups immigrated in large numbers after the passage of the civil rights laws. Prior to the 1980s, these groups were considered, and identified themselves, as white by the federal government. In 1980, the government started identifying them as minorities, thus giving them the same minority status as African Americans. These chapters trace the Mexicans' experience from colonial Mexico to the present, in an attempt to isolate and identify those independent variables that can best explain their current impoverished status.

Finally, the summary and conclusion chapter summarizes the major arguments of this book and offers evidence to support the major arguments advanced to explain the cause of group mobility and inequality.

Notes

1. W.E.B. Du Bois, *The Souls of Black Folk* (Greenwich, Conn.: Fawcett Publications, 1961), pp. 291-92.

2. See *Black Reconstruction in America* (New York: Atheneum, 1983) and *The Philadelphia Negro* (New York: Benjamin Blom, 1967).

3. Gunnar Myrdal, *An American Dilemma* (New York: Harper & Row, 1962), p. lxxi.

4. The Kerner Commission, *Report of the National Advisory Commission on Civil Disorder* (Washington, D.C.: Government Printing Office, 1969), p. 279.

5. See the Summary and Conclusion chapter for a discussion of these writers.

CHAPTER 1

A Framework for Studying Group Upward Mobility and Inequality

This chapter will consist of two parts. First, it will critically examine the methodological weaknesses of the current approaches to the study of the causes of ethnic and racial inequality. Second, it will advance a framework by which group mobility and groups' socioeconomic behavior can be evaluated with empirical accuracy and conceptual clarity.

Methodological Weaknesses

The first major weakness that this writer finds with the approaches to the study of group social upward mobility is that analysts have the tendency to start their mode of analysis with the American polity. Such an approach will automatically force them to make various assumptions about the cause(s) of group mobility that may or may not be true. These assumptions too often fit neatly into one of the traditional arguments that has been advanced to explain group success. For example, the typical argument found in the literature is the old story as to how an individual immigrated to America with nothing but the shirt on his back. He accepted a dirty and low-paying job and subsequently succeeded in building himself a financial empire as a result of hard work.

This same story has also been used to explain group success. Such a story can easily be misleading because it can be masqueraded as containing all of the prerequisites for scientific import by marshaling forward statistical data to support it. The inherent problem with this story is that it overlooks the human

capital that the individuals or groups bring with them. Throughout this study, I
will demonstrate that groups do not immigrate and advance socially and economically without possession of a certain amount of human capital. This human capital is acquired either in their homelands or by certain *de jure* or *de
facto* systems of protection that they receive after arriving in America. (See
below for a discussion of human capital.)

The second methodological weakness is that the current approaches do not
encourage students to classify groups' behavior according to their differences
and similarities. Examining the structural time periods during which groups
immigrated/migrated and the structural conditions both in the groups' homelands and in America will allow us to overcome this dilemma. It is worth noting
here, however, that the structural time period contemplated here is not synonymous with the "social time factor" discussed below. The latter addresses the
lengths of time that groups have been in America, while the former examines
the structural conditions limiting immigration to certain social classes within
these time periods. For example, the Immigration Act of 1917 restricted immigration to the professional, the educated, and the skilled immigrants. This condition is known as the "siphoning effect"; that is, it drew the cream of the crop
of immigrants/migrants and excluded the lower-and-under classes.[11]

The third methodological weakness is the tendency of social scientists to
fall into the intellectual trap of comparing groups' racial characteristics instead
of their interactions with their environment. This method prevents scientists
from comparing groups' behavior on a one-to-one basis. For example, social
scientists tend to compare African Americans' behavior with that of an aggregate of all-white ethnic groups. Their reference to the "melting pot" concept
serves as evidence that they assume that all white groups behave the same,
socially and economically, because of race.

Our greatest data-gathering institution, the United States Bureau of the Census, has helped perpetuate this assumption by collecting data in terms of African Americans, whites, and others. First, this method of data collecting induces
researchers to assume that groups' behavioral patterns are derived from their
biological make-up instead of historical interaction with the economic, political, and social institutions in their society. Second, lumping all white ethnic
groups together obscures the fact that each ethnic and racial group in America
constitutes a functioning subsystem–that is, a political or social unit–within
the whole social system that is "distinct from the rest of the population."[12] It
must be noted here that each group has a set of distinct behavioral patterns that
they developed over periods of time as a result of their interaction with the
economic, political, and social institutions in their homeland. These institu-

limited and defined groups' freedom to pursue certain occupations over generations.

The concept of race relations cycle lends further credence to the argument that ethnic and racial groups constitute subsystems within the whole social system. Stanley Lieberson has argued that racial groups attempt to establish the social order that approximates the one of their homelands in their early and initial stages of contact.[13] The groups with a superordinate social order superimpose their social order upon those ethnic and racial groups whose social order is subordinate to theirs. The latter groups do not totally abandon their social order but maintain a certain degree of autonomy within the framework of the superordinate social order.

In classifying these groups, it will be scientifically fruitful to make a distinction among the three types of subsystems that can be relatively identified as units of analysis within the whole social system; namely: formal, substantive, and normative subsystems. A formal subsystem is a membership system that functions as a distinct economic, political, or social unit within the whole social system and operates on a set of formal rules; that is, the court system, the school system, etc.

A substantive subsystem is a group that can be distinguished from other groups in the whole social system by, what Max Weber called, their "memories of colonization and migration." Classifying groups within this framework will prove fruitful in assessing the behavioral characteristics of the Latino groups. As we shall see, the U.S. Census Bureau mistakenly used language for the basis of categorizing immigrants from the Latin American countries. It lumped all immigrants (both white and Blacks) together and called them the fastest growing minority group in America. As will be discussed in later chapters, this categorization poses several methodological problems.

A substantive subsystem has an internal mechanism for self-containment, which fights against the radical intrusion of foreign membership in their workplaces and neighborhoods. In American society, such a subsystem is usually found clustered around certain organizations of work and has established rules for recruitment which give preference to members of their own.

A normative subsystem is also a group that can be distinguished from a substantive subsystem on the basis of its religious characteristics. Unlike the latter subsystem, a normative subsystem is held together because of its denominational beliefs. What distinguishes a normative subsystem from a substantive one is its economic base. For example, a normative subsystem can be used to explain the religious behavior of all denominational groups such as the Jews, the Catholics, the Protestants, etc., in America, but it cannot be used to explain the economic, political, and social behavior of these groups, as some analysts have attempted. A denominational group (a normative subsystem) is scattered throughout the country in various geographic areas and occupational categories. It is not all-inclusive of persons who can be distinguished from other groups by their memories of colonization and migration. It does not have an economic base by which we can find patterns of economic, political, and social behavior.

The definitions of normative and substantive subsystems often overlap when describing religious groups, but differ when used to describe ethnic groups. For example, the term "Jews" is used to describe both a religious group and an ethnic group. But because of the Jews' historic experience, they are highly concentrated in certain occupational categories and geographic areas. Therefore, we can find patterns of economic and social behaviors among them while the same cannot be found among all Protestants. Hence, for analytic purposes, we will classify all ethnic and racial groups as subsystems based on their memories of colonization and migration.

The fourth methodological weakness to the approaches to the study of the cause(s) of inequality is that writers have the extraordinary propensity to wipe the slate clean of groups' historical experience and begin their mode of analysis with their present day experiences. This approach inadvertently forces them to select variables–both dependent and independent–as their basic unit of analysis. In many instances, a close statistical correlation can be found between these variables and groups' behavior. The inherent problem with this approach is that it promotes the misconceptions about the cause(s) of groups' success or lack of success in America. Once such findings have been published, other writers, too often, are willing to jump on the bandwagon, thus further weakening the methodological approaches to this area of study.

For example, in 1965, Daniel P. Moynihan identified pathology as an independent variable. He advanced the argument that the high rate of single-female head of the family found among African Americans was the primary cause of their lack of social upward mobility.[14] He marshaled forward statistics which strongly supported his argument. However, pathology is a dependent variable caused by some independent variable(s). Notwithstanding this methodological weakness, Edward C. Banfield, a political scientist, immediately jumped on the bandwagon in his book, entitled *The Unheavenly City*.[15] He argued that the pathology of the African American community may be related to "their biologically inherited intelligence." He further argues that "strong correlations have been shown to exist between IQ score and socioeconomic status, and some investigators have claimed that these correlations are attributed to genetic factors."[16] In 1969, Banfield was followed by psychologist Arthur Jensen who carried this pathology argument a step further. He argued that the low status of African Americans was a function of their genetic inferiority, and there is nothing that society could possibly do to improve their socioeconomic status because such improvement presupposes an improvement in their IQ,[17] which is fixed at the point of conception.[18] These reports not only served as the backbone for critics of civil rights to advance the victimization arguments following the publication of the Kerner Commission Report on Civil Disorders but also as the basis to attack current civil and human rights measures designed to secure adequate advancement for African Americans.

One of the politically negative repercussions of the self-victimization argument is that it has an extraordinary tendency to induce proponents of civil rights to offer alternative arguments for the lack of groups' success and to make proposals to secure adequate advancement for them. This was precisely what happened in the 1960s when the government became actively involved in fighting poverty. For example, the internal colonial model advanced by Stokely Carmichael and Charles Hamilton was in response to the criticism of civil rights. They drew an analogy between the African American community and a colony and argued that the primary cause of the state of stagnation and deterioration of the African American community was that it was controlled politically and exploited economically by outsiders, which was a true statement. As a solution to the problem they suggested that African Americans needed to develop an ideology of self-determination.[19] These arguments and counter arguments continued to dominate the literature on the cause of ethnic and racial inequality from the 1960s to the present day.[19]

At the time that Carmichael and Hamilton had advanced the self-determination argument, President Lyndon B. Johnson had already declared a war on poverty as a part of his Great Society programs. The thrust of the poverty programs was to employ the government to take affirmative measures to eliminate poverty among African Americans, and other minority groups. Because of the civil rights movement and social unrest at the time, policymakers--and commentators alike—supported many of the Great Society programs at face value because they were seen as a panacea for resolving the social unrest plaguing society at the time.

The notion that the government should take an active role to eliminate poverty continued during the Nixon Administration. The Republicans found the self-determination argument advanced by Carmichael and Hamilton appealing because it was consistent with their ideology that social problems can better be solved through the private sector. They viewed many of the Great Society programs as "band-aid"approaches to African American problems because they consisted of establishing programs to train them for jobs that did not exist.[20] To resolve this dilemma, they unsuccessfully attempted to give the concept of self-determination the full blessing of the federal government by introducing the Self-Determination Act of 1968.[21] However, this bill was defeated by the Democrats. On the heels of their defeat, the Nixon Administration established several programs (known as minority programs) through executive orders that were designed to promote self-sufficiency among African Americans. These programs consisted of the implementation of affirmative action, establishing minority small businesses, A-8 Set Aside, minority contract programs, and so on.

Before these minority programs could emerge from their infancy, critics launched a protracted anti-civil rights campaign. Their objectives were multifarious. First, their attacks were directed toward casting doubt on the basic premise on which these programs rested in an attempt to convince policymakers that the African American problems should be taken off the public and official agenda.[22] Second, they attempted to argue that social programs contribute to ethnic and racial inequality instead of eliminating it. Finally, they argued that the cause of this inequality can be attributed to factors other than anything that white society has done to African Americans.[23]

The leading advocate against civil rights programs was an African American economist by the name of Thomas Sowell, who suggested that ethnic and racial inequality is not caused by discrimination but by such variables as age, geographical distribution, and fertility rates.[24] He summarily dismissed the role that government played in groups' upward mobility. He argues:

> What determines how rapidly a group moves ahead is not discrimination but the fit between elements of its culture and the requirements of the economy. To get ahead, you have to have some ability to work, some ability at entrepreneurship or something else that society values.[25]

Sowell's argument added fuse to the anti-civil rights propaganda machinery to take civil rights off the public and official agenda in the early 1980s. This movement continued throughout the 1990s into the present. Since the first publication of this book in 1987, there have been various arguments advanced purporting to explain the cause of African Americans' lack of success, all of which are laden with internal contradictions and inconsistencies. Their major default is that they are incapable of systematically identifying those independent variables that influence group behavior. As mentioned previously, Easton argued that theories that are not systematic may prove trivial. A critique of these arguments will shed some light on their inherent defects.

A CRITIQUE OF THE CURRENT THOUGHT PATTERNS

There have been numerous theories advanced to explain the causes of ethnic and racial inequality. In this study, we will examine only the major ones that have withstood the weather of time. They consist of the following: (1) time factors, (2) the Protestant work ethic, (3) racism, (4) the family structure, (5) individualism, and (6) bootstraps. These arguments are articulated within the framework of micro-analysis; however, the inherent problem with micro-analysis is that it forces scientists to narrow their focus at the outset. To validate their research, they have too often drawn from a micro-data base[26] in which they have established axioms and made assumptions about group behavior, which does not always withstand systematic scrutiny. Such methods of research have been partially responsible for the current debate over the causes of ethnic and racial inequality. A critique of each of these arguments will lend credence to this contention.

The Social Time Factor

It has often been argued that the "social time factor" can account for the lack of African Americans' and Puerto Ricans' economic success. This argument has two components. First, some writers have argued that the primary reason for is that they have not had enough time to get adjusted to American urban life.[27] This argument contends that as soon as they make this adjustment, they will adopt middle-class values and achieve economic success, as other immigrants have done. Second, this argument holds that these groups are the newcomers, and when they migrated to the cities, all of the skilled jobs were taken.[28]

The social time theory has several major flaws. First, it is too narrow in scope to explain the magnitude of the problems involved in racial inequality, and the evidence to support it is flimsy. Second, this argument does not account for the technological changes that have taken place in America since the New Deal. For instance, from this period to the present, the American economy has been transformed from smokestack industries to modern technology.[29] Numerous skilled jobs have been created with little, if any, remnants of the old industries. As we shall see in Chapter 8, European groups started acquiring skills only after the government intervened and started subsidizing their training in various national apprenticeship programs. These government subsidized programs were established during the 1930s and lasted to the 1970s and 80s. Until the implementation of affirmative action, African Americans were systematically excluded from participating in these programs solely on the basis of race.

Third, the lack of a pattern of achievement among certain white ethnic groups further weakens the time factor argument. For example, the Jewish immigrants of the late nineteenth century have achieved economic success at a much faster rate than the Irish Catholics, who preceded them by approximately two generations. Furthermore, if the social time factor were the independent variable involved in a group's economic success, the majority of the Irish Catholics should have been clustered at the top of the middle-class stratum of society around the 1920s. But statistics show that the Russian Jews who immigrated during the period between the 1880s and 90s were of a higher socioeconomic status in the 1920s than the Irish. Furthermore, except for the Anglo-Saxon Protestants and the other colonial immigrants, the Irish have been in American cities longer than any other ethnic group. It was not until government intervention with its New Deal programs that the Irish began to escape the slums. As will be demonstrated in Chapter 8, these programs not only subsidized workers in their training and wages but also provided them with a set of property rights which enabled them to secure adequate advancement.

Fourth, the "social time" theory overlooks economic conditions at the time of a group's migration. If the conditions of the economy were an independent variable, then both African Americans and Puerto Ricans should have achieved economic success at a faster rate than some of the European migrants. For example, African Americans migrated to the northern cities during the prosperous years of World Wars I and II. In fact, the war economy was one of the underlying causes promoting their migration North. Unlike the Irish and other poor immigrants who rambled around the country from city to city seeking employment, African Americans had jobs waiting for them when they arrived in the northern cities during the two wars. However, conditions were different during peacetime, as will be demonstrated in Chapter 6.

The Protestant Work Ethic

The Protestant work ethic is one of the most frequently used arguments to explain group success; however, this is more of an assumption than a scientific fact. Writers have attempted to equate this argument with Max Weber's analysis of the rise of the spirit of capitalism among the Protestants. The thrust of this argument is to shift the blame for African Americans' lack of socioeconomic success upon their own shoulders. It holds that the primary reason African Americans have not been able to escape the slums like other groups is that they have rejected the Protestant work ethic. The rejection of this value seems to be a central theme that scientists use to justify African Americans' oppression. For example, in 1968, Edward C. Banfield argued that, in order to get ahead, it requires the "ability to discipline oneself to sacrifice present for future gratification."[30] Twenty two years later, this argument was still a dominant theme in the literature as evidenced by the study conducted by Stanley Lieberson in 1980. He wrote that some scholars "have argued that personality, orientation to work, and expectations about work all affect a group's chances. In turn, it is claimed that [African Americans] on the aggregate had less favorable characteristics than did some of the European groups."[31]

Notwithstanding the lack of scientific import, the Protestant work ethic argument has to be rejected as an independent variable for two basic reasons. First, it did not help the Protestants, who created the work ethic, to escape the slums. The Protestants broke with the Catholic Church in the 1520s, but they did not start leaving the slums until after 1696 (some 171 years later), shortly after John Locke published his *Second Treatise of Government*. In this book, Locke spelled out the duty and responsibility of the government in protecting man's property rights. This duty and obligation derived from the fact that the government had an implied "social contract" by the mere fact men united themselves into a commonwealth; the chief end for men forming a commonwealth was the protection of their property. The government must do this, Locke argued, by adopting positive laws to determine the distribution of property.

It was only after the Protestants started demanding that the government fulfill its duty and obligation in protecting man's property rights that they started escaping the slums. Such protection was imperative because the Protestants considered the accumulation of property as evidence of individual salvation. Without such protection, man's salvation was in jeopardy. Any official of the King could knock on a farmer's door and demand his property in the name of the King. The refusal to comply with this demand constituted treason, which was a capital offense.

Another reason for rejecting the Protestant work ethic as an independent variable to explain group upward mobility is that if we look around today and try to identify the hardest working group, we will find the Mexican farm-migrant workers. This group works from sun—up to sun—down, seven days a week, during certain seasons. As long as they continue to work under the conditions which they are forced to work, they will never raise themselves above poverty.

The above arguments are not to be understood as a rejection of hard work as a value. It simply means that hard work by itself will not elevate groups or individuals to the middle class. Hard work is inherent in lower class status. As will be demonstrated throughout this book in general and particularly in Chapter 8 and 9, white ethnic groups did not make it to the middle class plateau by hard work but by the system of protection and the government subsides offered them in the form of free land, collective bargaining laws, fringe benefits, subsidized home mortgages, and so on.

The Family Structure Argument

The pattern of female-headed households found among African Americans was identified by Daniel P. Moynihan as the chief cause of their lack of economic success in urban America.[32] Subsequently, social scientists started referring to this high rate of female-headed households as broken families, and therefore, dysfunctional. This movement precipitated counter arguments. The family structure argument subsided somewhat around the 1970s. However, it was resurrected again in the early 1980s by African American conservatives. At the heart of this argument are the assumptions that (1) the family structure is an independent variable that can explain group upward mobility, and (2) the institution of slavery destroyed African Americans' nuclar family structure, consequently affecting their capacity to function in American society after emancipation.

Moynihan attempted to validate his family structure argument by comparing the economic success of the European ethnic groups and their apparently cohesive family structure with those of African Americans. Such comparison will always yield a close statistical correlation between race and group socioeconomic attainment because what is being compared is not racial but class behaviors.

Andrew Billingsley, Herbert Gutman, Robert Hill, and Charles Willie have offered counter evidence to Moynihan's theory that African American families are dysfunctional. Basically, they marshaled forth evidence to prove that the African American family was not particularly disorganized either during slavery or in the early period of African American migration.[33] Although the African American family may be headed by a female, they argued, it is still a functional unit.[34]

There are numerous other arguments—both pros and cons—about the role that family structure plays in a group upward mobility that need not to be rehashed here. Suffice it to say that these arguments are plagued with the same problems as the other arguments purporting to explain group upward mobility; that is, they are devoid of scientific import. What strips the family structure argument of its scientific import is the lack of a clear definition of a strong family structure. There are a lot of discussions, both pro and con, about this topic but no definition. Before family structure can be selected as an independent variable to explain group upward mobility, it first has to be defined in such a way as to withstand systematic scrutiny. Once defined, social scientists will be on a more solid scientific foundation to marshal forward evidence to support the argument that the family structure is an independent variable in group upward mobility.

For example, if a strong family structure is defined as a family having values of helping each other to get ahead and to share in solving each other's social problems, then we can find such patterns of behavior among immigrant groups, regardless of race and ethnicity. Writers can always find a close correlation between group upward mobility and family cohesiveness. A close examination of this pattern of behavior will reveal that race and ethnicity are coincidental variables. The independent variable will be the coping strategies that groups adopted for survival. This pattern of behavior can be found largely among the first generation of immigrants.

To use a metaphor, when a group immigrates to America, they travel by boat. Upon their arrival, they burn the boat. Once the boat has been burned, that is no possibility of returning home. Consequently, the group tends to turn its energy inward and focus on using whatever resources they have for survival. This necessitates lending each other a hand and sharing resources. This practice extends beyond the nuclear family to ethnicity. This type of behavior can best be described as group interdependency. Social scientists have misconstrued this behavior as an independent variable that can explain group upward mobility.

The pattern of group interdependency found among immigrant groups tends to fade out in the second and third generations as a result of the group internalizing the American cultural value of individualism. Once this cultural value is internalized, there will be very little evidence of a pattern of family members helping each other. The principle of individualism posits the notion that each individual is responsible for his own action. This principle is practiced more widely among the American middle class than among the lower class.

A close examination of the behavioral patterns of lower class families will reveal a higher degree of cohesiveness and family support. The reason for such support is not because of any emphasis placed on family values but the value of survival. They come to depend upon each other for survival because they do not have anything else on which they can rely. They are socially dispossessed and are not connected to the mainstream of society's income redistribution system. (This system will be explained later.) Consequently, they have neither job security, which offers them fringe benefits, nor a line of credit, such as credit cards, where they can purchase the basic necessities of life on credit. Such dispossession becomes a driving force that forces lower class populations to become interdependent.

The pattern of group interdependency has no respect for race or ethnicity. Such patterns of behavior can be found among immigrant groups such as the lower class Hispanic farm workers. Once this group began to internalize the American middle class value of individualism, then the principle of strong family values, i.e., group interdependency, begin to dissipate. This usually occurs during their second or third generation stay in America.

It must be noted here that group interdependence is not always found among lower class migrants. Take, for example, African Americans and the Puerto Ricans. They both are American citizens. The metaphor of burning the boat after migration does not apply to them. When they migrated from their origin of birth to the northern urban areas and, perchance, found it difficult to get adjusted, they always had the option of returning home with the intention of returning some day. They do not have to worry about immigration laws and the possibility of being unable to return to the urban areas again.

The notion of group interdependency and cohesiveness may, on the surface, seem to lose some of its scientific import once we consider behavioral patterns of some Asian groups. The group interdependency found among these groups is not necessarily a function of their coping strategies but more of their cooperative value system. They do not subscribe to the American cultural value of individualism which is based on competitiveness. Their cooperative value system prescribes them to seek to improve the status of the group. This behavioral pattern seems to be intergenerational.

The above analysis has pointed out some of the shortcomings of a micro-analysis in evaluating family structure as an independent variable in group upward mobility. What social scientists have been calling strong family structure and values have been patterns of group interdependency which is found largely among first generation of immigrants.

The family structure argument, both pro and con, have one thing in common; they ignore the role that the government plays in promoting family disorganization. Once reviewed within the framework of the liberal democratic theory, social scientists will find that the disintegration of the family structure is a function of government action. As we will see in Chapter 10, the ethnic group that is noted for having strong family values and ties began to tear apart at the seam before government intervention in the 1940s.

Viewed within the framework of the liberal democratic theory, we will be able to examine family structures in relation to public policy and the process of socialization. Specifically, we will be able to evaluate the impact of discrimination in educational policies and resource allocation based on race. For example, a review of the literature will reveal that the most famous landmark decisions handed down by the United States Supreme Court have centered around discrimination in education.[35] Therefore, educational policies should be a basic unit of analysis in studying family structures. Embedded in the system of education are key variables such as cultural values, family values, and groups' orientation toward work.

Racism and Racial Prejudice

"White racism is essentially responsible for the explosive mixture which has been accumulating in our cities since the end of World War II," states the Kerner Commission Report on Civil Disorder.[36] The inherent problem with this argument in explaining African Americans' lack of economic success is that it has (1) the tendency to explain everything and nothing at the same time, (2) an extraordinary propensity to cloud government actions that operated to deprive African Americans of their civil rights to acquire and possess property and to pursue a wide range of economic opportunities, and (3) a tendency to reduce scientists' analyses from a macro- to micro-analysis.

In our systematic comparative macro-analysis, the term "racism" needs a more precise definition than the one given in current literature. For example, Stokely Carmichael and Charles Hamilton constructed a schema in which the term *racism* could be viewed as covert (institutional) and overt (racial prejudice) actions.[37] Before Carmichael and Hamilton's definition, racism was thought of as an attitudinal phenomenon. Consequently, the critics' argument against anti-racist legislation was that attitudes could not be legislated. This argument overlooks the fact that racial attitudes are short-lived unless they are sanctioned by government actions.

The current definition of racism is too loose to fit into a systematic comparative macro-analysis. It allows European ethnic groups to falsely claim that they too have been victims of past discrimination; and that, they have overcome this adversity through hard work and strong family values. The corollary to this argument is that "We have made it and African Americans can do the same if they would only straighten out their sexual mores, live in a nuclear family, and internalize the Protestant work ethic."[38] Hence, this line of argument diverts social scientists' attention from government actions and focuses on self-victimization analyses.

Within our schema, the term "racism" is broken down to make a distinction between attitudinal phenomena, which are protected by the First Amendment (freedom of expression), and public policies, which operate to foreclose groups' freedom to acquire and possess property and pursue economic opportunities.

Under the United States Constitution, a citizen has a constitutionally protected right to express his opinion on any subject. However, there are certain constraints placed on his freedom for the purpose of regulating public safety and safeguarding the individual's property interest rights to his reputation. As will be demonstrated in this book, it was not simply a matter of racial attitudes that constrained African Americans' socioeconomic growth and development, but those public policies that they supported these attitudes.

It is scientifically unfruitful to argue that a group has become the victim of past discrimination unless government actions are selected as the basic units of analysis. The evidence to support such a contention would be flimsy at best. It follows then that, in order to validate an argument of past discrimination, social scientists must identify laws, regulations, statutes, or existing rules or understanding stemming from government action, which granted some groups rights to secure adequate advancements and at the same time deprived the same to other groups that were similarly situated.[39] Such denial must not be related to any proper government objective.[40]

In the present-day affirmative action policy, the courts use statistics to determine whether an agency is discriminating against a particular group. These statistics may prove useful to determine whether companies are in compliance with government regulations, but they are inadequate for scientists to use in an attempt to validate a public policy of past discrimination. Instead, these scientists must search for evidence of government action that operated (1) to foreclose a group's freedom to pursue those occupations common to life, and (2) to saddle them with the disability of race such as a stigma, or other disabilities, so as to foreclose their freedom to take advantage of these opportunities.

Within this schema, we can find sufficiently strong evidence to support the claim that African Americans have been the victims of past racial discrimination in the area of employment and educational opportunities. But evidence to support the argument that European groups have been victims of past discrimination is flimsy at best. What European immigrants have been calling past discrimination has consisted mostly of overt attacks on certain groups and an offensive propaganda campaign against them. These acts, in many cases, were short-lived and did not consist of government actions. But when the term past discrimination is used in this study, it is to be understood as government action, either *de jure* or *de facto*, which operated to deprive an entire group of the freedom to connect themselves to the mainstream of society's income redistribution system. (A definition of this term follows.)

The major problem with the term racial discrimination is that there is no legal definition of the term in the American system of jurisprudence. The lack of such definition has hamstrung the United States Supreme Court in making a consistent ruling on race every time it considers a case of "reverse discrimination." The California Legislature has addressed this problem by adopting a definition of "racial discrimination" from the Convention of the Elimination of All Forms of Racial Discrimination. This human rights treaty was adopted by the U.S. Senate in 1994. It defines "racial discrimination" as "exclusion."

Throughout this study, various forms of racism will be discussed which will include those racial doctrines, practices, and policies that operate to exclude an entire group from being connected to the mainstream of society's income redistribution system. There are two major racial doctrines that have historically been used to oppress racial groups: *romantic racialism* and *Social Darwinism.*[41] But there are numerous practices of racial discrimination such as *de jure, de facto, invidious discrimination*, and *insidious discrimination*[42] just to name a few. Regardless which form of racism we are considering, it must operate to exclude an entire group from connecting itself in substantial numbers to the mainstream of society's income redistribution system.

Racial discrimination is not found in skin color alone. Just because a group is nonwhite does not automatically subject it to a policy of racial discrimination. As we will see, race did not constrain the growth and development of the British West Indians, who are of African descent the same as African Americans. On the other hand, race does not guarantee a group success as we will demonstrate with the Irish-Catholics.

Finally, there is a big distinction between acts of racial discrimination and a policy of racism. An act of racial discrimination does not always operate to subordinate an entire racial group whereas a policy of racism does. An act of racial discrimination is short-lived as it was with the case of the Japanese being placed in the concentration camps during World War II. This act did not have a long-term effect on their socioeconomic growth and development. To have such an effect, a policy has to transcend a generation whereby certain agroup is stripped of its human capital. As will be demonstrated, this did not happen to the Japanese because they were incarcerated less than ten years.

In order to bring conceptual clarity in this study, the terms racism and racial discrimination will be defined as the "politics of exclusion." This form of discrimination is not to be found in the expression of racial slurs such as the use of the "n" word, but in those public policies that operate to foreclose an entire group's freedom to take advantage of a wide range of socioeconomic opportunities.

The Bootstrap Theory

Social scientists and commentators alike have often asked the following question: "Why do African Americans not pull themselves up by their own bootstraps as did the European immigrants?" This question is predicated on the false assumption that all European immigrants came over poor and poverty stricken. They accepted dirty and low-paying jobs, the argument goes, worked hard, and subsequently pulled themselves up by their own "bootstraps."[43] This argument is little more than partisan exaggeration. It has too often clouded the interrelationship between boots, bootstraps, and the economic success of groups. To clarify this issue, it is necessary to analyze the functions of the bootstraps concept separate from the boots.

In order to obtain a clearer understanding of this relationship, it is scientifically fruitful to formulate some hypotheses about (1) groups' status in their homelands before emigration, (2) the factors that precipitated their immigration/migration, and (3) their relative status in relation to dominant groups in their new place of settlement.

The most common factor precipitating emigration for most groups was the downward mobility they experienced in their homeland. There they were being pushed off the middle-class plateau onto the beachheads of the culture of poverty.[44] To avoid succumbing to the culture of poverty, they immigrated to America. However, when they arrived, they did not settle on the middle-class plateau but, unfortunately, on the beachheads of the culture of poverty in the new land. They remained there until the government issued them a set of bootstraps.

A pair of boots without bootstraps may prove useless in helping groups acquire economic security and success. The bootstraps are what fastens boots around a runner's feet so that he can run the race with ease. Once securely fastened to his feet, the runner can concentrate on winning the race and not having to worry about losing his boots during the race. In terms of a group's economic success, "bootstraps" serve as a system of protection that locks groups into the economic system and provides them with a sense of job security. According to the Weberian theory of social upward mobility, with such a secutity, a group can to plan for the future with calculation.[45] They will be in a position to take advantage of the many economic opportunities that society has to offer.

Hence, it takes more than hard work and the acceptance of dirty and low-paying jobs to escape the slums United States. From the end of slavery to the present day, African Americans have been forced to work hard at such jobs. They have done so not because of a cultural value to get ahead but out of necessity for survival. They attempted to follow the rules of success from their extreme manifestation. That is, they worked hard, delayed present gratifications for future ones only to discover that their freedom to job upward mobility had been foreclosed by a set of structural arrangements. It has been well documented that African Americans have worked hard to send themselves and their children to college only to find that their job opportunities were restricted to low-paying jobs such as janitors, elevator operators, dishwashers, or jobs as clerks at the Post Office. The political irony here is that they could have gotten the same jobs without obtaining even a high school diploma. This restriction is better known as "job ceiling" which was sanctioned by the government.[46] They did not have a system of protection. Let us turn to a discussion of the importance of this system of protection.

A Framework for Analyzing Group Mobility

Missing from the literature in the area of group mobility is an analytical framework that can explain a group's upward mobility on a systematic basis. As David Easton has perceptively noted, to repeat, research must be systematic. That is, theory must be supported by data and data must be tutored by the theory; otherwise, the research may prove trivial.[47] The approaches discussed previously (which are micro-analytical in nature) fall within this category because they have proven not to be systematic and thereby devoid of scientific import.

In order to add conceptual clarity and empirical accuracy to this area of inquiry, let us turn to developing a conceptual framework by which groups' upward mobility can be explained on a systematic basis (i.e., stating a proposition and drawing a conclusion). Such a conceptual framework must be a macro-analysis in nature and capable of withstanding systematic scrutiny. Take for example, the proposition if P, then Q. Let us assign P as the independent variable that represents the strong family structure argument. Let us assign Q as the dependant variable representing a group's rate of upward mobility. This proposition argues that P (strong family structure) causes Q (group upward mobility). In order for this statement to be true, every group that has sucin America has done so because of their strong family structure. If we can identify a group that has a reputation for a strong family structure and remained impoverished for more than two generations after their arrival in America, then this theory is false because it does not withstand systematic scrutiny. Such group success can be attributed to something other than their strong family structure. For example, the Jews have a reputation of having a strong family structure. As will be demonstrated, they arrived in the 1880s and '90s and remained pinned down on the beachhead of the culture of poverty (see page 26 for a definition of the term) for more than two generations. They only started escaping the slums after the 1950s.[48] Whatever caused them to escape the slums during this period was not their strong family structure, but something else, which will be discussed in Chapters 8 and 9.

The Liberal Democratic Theory

In all of the literature, it seems that writers have overlooked the utilitarian value of the liberal democratic theory in their analysis of the cause of group upward mobility and inequality. This oversight can be attributed, in part, to the fact that writers have viewed this theory as having one application: regressive; but it has another application: progressive. Traditionally, students have used the regressive application of this theory to justify individuals' right to own private property. A closer examination of this theory will reveal that its progressive application can be used to explain group mobility with a high degree of internal consistency. Particularly, it can be used to justify the need for progressive programs such as civil rights and affirmative action programs. Opponents have tried to downplay this application of this theory by arguing for a limited governmental role in civil rights. Throughout this study, it will be demonstrated that the progressive application of the liberal democratic theory is scientifically fruitful in explaining the cause of group mobility on a systematic basis.

The progressive application of the liberal theory can be found in John Locke's definition of property rights, i.e., life, liberty, and estate "which I shall call by general name, property."[49] Throughout his book, entitled *Second Treatise of Government*, Locke hammered home the duty and obligation of the government to adopt positive laws to determine the distribution of property.[50] The chief end for men forming a commonwealth, he argued, was "the preservation of their property; to which in the state of nature there are many things wanting."[51]

The progressive component of the liberal democratic theory can be found in Locke's hypothetical state of nature. In this state, Locke set out to demonstrate how men come to have a property interest in anything. For in the state of nature, he argues, man had the perfect freedom to do whatever he saw fit for the preservation of his nature. But when he joined other men to form a common-wealth, he transferred many of those rights to the commonwealth (the state or national government) to be regulated for the public good. One right, however, man can never transfer to the state is his right to preserve himself. Man, Locke argued, has an obligation to preserve himself. The commonwealth, according to Locke, has a duty and obligation to safeguard men's property rights to a means of subsistence. It must do this by adopting positive laws (i.e., affirma-tive action). Whenever the government fails to fulfill this obligation, then it forces men to resort back to their original state of nature (i.e., the natural state of war). In this state, Thomas Hobbes argues, "there is no place for industry; because the fruit thereof is uncertain."[52] The state of war, he maintains, does not consist of the "actual fighting: but known disposition thereto, during all the time there is no assurance to the contrary."[53]

Locke took Hobbes' notion of the natural state of war a step further. He argued that whenever the state fails to fulfill its duty and obligation to protect men's property rights to a means of subsistence, then they have the right to revolt. For the state would be indirectly asking them to take their own lives. This, Locke maintains, is a right that man does not have. Life is God given and man has no right to part with something that is not his to give.

Based on the political philosophies of both Hobbes and Locke, we can now see the dominant role that the liberal democratic theory has historically played in groups' economic growth and development, regardless whether we are ex-amining their experience in America or in their homeland. The theory of up-ward mobility applies in all cases.

From its very inception, America has adopted an economic system that is based on capitalism—which thrives on competition. At first, Americans relied on *laissez faire*, or the *invisible hand*, to regulate the economy. They soon dis-covered the defects of this system and gradually moved from this mode of domination to a mixed economy.

The concept of a mixed economy and the liberal democratic theory are in-separable. Here, one sees why James Madison was so concerned about safe-guarding man's natural rights against the tyranny of the majoritarian rule. In his Federalist Paper No. 47, Madison argued that there will be a "severe depri-vation" of natural rights when the accumulation of all powers (i.e., the legisla-tive, executive, and the judiciary) is concentrated in the same hands, regardless of whether it is in the hands of the minority or majority. Robert Dahl, a contemporary political scientist, restructured Madison's theory in the following propositions, which are applicable to the understanding of the basic causes of ethnic and racial inequality.

> If unrestrained by external checks, a minority of individuals can be expected to tyrannize over a majority of individuals. . . . If unrestrained by external checks, a majority of individuals will tyrannize over a minority of individuals.[54]

In a competitive market, we can expect management to tyrannize over the property rights of their employees unless external checks and balances are placed over its powers. There always exists an adversarial relationship between employers and employees. Employers, first of all, operate within the Adam Smith's *laissez faire* model, which subscribes to the principle of self-interest and self-preservation. Locke argues that the inalienable rights of the individual are preserved by his acquiring and accumulating property. That is, he is constantly working in his own self-interest to acquire more property. Therefore, it is within the self-interest of management to maximize its profits. One means of doing so is to reduce the cost of labor. This, in turn, reduces the rights of workers to acquire and possess property.

If we apply both the Madisonian theory of democracy and Lockean liberal democratic theory to explain groups' economic success, we can expect a severe deprivation of workers' civil and human rights to economic upward mobility. For there can be no group job upward mobility if all of the decisions concerning hiring, wage, promotion, and layoff are concentrated within the domain of managerial prerogatives. For employers will have absolute authority over the rights of employees to climb the economic ladder. As we shall see in later chapters, the late nineteenth-century immigrants were not able to elevate themselves to the middle-class plateau until the national government stepped in and adopted a set of positive laws to safeguard their rights to acquire and possess property. On the other hand, it refused to do the same for African Americans before the 1960s (i.e., the passage of the civil rights acts and other measures). Their rights have historically rested on the goodwill of their adversaries (employers) and competitors (European immigrants). Such construction is inconsistent with the liberal democratic theory, that is, a government of laws and not of men.

Now that we have discussed the progressive application of the liberal democratic theory, let us turn to constructing a theory that is capable of explaining groups' upward or downward mobility on a systematic basis.

A THEORY OF GROUP MOBILITY

In order for a group to "make it" to the middle-class plateau collectively, to hypothesize, it needs two things: a pair of boots and a set of bootstraps. A pair of boots consists of human capital. The term *human capital* is to be understood here in the same sense as it was defined by economist Gary Becker. He identified many variables as human capital, but for the purpose of this study, we are concerned only with the following four variables: (1) on-the-job training, (2) acquiring skills, (3) education, and (4) knowledge of how the economic and political systems work.[55] In order to acquire human capital, a group must have the freedom to interact in a human capital environment. This freedom can be protected either by *de facto* or *de jure* policy. (The terms freedom and liberty will be used interchangeably throughout this book as meaning "freedom" within the framework of the Lockean definition.) A *de jure* policy consists of a set of positive laws. A *de facto* policy exists by facts. That is, there are no laws restricting a group's freedom to take advantage of life opportunities that are common to society.

To compete on an equal footing in a competitive society, to hypothesize, a group must be guaranteed the freedom to acquire a sufficient amount of human capital. Without such capital, members of that group will not be able to take advantage of the wide range of economic opportunities that society has to offer. The government can adopt positive measures to promote equality of opportunities, but if members of a group do not have the necessary skills to take advantage of these opportunities then such an endeavor may prove fruitless. As we shall see in Chapter 3, this is precisely what happened to the Irish-Catholics.

Human capital also consists of social credentials such as academic degrees and other symbols of social values. These values can be acquired on an individual basis through hard work and adhering to the spirit and letter of the Protestant work ethic or, as Banfield has argued, by delaying present gratifications for future ones.[56] But in order to make it to the middle-class plateau collectively, a group needs a set of bootstraps.

A set of bootstraps must be government issued. It consists of a system of protection, either *de facto* or *de jure*,[57] that safeguards groups' freedom (1) to interact in a human capital environment, (2) to pursue those economic and employment opportunities that are considered common to life,[58] and (3) to connect themselves to the mainstream of society's income redistribution system.

Without a set of bootstraps, to hypothesize, a group will be pinned down on the beachheads of the culture of poverty by their competitors and adversaries until the culture of poverty itself begins to develop among them. Once developed, it has an extraordinary propensity for self-perpetuation from generation to generation, namely through process of intergenerational downward mobility. (A definition of this term follows.) This proposition of bootstraps will render the additional arguments such as a hard work, strong family structures and values, internalizing the Protestant work ethics, IQ deficit, and so on, null and void. It will allow students to conduct a systematic comparative analysis of group behavior with a high degree of internal consistency regardless of whether the students are studying the cause of group upward mobility or their downward mobility.

The culture of poverty is analogous to Hobbes and Locke's notion of the natural state of war. In this state, man's behavior can be predicted with a relatively high degree of accuracy. That is, he is going to do "whatsoever he thinks fit for the preservation of himself and others."[59] As will be demonstrated in Chapter 10, group behavior such as a high rate of crime, prostitution, gang killings, drug peddling, single-family structures, and welfare dependencies and more are nothing more than symptoms of a group that has been forced into the natural state of war. Historically, groups have remained in this state until the national government intervened by issuing them a set of bootstraps and means for acquiring a pair of boots (human capital).

The political significance of the relationship between bootstraps and the freedom that provides individuals to connect themselves to the mainstream cannot be overemphasized. This relationship can help social scientists to identify the independent variables that can best explain group inequality, thereby avoiding the pitfalls in which students of micro-analysis have fallen.

The bootstraps provide individual members within a group the freedom to connect themselves to the mainstream of society's income redistribution system. This system consists of trade, commerce, and real estate. It is the mother lode of society's system of wealth. Embedded within this system are various sources of income: (1) income from labor, (2) income from property, (3) supplementary income payments,[60] (4) subsidized mortgages, and (5) tax credit for home mortgages, as we shall see in Chapters 8 and 9.

Being connected to the mainstream of society's system of wealth is necessary for the individual to be able to take advantage of the wide range of economic opportunities that society has to offer. For example, the most commonly recognized system of accumulating wealth in America is the liberty to buy a home in an area where property values appreciate. As will be demonstrated in Chapter 9, the federal government spent billions of dollars in subsidies to construct homes in the suburbs between the period 1949 and 1969. It allowed the Federal Housing Administration to adopt rules and regulations that operated to foreclose African Americans' freedom to take advantage of these government *bonanza giveaways* solely on the basis of race. As a result, they were not able to grow and develop socioeconomically like other groups. As will be demonstrated in later chapters, many African Americans were able to become millionaires after the government adopted positive laws (the Fair Housing Act of 1968) to protect their freedom to take advantage of the opportunities in the real estate market.

Examining the relationship between a group's connection to components of the mainstream and their socioeconomic status in society can explain many of the disparities that social scientists have found in group behavior. The manner in which a group is connected to the mainstream determines their class status. What many of the social scientists have identified as racial characteristics have in fact been characteristics of class.

For example, the economic linkages to which an individual connects himself to the mainstream of society's income redistribution system will determine his capacity to accumulate wealth. This system, to repeat, consists of trade, commerce, and real estate. An individual has to be connected to two of these linkages in order to be able to take advantage of the socioeconomic opportunities that society has to offer. A trade consists of any skilled occupations such as artisans, craftsmen, and professionals. Commerce consists of the selling of goods and services for a profit. Real estate consists of real property such as housing, land, and commercial property.

In order to accumulate wealth in the American society, an individual has to be connected to two linkages of the mainstream (i.e., trade, commerce, and real estate). Those individuals who are connected to commerce are by operation connected to all three of these linkages. Managing commerce is also a trade. An analysis of how groups are connected to these linkages can explain the cause of inequality found between individuals and groups. Groups and individuals who are connected to all three linkages would always have a higher income than those who are connected to only two of these linkages. This proposition renders the traditional practice of comparing the income of whites with that of African Americans scientifically fruitless. Such a comparison tells us nothing about the economic linkages to which both groups are connected. For example, African Americans have found employment opportunities more favorable in the public sector than the private, whereas, whites have traditionally been employed in the private sector. By operation, the latter sector can offer a wide range of fringe benefits that the public sector cannot offer by law. These benefits have a determinative effect in determining income differences.

The government can adopt all sorts of policies designed to improve the conditions of life for society. These policies can be stripped of any racial bias, but if a racial group is not connected to the mainstream in substantial numbers, their members will not be able to take advantage of these opportunities. For example, the 1964 Civil Rights Act prohibits racial discrimination in public accommodations such as hotels and motels. But before anyone, regardless of race, can check into these facilities, they must have a valid credit card. In order to obtain such a card, they must have a job paying middle-class income. In order to obtain such a job, they must have a college education or some other job skilled. In order to obtain such training, these individuals must be granted the freedom to interact in a human capital environment.

Now that we have established a framework to evaluate the cause of group mobility, let us turn to stating the basic argument of this book.

No group or individual has been able to make to it the middle class without a system of protection, which could have been either *de jure* or *de facto*. Groups have acquired middle-class status as a result of conditions either in their homeland or after the government issued them a set of bootstraps upon their arrival to America.

Once a group reaches middle-class status, their mobility becomes intergenerational. The socioeconomic success that social scientists have been attributing to such variables as hard work, strong family structure, and the Protestant work ethic, have been a function of intergenerational mobility among that group. Many social scientists have fallen victims to the "fireside chats" that they have heard from their parents. In an attempt to inspire them, their parents tell them how they came over with nothing but the shirt on their back and how they were able to pull themselves up by their own bootstraps.

What is missing from these "fireside chats" is the fact that their parents immigrated with the necessary skills to compete in a competitive society. Their success is more a function of intergenerational mobility than their pulling themselves up by their bootstraps. Any immigrant over the age of 16 who immigrated legally after the passage of the 1917 Immigration Act was indeed in the middle class or were skilled workers. This phenomenon can explain why groups such as Asians and West Indians can come over and establish flourishing businesses in the so-called "ghettoes" and African Americans cannot. The former groups immigrate with the necessary entrepreneurial skills to compete successfully in a competitive society.

Intergenerational Mobility

The term *intergenerational mobility* will be used throughout this book to explain the upward and downward mobility of groups and individuals. Its basic premise is that groups that immigrate to America over the age of 16 are by operation in the middle class. The immigration laws restrict the poor and impoverished elements from immigrating. This principle does not apply to all Latino groups. Many members of this group immigrate without official papers, but those that immigrate officially are basically in the middle class, although their income may not be on the same level as other Americans.

The principle of intergenerational mobility can also be applied to American born citizens. This occurs when one person makes it to the middle-class plateau by acquiring a college education and undertakes measures to make sure that their children also acquire such an education. This is particularly true for African Americans who benefitted from affirmative action in the 1960s and 1970s. Because they have middle-class jobs, their children do not qualify for students' financial aid. This is the same situation that those whites who benefitted from the GI Bill found themselves during the 1960s and 1970s. Their income was too high for their children to qualify for financial aid.

In short, the conceptual framework developed previously, which is a comparative macro-analysis, developed above will allow students to examine more accurately those independent variables that can best explain the causes of ethnic and racial inequality without being forced to make various assumptions that cannot withstand systematic scrutiny. The following chapters will be case studies to support our basic argument.

NOTES

1. W.E.B. Du Bois, *The Souls of Black Folk* (Greenwich, Conn.: Fawcett Publications, 1961), pp. 291-92.

2. See (his books)

3. Gunnar Myrdal, *An American Dilemma* (New York: Harper & Row, 1962), p. lxxi.

4. The Kerner Commission, *Report of the National Advisory Commission on Civil Disorder* (Washington, D.C.: Government Printing Office, 1969), p. 279.

5. See, for example, John J. Appel, "American Negro and Immigrant Experience: Similarities and Differences," *The Alien*, ed. Leonard Dinnerstein and Frederic Cope Jaher (New York: Appleton-Century-Crofts, 1970), pp. 339–347; Philip M. Hauser, "Educational Stratification in the United States," *Sociological Inquiry* 40 (1970): 102-129; Irving Kristol, "The Negro Today is Like the Immigrant Yesterday," *New York Times Magazine* 11 (1966): 50–51, 124–142; Thomas Sowell, *Race and Economic* (New York: David McKay, 1975), pp. 100–102.

6. Christopher Jencks, *Inequality: A Reassessment of the Effect of Family and Schooling in America* (New York: Harper & Row, 1972), chapter 7.

7. David Easton, *A Framework for Political Analysis* (Englewood Cliff, N. J.: Prentice-Hall, Inc., 1965), p. 7.

8. See Chapter 10.

9. See Chapter 9.

10. Stephen and Abigail Thernstrom, *America in Black and White: One Nation, Indivisible* (New York: Simon & Schuster, 1997).

11. This concept is discussed extensively in Chapter 5 of this work.

12. Stanely Lieberson, "A Societal Theory of Race and Ethnic Relations," *American Sociological Review* 26 (December 1961), p. 902.

13. Lieberson, *A Piece of the Pie: Black and White Immigrants Since 1880* (Berkeley: University of California Press, 1980), Chapter 1.

14. Daniel P. Moynihan, *The Negro Family* (Washington, D.C.: The United States Department of Labor Policy Planning and Research, 1965), p. 5.

15. *The Unheavenly City* (Boston: Little, Brown and Company, 1968).

16. Ibid., p. 48.

17. Arthur R.Jensen, "How Can We Boost IQ and Scholastic Achievement?'' *Harvard Educational Review*: 39 (Winter 1969): 1-123. Jensen based his argument on a study conducted by C. Burt, "Intelligence and Social Mobility,'' *British Journal of Statistical Psychology* 14 (1961): 3-24. It was later discovered that Burt's research was manufactured.

18. These racial inferiority arguments will be discussed below.

19. Stokely Carmichael and Charles Hamilton, *Black Power: The Politics of Liberation in America* (New York: Vintage Books, 1967), p. 48.

20. See U.S. Congress, *Senate, Hearings on A. 3876,* 90th Congress, 2d session, July 24, 1968, p. S9284.

21. Ibid.

22. See the *Manhattan Report: Special Edition*, Manhattan Institute for Policy Research, Vol. 1, No. 8 (Winter 1982): 1-11.

23. For a discussion of how scientists are trying to shift the blame for racism to factors other than government actions, see Louis L. Knowles and Kenneth Prewitt, *Institutional Racism in America* (Englewood Cliffs, N.J.: Prentice-Hall, 1969), p. 10.

24. Thomas Sowell, *Market and Minorities* (Boston: Basic Books, 1981), p. 18.

25. "Culture–Not Discrimination–Decides Who Gets Ahead," *U.S. News & World Report* 91 (October 12, 1981): 74-75.

26. Herbert G. Gutman, "The World Two Cliometricians Made," *Journal of Negro Education* 60 (1):98.

27. Oscar Handlin, *Newcomers* (Cambridge: Harvard University Press, 1959).

28. For a discussion on this topic, see Michael Novak, "Further Thoughts on Ethnicity." *Christian Century* 10 (1973): 40-43; Bayard Rustin, "From Protest to Politics." *Negro Protest Thought in the Twentieth Century*, ed. Francis L. Broderick and August Meier (Indianapolis: Bobbs–Merrill, 1965), pp. 409-411; Sidney Wilhelm, *Who Needs the Negro*? (Cambridge, Mass.: Schenkman, 1970), p. 17.

29. John Kenneth Galbraith, *The Affluent Society* (New York: Mentor, 1969).

30. Banfield, *The Unheavenly City*, p. 48.

31. Lieberson, *A Piece of the Pie*, p. 14.

32. Moynihan, *The Negro Family*, p. 5.

33. Andrew Billingsley, *The Black Family in America* (Englewood Cliffs, N.J.: Prentice-Hall, 1968); Herbert G. Gutman,*The Black Family in Slavery and Freedom*, 1750-1925 (New York: Pantheon, 1976).

34. Charles Willie, *A New Look at Black Families* (Bayside, NY: General Hall, 1976); Robert Hill, *The Strengths of Black Families* (New York: Emerson Hall, 1971)

35. For a discussion of racism in the field of education, see *Legislative History of the Equal Employment Opportunities Act of 1972*, H.R. 1746 Senate, Subcommittee on Labor of the Senate Labor Committee on Labor and Public Welfare (H.R. 174, P.L. 92-261), Amending Title VII of the Civil Rights Act of 1964, pp. 416-420.

36. Kerner Commission, *Report on the National Advisory Commission*, p. 279.

37. Carmichael and Hamilton, *Black Power*, pp. 4-6.

38. Gutman, "The World Two Cliometricians Made," p. 226.

39. See the *Board of Regents of State College v. Roth*, p. 577.

40. See *Bolling v. Sharpe*, 347 U.S, 499-500 (1954).

41. These terms will be discussed in Chapter 6.

42. These terms will be discussed in the Summary and Conclusion chapter.

43. See Lieberson, *A Piece of the Pie: Black and White Immigrants Since 1880* (Berkeley: University of California Press, 1980), p. 3.

44. For a discussion of the theory of the culture of poverty, see Oscar Lewis, *La Vida* (New York: Random House, 1965), p. xiv.

45. For a discussion of the Protestant work ethic, see Max Weber, *The Protestant Ethic and the Rise of the Spirit of Capitalism* (New York: Charles Scribner's Sons, 1958).

46. See St. Clair Drake and Horce R. Clayton, *Black Metropolis* (New Your: Harper and Row, 1962(

47. Easton, p. 7.

48. For a discussion on this topic, see Chapter 8.

49. John Locke, *Second Treatises of Government*, Section 2.123.

50. Ibid., sec. 2.25.

51. Ibid., 2.124.

52. *Hobbes Selections,* ed. by Frederick J.E.Woodbridge (New York: Charles Scribner's Sons, 1958), p. 253.

53. Ibid.

54. Robert A. Dahl, *A Preface to Democratic Theory* (Chicago: The University of Chicago Press, 1956), p. 6.

55. See Gary S. Becker, "Investment in Human Capital: A Theoretical Analysis," *The Journal of Political Economy 70* (October 1962), pp. 9-49.

56. Banfield, p. 47.

57. David Easton, *A Framework for Political Analysis* (Englewood Cliffs, N.J. : Prentice-Hall, 1965), p. 7.

CHAPTER 2
The Colonial Immigrants, 1600–1776:
Anglo-Saxon, Dutch, French,
and Scots-Irish

This chapter consists of an examination of the economic, social, and political linkages that the colonial immigrants fashioned between themselves and the American polity in their initial and early stage of contact. The thesis of this chapter is that the vast majority of the colonial immigrants were not poor and poverty-stricken, as is widely discussed in the literature.[1] They were largely middle-class—primarily an emerging class of manufacturers who were "moderately prosperous and not the hopeless indigent."[2] Trailing this class were the uprooted yeomen, farmers, craftsmen, and merchants who were "skilled in industry, often independent in resources, and well trained in the intellectual controversies of religion and politics."[3] Their upward mobility was largely intergenerational.

The colonists immigrated to the colonies not so much to seek religious free-dom–although religion was a factor–as to escape their predicament. The In-dustrial Revolution had transformed European societies from a feudal system to an industrial one; in the process, it uprooted farmers, artisans, craftsmen and merchants. With diminishing need for their services, these groups found them-selves being pushed off the middle-class plateau onto the beachheads of the culture of poverty. To avoid such calamity, they immigrated to the colonies. If they had remained on these beachheads for more than a generation, they would have succumbed to the culture of poverty, by which the principle of intergenerational downward mobility would have kicked in.

When arrived in the colonies, they did not settle on the middle-class plateau, but on the beachheads of the culture of poverty. They remained there until their respective governments issued them a set of bootstraps in the form of free land under the headright system.[4] This free land connected them to the mother lode of America's income redistribution system. Thus, these bootstraps prevented even the penniless immigrants from falling victim to the culture of poverty. It is worth noting here, that although immigrants could have been penniless, they had the necessary skills to take advantage of life's opportunities.

An analysis of the adjustment of the colonial immigrants would not be complete without an examination of the role that Protestantism played in shaping and forming the basic ideals and institutions of America.

The Origin of Basic American
Ideals and Institutions

Although the colonial immigrants came from different countries, the majority of them were imbued with the doctrines of Protestantism. These doctrines provided the foundation on which basic American ideals and institutions were built. Again, the origin of these doctrines can be traced more to the Protestant Reformation rather than to Anglo-Saxon traditions.[5] From their extreme manifestations, these doctrines prepared the hearts and minds of the Protestants for the concept of a free government based on constitutional principles such as trial by jury, separation of power, freedom of religion and press, equality of economic opportunities, and the ownership of private property.

One of the doctrines of the Protestant Reformation movement was that man had an inherited right to approach God directly without the intercession of any priest, sacrament, or institution.[6] This doctrine in its totality provided the basis for individualism, freedom of thought, and ideals, all of which remain important components of modern democracy. It is equally important to note that John Calvin, one of the Protestant reformers, "demonstrated in his development of the Presbyterial type of church government" that "democratic principles function effectively through representative agencies."[7] Hence, these principles helped to politicize the Puritans for the concept of freedom and self-government. This was, perhaps, the underlying impetus prompting the Puritans to seize the reins of government in England from the royalty in 1640, returning them "in 1660 under conditions which established for all times the supremacy of Parliament."[8]

The concept of a free government based on constitutional principles was nurtured by Renaissance learning, which "encouraged successive generations of Englishmen to seek the restoration of primitive Christianity,"[9] thereby drawing them closer to the doctrines of Protestantism than to Anglo-Saxon institutions and ideals. These doctrines became the framework on which democratic institutions and ideals were established both in England and in America. They were also the magnets that drew the colonial immigrants together toward one common belief and, subsequently, facilitated their adjustment to American life.

Protestantism received its strongest support from the manufacturers, merchants, and lesser gentry class in Europe, particularly in England, France, Germany, and the Scandinavian countries.[10] These immigrants—except the Scandinavians—constituted the majority of the religious refugees during the colonial period.

The Changing Economic Conditions in Europe

At the beginning of the sixteenth century, England witnessed an increase in population growth after a century and a half of decline precipitated by the conditions of the Dark Ages.[11] In an attempt to sustain the effect of this new growth, economic conditions in Europe were structured so that every person was a part of an economic unit. The peasants and artisans were bound together by the organization of the agricultural life of the village. Neither one could move without the village officer telling them which strip was to be cultivated and which artisans could set themselves up in trade.[12]

The economic system during this period was for all practical purposes a closed system. The farm tenants' capacity to improve their lot by learning a trade was constrained by the apprenticeship program. The Statute of Apprenticeship of 1563 prohibited those below the rank of yeoman (a class of landowners below the gentry who cultivated their own land) from withdrawing from agricultural pursuits to become apprentices in trade.[13] Journeymen, apprentices, and day laborers made just enough for bare necessities.[14]

The inevitable consequence of the these constraints was a restricted population growth. As early as the thirteenth century, marriage was contingent upon the male's ability to obtain land in order to support his family.[15] As the population continued to increase, and land became more and more scarce, the European countries established the primogeniture system, the custom of passing the land down undivided to the oldest son. This system profoundly affected the age of marriage until the domestic woolen industry was introduced; it offered the male an alternative economic means by which he could support a family.[16]

The woolen industry was introduced into the English economy sometime during the last quarter of the sixteenth century. From this period onward, the economic conditions in Europe started breaking the bonds that had kept the peasants and artisans inextricably tied to an agricultural life. The woolen industry increased the demands for the manufacture of clothing, thereby discouraging agricultural production. These developments encouraged the fencing in of open farmland for raising sheep. As demands for woolen material continued to increase, the landowners started a protracted process of enclosure, which had the inevitable effect of forcing numerous farm tenants off the farms.[17] The process of enclosure promoted the practice of large-scale farming in which comparatively less labor was needed.[18] This process then created a labor surplus in Europe for the first time since the big plague.[19]

As the population began to shift from rural to urban areas, a class of merchants and manufacturers began to emerge among the craftsmen, artisans, and yeomen.[20] For a long period of time, the upper classes consisted of noblemen who earned their living by renting out their large plots of land to farm tenants. But with these economic changes, wealth was being redistributed to include manufacturers, merchants and traders, and other townspeople who were involved in foreign trade.[21] These changes began to restructure the social order of northern European countries. At the top of the social structure, there were the landowning aristocrats, who were followed by the rich merchants and yeomen, the poor farm tenants and husbandmen, the artisans and craftsmen, and the common laborers.[22] The new classes below the aristocracy were predominantly Protestants, who had bitter memories of the royalty's favoritism toward the aristocracy in renting the land under the feudal system.

The class of merchants and traders began to augment the English economy, which in turn created new and increasing demands for raw materials, which England herself could not produce. Consequently, England began seeking raw materials from abroad. Long before this class began to constitute a potent economic and political force in England—during the period between 1485 and 1603—the Tudor kings of England began to express a desire to make England a powerful and wealthy nation through the enlargement of her trade opportunities in competition with the rest of the world; however, England found the trade market somewhat dominated by other countries. In order to expand economically, she had to find new lands and territories from which raw materials could be obtained; consequently, she turned her attention to the New World.

As the emerging number of middle- and upper-class merchants and traders continued to grow, they created a need for overseas expansion. The groups who responded to the expansion were southern planters (who were representatives of the noble class) followed by the Puritans in the New England colonies.

The Southern Colonies

The establishment of the southern colonies was but one ploy within England's mercantile system at the time. During the seventeenth century, England established colonies around the globe for the purpose of strengthening its empire through the mercantile system.

The English Empire was the most complete embodiment of the ideal. The factories in the Spice Islands and on the coasts of India supplied the products of the Orient, not to be obtained elsewhere. Africa provided the Negroes, upon whose labor was based the production of sugar in the West Indies, which formed one of the mainstays of the Empire's commerce. St. Helena and Bermuda were strategic points on the Indian and American trade routes. Virginia and Maryland were wholly devoted to the staple crop of tobacco, which was another of the important elements in British trade. The fisheries of New Foundland provided England with an article to exchange with the Catholic countries of southern Europe for the wine, salt, and other products imported from them.[23]

Although the mercantile system promoted the establishment of colonies, the structural conditions there restricted immigration primarily to the aristocrats, a few indentured servants, and African slaves.

The first prominent English settlement in the New World was established in Jamestown, Virginia, in 1607 by a group of planters who were an extension of the upper class of England that showed loyalty to the King and the Anglican Church.[24] They consisted of "sons of noble families, others from lesser nobility, and still others from the English middle class."[25] The chief occupation of these early settlers was farming. They settled primarily in the colonies of Virginia, the Carolinas, and later Georgia, where the soil was fertile, and the long hot summers were conducive to farming.[26]

The aristocratic class attempted to establish the same economic and social order that approximated the one in their homeland: namely, large-scale farming and the plantation system.[27] The plantation system within itself placed constraints upon social mobility. The southern social system, structured in the Anglo-Saxon tradition, was based on the principle that a wealthy minority should control the government and hold this power by restricting the political activity of the majority. Larger estates were indispensable for agricultural production based on cheap labor; this labor was first supplied by white indentured servants and later by African slaves.

The structural conditions during this period necessitated the importation of numerous white indentured servants. Most of these servants cannot be considered to be synonymous with poverty-stricken individuals. They were the displaced artisans, craftsmen, yeomen, and farmers who had been reduced to the status of wage-earners or who, for some reason or another, found themselves in debt. The indentured system was a way by which individuals could extricate themselves from the humiliation of poverty. They could either rot in prison for their debts or indenture themselves and immigrate to the colonies. Many took the latter alternative.

The nature of the southern colonies was such that it discouraged the influx of poverty-stricken individuals and attracted skilled and industrious ones. First of all, the attempt to establish a colony in the New World was so precarious that the venture was too big for any individual or group to undertake alone. Therefore, in order to minimize the risk involved, the English adopted the con-cept of a joint-stock company from the Dutch. In essence, this company provided for three or more persons to invest in an adventure so that the loss, if any, would be shared. The company membership consisted of two types of people: adventurers and planters. The adventurers were the ones who invested capital but remained in England, while the planters settled in the colonies.[28]

For a period of ten years, the rate of return for these shareholders' investment was very meager. As a result, the planters had a hard time recruiting people to populate the colony, despite the fact that there was a surplus of labor in England, which was precipitated by the Industrial Revolution.[29] Laborers were reluctant to emigrate to the colonies because they were uncertain about whether a far-off land could offer them better opportunities than those existing in their homeland.

The settlement of the colonial immigrants was not made possible solely by private means. Government action was also required. The Charter of 1609 was designed both to raise capital for the voyage across the sea and to give the planters incentives (bootstraps) to settle in the New World. The charter stipulated that any person above the age of ten would be provided food, clothing, shelter, and one hundred acres of land for himself and for each member of his family after serving the company for a period of seven years.[30]

The colony was not attractive to the mass of the people in England, partly because it had not established a solid economic base. It was not until Thomas Dale began to administer the colony in 1712 that the cultivation of tobacco in Virginia began to offer the planters a stable economy.[31]

After an economic base had been built, the planters established the "head-right" system, which was designed to increase the population in the colony. This system promised each man 150 acres of land and 150 more for every able male servant that he brought with him, and 100 acres more for every woman and male servant under the age of sixteen.[32]

The headright system had both political and social motives. Politically, England was afraid that Spain would extend her colonies northward along the Atlantic coast as she had done on the Pacific. In order to provide a check upon this expansion, England created the headright system as an incentive to populate the New World.[33] The population of the colonies attracted those displaced farmers, artisans, and craftsmen who were able to survive in a distant land. This demand, therefore, drew heavily from the yeomen and farm tenants who were being reduced to common laborers in England. It seems logical—after an economic base had been established—that the colony would have been appealing to those farmers who could thus make their families economically secure and spare themselves the humiliation of being reduced to common laborers in England[34] where the principle of intergenerational downward mobility would have kicked in.

Socially, the headright system was designed to draw a skilled class of people to the colony. After the planters established the plantation system as their economic base, there was a need for additional labor to do the maintenance work, which required artisans and craftsmen. Much of this labor was supplied by the employment of the whole family in the early stage of settlement. And, in many cases, heavy work was done through communal work service.[35] But there was an additional need for artisans and craftsmen who were not attracted to the New World by the desire to become independent farmers.[36]

Because of the changing conditions precipitated by the economic expansion in England, the socioeconomic status of the artisans and craftsmen was reduced significantly. Many did not have enough money to pay for their passage to the New World. Their interest was not so much in obtaining land, but in pursuing their learned trades. Therefore, in order to increase this stock, the planters established the *indentured servant system*, which provided for persons to indenture themselves for a certain length of time in return for free passage to the colony.[37] They indentured themselves to the ships' captains, who, in turn, transported them to the colony and sold their bounties to the planters for a fee commensurate with the cost of the passage. Hence, the indentured system, as will be demonstrated in the later part of this chapter, was a vehicle for social upward mobility.

The economic conditions in the southern colonies provided such a high propensity for upward mobility for artisans and craftsmen that the planters were confronted with a pattern of runaway servants. The manufacturing industry in the colony required such small initial capital that the average enterprising craftsman or artisan could save enough money in a year or so to set himself up in an independent business.[38] This created a labor shortage for the planters. They were forced to to turn to African slaves in order to obtain a more permanent source of labor.[39]

The introduction of slaves had an immediate economic and political effect upon the southern colonies. Economically, the slaves began to provide a stable source of labor, which enabled the planters to plan their economic growth through calculation.[40] This source of labor precluded the possibility of an emerging middle class. This phenomenon is in conformity with historical developments in plantation system.

After the slaves were introduced, there was still a need for white servants to provide a buffer between the planters and the slaves. White servants were used as overseers and provided a defense for the planters against the Indians.[41] The demand for this type of labor called for a different breed of person than that called for by the headright system. The persons who responded to this labor demand usually came from the rank of disbanded soldiers, defeated rebels, orphans, convicts, and poor Protestants.[42] However, during most of the eighteenth century, the data indicate that this class of people never constituted a significantly large percentage of the population in the southern colonies. Although the data for the southern colonies on slaves and servants are not accurate, the figures that are available lend credence to the argument that the structural conditions limited immigration to the skilled and the well-to-do. The figures in Table 1 give some indication of the ratio of slaves to whites.

Table 1
Population of the Southern Colonies, 1755

Colony	White	Black
Maryland[a]	107,209	42,764
Virginia[b]	173,316	120,156
North Carolina[b]	50,000	30,000
South Carolina[b]	25,000	50,000

SOURCE: Abbot Emerson Smith, *Colonists in Bondage* (Chapel Hill: University of North Carolina Press, 1947), p. 332.
[a]These figures are based on Maryland census for the year 1755.
[b]The figures for Virginia and the Carolinas are based on estimation made by colonial officials of that time.

In 1755, the Maryland census indicated that there were "98,357 free whites; 6,871 servants; 1,981 convicts; 3,591 mulattoes; and 42,764 Negroes."[43] Therefore, since Virginia and the Carolinas were a part of the plantation system, these figures suggest that the numbers of white servants in these colonies were somewhat similar to those in Maryland.

The New England Immigrants: The Protestants

The New England immigrants were from a different breed of Englishmen than the southern immigrants. The former group came from a less noble class than the latter group. They were predominantly Protestants who were uprooted from England by the changing economic and political conditions, which occurred during the seventeenth century. Although they were not as wealthy as their southern counterparts, the structural conditions in the colonies defined the range of choice possibilities for them in a way that created an environment conducive to their early economic success.

The doctrine of Protestantism had already politicized the New Englanders for the establishment of a free government based on constitutional principles. Many European countries—except for the Netherlands, which had a tradition of religious tolerance—considered the Protestant Reformation a threat to the status quo. Subsequently, this view set in motion a series of religious persecutions and political exiles. The victims of these persecutions were left with only the New World as an outlet.[44]

The first religious refugee group to make contact with America was the Pilgrims, who landed at Plymouth Rock in 1620. It can be said without much exaggeration that the Pilgrims were the first ones to establish a form of modern democracy in America. This claim is manifested in the "`Mayflower Compact," which was signed in 1620 by forty-one men, who agreed to make just and equal laws and offer obedience to the same. The political significance of the Mayflower Compact is not only that it was the first form of democracy in America, but that it preceded democracy in England by some twenty years. It was not until 1640 that the Puritans seized the reins of government in England.[45]

It is with this religious group that our conceptual framework has meaning. The linkages they created in their initial stage of contact determined the subsequent behavioral patterns of the succeeding immigrants during this period. Their settling in the New World—free of English rule—served as a magnet to draw other nonconformists after them.

The concept of contact brings into consideration the broader question of superordinate and subordinate social order and the concept of race cycle, which consists of "competition, conflict, accommodation, and assimilation."[46] The theory of race cycle and contact holds that when one or more distinct ethnic groups migrate to a new area, each group has the propensity to maintain a social and political order approximating the one in their native land. Whenever such a situation occurs, the migrant groups not only differ, but often conflict with each other. As we will see, the Protestants, although they were from different countries and constituted different and distinct ethnic groups, did not differ significantly in the type of political order that they preferred: that is, a government based on constitutional principles. This group had a universal institution (Protestantism), which prescribed universal behavioral patterns toward democracy.

What the Pilgrims and other protestant groups had in common was that both groups were committed to the high ideals of Protestantism. It was their devotion to these high ideals and their heroic efforts to establish a colony in the New World that made an impact upon American colonial history.[47] Although the Pilgrims constituted a self-contained social unit, they did not dominate the New England colonies, because they were unable to propagate themselves sufficiently, and they did not have a constituency in England from which to draw additional immigrants. Therefore, by the turn of the seventeenth century, they were assimilated into their neighboring Puritan colonies of Connecticut and Massachusetts Bay.[48]

The Puritans, the second wave of Protestants, began to settle in New England in the 1620s. They settled in Massachusetts Bay, where a fishing post had already been established in 1623 by a group of Puritan merchants. The Puritan emigration was encouraged and financed by Puritan adventurers who wanted to establish colonies in New England along the Massachusetts Bay to promote fisheries in this region, thereby establishing commercial and trade linkages between England and the colonies.

Trade and commerce, nevertheless, offered the Puritans means by which they could become self-sufficient in their early stages of contact; therefore, they did not have to undergo the same hardships as the southern planters and the Pilgrims.

The majority who immigrated during this period came from the southeastern counties of England where the biggest industry was cloth making.[49] During the period between 1530 and 1625, the economic conditions in this area began to decline. As discussed earlier, people of all classes became disturbed by the decline in their social status, which was accompanied by the antagonism of Bishop William Laud, who attempted to make the situation very uncomfortable for nonconformists. Economically, these conditions had begun to push them off the middle-class plateau onto the beachheads of the culture of poverty. The mere fear of such deprivation gave them great incentive to emigrate to the new colonies, where land could be obtained free and where they could continue to practice Protestantism without interference.

The structural conditions of the colonies forced the Puritans to become industrious and self-sufficient in their early stages of contact. First, the geographic area in New England was not conducive to large-scale farming; therefore, it was economically advantageous for the Puritan farmers to concentrate on small intensive farming rather than extensive holdings as was typical of the southern colonies. Furthermore, the New England farmers often had sideline occupations such as manufacturing, fishing, and lumbering. Typical New England farmers were not solely dependent upon farming for a livelihood, but on their ability to produce goods for trade as well, thus connecting themselves to all three linkages of the mainstream (i.e., trade, commerce, and real estate).

Second, the New England colonies, unlike their southern counterparts, did not have any great single commodity that they could trade with England. They were forced to produce many of the necessities that the southern colonies were able to buy from England through trade. Hence, these economic conditions, buttressed by the Protestant work ethic, provided the basis for the subsequent emergence of a class of merchants and manufacturers in the colonies.[50] Out of basic necessity, the Puritans created an on-the-job training process overlapping trade, commerce, artisans, and craftsmen. This gave the individual the freedom to acquire the necessary human capital to survive in this new environment.

As time progressed, the Puritans started producing a surplus of domestic provisions for intercolonial trade. Massachusetts Bay became the trade center for the colonies and remained so until the construction of the Erie Canal in the nineteenth century.

With the exception of Pennsylvania, the differentiation in the economic and social structure of the Protestant colonies was not significant enough to merit an extensive elaboration here. Pennsylvania, however, differed from the other Protestant colonies in its immigration policies, and these policies had a profound effect upon the development of its economy. The New England colonies were structured to discourage the settling of non-Protestants.[51] Despite the fact that these colonies were founded on the basis of religious freedom, they entertained a degree of religious ethnocentrism, which provided the basis, perhaps, for subsequent class and race passion in America.

Unlike Pennsylvania, the New England colonies did not extend a welcoming hand to any religious group or sect that did not share the same religious values.[52] These differences in religious practices existed separately from the Protestant doctrines of self-government. The Pilgrims, Puritans, Quakers, and others seemed to prefer isolation for religious purposes, but they were united in their political beliefs.[53]

Pennsylvania was somewhat unique because it was a haven for many religious sects. This situation was in part responsible for its large and rapid population growth. When the King of England granted William Penn the colony of Pennsylvania in 1681—in consideration of a debt that the Crown owed his father and him—Penn decided to try out his ideals of Quakerism on a broader scale to ensure that his followers would be free from religious persecution.[54] He created the first heterogeneous colony by welcoming all religious sects. His action was due, in part, to the religious ethnocentrism that was practiced by the New England colonies—which excluded Quakers, Presbyterians, and Catholics by law.[55]

Penn was a firm believer in the doctrines of Protestantism—that is, a representative government and trial by jury, which he developed to its maximal efficiency in his colony. Because of his liberalism and his recruitment effort all over Europe, especially in Germany and France, the Pennsylvania colony grew faster than any other colony during the colonial period. His recruitment effort

led to an influx not only of people of religion but also of persons not socially and economically adjusted in Europe: criminals and paupers. The coming of these social variants was responsible for the opposition to free admission of aliens on a social basis; that is to the exclusion of criminals and to a method of control of those who were likely to become a burden to the colonies.[56]

Thus, Penn's liberal policies on immigration can be traced to the doctrines of Quakerism, which tended to "reduce all ranks of society to a spiritual level—spiritual democracy."[57] The doctrine has been translated in today's social science literature as social equality, equal opportunity, and social upward mobility. Again, Penn's liberal policies on immigration led the rest of the Protestant colonies to construct structural barriers (Alien Laws) to keep out those they thought undesirable.

As stated earlier, Penn went to Europe to recruit inhabitants to populate his colony. In the process of recruiting, Penn accepted all classes of people who were willing to settle in the new land. Many of the people who wanted to emigrate to the New World were poor, but skilled. The redemption system was created in order to make it possible for these people to emigrate. This system differed significantly from the white servitude system, in that the former system required the emigration of the whole family, while the latter provided for individuals. The redemption system appealed to Germans, who were driven from the Palatinate regions by the wars of Louis VII.[58] The Germans who came from this area were "disciplined in the habits of industry, frugality, and patience, and were particularly fitted for the laborious occupation of felling timber, clearing land, and farming."[59]

Many Germans who were fleeing from the Rhine arrived at Rothenburg to discover that they did not have enough money to emigrate to the colonies.[60] Merchants took whatever money they had, placing themselves and their goods on a ship and contracting to pay for the balance of their passage. Whenever they could not locate their friends in the New World, the ships' captains sold them into indentured servitude. Some German families came with the expectation of paying for their passage by indenturing their children. Since there was a shortage of labor in the colonies, many of the indentured children became apprentices to craftsmen and artisans,[61] thus immigrating into a human capital environment.

The redemption system in Pennsylvania had a positive social effect; it created a condition by which many young boys could learn a trade and thereby make themselves self-sufficient. The Pennsylvania German Society's *Proceedings*[62] indicate that the majority of the Germans who were in servitude were either apprentices, craftsmen, or artisans. Therefore, because of Pennsylvania's liberal policies on immigration and the redemption system, that colony acquired a class of craftsmen and artisans trained on a higher level than the rest of the colonies. Around the middle of the eighteenth century, "Pennsylvania held a leading place in the production of textiles, and she owed this position largely to the Germans who had settled in this province."[63] Pennsylvania led the rest of the colonies in establishing mills and factories. It was not until the end of the colonial period that the New England colonies began to establish their factories.[64]

Briefly, the policies of Pennsylvania toward immigration created a social and economic magnet that drew largely skilled people into its boundaries. These immigrants might have been without money upon their disembarkation, but the redemption and the apprenticeship system proved to be a set of bootstraps (both *de jure* and *de facto*) that enabled these individuals to elevate themselves up off the beachheads of the culture of poverty onto the middle-class plateau. As mentioned before, the manufacturing industries required so little capital that any enterprising laborer who had the technical know-how could easily set himself up as an independent merchant or artisan. Thus, human capital has proven to be the independent variable that can best explain these groups' success.

The New England colonies discouraged the influx of the white servitude and redemption servants, partly because they did not have a need for them. By doing so, they deprived themselves of many intellectual and industrious people.

It can be said without much exaggeration that it was Penn's early insistence upon social equality, freedom of the press, and equal justice that was responsible for Pennsylvania becoming the center for political agitation during the colonial period—and New York to a certain extent. Economically, Pennsylvania had an advantage over the rest of the colonies in developing its industry after the colonies emerged from under the yoke of the English mercantile system.[65]

The structural economic and political conditions in Europe prevented other European countries—with the exception of Spain—from gaining an economic foothold in North America. Germany and other countries suffered from a population decline due to the effect of the Thirteen Year War. Italy, however, suffered an era of economic retardation because of the decline in commerce in the Mediterranean and the deadly effect that malaria had upon its coastal plains.[66] Therefore, these structural conditions restricted emigration during the colonial period in almost all of the European countries, save England and the Netherlands (see Table 2). Before the end of the seventeenth century, the Dutch and

Table 2
Percent Distribution of the White Population According to Nationality As Indicated by Names of Heads of Families, 1790

Nationality as Indicated by Name	Percent
English	83.5
Scottish	6.9
Irish	1.6
Dutch	2.0
French	0.5
German	5.6
Hebrew[a]	-
All Others	0.1

SOURCE: Quoted in Maurice Davis, *World Immigration* (New York: Macmillan, 1936), p. 54, quoted from the 1908 U.S. Bureau of the Census, *A Century of Population Growth.*

[a]Less then one-twentieth of 1 percent.

French interests in the New World were limited to the establishment of trade posts.   The structural conditions in their homelands did not lend themselves to the creation of colonies in the New World. Their institutions and ideals, therefore, had little impact upon the formulation of American basic ideals and institutions. The Scots-Irish, however, constituted a large percentage of the colonial immigrants, but their ideals and institutions were shaped and formed by Protestantism in their homeland.

The Dutch Colony

When the Dutch settled in New York in 1624, they were primarily interested in expanding their commerce and trade industry. The Dutch had taken the lead in the commercial world, perhaps because of their pioneer's efforts in abolishing all restrictions on commercial activities in the sixteenth century.[67] Unlike those in the other European countries, the Dutch people were no longer tied to their villages and farms. They were free to farm and trade wherever and however their economic capacities allowed them.

The Dutch East India Company was chartered in 1602 with the powers of conquest, colonization, and government. It became a model for rival companies founded by the French and English. During the first half of the seventeenth century, the Dutch moved rapidly in forming a monopoly in commerce and trade on the shores of the Baltic, and in most of "the cities and states of Germany."[68] They also controlled commerce in Scotland, Ireland, and other British colonies—which was one of the reasons the British were powerless to stop them.

The Dutch perhaps could have established the dominant social, political, and economic institutions in America had they had the "pushing" forces typical of other countries. The Protestant Reformation, which was one of the dominant pushing forces in Europe, did not affect social conditions in the Netherlands, because the Netherlands had very liberal policies toward religion.[69] While religious persecution was a common practice for many of the northern and western European countries, the Netherlands welcomed all religious sects. Therefore, before the English conquest of the Dutch colony in 1664, the pushing force behind Dutch immigration to the New World was commerce and trade. The Dutch had little interest in the New World, other than for this purpose.

After the English conquered New Netherlands, New York became a haven for immigrants who were excluded from other colonies that practiced religious ethnocentrism. Thus, the Dutch colonists became Anglicized, for reasons we will discuss later. Their population in America consisted of traders, artisans, farmers, and a few indentured servants who were, in most cases, skilled workers.[70]

The French

France's first contact with America was initiated by her government in 1607. Her purpose was to explore the possibility of setting up trade posts.[71] The explorers pushed inland along the Great Lakes and rivers and established trading posts along the banks of both the rivers and lakes. The right to set up trading posts was granted to those merchants who were favorites of the King. Unlike the English, the French establishment of a colony in the New World was not a private enterprise venture.

The French colonial system was designed to discourage the development of agriculture and to prevent the growth of a large population. Its purpose was to strengthen its commercial system, which had been retarded by the country's frequent involvement in wars. The French did not have the manpower to establish an agricultural industry in the New World, so they adopted a policy of coexistence with the Indians.[72] They saw no serious problems in fraternizing and intermarrying with the Indians. This practice, in part, distinguished them from the English, who assumed a posture of superiority over the Native Americans.

Some consideration, however, was given to agriculture by the signeuries along the St. Lawrence River, but a shortage of manpower resulting from the wars forced France to place tight restrictions on emigration. The manpower shortage is explained in the following passage:

> Far different was the situation of France. One Army after another was called up from the villages, sent off to the front, and annihilated on the fields of battle. The peasantry was bled white, and in the last campaign of Napoleon, sixteen-year-old boys filled the places left vacant by their fathers. From this drain upon her manpower France did not recover.[73]

The restriction on emigration was applicable to all citizens except the French Huguenots and French Catholic religious refugees. The Huguenots were a selected "class of people, manufacturers and merchants, perhaps the most intelligent and enterprising."[74] They were driven out of France in 1685 when France ended its toleration for nonconformists (the revocation of the Edict of Nantes).[75]

The French Catholics, totaling 15,000,[76] settled in New York and Pennsylvania. The rest of the colonies were very hostile to the Catholics. Anti-Catholicism found its expression in legislative measures in 1674, when Massachusetts made it impossible for Catholics to become citizens.[77]

The French emigration to America before the American Revolutionary War never included large numbers of peasants and wage earners; it was limited to adventurers and the educated.[78] The structural conditions of France, as mentioned previously, restricted emigration to the French Huguenots, who happened to be predominantly middle class, educated, and merchants. In fact, the English government was instrumental in helping the French emigrate to America. Its purpose was to aid the French in establishing navy stores along the banks of the Great Lakes.[79]

By the end of the Revolutionary War, the French had become assimilated with the planters and professional classes. They had become "English in language and Protestant in religion, British in sentiment and policies. The fulcrum by which it [the assimilation] was accomplished was economic necessity, the lever was political preferment."[80] This assimilation was facilitated by the fact that the French felt no ties to their mother country, which was intolerant of their religious beliefs. The French Protestant ideals and institutions did not differ significantly from those of the English. This is precisely why the French ideals and institutions had little or no influence in shaping American institutions. French colonization ended when England passed a series of navigation acts designed to monopolize trading enterprises in North America.

The Scots-Irish

The Scots-Irish were the third largest ethnic group to emigrate to the colonies to stay. They were called "Scots because they lived in Scotia and they are called Irish because they migrated to Ireland."[81] They were uprooted from Ireland by a combination of economic, political, and religious factors.

Economically, the Scots-Irish had become successful manufacturers and merchants. The latter class was influential in getting Parliament to pass an act in 1698 forbidding the Scots-Irish from exporting any goods to any country save England. This act was one of a series of acts passed by Parliament to achieve maximum use of its commercial system known as mercantilism, a system used by many nations in the seventeenth and eighteenth centuries, designed to make the colonies dependent on their mother countries.

The mercantilism system strangulated the Scots-Irish economy. Their ships were excluded from colonial trade and their woolen manufacturers, who had developed a prosperous industry in Ireland, could no longer export their goods freely in the commercial system.[82] The industrial center in Ireland at the time was Ulster. When Parliament applied the principle of mercantilism to Ireland, it nearly destroyed Ulster's industry.[83]

Socially, the Church of England implemented a plan to make the Scots-Irish, who were Presbyterians, conform to its religious beliefs. To remain in Ireland meant that the Scots-Irish had to undergo radical changes in their religious and political behavior patterns, as well as experience economic retardation. To avoid this political, social, and cultural repression, the Scots-Irish decided to emigrate to America.

The Scots-Irish began immigrating to America at the beginning of the eighteenth century. By 1718, it was estimated that more than 4,200 Scots-Irish had settled in America. In their initial stage of contact with America, they occupied peculiar positions in the New World, a phenomenon due partly to their experience in Ireland and the structural conditions in America:

> At the time of their arrival in America the lands along the Atlantic coast were already well occupied. Thus, due to the religious exclusiveness of Massachusetts and the well-settled character of the country, as well as due to a more or less general feeling of hostility of the English colonists towards certain types of immigrants, they chose as their destination New Hampshire, Vermont, Western Massachusetts, and Maine, and, most of all, Pennsylvania, and the foothill regions of Virginia and the Carolinas. By nature typical pioneers, they pushed into Western Pennsylvania, Ohio, Kentucky, and Tennessee.[84]

The Scots-Irish did not want to settle in Massachusetts because that meant conforming to the state's church in order to be admitted to citizenship. This was one of the main reasons they had left Ireland. The Puritans of New England preferred that they settle on the frontier to serve as a buffer between the Indians and them. New York, however, was open to them because of the long-standing policy of Dutch religious tolerance, even after the English conquest.

The majority of the Scots-Irish, nevertheless, settled on the frontier, not because they were forced to do so, but primarily because they felt at home there. As frontiersmen, they had developed productive farms from the marshlands of Ireland. They were familiar with clearing forests for farm land.

In short, when the Scots-Irish immigrated to America, their hearts and minds were set on developing a free and self-governing society. Their ideals and institutions did not differ significantly from those of England. They had experienced a degree of autonomy in Ireland before England fully implemented its mercantile system. Hence, they encountered very few problems, if any, in adjusting to the American frontier. Since the majority of them were skilled workers and farmers, their subsequent socioeconmic status was characterized by intergenerational mobility.

Indentured Servants and Their Bootstraps

The culture of poverty did not develop among the indentured servants during the colonial period, because the structural conditions provided them with a system of protection that safeguarded their civil rights to acquire property and to pursue employment and economic opportunities. In fact, this system plugged a cork into the hole of the barrel from which the stream of poverty flows.

The culture of poverty usually develops among the second generation of migrant groups when structured conditions prevented the principle of intergenerational upward mobility from kicking in. The European practice of training the son in the crafts of his father was continued in the colonies. This practice perpetuated the class of artisans and craftsmen in America.[85] Many of the indentured servants, who were penniless when they made contact with the colonies, were prevented from falling victim to the culture of poverty, because the structural conditions of the colonies took their rights to acquire and possess property off the goodwill of their masters and placed them on a principle of law. This law was a set of legal codes which "required that masters should feed and clothe their servants and provide them with medical care, shelter, and certain 'freedom dues' prescribed in their contracts."[86]

The servant codes provided stiff penalties upon those masters who violated the servant rights. These codes gave the servant the legal right to "sue his master for breach of contract, in which case a local magistrate might free the servant, reduce the time of servitude, or order that compensation be given to him by his master at the end of his term."[87]

Once the servant completed his time of servitude, for example in the southern colonies, the law required that he be given "freedom dues" (bootstraps). These dues consisted of "fifty acres of land," which was granted "either by the master or the colony; in New England they consisted of tools, clothing, and livestock, or in lieu of these, many payments varying from two to five pounds."[88]

Any poor or penniless family that might have been standing on the threshold of the culture of poverty upon its disembarkation was prevented from falling victim to it because of the system of protection that the colonies provided for poor people to pull themselves up by their bootstraps. For example, if a poor man, for any reason, felt it necessary to place himself and his family into servitude, he might find such an endeavor to be a blessing in disguise, for he could indenture himself and his wife into servitude through which they could pay off their debts and look forward to "freedom dues" at the completion of their service. In the meantime, if they had any children, the boys had the great opportunity to be assigned to an apprenticeship. For such "apprenticeship was more than a form of labor: it was also a method of educating the poor and of implanting good morals."[89] After a boy came of age, he was prepared to walk into a labor market, where great demands for his skills awaited him.

In short, the indentured servant, the headright, and redemption systems were systems of protection that extricated the poor from the jaws of the culture of poverty and catapulted them onto the middle-class plateau.

To summarize, this chapter examined the economic linkages that the colonial groups fashioned with the American polity. These linkages were similar to those that they had fashioned with the polity in their homelands before they were uprooted. Because of the system of protection offered these groups by the structural conditions in the colonies or the government of their homelands, they did not fall victim to the culture of poverty. Both the uprooted peasants and the indentured servants were issued a set of bootstraps, which enabled them to elevate themselves to the middle-class plateau.

The next chapter will examine the political and economic linkages that the second wave of immigrants fashioned with the American polity.

Notes

1.   See Thomas Sowell, *Race and Economics* (New York: David McKay Company, 1975); Stanley Lieberson, *A Piece of the Pie: Black and White Immigrants Since 1880* (Berkeley: University of California Press, 1980); and Nathan Glazer, *Affirmative Discrimination* (New York: Basic Books, 1975).

2.   Abbot Emerson Smith, *Colonists in Bondage* (Chapel Hill: University of North Carolina Press, 1947), pp. 45-46.

3.   __, *Races and Immigrants in America* (New York: Macmillan, 1913), p. 25.

4.   See Chapter 1 for a discussion of the "bootstraps" concept, p. 20.

5.   Around the end of the nineteenth century, many historians argued that American basic ideals and institutions derived in essence from Anglo-Saxon sources. Social scientists have not yet questioned the validity of this thought pattern. For example, see Edward N. Saveth, *Historian and European Immigrants: 1865-1952* (New York: Columbia University Press, 1948), chapter 5.

6.   J. Minton Batten, *Protestant Background in History* (New York and Nashville: Abingdon-Cokesbury Press, 1946), p. 83.

7.   Ibid., pp. 90-91.

8.   Madison Grant, *The Conquest of Continent* (New York: Charles Scribner's Sons, 1933), p. 66.

9.   Batten, *Protestant Background*, p. 97.

10. Ibid.

11. Grant, *The Conquest of a Continent*, p. 66.

12. Oscar Handlin, *The Uprooted* (Boston: Little, Brown and Company, 1951), Chapter 1.

13. Ibid.

14. Jonathan D. Chambers, "Enclosures and the Rural Population: A Revision," in *The Industrial Revolution in Britain*, ed. A. M. Taylor (Boston:. D.C. Heath and Company. 1958), pp. 64-3.

15. See Phyllis Dean, *The First Industrial Revolution* (Cambridge: Harvard University Press, 1940).

16. Marcus Lee Hansen, *The Atlantic Migration 1607-1860* (Cambridge: Harvard University Press, 1940), p. 17.

17. Paul Mantoux, "The Destruction of the Peasant Village," in *The Industrial Revolution in Britain,* ed. A. M. Taylor (Boston: D. C. Heath and Company, 1958), p. 68.

18. For a discussion of enclosure, see Chambers and Mantoux in *The Industrial Revolution in Britain*, pp. 64-150.

19. Clarkson, *The Pre-Industrial Economy in England 1500-1750* (New York: Schocken Books, 1972). p. 31.

20. Mantoux, *The Industrial Revolution in Britain,* p. 72.

21. See Maurice Dobb, *Studies in the Development of Capitalism* (New York: International Publishers, 1963), chapter 1.

22. Marcus W. Jernegan, *The American Colonies: 1492-1700* (New York: Longmans, Green and Company, 1956), pp. 21-22.

23. James Truslow Adams, *The March of Democracy* (New York: Charles Scribner's Sons, 1932), p. 185.

24. Charles M. Andrew, *The Colonial Period American History* (New Haven: Yale University Press, 1938), p. 34.

25. Jernegan, *The American Colonies: 1492-1750*, p. 96.

26. Philip Bruce, *Economic History of Virginia in the Seventeenth Century*, 2 vols. (New York: Macmillan Company, 1896; reprint ed., New York: Johnson Reprint Corp., 19XX), Vol. 1, chapter 1.

27. Ibid.

28. Oliver P. Chitwood, *A History of Colonial America* (New York: Harper and Row Brothers, 1931), p. 63.

29. Mantoux, *The Industrial Revolution in Britain*, p. 68.

30. F. N. Thorpe, *The Federal and State Constitutions, Colonial Charter* (Wilmington, Del.: Scholarly Press, 1968), pp. 383–389.

31. L. G. Tyler, *Narratives of Early Virginia* (New York: Charles Scribner's Sons, 1907), pp. 239-244.

32. Warren B. Smith, *White Servitude in South Carolina* (Columbia: University of South Carolina Press, 1961), p.19.

33. Bruce, *Economic History of Virginia*, chapter 1.

34. Clarkson, *The Pre–Industrial Economy of England 1500-1700*, p. 246.

35. Chitwood, *A History of Colonial America*, p. 72.

36. Smith, *Colonists in Bondage*, chapter 2.

37. Ibid., p. 27.

38. Chitwood, *A History of Colonial America*, p. 211

39. For a discussion of slavery in Virginia, see James C. Ballagh, *A History of Slavery in Virginia* (Baltimore: The Johns Hopkins University Press, 1902; reprinted., New York: Johnson Reprint Corp., 1968).

40. For a discussion of labor and white servitude in Virginia, see Marcus W. Jernegan, *Laboring and Dependent Classes 1607-1783* (Chicago: University of Chicago Press, 1931); Theo D. Jervey, *Genealogical Magazine* 12 (1911): 163–178.

41. Warren B. Smith, *White Servitude*, p. 141.

42. Ibid., p. 38.

43. Ibid., p. 324.

44. John T. Adams, *The Founding of New England* (Atlantic Monthly, 1963), p. 74.

45. Grant, *The Conquest of Continent*, p. 66.

46. Stanley Lieberson, "A Societal Theory of Race and Ethnic Relations," *American Sociological Review* 26 (December 1961): 902.

47. See Charles Banks, *The Ancestry and Homes of the Pilgrim Fathers* (Baltimore: Genealogical Publishing Co., 1971).

48. See Alexandra Young, *Chronicles of the First Planters of the Colony of Massachusetts* (New York: Da Capo, 1971).

49. See Tables 5 and 6 in Margaret G. Davies, *The Enforcement of English Apprenticeship* (Cambridge: Harvard University Press, 1956), p. 115.

50. See Edmund Morgan, *The Puritan Dilemma: The Story of John Winthrop* (Boston: Little, Brown and Company, 1958).

51. See V. L. Parrington, *The Colonial Mind 1620-1800* (New York: Macmillan Company, 1920), pp. 42-43.

52. For a discussion of religious intolerance see, Sanford H. Cobb, *The Rise of Liberty in America* (New York: Research Service, 1970).

53. Hansen, *The Atlantic Migration*, pp. 5-6.

54. Lawrence Guy Brown, *Immigration* (New York: Longmans, Green and Company, 1933), p.44.

55. Jernegan, *The American Colonies: 1492–1750*, p. 209

56. Ibid., p. 209.

57. Karl Frederick Geiser, *Redemptioners and Indentured Servants in the Colony and Commonwealth* (New Haven: Tuttle, Marchouse and Company, 1901), p. 27.

58. Ibid.

59. Ibid., pp. 110-111.

60. Abbot E. Smith, *Colonists in Bondage*, p. 20.

61. Warren B. Smith, *White Servitude*, p. 49.

62. The Pennsylvania German Society, *Proceedings* 44 (October 1907): 10.

63. Chitwood, *A History of Colonial America*, p. 446.

64. Ibid.

65. See Victor S. Clark, *History of Manufacturers in the United States: 1607-1860* (New York: McGraw-Hill Book Co., 1929).

66. Robert F. Foerster, *The Italian Emigration of our Times* (New York: Russell and Russell, 1968), pp. 59-63.

67. Hansen, *The Atlantic Migration*, p. 7.

68. Andrew, *The Colonial Period*, pp. 22-23.

69. Carl Wittke, *We Who Built America* (Cleveland: Case Western University Press, 1964), p. 14.

70. Ibid.

71. Jernegan, *The American Colonies: 1492-1750*, p. 41.

72. See Thomas F. Gossett, *Race: The History of an Idea in America* (Dallas: SMU Press, 1963), p. 18.

73. Hansen, *The Atlantic Migration*, p. 24.

74. Commons, *Race and Immigrants*, p. 14.

75. Wittke, *We Who Built America*, p. 4.

76. Ibid., p. 23.

77. Brown, *Immigration*, p. 52.

78. Commons, *Race and Immigrants*, p. 25.

79. Wittke, *We Who Built America*, p. 5.

80. Arthur H. Hirsch, *The Huguenots of Colonial South Carolina* (Durham: Duke University Press, 1928), p. 90.

81. Commons, *Race and Immigrants*, p. 35.

82. Wittke, We Who Built America, p. 36.

83. Commons, *Race and Immigrants*, p. 35.

84. Roy L. Garis, *Immigrants Restriction* (New York: Macmillan Company, 1927), pp. 6-7.

85. See Oscar Lewis, *La Vida* (New York: Random House, 1965), p. xliv.

86. Curtis P. Nettels, *Roots of American Civilization* (New York: Appleton-Centure-Crofts, 1938), p. 320.

87. Ibid., p. 321.

88. Ibid.,

89. Charles Andrews, *Colonial Folkways* (New Haven: Yale University Press, 1919), p. 189.

CHAPTER 3

The Second Wave of Immigrants, 1820–1870: Irish, Germans, and Scandinavians

As demonstrated in the previous chapter, the structural conditions both in Europe and the colonies restricted immigration to America largely to those groups that had acquired the necessary human capital to compete successfully in a competitive society; their subsequent experience, in terms of upward mobility, was characterized as intergenerational mobility. This was the pattern of immigration up to the American Revolutionary War. This chapter consists of an examination of the political and economic linkages that the first and second wave immigrants fashioned with the American polity after the American Revolutionary War. Our units of analysis will be to critique (1) the structural conditions that uprooted these groups in their homelands, (2) the systems of protection that the government granted them to safeguard their freedom to interact in a human capital environment, and (3) the economic inducements (bootstraps) that the government offered them to connect themselves to the mother lode of America's income redistribution system.

During the whole of the eighteenth century, the majority of the peasants in Europe were either tied to the land by the feudal system or restrained from emigrating by various wars. After the first quarter of the nineteenth century, a combination of peace and the after effects of the Industrial Revolution began to loosen the bands that had kept the peasants tied to their villages. With this new birth of freedom, the peasants began wandering about in their homeland seeking employment. Around the first quarter of the nineteenth century, the economic conditions both in their homeland and in

America precipitated their immigration to America in waves in the 1830s, 1840s, and 1850s.[1]

The Germans and Irish began immigrating to America during the 1830s and 1840s, but the Scandinavians did not begin their immigration until after the American Civil War. The Scandinavians are being compared here with the Irish and Germans, who emigrated some twenty years earlier, to demonstrate that the "social time factor" plays a very minor role, if any, in the rate of group adjustment to American life.

The uprooting of the Germans and Irish was a result of the eighteenth-century Industrial Revolution.[2] This revolution set in motion a chain reaction that had a ripple effect on a vast number of economic and social phenomena, both in Europe, and America. Economically, the revolution created, in Europe new tools by which farmers could cultivate their farms, which in turn increased agricultural productivity and economic growth. This growth created a surplus of goods for the first time since the Dark Ages.[3]

Socially, the economic growth precipitated an increase in the population, which in turn had a profound effect upon the primogeniture practice, which was common in Europe, particularly in Germany and the Scandinavian countries.[4] This practice made provision, to repeat, for the eldest son to inherit the family land. He was obligated to provide for his sisters and brothers, mother, and retired father. He was, by all means, to keep the family on the same social and economic plateau as his father had done before him or suffer the humiliation of allowing his family to lose the social status they inherited.

Land in Germany and the Scandinavian countries was more highly valued than money. It was the sacred value that gave the peasant his social status and prestige in the eyes of his neighbors. If a man lived on his wife's land, he lost his dignity and was usually looked down upon by his peers.[5] Thus, with the exception of the Irish-Catholics, it was the fear of losing their social status and the possibility of being reduced to common laborers that prompted these groups to emigrate to America.

The American Magnet

Although the driving forces that uprooted the Germans, Irish, and Scandinavians were different during this period, the pulling forces in America were somewhat the same: that is, promises of improvement in their social and economic status. The conditions of life in both homelands, however, caused each group to be drawn by what we shall call different magnets:[6] an urban magnet, to which the majority of the Irish responded, and the agrarian magnet, to which the majority of the Germans and Scandinavians responded.

For more than two generations the structural factors both in Europe and America created a tradition where merchants, traders, craftsmen, and artisans settled in the cities, and the farmers moved into the interior and settled on the frontier. This tradition had a determinative impact in prescribing the classes of people populating American cities. There was very little opportunity in the city for the unskilled laborers. Before the federal government intervened, many states had passed laws designed to exclude those immigrants who seemed to be causing social problems such as pauperism, criminality, insanity, and so on.[7]

Economic conditions in America played an important role in the character of immigrants. The construction of the Erie Canal earmarked America's first large public works project. After the canal's completion, New York became commercially important to America by opening a direct line of transportation from the Atlantic Ocean to the interior by way of the Great Lakes. New York began to grow after the completion of the canal, and thereby created a great demand for construction workers. In addition, the majority of the eastern cities had fallen behind in their construction of warehouses, docks, stores, and offices because of the effect that the War of 1812 had upon the economy.[8]

Now in a state of recovery, contractors needed masons, stonecutters, carpenters, woodworkers, and a variety of other craft types.[9] They sent agents abroad to recruit cheap labor. News of opportunities for advancement in the building of canals, turnpikes, and later railroads was passed on. The recruitment of cheap labor abroad for construction of public works projects became a tradition that lasted until the beginning of World War I. The people who usually responded to this calling were the uprooted peasants and displaced artisans who normally constituted the bulk of the surplus labor.

A critique of the conditions of life in each group's homeland will shed some light on the subsequent adjustment and economic growth in America.

The Uprooted Germans

Beginning at the close of the eighteenth century and continuing up to the middle of the nineteenth, the German traditional primogeniture system crumbled as the population increased. In each generation, the land was divided to the extent that it could no longer support a family without the man engaging in day labor. "Thus, if a man with fifty morgen [acres] of land had six children, an equal division upon his death would give less than ten morgen."[10] Such a division would reduce their children to laborers, which in turn reduced their social status.

The social class system in Germany was tenaciously tied to the ownership of, and survival on, the land. The emergence of a new middle class of merchants and traders did not occur in Germany as it had in England a century earlier. The merchants and traders were the despised, but necessary, occupations, which the Germans relegated to the Jews. The Germans' social structure and value system had the following bearing during the whole of the eighteenth century:

> After the ruling prince, it was the officer who enjoyed the greatest respect, after him, or on an equal footing with him, the great landowner, after him the civil servant, then the industrialist, the artisan, the peasant, the worker. Lower than all these in social esteem stood the trading class as a whole—
>
> apart from exceptional cases and individual judgments as to its social value— and within this class again, during the whole of the eighteenth and nineteenth centuries, the merchant who dealt in money instead of real goods: the banker, the bank director, the stockbroker.[11]

As the Industrial Revolution began to spread over Europe, it called for a reorganization of Germany's rural economy; the expansion of the urban market for "foodstuffs" forced changes in the system of cultivation of land in which the application of new agricultural techniques for large-scale farming was a necessity.[12] In order to meet these new demands, peasants mortgaged their farms (after 1815) so that they could modernize them.[13] But the Germans were unable to negotiate this shift successfully because of a series of crop failures, accompanied by a diversion of credit from the agricultural industry to railroad building. This too was a product of the Industrial Revolution.

The stroke that really gave the peasants their final blow was the passage of the emancipation laws, which were intended to improve their status, but in fact added to their economic difficulties by requiring annual cash payment in lieu of the former feudal obligation. Increasingly, mortgages were being foreclosed, and numerous peasants were being pushed off their land. Fearing that they would lose their land and self-respect (being reduced to common laborers), many German peasants sold their land at any price and took their families to America. *pull*

However, many peasants and day laborers first drifted about the countryside seeking employment. Unlike those in other European countries, German factories had not developed to the stage where they could absorb the increasing surplus labor. As a result, thousands of peasants, artisans, and craftsmen were pushed out of the labor market and onto the beachheads of the culture of poverty.[14] The only feasible alternative left open to them—that is, to save their dignity and self-respect and, again, to avoid falling victim to the culture of poverty—was to emigrate to America.

The Early German Peasants

An analysis of the German peasants of the 1830s, 1840s, and 1850s would be incomplete if we restricted our mode of analysis solely to this period. The status of the Germans who emigrated during the period between 1780 and 1829 has to be considered. This group had established political and economic linkages with the American polity that had a profound *MP* effect upon the subsequent behavior patterns of the German immigrants.

The Germans who immigrated during the period between 1780 and 1829 settled on the frontier. The frontier could be divided into two components: North Central and South Central. The 1900 U.S. Census indicates that over 1,461,603 Germans settled in the North Central area, which covers states such as Ohio, Indiana, Illinois, Michigan, Wisconsin, Minnesota, Iowa, Missouri, North and South Dakota, Nebraska, and Kansas.[15] In the South Central area, they settled in states such as Virginia, the Carolinas, Kentucky, Tennessee, Mississippi, Louisiana, and Texas.[16]

The literature indicates that the Germans began settling in these areas when it was considered to be frontier land. They were lured to these areas *pull* by economic inducements offered to them by the government (i.e., free land under the Land Grant Act of 1800). Before the big immigration movement of the 1830s, the early settlers sent news back to relatives in Germany informing them of how they could obtain society's most sacred value—a home and a farm, "without money and without price."[17] A detailed analysis of the German immigrants before the 1830s is not the object of this study. Their settlement is only germane to the extent that it provides a panoramic view of the possible economic and political linkages the immigrants of the 1830s fashioned with the American polity in the initial stage of contact. These Germans served as forerunners for the newcomers. They provided them with assistance and information concerning frontier life and taught them how they could use the American political and economic systems to help them obtain a better life.

In addition to seeking a better life, the early German settlers were also interested in establishing a German state in America. They established a recruitment committee to encourage more farmers in Germany to emigrate to America. Many cities in the Midwest were named after cities in Germany, such as Berlin in Wisconsin, as a means to encourage farmers to immigrate to this area.[18]

The major political significance of the earlier settlers' recruitment efforts was that they had already established economic and political linkages by which the immigrants of the 1830s could move from the seashores of the East Coast directly to the frontier with ease.

German Peasants of the1830s, 1840s, and 1850s

The Germans who immigrated to America before 1848 were from a different class than those mentioned previously. They were political refugees and intellectuals who resisted the "reform ideas of the French Revolution."[19] Their resistance prompted the Baden government to enforce "strict censorship of the press, of public meetings and on the schools and universities."[20] Their resistance was unorganized, but it posed a threat to the political stability of the country. Consequently, government authorities became increasingly alarmed.

It was too expensive to incarcerate the thousands of political prisoners, but the authorities could ill afford to let them remain free to continue their political agitation. As a way out of this political dilemma, the government offered to pay free passage to America for the rank and file of this group. Hence, the political unrest during this period created what we referred to in Chapter 1 as the "siphoning effect," that is, conditions where only the intellectuals, middle and upper classes (the cream of the crop) immigrated.

The majority of the uprooted German peasants of the 1830s and 1840s settled in the North Central and Midwest states, such as Wisconsin, Minnesota, Illinois, Ohio, Indiana, and Iowa.[21] Some settled in the South Central states, as previously stated. They settled at a time when this country's most sacred value was the ownership of a family farm. In fact, the family farm was considered "the backbone of democracy."[22] This is evidenced by the number of land-grant laws passed by Congress over the years.

The Land Act of 1820 offered inducements to farmers by reducing the price of land from $2 to $1.25 per acre. Furthermore, it allowed the average farmer to secure 80 virgin acres of land on credit. This land giveaway, coupled with the notion that the "accumulation of wealth was everywhere recognized as a badge of success and symbol of power,"[23] provided the immigrants between 1830 and 1850 with a set of bootstraps on a silver platter by the government. The average family that had lost its farm in Germany could immigrate to the western frontier penniless and purchase a parcel of virgin land on credit; after a few "years of honest toil," he could meet all of his financial obligations.[24]

The Germans' adjustment on the frontier was similar, in many respects, to the Scots-Irish, who had immigrated some 100 years earlier (see Chapter 2). The climate and soil closely resembled that which they "had left at home. The products of the soil were the same as they had raised in Germany for generations—wheat, rye, oats, and garden vegetables."[25] This was true whether the immigrants settled in Wisconsin, Minnesota, or Texas.

Shortly after the Germans settled on the frontier, they automatically constituted a potentially powerful political bloc. This bloc became increasingly significant to the emerging "New Democracy." This was an era in which the "common man" politics came into vogue. The influx of immigrants added to the already emerging significance of the "New Democracy." The German immigrants who settled on the southwest frontier in the period between 1800 and 1825 helped provide Andrew Jackson with the political leverage to wrest the gauntlet of power away from the elite Eastern establishment in the election of 1829.

The newcomers did not hesitate to use the instrumentalities of government to protect their freedom to acquire property and to pursue economic and employment opportunities. They walked off the boat right onto a political battlefield, where the contest being fought was over the preservation of the common man's liberty and property rights. This was the period when the common man was imprisoned for his debts and "mothers were torn from their infants for owing a few dollars."[26] As we shall see, through political participation, these immigrants were able to secure various forms of release.

In short, the Germans emigrated from one agrarian background to a similar one without having to make radical changes in occupational pursuits. The concept of being an independent farmer, or the ownership of property, was

PUSH

valued both in America and Germany. It was precisely the fear of losing their land and subsequently their social status that pushed Germans to leave Germany. Their ability to settle on a large piece of land in America served to enhance their social status instead of demeaning it. As will be demonstrated in Chapter 10, few Germans ended up in the social disorganization statistics. This within itself indicates that the principle of intergenerational upward mobility was functioning among them.

The Settlement of the Intellectuals, Artisans, and Craftsmen

PULL

The majority of the artisans, craftsmen, and intellectuals did not follow the peasants out west to the prairie but settled in the cities.[27] The German intellectuals sought to improve the social status of the German paupers through organized labor.[28] It is worth noting that the German political refugees came from a different region than did the artisans, craftsmen, and peasants. The former group came from the Baden area while the latter group came from regions where political agitation had been less pronounced and "where business was poor and the future of trade and agriculture was unpromising."[29]

MP

The skilled workers and the intellectuals settled on the Atlantic Coast, where their skills were in great demand. As soon as they made contact with American polity, they began forming unions in their respective trades, in an attempt to wrestle their property rights to employment away from the good will of management and place them on a set of principles (i.e., a *de facto* system of protection). Assisting them in this area were the intellectuals who had been driven out of the Baden region for their political agitation.[30]

The economic conditions in America for artisans and craftsmen were lucrative during the period between 1790 and the 1830s and 1840s. Therefore, the primary concern of tradesmen was to establish a system of protection to safeguard their civil rights to pursue employment opportunities within their trade. They were trying to protect their wage rates (property rights) and the right to form a monopoly over the apprenticeship programs in order to "prevent employers from replacing journeymen with learners, runaway apprentices, and women at wages below union scale."[31]

In New York, for example, employers were arbitrarily and capriciously trying to diminish the wages of craftsmen and artisans through the process of competitive wage cutting–that is, "the workers in a local union in one city often found wages limited by wages received by similar workers in other cities."[32] To prevent this practice, the craftsmen began combining into national craft unions. The first national union, The National Trades Union, was formed in New York in 1834.[33]

Although there was no collective bargaining by which the German unions could engage, their power—both to control the number of persons entering the trade and to strike—was sufficient to take their liberty rights to employment off the goodwill of their employers and to place them on a set of established rules. This system served as a "safety net" to prevent the artisans and craftsmen from falling victim to the culture of poverty. This system guaranteed them the freedom to select their sons and relatives for the apprenticeship programs, thereby ensuring them the opportunity to learn a trade while remaining on the middle-class plateau on which they were born.

Obtaining better working conditions was not the only benefit the unions offered workers during this period. The 1820s through the 1840s marked the Jacksonian period and the emergence of "common man" political parties, which had as their primary aim to improve the lot of the working man. Through political participation, the workingmen were able to translate their personal preferences into public policies. For example, their most notable success during this period was in "bringing free public education, banking reform, mechanics' lien laws, the elimination of imprisonment for debts, and the political franchise for those who did not own property."[34] The election of Andrew Jackson provided them with a means of release. Through various laws and policies, the German farmers were able to take their liberty interest to pursue economic opportunities from the goodwill of their adversaries and place them on a principle of law.[35]

The Uprooted Irish

The conditions uprooting the Irish-Catholics of the nineteenth century were similar to the structural conditions that uprooted the Scots-Irish during the first quarter of the eighteenth century—the restrictive English commercial policy.[36] These policies had long-term political, social, and economic repercussions upon the social status of the Irish.

As mentioned in Chapter 2, the English Parliament passed a law in 1698 that destroyed the manufacturing industry that the Scots-Irish had developed. The Scots-Irish emigrated from Ireland between 1714 and 1720. From this period to the 1830s, Ireland had a predominantly agricultural economy. Underlying this agrarian economy were factors constraining the development of middle-class behavior patterns among the Irish-Catholics.

After the Cromwellian invasion of Ireland in 1650, England passed anti-Catholic penal laws, which in effect made the Irish poorer and kept them socially prostrated.[37] There were changes in land laws that destroyed the Irish security of land tenure and created a landlord class of foreign Protestants. The Irish could no longer own land and were forced to become farm tenants, renting their land. The inevitable consequence of such practices created a spiral rent system in which the land was rented to the highest bidder. These conditions progressed to the point where farming was no longer profitable. Each year the number of farms decreased at a relatively high rate.[38]

Below the status of farm tenants were the cottiers who, by the end of the seventeenth century, constituted the largest percentage of the population, embracing perhaps four-fifths of all Irish families.

The process by which the land was rented in Ireland discouraged the farm tenant from improving his rented land. There was no system of protection that safeguarded his interest to rent the land the following year. Any improvement farm tenants made to increase the productivity of their farms usually benefitted the landlord; no farm tenant had preference to the expired lease; it went to the highest bidder.[39] This practice deprived tenants of their inalienable rights to improve their lot in society. The self-interest of the landlords contradicted property interest rights of the tenants to improve their lot. The former simply maximized their profits by dividing their land into small plots to increase the number of plots to rent to tenants. By 1841, the landlords had divided the land into so many tiny-plots that it reduced the majority of the population of Ireland to mere subsistence.

When the Industrial Revolution swept Europe, the landlords began to consider ways to adjust Ireland's agricultural system to maximize their profits. They found this profit by furnishing wool for the machinery of the Industrial Revolution. Their efforts, however, were hamstrung by the fact that a large number of farm tenants had numerous tiny-plots of land. The landlords could not turn their land into pasture unless they pushed the farm tenants off their land. When the Corn Law, which protected Ireland's grain in the English market, was repealed in 1846, it destroyed Ireland's grain market and gave the landlords a free hand in modernizing their land by turning numerous tiny-plots into pastures.[40] This process sent hundreds of cottiers wandering across the Irish Sea to seek employment in England and Scotland. This migration was stimulated by demands for cheap labor in these countries—especially in England—where there was a great labor demand for the construction of the spreading chain of railroads.[41]

From 1820 to 1841, the Irish had developed a pattern of migrating from Ireland to England in the summer, seeking employment as common laborers, and returning home for harvesting in the fall. When the potato famine struck Ireland between 1845 and 1848, this pattern had developed into a tradition. This phenomenon is significant here because it will support, as we shall see, our hypothesis that ethnic groups do not deviate significantly from the linkages that they formed with a country's polity in their initial stage of contact.

During the potato famine, thousands of Irishmen wandered from town to town, begging; many died of starvation.[42] Aid was sent to the starving Irish by both Englishmen and Americans; however, this aid was not enough to relieve the grave situation, which worsened when the British ceased sending aid because of their policy of *laissez-faire* economics[43]—that is, government "was to keep its hands off private enterprise because such interference, they concluded, would destroy any local incentive to solve their own problems. The only aid, thereafter, that the Irish received from England was from the landlords. They subsidized masses of hopeless peasants to board emigrant ships in order (1) to speed up the removal of the peasants from their land, and (2) to expedite the process of turning farmland into pastures. While the Irish were being pushed off their land, they were simultaneously excluded from the European labor market because of surplus labor in certain countries. They were then confronted with two alternatives: die of starvation or immigrate to America. They opted for the latter and immigrated in waves from the 1830s until the end of the 1850s.

Linkages the Irish Fashioned with America

The magnet that attracted the Irish-Catholics to America, and the skills they brought with them, had the determinative impact on the economic linkages established in their initial stage of contact. The linkages they fashioned were with the unskilled portion of industry, unionization, and municipal employment.

The Irish broke the traditional pattern of immigrants' adjustment and settlement. For more than two generations, the structural factors both in Europe and America had created a tradition in which merchants, traders, craftsmen, and artisans settled in the cities, and the farmers moved into the interior and settled on the frontier. The reason the Irish broke this tradition of settlement was because they were predominantly unskilled workers. They were the only unskilled workers, except for the Germans, who were allowed to emigrate from Europe in the 1830s and 1840s. In England, for example, British officials attempted to restrict the emigration of England's skilled workers by invoking its half-forgotten statute of 1803, which required all British ships "to carry one passenger for every two tons of registry but limited foreign vessels to one passenger for every five tons."[44] The statute did not apply to the Irish, who were a burden to Britain. The British government wanted to rid itself of the unskilled Irish population, but until the economic vacuum was created in America, the poor Irish were not welcome in many places.[45] This new economic development in America promised the Irish a better future than the "rack" renting of small plots of potato patches—a practice that reduced them to the "morgen of subsistence in Ireland."[46]

MP

It is commonly thought that the reason the Irish refused to move to the interior was because they were poor and destitute peasants; consequently, they were forced to accept immediate employment upon disembarkation.[47] If the independent variable was physical property, the Irish could have saved enough money from their earnings to purchase the necessary apparatus for farming. As we shall see, this is precisely what the poor Scandinavians did. The Irish had developed the culture of poverty when they immigrated to America. Instead of moving into the interior, they developed a pattern of following various construction-work projects. As these projects terminated, they returned to the city with no intention of establishing themselves as independent farmers—a value which the American society cherished at the time.[48]

MP

The Irish did not pursue farming as an occupation because they had lost their skills for farming (i.e., human capital). As we have seen, the English government removed the system of protection that allowed the Irish to interact in an environment where they could acquire the skills for large-scale farming; consequently, they were restricted to the cultivation of small potato patches. Land used for growing the latter could support three times as many people as the same plot of land sowed with wheat. The landlords could raise more capital from their land by renting small plots to numerous peasants than they could by renting to farm tenants to grow wheat or corn.

The significant difference between the Irish-Catholics and the Scots-Irish was that the latter group had a tradition for large-scale farming (human capital) when they immigrated to America some one hundred years earlier. They also had developed skills for clearing marshlands. These skills, in part, facilitated their settling on the colonial frontier, but when the Irish-Catholics immigrated to America, they had lost these skills. Special efforts were made by private organizations to lure them out to the frontier,[49] but the Irish kept returning to the cities precisely because they did not have the skills for large-scale farming, which were indispensable for survival on the American frontier. *product of their enviornment*

MP

Irish Politics: Power and Job Security

Shortly after their arrival in America, the Irish entered politics for politi- *pull* cal power and job security. Prior to immigrating in the 1830s, they had witnessed for approximately a century how the Anglo-Saxon government had made a mockery of laws and how officials had used power to their advantage. The inequality of people under the law was engendered into the consciousness of the Irish the concept of power. Everywhere they turned, they were under the influence of power: the power of the Catholic church, and "the power of the landlords and the Anglo-Saxon government author-ity."[50] Hence, the Irish came to view power as an instrument to be used in the interest of those who possessed it. When they entered the politics, there was no uncertainty as to their purpose. They entered it to gain power. More plainly, for the first time in their lives, they saw the gauntlet of power, which had held them socially prostrate for over a century, lying in the ditch; they bent over, picked it up, and used it to place their freedom to economic op-portunities on a principle of law.

The Irish quickly identified themselves with the Democratic party be-cause of (1) their apparent lower-class status, and (2) the religious ethno-centrism practiced by the Protestants. Like the Germans, the Irish entered politics during the Jacksonian era.[51] It was the political ethos of the Jackso-nian era that helped mold their attitudes and practices in politics. During this era, the Irish learned that they could trade votes for tangible benefits such as jobs.

The Jacksonian politics that laid the foundation for the emergence of political machines marked the first time that the Irish had a system of pro-tection to pursue economic security. Being the most illiterate immigrants *pull* during the period between 1830 and 1850, the Irish sought jobs in the mu-nicipal government because these jobs (police, public works, and fire de-partment) required only rudimentary knowledge. Employment in the city bureaucracies offered the Irish a chance to leave the squalor of the slums and to obtain a small measure of economic security and personal respect. Again, this employment offered them a chance to transform from a sedentary peasant economy to one that offered them jobs in the form of job security as well as a chance to sink their culture's roots into the urban community.[52]

It is worth noting here that not all Irish were employed in the public sector. There were a limited number of jobs in this area. But they dominated the ones that were available in this area. As will be discussed later, they were also employed as craftsmen.

The significant aspect of the Irish entering politics during the Jacksonian era was that municipal jobs were low-paying and were looked down upon by the Protestants. As mentioned before, most of the urban dwellers were tradesmen, artisans, or craftsmen, and there was very little room for unskilled laborers such as the Irish before the Jacksonian era. Municipal jobs offered the Irish the same type of security as craftsmanship and artisanship offered other groups. In the last quarter of the nineteenth century, the Irish had full control of the municipal jobs within the great urban triangle formed by St. Louis, Washington, and Boston, when the immigrants of the 1880s appeared on American shores.[53]

The political linkages that were fashioned between the Irish-Catholics and the American polity were made largely through the Catholic church and the Irish saloons. The internal power structure of the church crystallized the attitudes and goals of the Irish toward the means and ends of government and gave them a base for their political organization. The dominant influence of the church in the Irish experience cannot be overemphasized. The parish and the church were closely associated with ward politics. The priests not only recruited parishioners for politics, but they also obtained patronage jobs for them. Securing jobs for the parishioners was both an organizational and a humanitarian concern for the priests. The greater the number of parishioners recruited, the greater the sum of money that could be raised for the church through donations. Therefore, every intercession that the priest made on behalf of his parishioners "strengthened the ties of politics, parish, religion, and the bonds of Irish solidarity and identity."[54]

Although the vast majority of the Irish who settled in the cities were contract laborers, there was a class of artisans and craftsmen among them. These skilled workers formed unions to protect their property rights to employment.

The Irish arrived in America when the labor movement was in its infancy. As we shall see in Chapter 8, the labor movement was slow in getting off the ground because companies employed a tactic called "combination of restraint in trade" to reduce unions' effectiveness.[55] The labor movement began crawling from its cradle in the 1840s and 1850s; after the Civil War, it picked up momentum to the extent that unions served as a *de facto* system of protection to safeguard the Irish property rights to employment. But even before the Civil War, the Irish had developed a propensity for organized labor. For example, in the 1850s, they "constituted three-fourths of the foreign-born masons, plasterers, and bricklayers in the [New York] city, one-half of the carpenters, and one-third of the painters."[56]

Since the Irish outnumbered the German skilled workers, they began to dominate the labor movement in the early 1850s. Around the middle of the decade, they began also to dominate the rank and file of the New York Tailors Trade Association and other unions that were on the rise as a result of America's growing economy.[57]

After the Civil War, the Irish began to organize the first mixed national body of labor (Noble Order of the Knights of Labor). As we have seen earlier, the German craftsmen formed a national union to encompass their own respective trades. But the Irish attempted to form a mixed national, on the assumption that all workers had "common interests and should join forces improving working standards."[58]

The political significance of the Knights of Labor is that the union bound unskilled and skilled workers together by its oaths and rituals. These bonds enabled the Irish to form a monopoly in certain areas and established the framework for the organization of work that determined the relationship between union workers and employers. The unions had the power to determine who, and how many, could be allowed to enter certain occupations. Naturally, the Irish used this power to protect the property rights to employment for their families, relatives, and kinships in both skilled and unskilled jobs. With such a structure, the Irish-dominated unions began to grow rapidly in size "in the 1870s and reached the peak of about 500,000 members in 1886."[59] In fact, their domination of the unions led the German miners, in 1902, to protest that the "Irish monopolized the union offices, favored their own people in the distribution of strike funds, and exploited their positions in the union for personal gains."[60]

As we shall see in Chapter 8, although the Irish were able to establish a *de facto* system of protection to safeguard their rights to employment, they were not able to elevate themselves to the middle-class plateau as a group until the passage of the National Labor Relations Act of 1937. That act provided them with a *de jure* set of bootstraps.

In short, although the Irish did enter other segments of the work force, their major occupation was public employment. Their political activity was expanded by their ability (1) to absorb politics into their everyday lives, and (2) make politics as desirable an occupation for themselves as non-political careers were for other ethnic groups. Therefore, the Irish political career was cast into the social structure of the old peasantry system, which they inherited from the European experience–that of the elder son pursuing the same occupation and political office as his father–that is, mentoring methodology. The Irish still followed this pattern to a large extent into the 1980s.

A Comparative Analysis of Irish and German Economic Linkages

The political and economic linkages that the Germans and Irish fashioned with the American polity in their early stages of contact reflected the amount of human capital that they brought with them. The Germans settled both in the cities and on farms, according to their chosen occupation. As we shall see in Chapter 7, they remained predominantly on the farm up until the 1960s. Then they began to shift their occupational pursuits in accordance with changes in technological development.

The Irish, however, did not pursue farming as an occupation, because they had lost their skills for farming and had developed a pattern of seeking employment as common laborers. The Irish immigrants outnumbered the Germans two-to-one, yet the Germans constituted the largest percentage of independent farmers during this period. For example, in 1850 and 1860, the Irish constituted 43.51 and 38.94 percent of the immigrants during this period while the Germans constituted 25.94 and 31.45 percent, respectively (see Table 3). If simple equality of opportunity was all that was necessary for group economic success, then the Irish should have taken up all of the jobs and available farmland when they first made contact with the American polity. The data overwhelmingly support the theory that both human capital and a system of protection are needed to ensure a group's economic success.

The Irish settled in the cities. Yet, the German artisans and craftsmen who settled there during the same period fared markedly better than the Irish in terms of the percentage employed in skilled occupations. Regardless of whether they were shoemakers (see Table 4), peddlers (see Table 5), or carpenters, the Germans were consistent in surpassing the percentage of Irishmen in certain skilled occupations.[61]

The Scandinavians

The forces that uprooted the Scandinavians were similar to those that uprooted the Germans some 40 years earlier. Their immigration and adjustment to American life supports one of our arguments; that is, if an ethnic group immigrates to a physical and economic environment that approximates the one of their homelands, they will encounter little, if any, difficulty in adjusting to the new environment.

The term "Scandinavian" is used here to describe ethnic groups who emigrated from Sweden, Norway, and Denmark. Significant numbers emigrated from these countries after the Civil War and up to the 1880s.[62] These ethnic groups were able to adjust to American life much faster than the Irish and, to a certain extent, the Germans. Their rapid adjustment can be attributed to the condition of life in their homeland and the economic conditions in America during the time of immigration.

The conditions of life that uprooted the Scandinavians were preponderantly economic.[63] First, the Scandinavian countries began to lose their prestige in the mid-1860s. Denmark was defeated by the Germans in 1864, "and the rise of a new power on the Baltic destroyed the hope of growing Scandinavianism."[64] Consequently, Denmark's defeat reduced the countries on the northern continent to subordinate positions. This defeat was accompanied by three depressing years of crop failure, which destroyed Sweden's capacity as a "grain-exporting country."[65]

Second, there was a reorganization of the economic and agricultural systems in these countries. In the 1830s, the Scandinavians changed from a barter economy to a money economy. The transition precipitated widespread speculation in land. This phenomenon increased the value of land in the rural districts from $5.8 million in 1833 to $67 million in the 1860s.[66] The bulk of this land was purchased through loans from mortgage associations. During the years of crop failure, the farmers were unable to pay the mortgages on their land at the same time that there was a rise in the construction of railroads and the expansion of the factory system—which demanded a large sum of capital. This new demand for capital increased the competition for money, a phenomenon that had the inevitable consequence of increasing interest rates and curtailing agricultural credit.[67] This constraint forced many farmers into bankruptcy. Those farmers who were able to hold on to their land were forced to dispense with their hired labor and cultivate their own land as best they could with the aid of their own families.[68] This in turn created a residual number of unemployed laborers; emigration was the only reasonable alternative.

As economic conditions were the primary force that uprooted the Scandinavians, there also existed economic conditions that were the pulling forces in America. At the close of the Civil War, America turned its attention toward populating the territory that it had conquered and ceded during the Mexican American War. This necessitated opening up the West and expanding the system of railroads.[69]

Table 3
Number and Percentage of Ethnic Groups in the United States, 1850-60

Origin	Census of 1860	Census of 1850	Proportion in 1860	Proportion in 1850
Ireland	1,611,304	961,719	38.94	43.51
Germany	1,301,126	571,225	31.45	25.94
England	432,692	278,675	10.44	12.61
British Amer.	249,970	147,700	6.05	6.68
France	109,870	54,069	2.66	2.44
Scotland	108,518	70,550	2.63	3.19
Switzerland	53,327	13,358	1.29	0.60
Wales	45,763	29,868	1.11	1.34
Norway	43,995	12,678	1.07	0.57
China	35,565	785	0.86	0.03
Holland	28,281	9,848	0.68	0.45
Mexico	27,466	13,317	0.66	0.60
Sweden	18,625	3,559	0.45	0.16
Italy	10,518	3,645	0.26	0.17
Others	60,145	37,870	1.45	1.71
Total foreign	4,137,175	2,210,866	100.00	100.00

SOURCE: Lawrence Guy Brown, *Immigration* (New York: Longmans, Green

and Company, 1933), p. 81.

Table 4

Percentage of Ethnic Groups Employed As Shoemakers in New York City, 1855

Origin	Percentage of Shoemakers to Total Gainfully Employed of the Same Nationality, 1855
Germany	8.13
Poland	5.37
France	5.33
Switzerland	4.84
England	2.88
Ireland	2.04
Scotland	1.78

SOURCE: Robert Ernst, *Immigrant Life in New York City: 1825-1863* (New York: King's Crown Press, 1989), p. 78.

Table 5

Percentage of Ethnic Groups Employed As Peddlers in New York City, 1855

Origin	Percentage of Peddlers to Total Gainfully Employed of the Same Nationality, 1855
Poland	9.06
The Netherlands	4.05
Germany	2.06
France	1.07
Scandinavia	.90
Ireland	.85
Italy	.84

SOURCE: Robert Ernst, *Immigrant Life in New York City: 1825-1863* (New York: King's Crown Press, 1949), p. 78

The tools that Congress decided to use to open up this new territory were the construction of the transcontinental railroad and the settling of farmers along the railroad lines. To achieve this end, Congress commissioned the Union Pacific Railroad Company to build the railroad and passed the Homestead Act of 1862 to provide economic incentives to attract farmers to settle on the prairies.

One of the major purposes for constructing the railroad was to tie the western market to the main arteries of the eastern economic system. To achieve this end, Congress gave generous federal loans and grants to the railroad companies, ranging from $16,000 per mile on the flat prairie land to $45,000 for mountainous country.[70] For every mile of track laid, the government gave the railroad companies twelve square miles of land. This amounted to 640 acres of land per square mile.

In order for the railroad companies to ensure themselves a profit, they needed farmers to settle on the prairies. To achieve this goal, they sent agents to the Scandinavian countries to recruit settlers. In some instances, they offered them free transportation to America if they would agree to settle on the prairies.

When the Scandinavians made contact with the American polity, they also were handed a set of bootstraps on a silver platter. They arrived just in the nick of time to be the beneficiaries of government giveaways—free land provided by the Homestead Act. This act provided for farmers to settle on 160 acres of land free. After living on it for five years and making minor improvements, they could purchase the land for the incredibly nominal fee of $10.

These government giveaways (bootstraps), coupled with the new transportation system that linked the Scandinavian farmers with the main arteries of the economic markets back east, served as a system of protection, which prevented the Scandinavians from falling victim to the culture of poverty in their initial stage of contact. Again, the government giveaway of land also served as a safety net that prevented the second generation of Scandinavians from falling victim to the culture of poverty. This land served as a set of bootstraps by which the Scandinavians were able to pull themselves up to the level of the middle-class plateau. Whatever hardships there were, they were short-lived because farmers were part of the common-man movement, which sought release through political participation.

With the full blessing of the federal government, the Scandinavians were able to pursue their goal of becoming landowners—one of America's most sacred values at the time—and to improve their social and economic status. The Scandinavians were not forced to undergo a prolonged period of agony and deprivation either in their homeland or in America. Their immigration to America was precipitated not by religious persecution or political oppression but because the economic conditions in their homeland had begun to push them off the middle-class plateau onto the beachheads of the culture of poverty. They did not stay on these beachheads long enough to lose their skills for farming, as was typical for the Irish, or their other human capital that they had acquired.

The Scandinavians emigrated from one wheat-growing environment to another. They were, by occupation, predominantly farmers who settled heavily on the prairies of the Mississippi Valley along the railroads, as those were completed. The majority of the Norwegians settled in Wisconsin, Minnesota, Iowa, and northern Illinois. The Swedes concentrated in the upper Mississippi Valley and in the northern areas, such as St. Paul, Minnesota, and Chicago, Illinois. The Danish, who constituted 50,000, settled in Iowa, Minnesota, and Illinois.[71]

The Scandinavians did not settle in the cities, as did the Irish. Even those Scandinavians who were relatively poor upon disembarkation, and who were forced to work for the Northern Pacific Railroad at $1.50 a day, were eventually able to save enough money to purchase a farm, usually in a period of two years or less.[72] The major difference between the poor Scandinavians and their Irish counterparts was that the former had not been off the farm long enough to have lost their skills at farming. Where the Irish had been off the farm for two or more generations before emigration, the Scandinavians had been uprooted less than half of one generation. There were also tradesmen, artisans, and merchants among the Scandinavians. This group settled in the cities with little or no difficulty.

The Scandinavians were predominantly Protestant, and they supported the ideals associated with the accumulation of property and wealth, individualism, and free government based upon constitutional principles. Many values of the Scandinavian people coincided with the American value system. Success in America during this period was manifested in being an independent farmer. The federal government handed to the Scandinavians on a silver platter.

In short, this chapter has supported our argument that what determines a group's success is the human capital (boots) that they bring with them and the system of protection (bootstraps) that the government offers them.

Notes

1.   See Robert Ernst, *Immigrant Life in New York City: 1825-1863* (New York: King's Crown Press, 1949), pp. 1-2.

2.   Oscar Handlin, *Boston's Immigrants* (Cambridge: Harvard University Press, 1959), p. 30.

3.   Brinley Thomas, *International Migration and Economic Development* (Paris: UNESCO, 1961), p. 9.

4.   Oscar Handlin, *The Uprooted* (Boston: Little, Brown and Company, 1951), pp. 24-28.

5.   Ibid.

6.   The term "magnet" is to be understood here as the place where ethnic groups formed a pattern of settlement in their early contact with America.

7.   Lawrence Guy Brown, *Immigration* (New York: Longmans, Green and Company, 1933), pp. 79-132.

8.   Marcus Lee Hansen, *The Atlantic Migration: 1607-1860* (Cambridge: Harvard University Press, 1940), pp. 83-84.

9.   Ibid.

10.   William I. Thomas and Florian Znaniecki, *The Polish Peasant in Europe and America* (New York: Alfred A. Knopf, 1927), p. 117.

11.   F. R. Bienenfeld, *The Germans and the Jews* (Chicago: University of Chicago Press, 1960), pp. 5-6.

12.   Maldwyn A. Jones, *American Immigration* (Chicago: University of Chicago Press, 1960), p. 97.

13.   Ibid., p. 110.

14.   Hansen, *The Atlantic Migration*, chapter 5.

15.   Albert Bernhardt Faust, *The German Element in the United States* (New York: Arno Press and the *New York Times*, 1969), p. 388.

16.   Ibid., p. 431.

17.   Ibid., p. 436.

18.   Ibid., pp. 490-501.

19.   John F. Kennedy, *A Nation of Immigrants* (New York: Harper Torchbook, 1964), p. 52.

20.   Ibid.

21.   Ibid., chapter 15.

22.   Thomas A. Bailey, *The American Pageant: A History of the Republic* (Boston: D.C. Health and Company, 1956), p. 574.

23.   Ibid., p. 320.

24.   Faust, *The German Element*, pp. 476-477.

25.   Ibid., p. 475.

26.   Bailey, *The American Pageant*, p. 228.

27.   Kennedy, *A Nation of Immigrants*, p. 52.

28.   Handlin, *The Newcomers* (Cambridge: Harvard University Press, 1959), p. 18.

29.   Hansen, *The Atlantic Migration*, p. 275.

30.   See definition in Chapter 1 for an explanation of *de facto* and *de jure* systems of protection, pp. 34–35.

31. Lloyd G. Reynolds, *Labor Economics and Labor Relations* (Englewood Cliffs, N.J.: Prentice–Hall, 1970), p. 325.

32. E. Edward Herman and Alfred Kuhn, *Collective Bargaining and Labor Relations* (Englewood Cliffs, N.J.: Prentice-Hall, 1981), p. 8.

33. Reynolds, *Labor Economics*, p. 8.

34. Herman and Kuhn, *Collective Bargaining*, p. 7.

35. Ibid.

36. Marcus W. Jernegan, *The American Colonies* 1492-750 (New York: Longmans, Green and Company, 1956), p. 310.

37. Handlin, *Boston's Immigrants*, p. 38.

38. Edmund Curtis, *A History of Ireland* (London: Methuen and Company, 1968), pp. 319-320.

39. Arnold Scrier, *Ireland and the American Emigration 1850–1900* (Minneapolis: University of Minnesota Press, 1918), p. 12.

40. Edward M. Levine, *The Irish and Irish Politicians* (Notre Dame, Ind.: University of Notre Dame Press, 1966), p. 54.

41. Handlin, *Boston's Immigrants*, p. 43.

42. See Sir Charles G. Duffy, "The Distressed Conditions of Ireland, 1847: An Irish View," in *Historical Aspects of the Immigration Problem*, ed. Edith Abott (Chicago: University of Chicago Press, 1926), pp. 116-120.

43. Levine, *The Irish*, pp. 55–56.

44. Hansen, *The Atlantic Migration*, pp. 82–83.

45. See Cecil Woodham Smith, *The Great Hunger, Ireland 1845-1849* (New York: King's Crown Press, Columbia University, 1962), chapters 1-6.

46. John E. Pomfret, *The Struggle for Land in Ireland: 1800-1923* (Princeton, N.J.: Princeton University Press, 1930), p. 23.

47. Jones, *American Immigration*, p. 121.

48. Carl Wittke, *We Who Built America* (Cleveland: Case Western University Press, 1964), p. 136.

49. Kate H. Claghorn, "The Foreign Immigrant in New York," United States Industrial Commission, *Reports on Immigration*, 42 vols. (Washington, D.C.: Government Printing Office, 1901), 15: 442-494.

50. Levine, *The Irish*, p. 47.

51. Ibid., p. 112.

52. Lawrence Funchs, ed., *American Ethnic Politic* (New York: Harper & Row, 1968), p. 19.

53. For a discussion of the urban triangle, see Handlin, *Boston's Immigrants*, chapter 3.

54. Levine, *The Irish*, p, 131.

55. This topic will be discussed in Chapter 8.

56. Wittke, *The Irish in America* (Baton Rouge: Louisiana State University Press. 1956), p. 217.

57. Ibid.

58. Ibid., p. 222.

59. Ibid.

60. Ibid., p. 225.

61. Ernst, *Immigrant Life*, pp. 1-2.

62. Wittke, *We Who Built America*, p. 257.

63. Florence Edith Janson, *The Background of Swedish Immigration: 1840-1930* (Chicago: University of Chicago Press, 1931), p. 223.

64. Wittke, *We Who Built America* p. 257

65. See G. M. Stephenson, *A History of American Immigrants* (Boston: Ginn and Company, 1926), chapter 2.

66. Wittke, *We Who Built America*, pp. 257–258.

67. Alfred O. Frankelsurd, *The Scandinavian-American* (Minneapolis: K. C. Halter Company, 1915), p. 35.

68. Janson, *The Background of Swedish Immigration*, p. 225.

69. Frankelsurd, *The Scandinavian-American*, p. 36.

70. See John Moody, *The Railroad Builders: Chronicles of America* (New Haven: Yale University Press, 1919).

71. Wittke, *We Who Built America*, p. 280.

72. Ibid., p. 219.

CHAPTER 4

Italian and Jewish Immigrants, 1880–1910

In Chapter 1, it was demonstrated how scientifically fruitful it was to identify (as units of analysis) ethnic groups based on their memories of migration and colonization instead of religious denominations (normative subsystems). Such an analysis will allow us to examine a group's behavior on a systematic basis. We will begin our mode of analysis by examining the conditions of life in the homelands both of Italians and Jews and trace their emigration from their homeland to America. Examining those economic and political linkages that they fashioned with the American polity in their initial stage of contact.

The basic argument in this chapter is that, although these groups were non-Protestants, they did not fall victim to the culture of poverty as did the Irish Catholics because of: (1) the human capital they brought with them, and (2) the *de facto* system of protection that assisted them in getting adjusted to their new environment. It will further be argued that, although these groups did not develop the culture of poverty as did the Irish Catholics, these groups remained pinned down on the beachheads of the culture of poverty until after the 1940s, approximately two generations afterward. It was only after this period that the government issued them a set of bootstraps which catapulted them onto the middle-class plateau. (This will be demonstrated in Chapter 8.)

In studying immigration during the period from 1880 to 1910, we will omit other ethnic groups who immigrated during this period, such as the Slavs, because these groups consisted of numerous ethnic groups, and data about them are incomplete. For instance, the term "Slavs" covers

Poles, Slovaks, Croatians, or Slovenians, Ruthenians or Russniak, Moravians, and Bohemians and Serbians and Montenegrins, Russians, and Dalmatians and Bosnians and Herzegovinians.[1]

The greatest difficulty lies in an attempt to assess the adjustment patterns of the Poles. The U.S. Census Bureau is not allowed to ask questions concerning religious affiliation. Therefore, a clear distinction between Catholic Poles and Jewish Poles is almost impossible from the available data. The greatest difficulties lie with the Jews; the following passage illustrates some of the inherent difficulties in studying them:

> In 1905 there entered at our ports 92,388 Jews from Austria; those who came from the Polish provinces of Russia and Austria (that is probably the greater part of them) appear in the census simply as "native of Poland" and quite distort the facts. Especially as regards to their concentration in cities. The Polish Jews make the census figures for "natives of Poland" almost meaningless as regards Poles.[2]

Therefore, we are going to restrict our analysis to the Italians and Russian Jews, where the data are clear and complete.

Conditions of Life in Europe

The third wave of immigrants differed markedly from the previous groups. For the first time, the immigrants did not consist predominantly of farmers and Protestants. Instead, they were urban dwellers who sought non-agricultural occupations. Their immigration was precipitated both by economic and political factors. For example, the Italians' immigration can be characterized as purely economic. Their country was experiencing a severe overpopulation problem coupled with several years of a depressed agricultural industry. Many Italians immigrated to America with the idea (1) of earning a fortune and returning home to fulfill their lifelong dream of purchasing a farm, or (2) earning enough money to return home and retire in comfort for the rest of their lives. The Russian Jews' immigration, however, was characterized by political oppression and religious persecution. They became scapegoats for the economic ills that Russia was experiencing at the time.

Both the Italians and Russian Jews saw America as a place where they could escape their predicaments. They began immigrating in droves in the early 1880s and continued up to 1914, when the European countries began rumbling up their war machinery in preparation for World War I.

The American Magnet

The Italians and Russian Jews immigrated to America on the heels of the "common man" movement. Out of this movement, workers managed to develop a *de facto* system of protection, which safeguarded their rights to acquire property and to pursue a wide range of economic opportunities. The property rights that they sought were the conditions of employment, which included job security, wages, arbitrary layoff, and other related fringe benefits. This system is referred to here as *de facto* in contrast to *de jure* because collective bargaining was not sanctioned by the federal law; this, as we shall see, came with the adoption of the National Labor Relations Act. Despite its limitations, the immigrants during this period were able to wrestle from employers some measures of job security. Specifically, they were able to place constraints on managerial prerogatives to hire and arbitrarily dismiss their employees or reduce their wages. Up to this period, conditions of employment rested largely on the goodwill of management instead of on a set of established procedures.[3] From this period onward, the unions, which were coming of age, shared in these decisions. Politically, the unions prevented these immigrants from developing the culture of poverty. However, it did not catapult them onto the middle-class plateau. They were not able to make such an accomplishment until after the New Deal programs began to take affect (see Chapter 8).

Economically, these immigrants arrived in the nick of time to ride in on the high tide of an economy that was rapidly expanding and shifting its wealth from rural areas to industrial ones. For example, in 1850, the rural districts accounted for over half of all the wealth in America. But by the 1880s this amount had decreased to 25 percent: $3 billion for rural areas compared to $49 billion for urban and industrial areas.[4]

At the end of the nineteenth century, America was emerging as a prosperous and powerful industrialized nation. In order for a nation to grow economically, there must be available an adequate supply of labor to meet the labor demands. America had a tradition of utilizing the European surplus labor to meet its labor demands and to promote its economic growth. Some scholars have argued that America's policy of turning to Europe for its labor supply (white Europeans) instead of turning to the American South for Black labor was indeed a racial policy. Also, if America had utilized the untapped southern Black labor supply, then questions of Blacks' economic status would have been solved long ago.[5] Racism did play a role in these decisions. However, there were other economic factors as well.

From an economic perspective, the American South—until the turn of the twentieth century—could ill afford to relinquish its labor force without significantly undermining the United States' economy. There was no conceivable way by which the South could have replaced its labor supply without seriously retarding the economy of the United States. The South produced cotton, which was indispensable to the flourishing northern manufacturing industry.

The institution of slavery had been abolished. The climate in the South was so hot that many Europeans did not have a tradition of enduring such a climate. Furthermore, there was very little unoccupied land for independent farmers. America did not need farmers at that time, but laborers to construct railroads, subways, terminals, and bridges.[6] This was the magnet that drew European immigrants to American shores during this period.

The Uprooted Italians

The important phenomenon about the Italian peasants and their immigration to America is the condition of life that forced them off their farms. Italy, unlike other European countries, did not undergo economic development during the eighteenth century as did other European countries. As a result, the industrial development was retarded in Italy.

The lack of industrial development had a profound effect upon the economic status of the peasants. They continued to employ old methods of farming while the northern European countries were implementing new equipments and scientific techniques. The lack of the Italians' success in this area can be attributed to the system of land ownership that gave the farm tenants very little incentive to make improvements on their land, as was true with the Irish. This system was designed for the landlord to realize the greatest share of the profit. Any improvement that the farm tenant made to increase the productivity of the land went not to him, but to the landlord because the farm tenant did not have property interest rights (that is, preference) to his expired lease.

Accompanying this oppressive land system was an increase in population. The population of Italy increased from somewhat fewer than 27 million in 1871 to more than 34 million in 1905.[7] Of this total population, over half the adult male population was engaged in agricultural pursuits. This class, which consisted of farm tenants and day laborers, played a very significant role in the Italian economy because the craft and trade populations were depending upon them for their existence. A decline in their productivity would automatically affect the trade and craft class.[8]

The use of an unequal land system increased the number of common laborers in Italy during the mid-nineteenth century. Regardless of how hard they worked, the common laborers could not raise themselves above mere subsistence. The most attractive alternative for them to improve their lives was emigration.

Economically, as the population of Italy increased after 1871, the staple crops (i.e., olive oil, wine, and wheat) remained stationary.[9] Italy tried to stimulate her industries through protective tariffs, but this measure only benefitted the North, where industry was situated.[10] Also, the rainfall in Southern Italy was so infrequent that even the richest soil produced meager crops.

Italian farmers, despite the oppressive land system, undertook various measures to improve the productivity of their land. They employed such methods as irrigation and fertilization, but these methods proved to be ineffective because of the lack of rainfall.[11] Even the occasional rainfall had very little effect upon the crops. The soil had difficulty retaining water for any length of time due to deforestation, which the Italians had undertaken to make room for new farmland. As we shall see, the skills of irrigation, tillage, and fertilization proved to be very advantageous for the Italian farmers when they immigrated to America.

The peasants were not the only ones who were having problems surviving in Italy. As the country became more industrialized, artisans and craftsmen were being displaced by modern technology. Their products could not be matched by low-cost, factory-made items. They simply could not live on the low wages offered by factory employment.[12] In the 1880s, therefore, there were two classes of unemployed Italians–the skilled workers and the peasants. The only alternative left for these classes to improve their lot was through emigration.

The Italians had begun emigrating from Italy in the 1860s. Their emigration, however, remained relatively small until the 1880s. After this period, the Italians emigrated in much larger numbers. This increase can be attributed to the Italian government, which was one of the few governments that encouraged emigration.[13] It provided a system of protection for its emigrants on their voyage to their designated country and kept a protective interest in them in their new country.[14] The Italian government found it not only socially and politically beneficial to encourage emigration, but also economically advantageous. Emigration provided the Italian government with additional revenue for its failing economy. It was estimated that the immigrants sent from $30 million to $80 million a year back to Italy to their families and relatives. This revenue boosted the Italian economy, especially in the small towns and villages. Numerous such villages emerged from poverty-stricken status to prosperous towns because of this additional revenue.[15]

The Italians' emigration was not restricted to the States. They emigrated to almost every country that had a demand for unskilled labor. The Italians from Northern Italy preferred to emigrate to South America–Argentina and Brazil in particular. These two countries were particularly attractive to the Italians because of their favorable agricultural opportunities. The average Italian peasant who had lost his farm or was forced into day labor could emigrate to Brazil and purchase a farm for very little capital.[16] The Argentine and Brazilian governments were particularly interested in the Italian farmers because of their desire to populate the land. To facilitate their immigration to South America, the Buenos Aires Association, which was an employer organization, sent a delegation to Europe to explore various possibilities by which it could organize immigration to Argentina on a systematic basis.[17] This phenomenon created a pattern by which the Italian agricultural workers could emigrate directly from Italy to Argentina. In other words, they were emigrating from a physical environment without discontinuity in occupational life style. As has been demonstrated, this type of emigration facilitates an ethnic group's adjustment.

From 1876 to 1920, the total emigration from Italy had the following distribution: "To the Americas-North and South-about 9,000,000; to Europe, 7,500,000; to Africa, some 300,000; to Asia, about 11,000; and to Oceania, a little more than 40,000."[18] Although the Italian emigration to other countries is interesting, we are concerned primarily with their immigration to America and an examination of the economic and political linkages (trade, commerce, and real estate) they fashioned between themselves and the American polity in their early stages of contact.

Linkages the Italians Fashioned with America

The linkages that the Italians fashioned with America in their early stage of contact were with agriculture, craftsmen, artisans, contract labor, and small business.

The number of Italian farmers who immigrated to America was minute. The expanding American industry was more attractive to the class of displaced artisans and craftsmen than it was to the agricultural workers who emigrated to South America. According to the United States Bureau of the Census of 1890, 16 percent of the Italians were engaged in agriculture and 16 percent were in domestic and personal service.[19]

The skills that the farmers developed in Italy of tilling, fertilizing, and irrigating swampy and unproductive land proved to be advantageous for those who wished to pursue farming in America.[20] They purchased swampy and unproductive land on both the East Coast and in the South and turned it into productive farmland through irrigation and fertilization. Thus, the Italians were noted for being among the first in America to use fertilizer to increase the productivity of farmland. On the abandoned farmland, they were able to raise sugar cane, corn, strawberries, peaches, and apples in eastern and southern states, such as Arkansas and Louisiana.

The fact that many Italians settled in the South seemed to refute the generally-held view that immigrants refrained from immigrating to the South in the early part of the nineteenth century because they disliked the institution of slavery, and after slavery, because they disliked being associated or working closely with Blacks. The primary reason that the previous immigrants refrained from immigrating to the South was because they did not have the necessary skills conducive to the southern agricultural industry; also there was very little, if any, unoccupied land. For example, before the mass immigration of the Italians to America, numerous Italians settled in and around New Orleans, where their main occupation was fishing, a practice that they developed in Italy. The Italians had a tendency to settle in any part of the United States where conditions allowed them to utilize their skills. They settled particularly on the abandoned farmland in the Midwest around Rockford, Davenport, Joliet, Peoria, East Moline, etc.[21]

The system of protection that the Italians used to prevent the class of unskilled workers from falling victim to the culture of poverty in their initial stage of contact was the *padroni* system. This system constituted a *de facto* system of protection, which safeguarded their freedom to interact in four human capital environments: employment, on-the-job training, commerce, and banking.

The first task of the *padroni* system was to find work for the newly arrived immigrants. This task inadvertently elevated the system to a level where it became a system of employment and distribution of the newly arrived immigrants throughout the United States.

Employment-wise, the *padroni* system was a life-saver for the newly arrived immigrants. It facilitated their adjustment to the American polity by assisting them in finding employment and offering them financial assistance until they could find employment.[22] This system enabled the Italians to develop an employment pipeline by which workers could be transported from the shores of Italy to the main arteries of the economic system in America. For example, the Italians knew precisely where they were going in America and the type of job that was waiting for them at the end of the pipeline. This differed significantly from the Irish, who had to travel around the country from city to city looking for work.

Incorporated in the *padroni* system was a built-in system of on-the-job training, which was made possible by the pattern of immigration. The Italians of small towns and villages in Italy created a pattern of settling among other Italian immigrants from the same villages. The new immigrants seemed to pursue the same occupations as their fellow immigrants, regardless of whether or not they had skills for these occupations. This practice, in turn, served as an on-the-job training program for the unskilled workers.[23] Skilled workers from Northern Italy moved directly into the interior, where they were employed as marble cutters, miners, and mill hands. Many other immigrants were skilled mechanics, masons, stonecutters, bricklayers, carpenters, and cabinet makers. These immigrants resided in New York, where there was a high demand for their skills.[24]

In addition to employment, the *padroni* system provided services that the Italians could not get elsewhere, such as banking, letter writing, and buying and selling real estate property. Among these services, banking proved to be the most significant one. It created an environment whereby the Italians could acquire banking skills by interacting in a money-lending environment. For example, long before the Italians were able to establish their own banks, the average Italian found that he could entrust his money for safekeeping with the *padroni* system until he was ready to return home to Italy, or he could borrow money from it to purchase a farm or to establish his own business. This practice enabled some heads of *padroni* systems to turn this system into a bank, thereby becoming bankers because of the experience they gained in handling money.[25] In New York City, where the majority of the Italians resided, it was estimated by the "Big Five" banks that Italian savings constituted from 15 to 33 percent of their depositors; and they speculated that more than this amount was deposited in the Italian banks and the *padroni* system.[26]

These banks assisted the Italians in branching off to other fields of business. For example, many banks were established to facilitate the Italian saving and commercial business in America and their homeland. Some of the Italian banks established during this period still exist today; one of the largest in the country, Bank of America, has its headquarters in San Francisco.[27]

In addition to their banking system, the Italians established a significant foothold in small business. Groups' success in business, to recapitulate, is highly contingent upon (1) managerial skills they brought with them, and (2) the system of protection that safeguarded their freedom to interact in a business environment after making contact with the American polity. The Italians' success in business lends credence to this theory. For instance, the Italians (who are Catholics) were able to do better in entrepreneurship than the Irish-Catholics, primarily because they had acquired the entrepreneur shills when they made contact with the American polity. They succeeded in business not by trying to pursue those businesses already developed in America, but by introducing new types of business and new concepts; for example, macaroni, artificial flowers, organ grinding, and confections.[28]

The Italians were particularly noted for introducing fruit and vegetable stands to the American small business market. This was made possible by other Italians who engaged in small farming in the outskirts of the city. They furnished the peddlers and the pushcart markets with fresh vegetables and fruits. The method of pushcart selling was somewhat new to America. At the time the Italians immigrated, greater value was placed upon the ownership of large independent farms.[29] It appears that almost all of the industries that the Italians later began to monopolize were closely related to customs and traditions of their homeland. For example, the Italians were heavily concentrated in shoemaking, tailoring, barbering, and the manufacturing of cheese. The Northern Italians were heavily concentrated in mining and masonry. The significant differences between the Northern and Southern Italians lie in manufacturing. In America, the Northern Italians constituted 4,018 of the Italian manufacturers, while the Southern Italians constituted 162 in 1910.[30] This dissimilarity can be explained by the fact that the Italian manufacturing industry was situated in Northern Italy, while the Southern Italians were predominantly farmers.

In short, the structural conditions in both Italy and America restricted the Italian immigration largely to craftsmen, artisans, merchants, and a few farmers until after World War I. Congress passed the Immigration Act of 1917 which restricted immigration to skilled and literate adults,[31] thus truncating the immigration of the unskilled and illiterate peasants. This act prevented the culture of poverty from developing among them, as it did among the Irish-Catholics. There were enough craftsmen and artisans among them to provide a sufficient on-the-job training program for the unskilled, thus allowing the principle of intergenerational mobility to kick in. This system of training was facilitated by the *padroni* system. It was primarily through this system that the Italians were able to fashion linkages between themselves and the American polity. This system was later used to transform the Italian workers into the labor unions, which provided them with a high degree of economic security. When the federal government clothed the labor unions with a *de jure* system of protection and subsidized their apprenticeship programs, the Italians were able to catapult themselves onto the middle-class plateau, as we shall see in Chapter 8.

Conditions of Life of the Jews in Europe

The Jews who emigrated to the United States during the last part of the nineteenth century and the early part of the twentieth century came largely from the Russian Empire, Austria-Hungary, and Romania. They were not up-rooted from the land, as was typical of the Italians, but they were driven out of the Russian Empire because of the peculiar economic positions that they held.[32] They dominated the trade and commerce throughout the empire. At the close of the nineteenth century, Russia attempted to undergo industrial development. In order to do so, it had to take control of trade and commerce, which the Jews had controlled since the Middle Ages.[33] The Jews' concentration in these fields was due not to a calculated effort on their behalf to achieve economic upward mobility, but to their response to a set of structural conditions that foreclosed their freedom to pursue those occupations that were common to life and that society valued.

In order to better understand how the Jews came to dominate the trade and commercial system, it is necessary to examine the social role that the ghetto played in offering the Jews a system of protection to acquire human capital in those occupations that had a propensity for producing high income in America.[34] Long before it became compulsory, the Jews found it to be socially and eco-nomically advantageous to live in separate parts of the city, primarily to pre-serve their religious practices and to promote their economic enterprises.[35] Through the years, the ghetto became a symbol of isolation and acted as a social wall that kept them apart from the Christians. Whether by decree, law, or their own volition, the Jews developed the ghetto into a universal institution. This was particularly true in those countries that granted them full citizenship—as in the Netherlands. The Jews were forced into trade and commerce because, during the Medieval period, the church prohibited them from engaging in pres-tigious occupations, such as handicrafts, artisanry, and farming.[36] These occu-pations were reserved for the Christians. In other words, the church forced the Jews into those occupations, which were despised but necessary.

One of the despised occupations that proved to be economically advanta-geous for the Jews when they emigrated to America was banking. They had been engaged in banking, or money lending, ever since the medieval period. At that time, they developed the concept of lending money for interest.[37] The Chris-tian church had long considered the lending of money for interest to be forbid-den by the Scriptures and to be antagonistic to the laws of nature. Lending money had no impact upon the Jewish religion; it was simply an occupation.[38]

Besides lending money, the Jews were able to develop a system of trade and commerce. This system was unparalleled in the circle of Christians. This can be accounted for by the fact that the Jews were not tied to the serfdom or feudal system. Trade and commerce provided a universal institution by which the Jews could travel from one community to another to ascertain the needs and wants of the Christians. This institution in turn provided a system of secret correspondence for international commerce. The Jews consequently gained a distinctive advantage over the Christians, who were forced to rely upon them for international trade.

For a long period of time, the Jews were the only link between the Orient and the Western World. They have been given credit for introducing Oriental products such as tobacco, sugar, and coffee into the West.[39] They also initiated the exchange of wool and clothing between England and Spain, which later became England's staple industry. Therefore, from the Middle Ages to the beginning of the Industrial Revolution, the Jews formed a monopoly over certain forms of international commerce. The wheels of the Industrial Revolution broke this monopoly as a new class of merchants and manufacturers emerged among the Christians, especially in England, as was discussed in Chapter 2.

It may seem on the surface somewhat ironic that the Jews were able to travel from one country to another and conduct trade with the Christians, their oppressors, but the Jews considered trade an abstract phenomenon in which all emotions fell into the background. They felt free to trade with their enemies because there were no personal prejudices involved. "The less personal, the less emotional, and the more impersonal, the more abstract the attitudes of the trader, the more efficiently and the more successfully can he exercise his function."[40] From this statement, it can be inferred that the Jews created the impersonal relationships involved in business: that is, they were able to detach personal and familial ties from business, a concept that Max Weber later attributed to the Protestants.

The Jews dominated the business enterprises in almost every country in Europe until those counties began to undergo industrial development. When this occurred, the Jews were pushed out of the occupations previously reserved for them. As we have seen in Chapter 2, the origin of the Industrial Revolution, which can be traced to England, started in the late seventeenth and early eighteenth centuries. During this time, a new middle class of merchants and manufacturers emerged in England, and social prestige shifted from the aristocrats to this new middle class, who began to gain prestige in the public eye, pushing the Jews gradually out of trade and commerce, leaving them with only money-lending in England. It is also worth noting here that it was precisely trade and commerce on which the British Empire flourished.[41]

The Russians, however, were almost two centuries behind the English in developing industrially. Consequently, the Jews remained in commerce and trade in Russia until the latter part of the nineteenth century. Statistics show that in 1897, the Jews constituted only 4.5 percent of the total population in the Russian Empire, but they constituted 10 percent of those engaged in manufacturing and the mechanical pursuits, and 36 percent of these engaged in commerce.[42] When compared to the rest of the Russian population, the Jews were engaged predominantly in industry and commerce in the Russian Empire. The majority of them were concentrated in those parts of the Russian Empire where commerce, manufacturing, and mechanical pursuits took place, namely the Jewish Pale, or the "Pale of Settlement." This territory consisted of 25 provinces— 10 in Poland, 3 in Lithuania, 3 in white Russia, and 9 in southwestern and southern Russia.[43]

In the Pale of Settlement, the Jews constituted 12.1 percent of the total population, 32.1 percent of all those engaged in manufacturing and mechanical pursuits, and 76.7 percent of those engaged in commerce. They also showed significant achievement in the professional services. Here, they constituted 21.7 percent of the professionals, while only 2.9 percent of the total population of the Russian Empire was engaged in these occupations, as indicated in Table 6.

Table 6
Distribution of the Jews in Occupations in the Pale of Jewish Settlement, 1897

Group Occupations	Total	Jews	Percent of Total
Agricultural pursuits	6,071,413	38,538	.63
Professional service[a]	317,710	67,238	21.7
Personal services	2,138,981	250,078	11.7
Manufacturing and mechanical pursuits	1,573,519	500,844	32.1
Transportation	211,983	44,177	20.11
Commerce	556,086	426,628	76.7

Source: *Emigration Conditions in Europe* (Washington: Government Printing Office, 1911), p. 292.
[a]In order to make these figures comparable to figures in the United States, saloon keepers are included in personal services.

This table shows that the Jews constituted the majority of the commercial class and, to a certain extent, a significant part of the industrial class in the Pale of Settlement. In other words, what was true of the Jewish occupations in the whole Russian Empire was increasingly true in the Pale of Settlement. They were mainly artisans engaged in the manufacturing of shoes and wearing apparel. Over half of the tailors and shoemakers in the Pale were Jews, and they constituted a high proportion of those engaged in food production, the building trade, metal working, and the wool and tobacco industries.[44] The practical political and economic importance here is that the Jews became increasingly essential to the economics of the Pale.

Russia's staple industries during the latter part of the nineteenth century were grains, cattle, furs, and hides. The majority of the Jewish merchants in the Pale were dealers in these products, and the Russian peasants depended heavily upon the Jews to export their products. Where the Russian merchants were somewhat unfamiliar with the most elementary principles of trade, the Jews were more advanced in their skillful use of credit and their well-organized commercial system. Thus, the Jews played an important role in the organization of the Russian grains in the Pale and along the Black Sea.[45]

The social characteristics of Jews in the Russian Empire are of immense significance here because their status there will explain, in part, how they were able to achieve economic success in America at a faster rate than other ethnic groups. The Jews were mostly urban dwellers while the non-Jews were predominantly rural:

> In all Russia, 51 percent of all Jews lived in incorporated towns, as against only 12 percent of the non-Jews. Though the Jews constituted 4 percent of the total population, they constituted 16 percent of the town population. In the Pale, where they constituted 12 percent of the total population, they comprised 38 percent of the urban population.[46]

As far as social class was concerned, the Jews had a distinct advantage over the non-Jews, partially because of their urban concentration and occupational pursuits. In Russia, townsmen ranked higher in social status than the peasants; the latter constituted 86 percent of the total Russian population.

Traditionally, the urban population constituted a higher cultural standard than the rural population, and in most cases, the urban population had a higher literacy rate than the rural population. The Russian census of 1897 revealed that the Jewish population contained one-and-one-half times as many literates as the total population of Russia, which indicates that the Jews traditionally placed a higher value on education than the rest of the Russian population.[47]

The economic and social status of the Jews in Romania and Austria-Hungary was somewhat the same as it was in Russia. The principal trades in which two-thirds of the Jewish industrial workers were concentrated in were "tailors, shoemakers, tanners, joiners and planers, and bakers."[48] The Jews in Romania differed somewhat from the Jews in Russia in that the former were concentrated in the glass, clothing, wood and furniture, and textile industries; they controlled these enterprises.

Socially, the Romanian Jews presented the same social characteristics as the Russian Jews. Eighty percent of the Romanian Jews lived in either towns or villages and their educational standards were somewhat higher than the former.[49] However, their standard differed from the Jews' educational attainments in that the Romanian Jews had a higher literacy rate than the total Romanian population only in the age groups above fifteen, but the Romanian urban population between the ages of seven and fifteen had a higher rate of literacy than the Jews.[50] This is attributed to specific restrictions that the Romanian government placed upon the Jews' education. It placed a 10 percent quota upon the number of Jews who could attend public schools, despite the fact that the government provided only a small number of public schools. It also limited the number of private schools that Jews could establish on their own behalf. The Romanian government feared that the widespread cultivation of the majority of the Jewish population would pose a threat to the security of the state.[51] Large sums of Russian monies were spent on loan interest, armaments, new highways, and on an exceptional police force and its administration; very little money was spent for the educational needs of the people.[52]

The economic position of the Jews in Austria-Hungary, to a large extent, paralleled that of the Russian and Romanian Jews. Seventy-three percent of the Austrian-Hungarian Jews were engaged in either commerce or trade. Statistics show that 44 percent were engaged in commerce and trade, and 29 percent were engaged in farming in Austria-Hungary (because the restrictions placed upon the Jews engaged in farming there were not as severe as the restrictions in Russia). In Russia, Jews were forbidden by law to buy or rent land anywhere except in towns; but in Poland these restrictions applied only to the land that belonged to the peasants. The Jews had slightly more opportunity to engage in farming in Poland than they did in Russia.[53]

Socially, the Jews in Austria-Hungary presented somewhat the same social characteristics as did the Jews in Russia and Romania.[54] In almost all of the cities that were situated in the Pale of Settlement, which constituted 40 cities with a population of over 5,000, the Jews constituted 34 percent of the total population.[55]

In short, our examination of the occupations, education, economic functions, and social characteristics of the Jews in Eastern Europe has revealed that they constituted a large proportion of the industrial class in each country. When the Jews began to emigrate to America, they differed somewhat from the Italians and the Irish. Instead of being uneducated and poverty stricken, they were predominantly literate and skilled.

The Jewish Exodus from Russia

In the early 1860s, the Russian Empire began to undertake industrial development. In order to do so, it had to reorganize its economy and to conform with the rest of the western world. Such reorganization necessitated the abolition of the feudal system and the inevitable consequences of freeing numerous peasants from the land. After Russia emancipated its serfs in 1861, the economic conditions became unstable. As time progressed, the peasants' living conditions became increasingly precarious, as their government needed to raise money for the construction of highways and railroads. At just about that time, the peasants turned their attention upon the Jews (who were the merchants and the middlemen) and blamed them for the miserable conditions.[56] The peasants began a series of anti-Semitic campaigns, which erupted into a riot in 1881. In 1882, the Russian government took up the persecution of the Jews by implementing the so-called "May Laws," which placed restrictions upon Jewish worship. They also barred Jews from agriculture, industry, the professions, public office, and equal access to educational opportunities.[57] In addition, a policy of "pogroms" (persecution of the Jews) was adopted.

The persecution of the Jews in the Russian Empire proceeded in a systematic manner from 1881 to 1891."[58] Under the ministry of Count Ignatieff, pogroms took place on a wide scale. The pogroms resulted in 21,500 Jews emigrating from the Russian Empire. But in 1882 and 1883, when the pogroms were forbidden because of a change in ministry, the Jews' emigration from the Russian Empire dropped to 11,920.[59] In May of 1882, a law was passed that prohibited Jews from cultivating any land or residing in villages outside of Pale of Settlement. This law precipitated another large exodus of Jews from the Russian Empire. As Table 7 indicates, the number of Jews who emigrated from the Russian Empire during the period between 1889 and 1899 was 24,275.[60]

The early part of 1904 marked the beginning of the Russian Civil War, which was followed by the Bolshevik Revolution. Both events significantly disorganized the economic life of Russia and had a profound effect upon the state of Jewish people. Because they were involved in trade and commerce, they felt the impact of these events differently than the rest of the population. The anti-Semitic feelings were more extreme than previously expressed, thus encouraging thousands of Jews to emigrate from Russia. They emigrated to many parts of the world, but the majority of them came to the United States.

The only other ethnic group that matched the Jews in proportion of skilled occupations during this period of immigration were the Cubans, who constituted 22,396 of the immigrants. Of the Cubans, 66 percent were recorded as skilled workers.[61]

Table 7
Number of Jews Emigrating to the United States from Russia, 1889-1906

Year of Emigration	Number
1889-1899	24,275
1899-1900	37,011
1900-1901	37,660
1900-1902	37,846
1902-1903	47,689
1903-1904	77,554
1904-1905	92,388
1905-1906	125,284

SOURCE: *Emigration Conditions in Europe* (Washington: Government Printing Office, 1911), p. 280.

Table 8 indicates that more than 67 percent of the Jews who emigrated to America during this period were skilled workers. If the number of professionals, merchants, and dealers was added to the figures of the skilled workers, then it could be said that 73.7 percent of the Jews were skilled workers when they first made contact with America (see Table 8).

As stated previouslyto, the Jews were forced into industrial occupations in Europe not because of their desires to obtain a higher economic status than the rest of the populations but in response to the oppressive policies applied to them by the countries in which they lived. For instance, in Germany, Russia, and Switzerland, the Jews were highly concentrated in the legal professions.[62] The Christians scorned those occupations because lawyers were looked down upon as "debt collectors," a labeling which did not occur in England and France.[63] Ever since the Middle Ages, the Jews have been referred to as "people of the Books,"[64] because they ran the printing presses in many of the European countries after the Renaissance period. These endeavors prescribed a high degree of literacy. The same is true with banking, newspapers, theaters, and stock occupations that the Jews dominated in Europe at various times in history in those countries.

Table 8
Jewish Immigrants Reporting Occupations, 1880-1910

Group	Number	Percent
Professional	7,455	1.3
Skilled laborers	395,823	67.1
Laborers	69,444	11.8
Servants	65,532	11.1
Merchants & dealers	31,491	5.3
Farm laborers	11,460	1.9
Farmers	1,008	.2
Miscellaneous	8,051	1.3
Total	590,264	100.0

SOURCE: Samuel Joseph, *Jewish Immigration to the United States: From 1881 to 1910* (New York: AMS Press Inc., 1967), p. 187.

Linkages the Jews Fashioned with America

The political linkages that the Jews fashioned with the American polity in their initial stage of contact were markedly different from those fashioned by other groups. In their response to political and economic oppression in Europe, the Jews had developed an immense amount of human capital, which allowed them to align themselves with a broad segment of the American economy. For example, they were able to fashion linkages with entrepreneurship, labor unions, and various learned professions which were part of the mother lode of society's income redistribution system. In fact, two-thirds of the Jews originally settled in the four largest industrialized cities: New York, Chicago, Philadelphia, and Boston.[65]

Since the Jews had over 500 years to develop their entrepreneurship skills, it was obvious that they would pursue entrepreneurship upon their disembarkation. The scientific significance of examining the Jews' entrepreneurial pursuits is that this study will shed some light on how the Jews were able to broaden their choice possibilities in America by creating jobs for themselves. They were able to do this because of the entrepreneurial skills that they possessed when they immigrated.

One of the entrepreneurial skills that the Jews brought with them was the ability to detect a need for goods and services and to design a delivery system to provide them. This practice helped significantly to develop America's system of redistribution of goods. From this system, the Jews were able to create numerous jobs for themselves over a period of years. For example, the occupations of the drummer and the peddler were created as a result of this system.

As the American economy grew, the peddler and drummer business increased to the extent that the Jews were able to develop a chain of retail stores, which later came to play a major role in the development of the American economy. The origin of many of the chain retail stores in America can be traced to the works of a peddler or a drummer. These chain stores, however, were not developed overnight. They developed as a result of the principle of intergenerational mobility coming into play among them. The significant aspect here is that the persons who started these stores learned their skills by interacting in a human capital environment at some point in their lives. For example, names such as Macy's, Gimbel's, Strauss, Sears & Roebuck and Co., Rosenwald, and so on, can be traced back in some shape or form to an enterprising peddler or drummer.[66]

Another advantage that the Jews had over other immigrants was their experience in international trade. Over the years, they developed some unique skills in this area. When they made contact with America, they were able to utilize these skills to help other Jewish entrepreneurs develop their businesses. In many instances, the Jewish entrepreneurs who engaged in international trade were utilizing their international connections in trade—that is, the economic linkages fashioned with Jews in other countries.

Another advantage of international trade was that it enabled the Jews to go abroad and recruit capital for business investment. Money was sought by banking families, such as "Seligman, Schiff, Loeb, Lehman, and Warburg who helped recruit overseas capital for investment in the United States."[67] With this capital, the Jews were able to start new enterprises and purchase existing ones, particularly in the garment business.[68]

Although a considerable number of Jews were engaged in business, the majority of them were employed as craftsmen, artisans, and common laborers. The significance of this class of workers is that they contributed to the development of the income redistribution system through organized labor.[69] The Jews immigrated at the time the labor movement had begun to become political potency by influencing public policy, as we shall see in Chapter 8 . The American Federation of Labor (AFL) had made significant headway in wresting the power to determine workers' conditions of employment off the goodwill of management and placed them on a set of *de facto* principles. The Jews arrived just in time to ride in on the high tide of this movement.

Immediately upon their arrival, the Jews formed the United Hebrew Trades with its primary aim of improving the working conditions of the Jewish workers. The Jews were very labor conscious when they made contact with America. According to Oscar Handlin:

> they had the advantage–or usually it proved an advantage–of leadership by a tiny but very aggressive minority of intellectuals and intellectually-minded workers trained in the most advanced trade unions of Europe, men who brought to New York and Chicago experience learned in the Russian *bunds* and in the English labor movement. These thinkers, having escaped from European oppression to the freedom of tenement and sweatshop, were radicals, anarchists, and socialists of many varieties. They regarded the trade union as an instrument in the battle against capitalism, a means of mobilizing the laboring masses for the inevitable struggle for power.[70]

Through the United Hebrew Trades, the Jews were able to organize work in both crafts and light manufacturing, where the Jews were highly concentrated. The Jews were much easier to organize because, in many instances, both the workers and the employers were Jews.[71] The employers did not seek court injunctions to block their employees from organizing, as was the case with non-Jewish employers. "There was indeed no love lost between the 'German' manufacturer and the 'Russian' proletarian; common religion, at first, actually heightened friction. But they could at least talk with each other."[72] With this relationship, the leaders of the United Hebrew Trades were able to organize 89 unions by 1910 with a total membership of over 100,000 in the three large industrialized cities: New York, Philadelphia, and Chicago.

The United Hebrew Trades eventually merged with the AFL. The Jews became deeply involved in union politics. From their rank, emerged giant labor leaders, such as Samuel Gompers, who headed the AFL from 1886 to his death in 1924. The Jews' union activities need not be rehashed here. It suffices to say that they used the unions as instruments (1) to secure political and economic gains, and (2) to protect their freedom to acquire property and to pursue a wide range of economic and employment opportunities. As we shall see in Chapter 8, the unions catapulted the Jews onto the middle-class plateau after the federal government clothed the unions with a *de jure* system of protection.

In short, although the Jews immigrated with the necessary human capital to compete successfully in the American society, a large percentage of them remained pinned down on the beachheads of the culture of poverty for more than two generations. Although they were able to execute the principle of intergenerational upward mobility among themselves to preserve many of their skills, they were not able to catapult themselves to the middle-class plateau until after government intervention (i.e., the liberal policies adopted during and after the New Deal). As we shall see in Chapter 8, the Jews did not actually escape the slums until the 1950s.

Notes

1.   G. M. Stephenson, *A History of American Immigration* (Boston: Ginn and Company, 1962), p. 87.

2.   Emily Greene Balch, *Our Slavic Fellow Citizens, Charities Publication Committee* (New York: John Wiley and Sons, 1910), pp. 457–459.

3.   For a discussion of the problems that workers underwent to establish principles of collective bargaining, see Douglas L. Leslie, *Labor Law* (St. Paul, Minn.: West Publishing Company, 1979), chapter 1.

4.   Solon J. Buck, *The Agrarian Crusade, A Chronicle of America Series* (New York: United States Publishers Association, 1920), p. 101.

5.   The Kerner Commission, *Report of the National Advisory Commission on Civil Disorder* (Washington, D.C.: Government Printing Office, 1968), pp. 287–292.

6.   Andrew F. Rolle, *The American Italians: Their History and Culture* (Belmont, Calif.: Wadsworth Publishing Company, 1972), p. 57.

7.   Ibid.

8.   Robert F. Forester, *The Italians Emigration of Our Times* (New York: Russell and Russell, 1968), p. 87.

9.   Ibid., p. 38.

10.   Stephenson, *A History of American Immigration*, p. 65.

11.   Forester, *The Italian Emigration*, p. 51.

12.   Lawrence Frank Pisani, *The Italian in America* (New York: Exposition Press, 1957), pp. 46-47.

13.   Joseph H. Senner, "Immigration from Italy," *North American Review* 5 (June 1896): 49–57.

14.   Stephenson, *A History of American Immigration*, p. 64.

15.   John R. Commons, *Races and Immigrants in America* (New York: Macmillan, 1913), p. 79.

16.   Stephenson, *A History of American Immigration*, p. 69.

17.   Ibid., pp. 67-69.

18. The Federal Writers' Project, *Italians of New York* (New York: Arno Press and the New York Times, 1969), p. 43.

19. Edward P. Hutchinson, *Immigrants and Their Children: 1850-1950* (New York: John Wiley and Sons, 1956), p. 121.

20. Kate H. Claghorn, "The Foreign Immigrant in New York City," United States Industrial Commission, *Reports on Immigration*, 42 vols. (Washington, D.C.: Government Printing Office, 1901), 15: 475.

21. Daniel J. Elazar, *Cities of the Prairie* (New York: Basic Books, 1970), p. 77.

22. Pisani, *The Italian in America*, p. 85.

23. The Federal Writers' Project, *Italians of New York*, p. 2.

24. Claghorn, "The Foreign Immigrant," p. 475.

25. Ibid.

26. Ibid.

27. Pisani, *The Italian in America*, p. 99.

28. The Federal Writers' Project, *Italians of New York*, p. 2.

29. Ibid., p. 72.

30. Reports of Immigration, *Statistical Review of Immigrants 1820-1910*, 42 vols. (Washington, D.C.: Government Printing Office, 1920), 3: 132.

31. Maldwyn A. Jones, *American Immigration* (Chicago: University of Chicago Press, 1960), pp. 269-70.

32. Major W. Evans-Gordon, *The Alien Immigrant* (London: William Heinemann, 1903), chapter 4.

33. Israel Abrahams, *Jewish Life in the Middle Ages* (London: Macmillian, 1897).

34. Louis Wirth, *The Ghetto* (Chicago: University of Chicago Press, 1929).

35. Ibid.

36. Ibid., p. 24.

37. Abrahams, *Jewish Life in the Middle Ages*, pp. 240-241.

38. Max Weber, *The Protestant Ethnic and the Rise of the Spirit of Capitalism* (New York: Charles Scribner's Sons, 1958), chapters 2-5.

39. Abrahams, *Jewish Life in the Middle Ages*, p. 214.

40. Wirth, *The Ghetto*, p. 25.

41. F.R. Bienenfeld, *The Germans and the Jews* (Chicago: University of Chicago Press, 1960), p. 3.

42. Samuel Joseph, *Jewish Immigration to the United States: From 1891 to 1910* (New York: Columbia University Press, 1914), p. 158.

43. Immigration Commission, *Emigration Conditions in Europe* (Washington, D.C.: Government Printing Office, 1911), p. 265.

44. Joseph, *Jewish Immigration*, p. 44.

45. Ibid., p. 45.

46. Ibid., p. 46.

47. Evans-Gordon, *The Alien Immigrant*, chapter 5.

48 Joseph, *Jewish Immigration,* p. 49.

49. Ibid., pp. 48–49.

50. Ibid., p. 50.

51. Immigration Commission, *Emigration Conditions in Europe*, p. 280.

52. Ibid.

53. See the tables in the back of Joseph, *Jewish Immigration*, and Immigration Commission, *Emigration Conditions in Europe* for a comprehensive view of the social and economic characteristics of the Jews in the Russian Empire.

54. Joseph, *Jewish Immigration*, pp. 51–52.

55. Ibid., p. 52.

56. Commons, *Races and Immigrants*, pp. 91-93.

57. Jones, *American Immigration*, p. 201.

58. Immigration Commission, *Emigration Conditions in Europe*, p. 280.

59. Ibid.

60. Ibid.

61. See Table 20 in the appendix.

62. Thorstein Veblen, "The Intellectual Pre–Eminence of Jews in Modern Europe," in *Essays in Our Changing Order*, ed. Leon Arozrooni (New York: Viking Press, 1934), pp. 219-231.

63. Bienenfeld, *The Germans and the Jews*, p. 17.

64. Ibid., p. 9.

65. Oscar Handlin, *Adventure in Freedom* (New York: McGraw-Hill Book Company, 1954), p. 99.

66. Ibid., pp. 174-210.

67. Ibid., p. 90.

68. Ibid., pp. 92-93.

69. Ibid., pp. 174-210.

70. Ibid., p. 132.

71. Ibid., p. 136.

72. Ibid.

CHAPTER 5

Immigration of Racial Minority Groups Prior to the 1964 Civil Rights Act: Japanese, West Indians, and Puerto Ricans

At the offset, it must be noted here, there are some serious methodological problems in studying racial ethnic groups. One of the inherited problems is that analysts seem to lump all racial ethnic groups into one category and seek to analyze their behavioral pattern based on racial characteristics. This approach overlooks the independent variables that can best explain their behavioral patterns which shape these behaviors (i.e., their interaction with the structural conditions of their homeland). Prior to the adoption of the 1964 Civil Rights Act, this methodological problem did not occur because there were only two major groups: whites and African Americans. Although special surveys were conducted of these groups, the Japanese and Puerto Ricans were largely classified as white by the U.S. Census Bureau. These groups only started claiming minority status after the government started attaching benefits to this status.

The second major problem with studying racial groups is that analysts tend to treat all racial groups as though they have a minority status. Skin color within itself does not give a group a minority status. Instead, they must fit within the U.S. Supreme Court's definition of minority status; they must have the "traditional indicia of suspectness" and have been "saddled with such disabilities, or subjected to such a history of purposeful unequal treatment, or relegated to such a position of political powerlessness as to command extraordinary protection from the majoritarian political process."[1] (Hereafter, reference to the term "minority status" will be referred to those groups that have been "saddled with the disabilities" of race.)

Our study of the Japanese and British West Indians in this chapter will lend support to our argument that skin color within itself does not constrain a group's economic growth and development.

In an attempt to overcome these methodological problems and, at the same time seek conceptual clarity and empirical accuracy, racial minority groups will be treated within the historical context of their immigration to the United States. In this chapter, we will discuss the three racial groups that immigrated before the adoption of the 1964 Civil Rights Act: the Japanese, West Indians, and Puerto Ricans. Because of their long historical experience, African Americans will be treated separately in the next chapter. The Southeast Asians and Latinos will be discussed in separate chapters because they immigrated in large number after the passage of the Civil Rights Act, which provided them with a system of protection.

This chapter will be directed toward demonstrating that racial groups can overcome the effect of race if they are granted a *de facto* or *de jure* system of protection that allows them to interact in a human capital environment. This human capital, coupled with a system of protection, will enable them to compete successfully in a competitive society regardless of their race. It can also prevent them from succumbing to the culture of poverty. Their subsequent mobility can be characterized as largely intergenerational.

The major reason, to hypothesize, that the Japanese and British West Indians did not succumb to the culture of poverty—and Puerto Ricans did—was because of (1) the human capital that they brought with them, (2) the system of protection that safeguarded their freedom to acquire and possess property, and (3) their freedom to pursue a wide range of employment opportunities in their initial stage of contact. On the other hand, the Puerto Ricans fell victim to the culture of poverty because (1) they did not have a system of protection, either *de facto* or *de jure*, which granted them the freedom to interact in a human capital environment, either in their homeland or place of immigration, and (2) there was a set of *de facto* and *de jure* public policies that foreclosed their freedom to connect themselves to the mother lode of society's income redistribution system. Consequently, the principle of intergenerational mobility did not kick in among them to elevate them from the beachheads of the culture of poverty.

The Japanese

The status of the Japanese in the United States has long been anomalous because they once were considered unassimilable. Yet they have not constituted a problem of social disorganization, as has been typical of the Irish. They are not Protestants; yet they have acquired what many so-called Protestant values. Like the Jews, the Japanese are highly represented in the liberal professions. According to the 1970 U.S. Census, for example, they ranked high in the social mobility indicators (educational attainments and income) when compared to twelve other ethnic groups studied in this cohort. Furthermore, the Japanese have achieved a high level of economic security. Harry H. L. Kitano attempted to explain this phenomenon in the following passage:

> If, however, successful adaptation to the larger society consists mainly in acculturation, measured by the ability of a group to share and follow those values, goals, and expected behaviors of the majority, then the Japanese-American group has been very successful. Japanese-American values, skills, attitudes, and behavior apparently do not differ markedly from those of the average American. "Scratch a Japanese-American and find a white Anglo-Saxon Protestant" is a generally accurate statement.[2]

False

Many scholars attempt to attribute Japanese success to their strong family structures and values.[3] These scholars have simply identified the wrong variable in determining this group's economic success. The most fruitful and scientific question that one needs to ask along these lines is: What set of structural arrangements were the Japanese responding to that enabled them to develop such a high level of economic stability? In order to answer this and other related questions, let us turn to Japan and begin examining those structural conditions that granted them the freedom to interact in a human capital environment.

Conditions of Life in the Japanese Homeland

Unlike the European emigrants, the Japanese were not uprooted in their country by political oppression. Their emigration from Japan was characterized largely by an attempt by Emperor Meiji to modernize Japan in 1868. To achieve this goal, he signed the Magna Carta of Japan, which consisted of five Articles. One of these Articles dictated that "knowledge shall be sought throughout the world, so that the foundation of the Empire may be strengthened."[4] Before Emperor Meiji came to power, approximately 43 percent of the boys and 10 percent of the girls had some kind of schooling. After he signed the Magna Carta of Japan, education was made available to all. This provided the basis for a rapid increase in the literacy rate. By 1940, every educable Japanese child had an almost total uniformity of education in the first six years of schooling. This produced a "homogeneity of popular intellectual culture which has probably never been equaled in any society of 70 million people."[5]

The Japanese families were able to internalize the Articles of the Magna Carta of Japan because of their family tradition. The whole family was politicized to adopt a cooperative value system, which applied not only to family members but also to the entire empire of Japan. Everyone was obliged to work toward the improvement not for individual achievement but for strengthening the Empire. Before Meiji came to power, the Japanese government had a long-standing ban on emigration, which had lasted for three-and-a-half centuries.[6] Meiji lifted this restriction in 1868, when he decided to place Japan in competition with the Western world in terms of economic and military power. In doing so, he encouraged the Japanese to travel abroad to acquire Western knowledge—that is, human capital.[7] Within two generations, the Japanese family had internalized the Magna Carta of Japan into its cultural values. When the Japanese began immigrating to America, these cultural values were reflected in their behavior patterns.

The American Magnet

The factors that precipitated the large immigration of Japanese were the labor vacuum in Hawaii created by the Chinese Exclusion Act of 1882 and the stagnant agricultural economy of Japan. The large sugar plantations in Hawaii were in desperate need of laborers to cultivate cane. The plantation owners sent recruiters to Japan, the West Indies, the United States, and many European countries seeking laborers.[8]

The most successful recruitment effort was carried out in Japan was by Robert Walker Irwin, an American businessman living in Japan and acting as consul general to Hawaii in the 1880s. He was successful in organizing the labor supply that the sugar planters so desperately needed because of the social conditions in Japan—widespread unemployment and social unrest.[9] In the southwestern part of Japan, the population was densely settled and had to survive on an inadequate subsistence of farming and fishing. Since the sugar planters of Hawaii were seeking laborers with an agricultural background, Irwin concentrated his recruitment efforts in this area.

Japanese Contact with America

When the Japanese made contact with the American polity, they were not issued a set of bootstraps as was the case with the Germans and Scandinavians. Because of the structural conditions in Hawaii, they were not able to form labor unions to take their rights to favorable conditions of employment off the goodwill of their employers and place them on a set of *de facto* principles, as was the case of the Jews and Italians. Instead, the Japanese immigrated into an environment that was characterized by a severe labor shortage. This shortage provided them with a system of protection that granted them the freedom to interact in a human capital environment. *bootstraps*

Under the Irwin recruitment system, a pattern of immigration was developed between Japan and Hawaii, which lasted up until the immigration restrictions of 1924. Japanese immigration was first restricted to Hawaii, but the labor shortage created by the Chinese Exclusion Act of 1882 precipitated their immigration to the western states—that is, California and Washington—to meet the labor demands in the mines, canneries, lumber camps, railroads and farms, and in the domestic industry.[10] Before 1890, the number of Japanese immigrating to America was very low. For example, between the period 1861 and 1880, only 367 Japanese were reported immigrating to America. However, between the period 1881 and 1890, their number increased to 2,270 and continued to increase up to 1907 (see Table 9).

Table 9
Number of Japanese Immigrated to the United States, 1861-1940

Period	Numbers	Percent of All Immigrants
1861-1870	218	0.01
1871-1880	149	0.02
1881-1890	2,270	0.04
1891-1900	27,982	0.77
1901-1907	108,163	1.74
1908-1914	74,478	1.11
1915-1924	85,197	2.16
1925-1940	6,156	0.03

SOURCE: William Petersen, *Japanese Americans: Oppression and Success* (New York: Random House, 1971), p. 15.

From 1901 to 1907, the Japanese immigration reached its peak; Japanese constituted 1.74 percent of all immigrants for this period. From 1915 to 1924, Japanese immigration to America increased to 2.16 percent of the total immigrants: 85,197.[11] This increase in percentage can be accounted for by the restrictions that World War I placed on European immigration. From 1925 to 1940, and up to the time that Japan and America went to war, Japanese immigration to America averaged a fraction under 400 per year.

When the Japanese began immigrating into Hawaii, they were predominantly agricultural workers. Because of their longstanding policy of isolation, the Japanese had not created a class of merchants comparable in size or aggregated wealth to that of the Western World.[12] Consequently, their early contact with America (Hawaii) was characterized by a residual of farm laborers. An examination of their subsequent concentration in entrepreneurship and skilled occupations may seem on the surface to refute one of our basic arguments—that these behavior patterns are developed by interacting in a human capital environment in their homeland. But this anomaly can be explained by examining the way in which the Japanese responded to the structural conditions of Hawaii.

In Hawaii, the Japanese were able to develop behavioral patterns for skilled occupations and entrepreneurship because of the *de facto* system of protection that the conditions in Hawaii provided them. These conditions granted them the freedom to interact in an entrepreneurial environment. First, Hawaii was not an attractive place in which to live during the latter part of the nineteenth century. There was a shortage of craftsmen and artisans, who were needed for necessary construction on the island. Reluctantly, the few white craftsmen and artisans gave a limited number of Japanese the positions as assistants to skilled workers.[13] Over the years, this practice created a residual of skilled workers as the number of white skilled workers began to decrease further.

It must be noted here that the attempt to keep the Japanese out of the crafts was not an incident that happened in isolation; it was part of the Social Darwinist movement that surfaced after the Civil War. The thrust of this movement was an attempt to make facts conform to theory. This argument holds that nonwhite populations were genetically inferior to whites. To make facts conform to theories, there were concerted efforts made to ensure that the Japanese be prevented from pursuing those occupations that would require the use of the mind.

As the Japanese increased the size of their skilled workers, a law was passed in 1903 designed to foreclose their freedom to pursue skilled occupations; but it was difficult to enforce this law because of economic necessity.[14] From 1903 through World War I, American industry underwent an expansion and thus tied the majority of the skilled white workers to industrial plants in the Midwestern and Eastern states. As a result, it became increasingly difficult for plantation owners to recruit skilled workers to Hawaii. Consequently, they were forced to use available Japanese laborers. Over a period of two decades these conditions allowed for the emergence of a class of skilled workers.

Because of the shortage of white entrepreneurs, the Japanese were able to develop skills necessary for occupations in entrepreneurship.[15] First, there was a demand for goods that could be obtained only from Japan. This demand offered the Japanese opportunities to become importers and merchants. They eventually formed a monopoly in the retail grocery and dry-goods stores in Hawaii.[16] Thus, when the Japanese began immigrating to America at the turn of the twentieth century, they had developed a class of merchants and crafts- MP
men.[17]

Migrating to the Mainland

When the Japanese first immigrated to the mainland, they filled the labor shortage in domestics and personal services and farm labor. Because they had developed the skills for small intensive farming in Japan, they began buying and leasing small plots of farmland. Between 1910 and 1920, Japanese farmers owned 16,000 acres of farmland and leased another 137,000 acres in California. By 1921, they owned 1.67 percent of the cultivated farmland, while constituting only 2 percent of the total population of California.[18] This rapid increase in independent farming resulted in a decrease in the number of Japanese farm lands and an increase in competition in the produce industry.[19] Consequently, California farmers concluded that the Japanese posed serious threats to their economic security. Because of their propensity for small farming, the Japanese recreated the labor shortage in the United States, which they were brought in to relieve in the 1880s.

In order to check the diminishing agricultural labor supply, the California legislature passed anti-alien laws prohibiting the "ownership or leasing of land by aliens ineligible for citizenship and the purchase of land by American-born children of such aliens under parents' guardianship."[20] The alien laws were designed to foreclose the Japanese immigrant's freedom to acquire property in his American-born child's name. However, because of the human capital they brought with them, the Japanese constantly employed various tactics to circumvent these obstacles. This was the case up to the time that their land was confiscated in 1942, when the entire Japanese population was placed in American concentration camps.[21]

The Japanese immigrants' skills for small intensive farming enabled them to corner and monopolize the fresh vegetable market in California, which was a multimillion-dollar market at the time. For example, for those marketable crops in which they specialized, they operated 3.9 percent of all the farms in the state and harvested 2.7 percent of all the cropland. But, they produced:

—ninety percent of the snap beans for marketing; celery, spring and summer; peppers; strawberries;

—fifty to ninety percent of the following: artichokes; cauliflower; celery, fall and winter; cucumbers; fall peas; spinach; tomatoes;

—twenty-five to fifty percent of the following: asparagus, cabbage, cantaloupes, carrots, lettuce, onions, watermelons.[22]

This growing monopoly over a multimillion-dollar market was the underlying reason why the Japanese were placed in the concentration camps. If national security were the primary reason, as policymakers stated, they would have placed the Japanese in the concentration camps until the end of the war and released them afterward. Instead, they confiscated their land and did not return it after the war. Some Japanese, however, were able to retain their property by deeding it over to African Americans for safekeeping for the duration of the war. After the war, they deeded this property back to them.

The concentration camps did not have the same devastating effect upon the Japanese social structure as the institution of slavery had upon African Americans, as we shall see. The Japanese were stripped only of their physical capital and not their human capital. It can be argued that they were pushed off the middle-class plateau onto the beachheads of the culture of poverty the same as many of the other European immigrants. But they did not remain there long enough to succumb to the culture of poverty. As we have seen with the Irish, it takes more than two generations to destroy human capital within an ethnic group. When the census was taken of the Japanese in 1960, they had no deficit in human capital compared to other groups studied in this cohort. For example, the average percentage of professionals for this cohort was 6.2 percent; the average for farmers and farm managers was 9.7 percent; the Japanese had 15.3 percent. However, they were below the average in the craftsmen category; the cohort was 20.8 percent while the Japanese accounted for 9.7 percent. This difference can be accounted for by the locations of the major industries. The

Japanese were concentrating in the Western states whereas most of the industries were located in the Midwest and Eastern states. However, between 1950 and 1970, the industries began to shift to the West. As a result, the Japanese began to show a marked increase in the craftsman's category. In fact, they surpassed the average for this cohort; the Japanese had 22.2 percent and the cohort was 18.3 percent.[23]

Besides the agricultural industry, the Japanese showed remarkable gains in entrepreneurship on the mainland. "By 1919, for example, 45 percent of the hotels and 25 percent of the grocery stores in Seattle were Japanese owned."[24] The U.S. Bureau of the Census in 1930 recorded that 40 percent of the Japanese males were entrepreneurs. And, it was recorded in 1929 that the Japanese and Chinese retail stores were proportionately more numerous than those of whites.[25] Both the Japanese and the Chinese were able to gain a foothold in the economic system despite structural barriers and racism, which were designed to foreclose their freedom to acquire property. This achievement brings into consideration the broader question of how these racial minority groups achieved success in business in America while African Americans and the Puerto Ricans are still experiencing difficulties.

The argument that has so often been advanced to explain why African Americans have been unable to achieve economic stability is this: because of racism, they were unable to obtain the initial capital to start a business. It is then reasonable to ask how the Japanese and the Chinese overcame this barrier. Both the Japanese and Chinese were able to obtain initial capital to start a business because of their ancient tradition of raising capital through a rotating credit system (human capital).[26] This method of raising money provided an opportunity for them to start their small businesses.

It worth noting here that the most important variable in determining an individual's success in business is the amount of human capital he/she processes (managerial skills). In interviewing small-business managers and through personal observations, this writer has found this theory to hold true. A person who has the necessary managerial skills to run a successful business also has the skills to raise the necessary funds to start a business. The rotating credit system supports this argument. Traces of the rotating credit system can be found in southern China, Japan, and West Africa. As we shall see, the rotating credit system will, in part, explain how the British West Indians were able to gain an economic foothold in New York City while African Americans and Puerto Ricans have not. Let us for the time postpone further discussion of these groups and consider a full elaboration of the rotating credit system.

The concept of the rotating credit system seems to have been developed in China some 800 years ago;[27] the Japanese adopted it from the Chinese in the thirteenth century,[28] and some evidence of its existence can be found in West Africa as early as 1794.[29] The method of the rotating credit system varied in each country, but its mechanical operation achieved the same end–raising initial capital for business.

The Chinese rotating credit system was called *Hui*; the Japanese, *Tanomoshi* or *Mujin*; and the West African, *Esusu* or *Dashi*. Since the principles of the rotating credit systems are basically the same, the following passage, which explains the operation of the Chinese system, will suffice to explain, generally, how the system itself works.

> The Chinese have a peculiar method of obtaining funds without going to commercial banks. If a responsible Chinaman needs an amount of money, he will organize an association, each member of which will promise to pay a certain amount on a specified day on each month for a given length of time. For instance, if the organizer wants $1,300, he may ask 12 others to join with him and each will promise to pay $100 each month for 13 months. The organizer has the use of the $1,000 the first month. When the date of the meeting comes around again, the members assemble and each pays his $100, including the organizer. All but the organizer, who has had the use of the money, bid for the pool. The man paying the highest bid pays the amount of the bid to each of the others and has the money. This continues for 13 months. Each man makes his payment each month, but those who have already used the money cannot bid for it again. By the end of the 13-month period, each will have paid in $1,300 and have had the use of the whole amount.[30]

The full extent to which the rotating credit system has been used by the Chinese, the Japanese, and the British West Indians is unknown. However, the system gives us a logical explanation for their success in business in a competitive and pluralistic society where the large money-lending institutions have a tradition of not lending money to small and new businesses.[31] The greatest benefit that this system had was to widen the range of choice possibilities for groups in their initial stages of contact with America.

As will be demonstrated in Chapter 10, the Southeast Asian refugees of the 1970s and '80s also use this rotating credit system. In discussing this topic in class, this writer has learned from his Asian students that this system is used widely by this group to purchase not only businesses but also to raise the down payment on a home. Instead of getting the group to agree to pay $100 a month, they would agree to pay $5,000 a month. This practice is hard to verify because these groups do not discuss the details of this system outside of their inner circle, but the high rate of home ownership and low rate of loan rejections by the banks lends credence to this theory. (See Table 21 in Chapter 9.)

In short, the Japanese were able to acquire the necessary human capital both in Hawaii and the mainland. They were able to acquire these skills there because of the vacuum of skilled labor. On the other hand, they were able to acquire skills in the craftsmen category in the Western states because unionization was at a minimum. It was not until the late 1960s that the labor unions made any headway in the western states, like California and Washington. These states were among the last to repeal their right-to-work laws. Therefore, the unions were unable to foreclose the Japanese workers' freedom to acquire skills, as they did to African Americans in the midwestern and eastern states (see Chapter 6). Consequently, the Japanese were able to perpetuate and expand MP their class of craftsmen by executing the principle of intergenerational mobility.

The British West Indians

Recently, social scientists have paraded the relatively high rate of economic success of the British West Indians as evidence that *race* is not a factor in determining groups' economic success. This is particularly true when these scientists are attempting to cast doubt on the need for an affirmative action policy for African Americans. They quickly point out that both groups were victims of perpetual slavery. Yet, the West Indians have shown a remarkable degree of economic success while African Americans have not. This section will be directed toward offering a scientific explanation as to why the West MP Indians are able to succeed in spite of their skin color.

In analyzing the West Indians, the structural conditions of the islands will be compared to the structural conditions of the American South to isolate the system of protection that allowed the West Indians to acquire human capital.

The argument that is advanced in this section is that the primary reason the British West Indians were able to fare so well economically was because they had a system of protection both in their homeland and their place of immigra- MP tion that granted them the freedom to interact in a human capital environment. Thus, the human capital they brought with them and the system of protection that America provided them to safeguard their freedom to acquire and possess property and to pursue a wide range of employment and economic opportunities prevented them from succumbing to the culture of poverty.

Structural Conditions in the West Indies

The structural conditions in the British West Indies were not designed to foreclose the West Indians' freedom to acquire the necessary human capital to compete in a competitive society, as they were for African Americans in the American South. Social stratification in the West Indies displayed some basic differences when compared to the latter structure.[32]

At the top of the social hierarchy in West Indian society were the British aristocrats (plantation owners), whose primary purpose for residing on these islands was economic. Below the aristocrats were the Black masses. There was no conflict over tangible values because it was clear the aristocrats owned the land as they did in the American South.

The major difference between the aristocracy of the American South and that of the British West Indies determined in part the race relations between African Americans and whites in both areas. In the American South, the aristocrats lived on the plantation with their wives and children. But in the West Indies, the planters themselves lived on the plantation, and their wives and children for the most part were tucked safely away in England, where they could enjoy the cultural and social life of their mother country. Their children attended school in England and came to the islands only on short visits.[33] As a consequence, the plantation owners' families were far removed from the threats posed by the loss of those intangible values that were an inextricable part of the white southerners' way of life–that is, white supremacy.[34]

Comparatively, the economic conditions that created a vacuum for handicrafts, artisans, and entrepreneurs in the West Indies were absent in the American South. The majority of the goods the South consumed were manufactured. Thus, items such as shoes, dresses, suits, overalls, and hats were readily available both to African Americans and whites through the plantation stores, the towns, or the mail order houses; in the West Indies, these items were made by Black artisans and craftsmen.[35]

Long before their emancipation, the structural conditions of the West Indies were redesigned to encourage slaves to develop a propensity for economics. Society was restructured not for any humanitarian reason but through economic necessity. The following passage epitomizes this necessity:

> Administrative necessity, furthermore, induced the West Indian slaveholders to institutionalize the operation of a slave economy. This indulgence reflected the shortage of whites which relieved West Indian slaveholders of the administrators necessary to supervise subsistence farming as an organized function of the plantation.[36]

These activities created a sense of economics among slaves in the West Indies. In 1820, the British Parliament passed the Consolidated Slave Act, which required slaveholders to provide rights, land, and free time for the slaves to cultivate their own land. All slaves did not wish to cultivate land; some of them pursued a trade or a craft, which encouraged the exchange of goods and thereby created small markets.

The whites did not attempt to interfere with the slave economy. They were afraid that such interference might initiate an insurrection. Thus, slaves in the West Indies preserved elements of their African heritage that seem to have been destroyed among African Americans in the South. It was out of necessity, however, that the plantation owners allowed African Americans in the West Indies some degree of autonomy. This was due to the absence of a large number of lower-class whites. The absence of this lower-class group in the West Indies and its presence in the American South was an important structural difference.

In addition to a *de jure* system of protection that encouraged the West Indians to develop a propensity for economic self-sufficiency, structural conditions operated as a *de facto* system of protection. The political significance of this system is that it granted the West Indians the freedom to interact in a human capital environment after their emancipation. As a consequence, they were able to acquire the necessary skills to compete successfully in a competitive society. Once acquired, these skills were passed down to their children through the principle of intergenerational mobility.

The most profitable skill the British West Indians acquired in their homeland that enabled them to compete successfully in America was entrepreneurship. For example, the majority of the businesses that came under the heading of ethnic demands were owned and operated by the West Indians. On the contrary, in the American South, African American entrepreneurs were confined to shoeshine stands, beauty parlors, barber shops, funeral homes, and other service enterprises that the lower-class whites considered below their dignity.[37]

Because there was not a white middle class living on the islands, the British West Indians had the freedom to pursue many middle-class occupations, such as liberal professionals, doctors, lawyers, civil servants, and so on. Contrastly, these occupations were set aside exclusively for middle- and lower-class whites in the American South by practice and law.

In British and French West Indies' society, there were few, if any, structural conditions designed to foreclose the West Indians' freedom to acquire the necessary human capital to achieve economic stability.[38] The Black middle-class in the West Indies consisted mostly of mulattoes who were sons and daughters of the white aristocrats, or persons related to them in some other way. As the white aristocrats left the islands, they either willed or sold their land to their mulatto children.

As time progressed, mulattoes and middle-class became synonymous. Being a mulatto automatically placed a person psychologically in the middle class, while being Black automatically placed him in the lower and ultimately poorer classes. But this class line did not foreclose the freedom of the West Indians to elevate themselves above their lower class status. Many dark-skinned populations were able to elevate themselves onto the middle-class plateau by the accumulation of wealth, acquiring an education, and through personal achievement.[39] The most important variable here is that there were no structural barriers to foreclose their freedom to do so.

The British West Indians' emphasis on education was in the professions. Unlike African Americans, who were forced into "industrial education," the British West Indians were interested in the theoretical aspects of education and not solely in the practical sides.[40] Not only did they pursue the liberal professions in some of the best universities in England and in France, but:

> various islands' scholarships, e.g., the Rhodes scholarships and the Cambridge scholarships, selected students of unusual ability from the elementary schools of higher education. These scholarships enabled students of poor nurture but gifted with superior intelligence to rise above the social level of which they originally belonged.[41]

Prior to emancipation, the training of Blacks for the liberal professions was confined to European universities. The school that was built in the West Indies was located in Jamaica and was designed to tutor teachers for elementary schools.[42] The elementary schools were the most important social institutions to prepare the West Indians to enter middle-class employment.

There was no public policy of racial segregation in the public schools. Consequently, the growing West Indian child was not subjected to a public policy that denoted them as being racial inferior, as was the case with African Americans. The only separate schools in the West Indies were those schools designed to remove the language handicap for the Asiatic populations. But in the United States, however, four-fifths of all African-Americans' schools of higher education were segregated by law.[43]

Unlike African Americans, the British West Indians were not forced into a political socialization process, which was designed to stamp a feeling of natural inferiority into their hearts and minds.[44] Becoming docile and accommodating was not a precondition for the government to safeguard their freedom to connect themselves to the mainstream of society's income redistribution system. Instead, they were "taught from early infancy to stand up for their rights."[45] As a result of this process, the British West Indians were able to develop a tradition as argumentative "aggressive-type" people, and their "program and principle of accommodation has singularly been different from that" of African Americans.[46] Above all, the West Indians were socialized to assert their manhood in a society, like those in America and in England, which praised "heroism" and "strength," "assertion of manhood," and which condemned weakness as personal inadequacy and inferiority.[47] Hence, there is a contradiction in the American value system. It praised heroism and strength among white males; and at the same time, it promoted personal inadequacy and inferiority among African Americans.

When British West Indians first arrived in America in the early part of the twentieth century, they vociferously opposed any manifestation of discourtesy from whites, and such

> designation as "George," "Sam," which was the white American frequent manner in addressing Negro men, was so emphatically resented by the West Indians, that many employers refused to hire them on that account, complaining that the West Indians did not make good servants.[48]

In short, the structural conditions of the British West Indians' homeland offered them a system of protection to acquire the skills necessary to compete successfully in an industrial and competitive society.

The West Indian Migration

With the war drawing a large number of white men out of the labor force and the southern whites trying to keep African Americans in the South, industry began to focus on the untapped labor force in the West Indies in general and the British West Indies in particular because the latter had one of the largest labor forces.[49] Economic conditions in the West Indies played an important role in Black migration from this area. In the 1890s, the island's staple crops—sugar and lime—had begun to decline. The aristocrats attempted to substitute their staple crops with cotton in the first decade of the twentieth century. This new crop, however, was not enough to employ the labor surplus that emerged at the end of the first decade of the twentieth century.[50]

The labor force in the West Indies was predominantly Black.[51] The West Indians had begun immigrating to the United States in small numbers in 1901. From 1901 to 1910, it is estimated that 15,356 African Americans immigrated to the United States. But the largest number of British West Indians immigrated to the United States between the years of 1920 and 1924, totalling 27,373.[52]

One important factor that differentiated the British West Indians from the African Americans and Puerto Ricans was that British West Indians were from the British Commonwealth, and they had to immigrate under the provisions of the Immigration Act of 1917. This act excluded all persons over the age of sixteen who could not read or write, or had no specific skills. The practical political significance here is that such restrictions only allowed the middle-class, skilled workers, and the upwardly-mobile West Indians to immigrate to the United States.

Of the 6,873 West Indians who immigrated between the years of 1899 and 1990, 46.8 percent of them were classified as skilled workers and 8.3 percent were in the professional occupations. If we were to compute the skilled and professionals together, we would have more than 66.1 percent of the British West Indian immigrants in skilled occupations. Of the 6,873, only 6.4 percent fell into the labor category, and 35.7 percent fell into other skilled occupational categories.[53] The latter percentage consisted mainly of women and children. The economic implication here is that more than 90 percent of the British West Indians who immigrated to the United States had the skills necessary to compete on a level playing field. This large number of skilled and educated individuals helped prevent the culture of poverty from developing among them in their initial stage of contact.

Because a policy of accommodation and docility was not imposed on them on the islands, the British West Indians actively pursued skilled occupations on a broad scale. They were more aggressive than African Americans along these lines and fared much better. They had no fear of the deprivation of their life, liberty, and property at the hands of their adversaries and competitors, because they had the full protection of the federal government while African Americans and the Puerto Ricans did not. For example, when the labor unions attempted to foreclose their freedom to practice their trades, the West Indians had the option of calling upon the British Consul, who in turn would register a diplomatic protest with the United States government. This protest won them immediate release from racial oppression and job discrimination. African Americans, as we shall see, did not receive such a system of protection until the passage of the Civil Rights Acts of the 1960s, and these acts were not nearly so effective as the protection that foreign subjects received under the foreign diplomatic policy.

Shielded with such a system of protection, the British West Indians were able to maintain their middle-class status. Although they experienced some discrimination, it was not systematic enough to foreclose their freedom to connect themselves to the mother lode of society's income redistribution system. Because of the system of protection that West Indians received as foreign subjects, they were, and are still today, slow in taking out American citizenship papers. The average West Indian knows that once he gives up his foreign accent and citizenship status, there is the grave possibility that he/she will be subjected to the same form of police brutality and systematic discrimination as African Americans.

In short, the analysis of the West Indians demonstrates that racism can be overcome over a period of time if a group is granted a system of protection to interact in a human capital environment. They will acquire the necessary human capital to create new choice possibilities to offset the effect of racism, and allow the principle of intergenerational mobility to kick in among their offsprings.

The Puerto Rican Migrants

Although the Puerto Ricans came from one of the islands in the West Indies, they were not immigrants but migrants. Puerto Rico became a province of the United States as a result of the Spanish-American War. Therefore, the Puerto Ricans are American citizens. Their mobility from the island to the United States was one of migration and not immigration as was the case with the British West Indians. As a result, their migration was not restricted to the skilled and well-to-do, as was the case with the West Indians and, to a small extent, the Japanese. Therefore, an analysis of their migration to the states and their subsequent behavioral patterns will lend credence to our basic argument that acquisition of a sufficient amount of human capital is necessary to prevent a group from falling victim to the culture of poverty.

Structural Conditions in Puerto Rico

The experience from which the Puerto Rican migrants emerged differed markedly from the West Indians'. The Puerto Ricans had not acquired the necessary human capital to elevate themselves onto the middle-class plateau, because the island of Puerto Rico had been under Spanish control for more than 400 years.[54] As we shall see in Chapter 11, the development of the Spanish economy was hamstrung by its political calamities and economic structure (i.e., mercantilism).

At the turn of the twentieth century, Spain's economy was predominantly agricultural. It had not developed its industry to canning and packaging food-stuffs, as was typical of United States industries. The Puerto Rican merchants, however, had developed a marketing system by which they bought rice, peas, beans, and other foods from Spain in bulk supply without brand names.[55] The United States, however, had begun to move rapidly toward packaging and la-beling food products.

When the United States took control of the island in 1898 after the Spanish American War, there were only two or three sugar centrals, and the rest of the industries—such as repair shops, mills, and the textile industry—were on the handicraft level. These industries opened with a small number of employees and machines. There were, however, a few cigar and cigarette factories; but shortly after 1901, the American Tobacco Company set up a subsidiary on the island and gradually bought up all such factories and gained complete control of these industries. This was the beginning of the cigar and cigarette mechanization process on the island. By 1909, the American Tobacco Company had driven more than 75,000 workers out of this business, consequently making Puerto Rico's own tobacco factories obsolete. Within a period of ten years, only 500 persons were employed in the island's tobacco industry.[56]

After Puerto Rico was included in the United States tariff system by proclamation of President William McKinley in 1901, their merchants began importing goods from the mainland and thereby establishing their first trade system with the United States. By the end of that year, the United States was supplying Puerto Rico with seven-eighths of its value import while one-eighth was supplied by Spain and the rest of the European countries.

Like all other colonized nations, Puerto Rico's economy was designed to discourage native-born economic development. After the United States gained control of Puerto Rico, the island's system of land tenure was designed to accentuate agriculture. When the sugar industry was introduced, there was a consolidation of small farms into large ones. This consolidation became the catalyst for creating the culture of poverty among the Puerto Ricans. Their socio-economic growth and development had already been constrained by the mercantilism system of Spain. (This system will be discussed in Chapter 12.) This consolidation of small farms into large plantations further promoted the development of the culture of poverty, because it flourished on cheap and unskilled labor. This system also had the same operative effect upon the class of Puerto Rican artisans and craftsmen as the Industrial Revolution had upon the English peasants. That is, it discouraged the development of a class of skilled workers.

From the end of World War I up to the mid-twentieth century, only sugar mills and needle trades were operating in Puerto Rico. Needle work was the largest hand-production industry in Puerto Rico; it was operated by women, who learned the trade through the Catholic schools. These schools required all females to learn needlework. When America took control of the island, makers of linens and women's and children's clothing sent representatives to the island to contract handwork designs with the natives. By the end of World War I, a tradition had been established whereby Puerto Rican women produced handwork for American industry.

During the same period (1899-1930), the island experienced an astronomical population growth. In 1899, the population was 953,000; it increased to 1,554,000 by 1930–with a density of one person per square mile.[57] By 1930, Puerto Rico was one of the most overpopulated islands in the Caribbean.

As in other parts of the Caribbean, the population in Puerto Rico consisted of whites, mulattoes, and African descendants. Puerto Rico, however, differed from the rest of the Caribbean, in that, while other island populations were predominantly Black, Puerto Rico was 74.3 percent white and 25.7 percent Black (see Table 10).

Table 10
Population of Puerto Rico by Race, 1950

Race	Number	Percent
Whites	1,146,719	74.3
Blacks	397,156	25.7
Other races	38	

SOURCE: U.S. Census of 1930, *Outlying Territories and Possessions*, Table 2, p. 136.

Despite their large percentage of whites, Puerto Ricans did not fare as well as the British West Indian immigrants, who were predominantly Black. Again, this supports one of our basic arguments, that race alone does not promote or constrain a group's economic mobility. The focus of analysis must be on government action.

The basic difference between these two Caribbean groups was in educational attainment. Under United States control, the island of Puerto Rico's literacy rate did not increase to any significant degree before the 1950s. When Puerto Ricans began to migrate in large numbers to the United States after World War II, 40 percent of the population was still illiterate.[58]

The Puerto Ricans began migrating to the United States in 1908. Their numbers did not increase above 8,000 until after World War II. As has been demonstrated throughout this book, whenever economic instability occurs in any given society the first to emigrate are the merchants and traders, aristocrats, the political elites, or the well-to-do. From 1908 to 1930, economic and social conditions in Puerto Rico were somewhat stable. Puerto Ricans who migrated before the 1930s were small merchants involved in cigar and cigarette making. By the beginning of the 1930s, Puerto Rico had begun to feel the impact of its population growth. At the close of World War II, America experienced a period of economic prosperity that created a labor shortage. Puerto Ricans became the logical source for cheap labor because the American South had released most of its surplus labor, and many of the European countries were trying to recuperate from the war.

Puerto Ricans' Contact with the United States

After the war, the transportation link between Puerto Rico and the United States improved significantly. Airplane fares to New York, which had been $180, dropped to $75 on regular lines and as low as $35 on certain special flights.[59] Puerto Ricans migrated directly to New York City, where they were employed in the garment factories. In 1950, 187,000 Puerto Rican adults and 58,460 Puerto Rican children were living in New York City.[60] The greatest number of Puerto Rican migrants to reach New York City was during the period between 1952 and 1953, when more than 58,507 entered the city.

One interesting factor about this transition is that there was a large vacuum for labor in the garment manufacturing and processing industry, which allowed the women to employ skills that they had acquired in Puerto Rico. Their migration was caused in part by extremely low salaries and the spiraling cost of living in Puerto Rico. Mechanization, however, did raise the standard of living on the island, but it did not significantly improve the lot of the Puerto Ricans. As the standard of living increased, so did the demand for goods, all of which had to be imported.[61] This discouraged the development of a large class of entrepreneurs, whereas the situation was the opposite with the West Indians.

One social consequence of the Puerto Ricans' migration to the mainland is the number of workers who were downgraded in occupational pursuits in their

initial stage of contact with the northern industrial society. As Table 11 indicates, 42 percent of the men and 34 percent of the women experienced down-
grading in occupational pursuits. These migrants consisted of skilled, white-
collar workers, and semiskilled workers.

The downward mobility of the Puerto Ricans was very much contingent
upon the status of the American economy. Upon their arrival in New York, the
Puerto Ricans were forced to accept jobs on a much lower level than the ones
they had in their homeland. The downward job mobility for the Puerto Rican
women was in the white-collar and skilled categories. However, there was a

Table 11
Last Occupation in Puerto Rico to First Occupation in New York by Sex

Direction Mobility	Men	Women
Upward	13%	15%
Stable	45	51
Downward	42	34
Total (100%)	(265)	(258)

SOURCE: C. Wright Mills end Clarence Senior, *The Puerto Rican Journey* (New York: Harper and Brothers, 1950).

large percentage of Puerto Rican workers who remained on the same occupational level as they had in Puerto Rico. This group consisted of 45 percent of
the men and 51 percent of the women who worked in the garment manufacturing and processing industry. This industry required precision in dexterity, and
the Puerto Ricans, over the years, had developed a tradition for this in the
needlework business.

The garment manufacturing industry was among the lowest paying industries in New York. Historically, it has been attractive to almost all waves of
immigrants who lacked specific skills in their initial stage of contact.

Socially, the Puerto Ricans were very slow to learn the English language,
and they avoided any radical attempt to rid themselves of any stigma of Spanish culture, particularly if they were Black or mulatto. If the latter two groups
rid themselves of their Spanish accent, they would automatically be considered
to be African Americans by whites and be subject to the discourtesy and systematic discrimination with which white Americans were accustomed to treating African Americans. Consequently, the Puerto Ricans tried at all costs to

keep at arms' distance from African Americans because to be associated with the latter was to accept all the ascriptive inferior status that white society had systematically assigned to the population.

The migration of the Puerto Ricans did not radically improve their social status. Possibly the most significant positive factor about their migration is that it reduced overcrowding on the island. Economically, the Puerto Ricans did not make any remarkable showing in entrepreneurship like the British West Indians. According to Daniel P. Moynihan and Nathan Glazer, the Puerto Rican Migration Division estimated that there were more than 4,000 Puerto Rican-run businesses in the city of New York.[62] They took these figures, indicative of Puerto Rican advancement in business, as showing their superiority to African Americans. But a close examination of these businesses reveals that they were on the same level, though different in style and form, as the businesses that African Americans owned and operated in their communities; namely, these were businesses that received little or no competition from whites. For all practical purposes, these businesses were structured to meet ethnic consumer demands; that is, businesses such as "bodegas, little Spanish American food shops, on the side streets."[63] But the majority of the grocery stores in the Puerto Ricans' communities were owned and operated by the white ethnic groups, as was typical of the African American community. Service businesses such as barber shops, drug stores, and pool halls that catered exclusively to Puerto Rican clienteles were owned and operated by Puerto Ricans.

Their occupational pursuits were hierarchically structured at the bottom of the American economic ladder, and they were systematically excluded from many of the low-paying jobs because of language barriers. They were particularly excluded from domestic services and other low-paying jobs that carried as a prerequisite knowledge of the English language. Other service occupations that did not require knowledge of the English language, such as unskilled jobs in the city factories, hotels, and restaurants, employed large numbers of Puerto Ricans.

The Puerto Ricans were used as buffers to undercut the wage demands of African Americans. The former group was willing to work on the same job with the latter but at lower wages. This situation in itself precipitated resentment among African Americans toward the Puerto Ricans.

The Puerto Ricans had some experience with trade unions when they migrated to New York. They joined the International Cigar Makers' Union and the Spanish-speaking branch of the International Ladies' Garment Workers' Union. On the whole, the Puerto Ricans did not care much for the trade unions because the unions practiced discrimination. Unlike the British West Indians, the Puerto Ricans could not call upon any foreign consul to seek release from job discrimination.

The Puerto Ricans arrived in the states after the National Labor Relations Act had been fully implemented by the labor unions. As we shall see in Chapter 8, the political significance of this act is that it took workers' rights to decent conditions of employment off the goodwill of management and placed them on a principle of law. As the unions became more powerful, they augmented their power to foreclose the freedom of African Americans and Puerto Ricans to connect themselves to the mainstream of society's income redistribution. As mentioned in Chapter 1, this mainstream contains an awesome amount of government subsidies, which can only be obtained by being attached to it. These two groups were excluded from participating in this system. Subsequently, their exclusion provided the foundation for the development and perpetuation of the culture of poverty among Puerto Ricans and African Americans.

Although America was a nation of wealth at the time of their migration, they found very little release from the yoke of poverty at the end of their voyage. There were no government-issued bootstraps waiting for them, as there were for the Germans and Scandinavians who found acres of free land waiting for them, or universities to educate and to elevate their children onto the middle-class plateau. Nor were they able to benefit from a system of protection provided by the unions, as did the Jews, Italians, and Poles (see Chapter 8). The conditions in their homeland did not allow them to amass the necessary human capital to compete successfully in a capitalistic society, as did the Japanese and West Indians. In short, the Puerto Ricans left their homeland to escape the jaws of poverty just to be pinned down on the beachheads of deprivation and degradation in America.

Notes

1. *San Antonio School District V. Rodriguez, 411 U.S. 1 (1973)* 30.

2. Harry H. L. Kitano, *Japanese Americans: The Evolution of a Subculture* (Englewood Cliffs, N.J.: Prentice-Hall, 1969), p. 3. The acquisition of some selected middle-class values has been documented by empirical study. See Abe Arkoff, "Need Patterns in Two Generations of Japanese Americans in Hawaii," *Journal of Social Psychology* 50 (August 1959): 75-79.

3. William Caudill, "Japanese-American Personality and Acculturation," Psychology *Monographs* 45 (February 1942): 3-102.

4. William Peterson, *Japanese Americans: Oppression and Success* (New York: Random House, 1971), p.157.

5.   R. F. Dore, "Japan As a Model of Economic Development," *European Journal of Sociology* 5 (1964): 138.

6.   Maldwyn A. Jones, *The American Immigration* (Chicago: University of Chicago Press, 1960), p. 204.

7.   Petersen, *Japanese Americans*, p. 157.

8.   Hilary Conroy, *The Japanese Frontier in Hawaii: 1868-1896* (Berkeley: University of California Press, 1953), pp. 9-13.

9.   Petersen, *Japanese Americans*, p. 9.

10.   Carl Wittke, *We Who Built America* (Cleveland: Case Western University Press, 1964), p. 480.

11.   Petersen, *Japanese Americans*, p. 16.

12.   Ibid., p. 153

13.   U.S. Bureau of Labor Statistics, *Report of the Commissioner of the Labor on Hawaii: 1902* (Washington, D.C. Government Printing Office, 1903), p. 31.

14.   Ibid., p. 45-55.

15.   Conroy, *Japanese Frontier*, p. 25.

16.   Peterson, *The Japanese Americans*, p. 100.

17.   Ibid.

18.   Wittke, *We Who Built America*, p. 481.

19.   Ivan H. Light, *Ethnic Enterprise in America* (Berkeley: University California Press, 1972). p. 9.

20.   G. M. Stephenson, *A History of American Immigration* (Boston: Ginn and Company, 1926), p. 274.

21.   See Edward S. Corwin, *Toward War and the Constitution* (New York: Knopf 1947).

22.   U.S. Congress, House Select Committee, *Investigation of National Defense Migration*, 77th Congress, 2d sess., 4th Interim Report (Washington, D.C. Government Printing Office, 1953), pp. 117-118.

23.   See Tables 24 and 26 in the appendix.

24.   Light, *Ethnic Enterprise*, p.10.

25.   U.S. Department of Commerce, Bureau of the Census, *Fifteenth Census of the United States: 1930.* vol. 1, Distribution, pt. 1. "Retail Distribution" (Washington, D.C.: Government Printing Office, 1933) ; Table 12-C, p. 180, and Table 12–B, p. 615.

26.   Shirley Ardener, "The Comparative Study of Rotating Credit Association," *Journal of the Royal Anthropological Institute* 94, pt. 2 (1964): 201-229.

27.   See Daniel H. Kulp, *Country Life in the South China*, 2 vols. (New York: Columbia University, Press, 1925).

28.   See John F. Embree, *Suye Mura: A Japanese Village* (Chicago: University of Chicago Press, 1939).

29.   Ardener, "The Comparative Study," p. 209.

30.   Helen F. Clark, "The Chinese of New York Contrasted with Their Foreign Neighbors," *Century* 53 (November 1896): 110.

31. Alfred R, Oxenfeldt, *New Firms and Free Enterprise* (Washington, D.C.: American Council on Public Affairs, 1943).

32. D.A.G. Waddel, *The West Indies and the Guianas* (Englewood Cliffs, N.J.: Prentice-Hall, 1967).

33. Barrington Dunbar, "Factors in Cultural Backgrounds of the British West Indian Negro and the American Southern Negro That Conditioned Their Adjustment in Harlem" (Master's Thesis, Columbia University, 1936), p. 26.

34. For a discussion on racism and white supremacy, see Thomas G. Gosset, *Race: The History of an Ideal in America* (Dallas: SMU Press, 1963), chapters 1-5.

35. Dunbar, "Factors in Cultural Backgrounds," p. 7.

36. Light, *Ethnic Enterprise*, p. 38.

37. E. Franklin Frazier, *The Negro in the United States* (New York: Macmillan, 1965), Chapter 13.

38. Stuart B. Philpott, *West Indian Migration: The Monserratt Case* (New York: Athlone Press, 1973), p. 65.

39. Dunbar, "Factors in Cultural Background," p. 13.

40. Ibid., p. 26.

41. Ibid.

42. Ibid.

43. Ira De A. Reid, *The Negro Immigrant* (New York: Columbia University Press, 1939), pp. 48–49.

44. See E. Franklin Frazier, *Black Bourgeoisie* (New York: Collier-MacMillan, Ltd., 1957), p. 112.

45. Reid, *The Negro Immigrant*, p. 110.

46. Ibid., p. 49.

47. See William H. Grier and Price M. Cobbs, *Black Rage* (New York: Bantam Books, 1965), chapter 4.

48. Roi Ottley and William J. Weatherby, eds., *The Negro in New York* (New York: Oceana Publications, 1942), p. 191.

49. See Table 20 in the Appendix.

50. Philpott, *West Indian Migration*, p. 27.

51. See Table 20 in the Appendix.

52. Reid, *The Negro Immigrant*, p. 236.

53. U.S. Immigration Commission, *Statistical Review of Immigration 1820-1910* (Washington, D.C.: Government Printing Office, 1911), p. 96.

54. C. Wright Mills and Clarence Senior, *The Puerto Rican Journey* (New York: Harper and Brothers, 1950), p. 43.

55. Thomas C. Cochran, *The Puerto Rican Businessmen* (Philadelphia: University of Pennsylvania Press, 1959), p. 23.

56. Ibid., p. 33.

57. Martin B. Sworkis, *The Impact of the Puerto Rican Migration on Governmental Services in New York City* (New York: New York University Press, 1957), p. 7.

58. Lawrence R. Chenault, *The Puerto Rican Migrant in New York City* (New York: Columbia University Press, 1938), p. 43.

59. Mills and Senior, *The Puerto Rican Journey*, p. 44.

60. Puerto Rico. Department of Labor. *Migration Division. A Summary in Facts and Figures* (New York: Commonwealth of Puerto Rico, Migration Division, Department of Labor, April 1957).

61. Chenault, *The Puerto Rican Migrants*, pp. 124-125.

62. Ibid., p. 79.

63. Christopher Rand, *The Puerto Ricans* (New York: Oxford University Press, 1958), p. 7.

CHAPTER 6

The Chief Causes of Economic Inequality Among African Americans

Since the Kerner Commission Report posed the question "Why have African Americans been unable to escape the slums as did the European immigrants?" social scientists have been busy cranking out voluminous reports and studies that try to explain the reasons why.[1] Among these reports is a body of literature that purports to present a new view of slavery.[2] The thrust of these writers, it seems, is to drive home the point that the institution of slavery had a positive effect upon African Americans. For example, Nathan Glazer, who has written extensively in this area, wrote: "Whatever blame there was for the unsatisfactory conditions of [African Americans] after the Civil War thus rested with a class that no longer exists (the master class), or unfortunately, with [African Americans] themselves."[3] This statement epitomizes the arguments that critics have advanced since the publication of the Kerner Commission Report. Their arguments are directed toward shifting the blame for the low socioeconomic status of African Americans on their backs instead of anything that society has done to them. This effort was escalated during the Reagan administration and continues to the present day. It can be found in expressions such as "individual responsibility," "self-help," "the blaming the system," "individualism," and so on.

The focus of this chapter is to demonstrate that the present-day conditions of African Americans are a function of the government failure to fulfill its duty and obligation to protect their freedom to grow and develop as it has done for other groups. This failure hamstrung their ability to activate the principle of intergenerational mobility among them on the same level as other groups that received such protection.

Since the theme of this work is that groups' economic success is contingent upon their freedom to acquire and to possess property, we will begin our mode of analysis at the signing of the Emancipation Proclamation and trace the conditions of African Americans' experience from this period up to the time of their migration. Emphasis will be placed on demonstrating how their civil rights have persistently been placed on the good will of their competitors and adversaries. At the same time, the government adopted positive measures to protect the European immigrants' freedom to connect themselves to the mainstream of society's income redistribution system.

Placing a group's civil rights on the goodwill of their adversaries and competitors contradicts the Madisonian theory of democracy for a free society. Madison argued, to recapitulate, that there can be no liberty either for the minority or the majority, as long as the powers to legislate, execute, and judge are concentrated in the hands of the same individuals, whether these individuals are in the minority or the majority.[4] This theory applies equally to the freedom of groups to pursue their goal of becoming economically self-reliant.

The question of whether or not the present-day blame for African Americans' unsatisfactory conditions should be placed on African Americans themselves or on some external factors can be settled by asking this one fundamental question: Is there sufficient evidence to support the contention that African Americans' civil rights, historically, have rested on a principle of law or instituted upon the goodwill of their adversaries and competitors? If the latter is the case, then the blame must rest with the structural arrangement of the political system that failed to safeguard their freedom to connect themselves to the mother lode of society's income redistribution system.

Emancipation Without a Set of Bootstraps

In an attempt to explain the cause of inequality among African Americans, social scientists too often compare the manner in which African Americans were brought over to America to that of the European immigrants. Such comparison inevitably forces scientists to focus on family structure as an independent variable. What usually follows from such analysis is a mechanical elaboration of how the institution of slavery detribalized and annihilated African Americans as human beings, destroying the memory systems that transmit group culture and values in a positive manner from generation to generation.[5] These arguments are basically true—although they are dependent variables. What scientists have overlooked in their analyses are the independent variables, such as the government's failure (1) to issue African Americans a set of bootstraps after emancipation, as it did the European immigrants; and (2) to provide African Americans with a system of protection that would safeguard their civil rights to enter the mainstream of society's income redistribution system as it has done for other groups.

The core of African Americans' present-day lower socioeconomic status can be traced back to the failure of the government to undertake land reform after the Civil War. Specifically, the government abandoned its policy of granting freed slaves "freedom dues," which was a universal practice at that time. When a person was freed from slavery, his master could not simply say: "You're now free to go, and I wish you well." He had the legal obligation to grant him some kind of a stake. As was demonstrated in Chapter 2, the colonial government mandated that masters grant their indenture servants freedom dues at the time of their emancipation. This concept of freedom dues can be traced back to the scripture, which the colonial immigrants relied on heavily.

When the Jews were freed from Egypt and migrated into the wilderness, God told them to go back to their former masters and asked them for "lent" in the form of silver and gold.[6] This edict could be seen as symbolic as to how future masters were to treat their emancipated slaves. This is evidenced by the fact that God, being the alpha and omega, could have provided them with all of the silver and gold that they needed. Congress, it must be noted, did pass a law to grant every newly freed slave family 40 acres and mule. But President Johnson vetoed the measure.

If America had followed through with its proposal to allocate each ex-slave family forty acres and a mule after emancipation, it would have served as a dike against the stream of the culture of poverty. Such measure would have anchored African Americans at the dock of economic self-reliance within the first generation of their emancipation. Their subsequent mobility would have been characterized by intergenerational upward mobility. But the northern industrialists who held the reins of power over the southern economic system after emancipation were not interested in designing a system of protection to ensure African Americans' full enjoyment of American democratic values such as income, safety, and deference.[7]

The rationale that policy-makers gave at the time for not allocating ex-slave families forty acres and a mule was anchored in the American democratic assumption that anyone who wanted to could pull himself up by his bootstraps. Parceling out land, they further argued, would add to the huge national debt.[8] But this argument was a contradiction to the existing public policy. At the time that policymakers were arguing against giving African Americans forty acres and a mule, Congress had passed the Homestead Act of 1862, which, as we have seen, constituted a set of bootstraps on a silver platter (i.e., free land) for the Germans and Scandinavians. Instead of offering these groups just forty acres, the government gave them 160 acres of land, under the Homestead Act, and provided them with colleges and universities under the Morrill Act of 1862 as a means to educate their offspring. These institutions had the operative effect of truncating the culture of poverty from developing among them.[9]

Offering ex-slaves a set of bootstraps after emancipation was nothing new to the modern world. When Russia freed her slaves in 1861, she not only gave them the land on which they had previously worked, but provided them with a system of protection that safeguarded their freedom to purchase land. Before Russian slaves were freed, Alexander II issued several "rescripts" to the nobles in Libenean providence asking them seriously to consider the possibility of emancipating their serfs, on the basis of the following mandatory principles: "(1) the right of the emancipated serf to buy the plot of land on which he lives, (2) the right to buy a parcel of land based upon his needs and ability to pay."[10] To ensure their orderly and proper adjustment to their new status, Alexander II established a statute of "temporary obligation," which allowed the newly freed slaves to enter into an agreement for a period of twenty years to purchase land from the landowners.[11] The operative effect of this time period was that it allowed the slaves to develop a sense of self-determination at their own pace.

The twenty-year period in which the Russian slaves could purchase land from their former masters is of political significance here. The time period constituted almost a generation in which the skills for economic self-reliance (i.e., acquiring human capital) could be developed among the newly freed slaves. On the contrary, the system of protection that America gave her slaves to purchase land–the Confiscation Act of 1861–lasted fewer than five years.[12] The act allowed the federal government to confiscate the land of the Civil War rebels and prevented them from owning land afterward. Consequently, millions and millions of acres of land were suddenly made available for anyone, except the ex-confederates, to purchase. African Americans took advantage of this opportunity by purchasing a large portion of this land without government assistance (i.e., under the Freedmen's Bureau).

The Freedmen's Bureau and the Quest for Economic Self-Reliance

Despite the fact that the government refused to issue African Americans a set of bootstraps, African Americans still would have achieved economic self-reliance within a generation, if their freedom to pursue economic opportunities had been placed on a principle of law. Upon the heels of their emancipation, African Americans had an extraordinary craving for land. They perceived owning land as being a precondition for real emancipation.[13] With the aid of the Freedmen's Bureau, African Americans moved at a miraculously rapid pace in acquiring land with their own resources. The Freedmen's Bureau was "financed not by taxation but the tolls of ex-slaves; the total amount of rent collected from land in the hands of the bureau, paid mostly by Negroes, amounted to $400,000, and curiously enough it was this rent that supported the bureau during the first years."[14]

Under the Freedmen's Bureau Act of 1865, Congress gave the President the authority to appoint a commissioner of the bureau. This act temporarily gave the ex-slaves a system of protection that safeguarded their civil rights to purchase land. The commissioner had the authority to lease unoccupied tracts of land, not exceeding forty acres, to ex-slaves and white refugees for a period of three years. At the end of this period, the tenants had the right to purchase the land.[15]

Further evidence of the ex-slaves' propensity for self-reliance was their enthusiastic support of the Freedmen's Saving and Trust Company. The bank was chartered by Congress in March of 1865. It emanated from the effort of several "union commanders to establish banks in their departments for Negro soldiers."[16] The bank was established by a group of philanthropists.[17] This group took great care to ensure that the bank was established on solid business principles. For example, the group provided that at least two-thirds of the bank's deposits were to be use to purchase government securities. The bank was authorized to use any surplus funds to promote the cause of education among African Americans. Under this charter, the bank was allowed to pay a maximum interest of 7 percent.

The Freedmen's Savings Bank probably was the wealthiest and most financially secure bank in the country at the time. It was reported that in 1874 its total deposits reached approximately $57,000,000.[18] Because two-thirds of these deposits were secured by government bonds, the only way that the bank could have gone under was for the federal government itself to have collapsed, which, at the time, rested within the realm of the impossible. Again, the Freedmen's bank was the only bank in the country chartered by the federal government, and it had a captive clientele of approximately 4 million potential depositors. This factor contributed to its rapid growth in a very short period of time (see Table 12).

Although the bank's headquarters was located in Washington, D.C., it had 34 branches situated throughout the South and in several northern states, including New York and Pennsylvania.[19] Around the 1870s, the board of trustees of the bank changed hands and the solid foundation on which it rested began to crumble. The new trustees were attracted to the bank's enormous assets. In 1870, they introduced a bill in Congress to amend the bank's charter so that

Table 12
The Freedmen's Saving and Trust Company Financial Statement for the Month of August, 1872

BRANCHES	Deposits for the Month	Drafts for the Month	Total Amount of Deposits	Total Amount of Drafts	Balance Due Depositors
Atlanta, Ga.	$9,419.68	$11,242.30	$245,200.27	$223,020.17	$22,180.10
Augusta, Ga.	10,771.99	9,217.94	367,653.16	284,406.14	83,247.02
Baltimore, Md.	29,755.52	18,644,.57	1,278,042.32	996,371.98	281,670.34
Beaufort, S.C.	189,600.74	184,924.40	2,99,873.30	2,944,441.88	49,431.42
Charleston, S.C.	67,668.83	84,464.53	3,100,641.65	2,795,176.24	305,465.41
Columbus, Miss.	2,426.15	4,364.34	132,036.46	121,776.67	10,259.79
Columbia, Tenn.	2,552.55	2,086.05	34,088.97	15,738.76	18,350.51
Huntsville, Ala.	7,343.50	10,127.61	415,617.72	364,382.51	52,235.21
Jacksonville, Fla.	67,292.09	57,307.54	3,312,424.55	3,234,445.72	77,978.83
Lexington, Ky.	14,383.85	11,221.13	238,680.22	188,308.76	50,371.46
Little Rock, Ark.	7,871.27	9,506.37	172,392.10	154,914.42	17,477.68
Louisville, Ken.	18,311.01	17,535.75	1,057,587.71	914,504.61	143,083.10
Lynchburg, Va.	3,104.48	1,242.56	36,880.98	18,354.87	18,526.11
Macon, Ga.	6,808.98	7,061.52	197,050.01	156,308.75	40,741.26
Memphis, Tenn.	20,045.40	27,197.06	1,039,097.05	213,861.71	24,244.37
Mobile, Ala.	11,136.05	18,645.62	1,039,097.05	933,424.30	105,672.75
Montgomery, Ala.	8,522.90	8,679.60	238,106.08	213,861.71	24,244.37
Natchez, Miss.	25,548.53	15,005.17	649,256.70	612985.74	36,270.96
Nashville, Tenn.	15,731.46	17,098.58	739,691.88	625,166.40	114,525.48
New Berne, N.C.	38,113.83	37,775.73	1,057,688.32	1,001,645.74	56,042.58
New Orleans, La.	193,145.48	207,878.53	2,393,584.08	2,171,056.95	222,527.13
New York, N.Y.	133,209.58	17,757.38	1,048,762.05	915,047.59	132,714.46
Norfork, Va.	16,771.88	17,757.38	1,048,762.05	916,047.59	132,714.46
Philadelphia, Penn.	11,451.12	9,887.49	357,924.82	278,641.10	29,653.38
Raleigh, N.C.	5,663.29	4,660.18	231,685.82	202,032.44	169,219.26
Richmond, Va.	64,112.51	53,900.72	1,082,152.71	912,933.45	169,219.26
Savannah, Ga.	30,951.23	27,066.33	1,031,173.38	893,321.30	137,852.02
Shreveport, La.	20,688.72	20,599.02	615,876.74	526,490.86	31,996.24
St. Louis, Mo.	26,323.93	20,599.02	915,876.74	526,490.86	89,385.88
Tallahassee, Fla.	4,589.45	4,526.75	361,614.57	329,618.33	31,996.24
Vicksbourg, Mis.	61,691.73	60,068.28	7,438,918.17	6,406,092.39	1,032,825.78
Washington, D.C	323,55.79	296,321.26	7,438,918.17	6,406,092	1,032,825.78
Wilmington, N.C.	10,714.10	12,632.65	457,360.75	407,512.51	49,848.24
Alexandria, Va.	1,929.91	685.80	14,091.77	1,626.35	12,465.42
	$1,461,207.52	$1,364,899.9	$38,245,163.8	$34,000,685.77	$4,244,478.03

SOURCE: George Washington Williams, *A History of the Negro Race in America* (New York: G.P. Putnam's Sons, 1883), p. 410.

one-half of the deposits already invested in government bonds could be invested in other notes and real estate mortgages.[20] This law opened the bank's vault to predators, and the hard-earned savings of the newly freed men were lost within a period of three years.

Many of the predators were not just the average man on the street. They were young men who later formed the "new nobility of industry" during the latter part of the nineteenth century. Among them was Jay Cooke, the banker and the financier.[21] The exact amount of money he took from the bank is not known. However, John Hope Franklin, a renowned African American historian, noted:

> At the time when his business was tottering, Jay Cooke borrowed $500,000 at 5 percent interest, and Henry Cooke together with other financiers unloaded bad loans on the bank. After the big financial houses failed in 1873, there was a run on the bank, and many speculating officials resigned, leaving Negroes to take the blame.[22]

The practical political repercussion that the bank charter amendment had upon African Americans' status is that it took their freedom to pursue a goal of self-reliance off a principle of law and placed them at the mercy of their competitors and adversaries. This measure helped to foreclose African Americans' freedom to purchase land on their own. Furthermore, many southern state governments opposed the branch banks in their states because they had no control over them. And they could not carry out their policy of re-instituting slavery through the guise of the Black Codes unless they could make African Americans totally dependent upon their goodwill. *Money was no good.*

To further foreclose African Americans' freedom to become self-reliant, President Andrew Johnson issued his Proclamation of Pardon for the ex-confederates. From this day onward, these individuals were able to reclaim their land. Before the general pardon, they could not legally "reclaim their property until they had been pardoned and had taken the oath."[23] President Johnson had declared before the war that the large plantations would be seized and divided into small farms. But his issuance of the pardon contradicted this practice.

The condition of African Americans shortly after issuance of the general pardon began to take a nose-dive from which they were unable to recover to the present day. African Americans who had bought land with their hard-earned money were driven off it by the terrorist actions of the Ku Klux Klan, which was created shortly after the Civil War. The influence of the Freedmen's Bureau began to diminish because Congress significantly curtailed its funds and authority. For example, in 1865, the Bureau controlled approximately 800,000 acres of land. In 1868, these acres had been reduced to fewer than 140,000.[24]

President Johnson's Proclamation of Pardon affected African Americans more than economically; it also affected them psychologically; it caused them to lose the faith that the federal government would grant them a fair deal. Despite the pardoning of the ex-confederates, however, many African Americans were able to buy land throughout the South before the Freedmen's Bank collapsed in 1874. For example,

> Virginia Negroes acquired between 80,000 and 100,000 acres of land during the late sixties and early seventies. There were soon a few prosperous Negro farmers with 400 to 1,000 acres of land and some owners of considerable city property. Georgia Negroes had bought, by 1875, 396,658 acres of land, assessed at $1,263,902, and added to this they had town and city property assessed at $1,203,202.[25]

The Black Codes and Their Effect on African Americans

The public policy that had the most profound effect on restraining African Americans' freedom to develop a pattern of self-reliance was the Black Codes. Although the stated purpose of these codes was to regulate labor, their operative effect was to reduce the socioeconomic status of African Americans to a subordinate position to whites both "in-law" and "in-fact." To achieve this end, southerners attempted to divorce African Americans' minds from the land by creating conditions whereby they could be tied to the plantation system physically without becoming psychologically a part of it. This was the same status that African Americans had during slavery. The major difference between this condition and slavery was that under the former condition, the slave-masters had to pay for their slaves; but afterward, they could get free labor by re-enslaving African Americans through these codes.[26] They had political, social, economic, and psychological effect upon their growth and development.

Political Effect

The political effect that these codes had upon African Americans was that they operated to foreclose African Americans freedom to enjoy those rights created by the Emancipation Proclamation, and the Thirteenth, Fourteenth, and Fifteenth Amendments to the Constitution.[27] The southerners copied the Black Codes from the debt-slavery system that the Spaniards used against the Mexi-

Codes from the debt-slavery system that the Spaniards used against the Mexicans until its independence in 1821. The codes became political tools by which employers fenced African Americans in on the plantations in such a way that they could not leave even if they desired to do so. For example, the codes stipulated that African Americans were free to choose their employers at the end of each year. But this was possible if, and only if, they had cleared their debts with their former employer. However, the employer had the sole authority to determine whether or not the tenants' debts were cleared; he kept the books. Any discrepancy that the tenant found in the employer's record-keeping was settled by the employer himself. Under the Black Codes, African Americans could not dispute the white man's word, because such a dispute constituted an act of disobedience, and the employer had the authority to fine them $1 for every offense.[28]

The codes gave plantation owners the legal right to work African Americans a whole year without paying them a penny. There was no redress that African Americans could resort to for a denial of their basic constitutional rights. Thus, these codes institutionalized the white man's words as the law of the land as far as African Americans were concerned—a practice that lasted until the civil rights movement of the 1950s and 1960s.[29]

Social Effect

The absolute authority that the Black Codes gave whites over the lives of African Americans significantly affected their social development. They prescribed the African American male to a caste system, which molded his social and political behavior into a "Sambo" or "Uncle Tom" personality type.[30] For example, these codes prescribed that African Americans males conduct themselves "properly": that is, they demanded "obedience to all proper orders" that his employer gave him.[31] The social significance of this law was that the term "obedience to all proper orders" was left solely up to the arbitrary and capricious interpretation of the employer. The employer had the discretion to interpret "proper orders"–ranging from leaving home without permission to impudence, swearing, or indecent language to or in the presence of the employer, or members of his family, or his agent; to quarreling or fighting among one another.[32] Thus, the authority to levy penalties for disobedience was the tool by which employers could foreclose African Americans' freedom to develop their skills and talents. The operative effect of this practice was that the Black Codes became the catalyst that prevented African Americans from developing a sense of self-reliance and, thereby, creating the sense of dependency they currently have.

Economic Effect

Economically, the Black Codes were a public policy that kept African Americans legally in slavery without the economic liability that accompanied the institution of slavery. For example, the life of an adult male slave had a value ranging from $500 to $1,400. After slavery, this value was removed and the life of an African American worker became penniless to the plantation owners;[33] they were free to hang them at will, while during slavery such an act would have constituted an economic loss to the slave-master.

As we have seen, African Americans had a burning desire to purchase land after their emancipation. In order to develop economically, a group must have a system to protect their freedom to interact in a human capital environment. The codes not only prevented African Americans from interacting in such an environment, but also foreclosed their freedom to take advantage of a wide range of other economic opportunities in society.

Psychological Effect

In addition to foreclosing African Americans' freedom to pursue a wide range of occupations, the Black Codes constrained the full development of their personalities–that is, discouraged the development of a sense of self-determination. These codes not only denied African Americans the enjoyment of America's basic ideals, such as freedom of speech, assembly, petition, and expression, but also societal goal values (i.e, shared power, income, safety, and deference).[34]

The American democratic values that the Black Codes denied African Americans were as important to the development of their personalities as air is to fire. The political significance of democratic values in relationship to the development of the personality has been thoroughly analyzed by Harold D. Lasswell. The whole of his writings was dedicated to analyzing the relationship between public policy and society's respect for human dignity.[35]

Lasswell demonstrates that there is a close relationship between public policy and the development of individuals' personalities. He argues that the individual's personality is developed by the degree to which the environment increases or decreases societal goal values. The personality, he argues, "is an on-going concern which is constantly relating itself as a whole to the environment in which it lives."[36] It expects to acquire societal goal values and, when certain design factors deprive it of these expectations over a period of time, it "exhibits substitutive activities. These substitutive activities . . . will be in the direction of restoring the level of expectation which is usual for the person."[37] In analyzing the sociology of African Americans, E. Franklin Frazier found that the African American middle class had substituted American goal values, such as owning a home in the suburbs (appreciative goods), with purchasing conspicuous consumption goods (depreciative goods).[38]

The Doctrines of Racism and the Institutionalization of Racial Inferiority

There are two doctrines of racism that have been adopted to control African Americans: *Romantic Racism* and *Social Darwinism*. Both of these doctrines provided the basis for the formulation of those policies that fostered racial inequality. The doctrine of romantic racialism was adopted in the 1830s.[39] We are going to defer discussing the impact that this doctrine had in formulating public policies of repression until Chapter 8. Instead, we are going to focus on Social Darwinism, which had its greatest expression after the Civil War.

The Black Codes within themselves were not sufficient to place African Americans in a position of economic, social, and psychological inferiority. The southerners and northern industrialists felt it necessary to adopt a doctrine of racism to achieve this end. This doctrine is better known as "Social Darwinism." The Social Darwinists extended the interpretation of the biological theory of evolution into a theory of the development of a society of conflict in which the stronger and more advanced race would naturally triumph over the inferior and weaker race.[40]

The Social Darwinian Theory received its maximal significance in the concept of the "white man's burden" and "manifest destiny," which had the inevitable political consequence of conditioning African Americans to become docile and accommodating people. Briefly, these concepts that were advocated by social scientists and churchmen alike argued that white Americans were destined either by natural force or by the will of God to rule North America and possibly the rest of the world. In addition, all non-whites were incapable of self-government. This creed, in effect, gave the white race a moral and theological justification for genocide of the non-white races.[41]

As Social Darwinism began to permeate the American thought pattern, the power elites had problems keeping African Americans in the South. These

problems centered around several factors. First, there was Horace Greeley call-
ing, "Go West, young man, go West." Second, economic conditions for African
Americans had begun to worsen. With the collapse of the Freedmen Saving
Bank, African Americans were unable to secure capital to purchase land. With
their inability to elevate themselves economically through the tenancy and sharecropping systems, coupled with cruel treatment by landlords and merchants,
African Americans had little incentive to remain in the South. As early as 1879,
African Americans began abandoning the South and adhering to Greeley's call
to go West. To encourage their migration, Henry Adams of Louisiana and "Pop"
Singleton of Tennessee started organizing African Americans for the westward
movement. Consequently, thousands of them began migrating from Mississippi, Louisiana, Alabama, Georgia, and Tennessee. "Adams claimed to have
organized 98,000" African Americans from Tennessee alone.[42]

This westward movement posed a serious threat both to the southerners
and the northern industrialists' plans for economic development of the South.
If left unchecked, they felt that this movement would rob the South of its irreplaceable cheap labor force—which was necessary for growing cotton.[43] To
remedy this problem, whites needed two things: a policy of social control and
an African American propagandist whom they could trust and control to impose their policy of subordination on African Americans.

The purpose of the social control policy was to convince African Americans not to subscribe to Horace Greeley's urgent plea to "Go West, young man,
go West," but instead to stay in the South. To this end, the industralists recruited Booker T. Washington as the chief spokesman for the African American race.[44]

This effort to keep African Americans in the South is manifested in
Washington's famous "Atlanta Compromise" speech, which he gave at the Exposition in 1895. He told African Americans:

> To those of my race who depend upon bettering their conditions in foreign
> land, or who underestimate the importance of cultivating friendly relations
> with the Southern white man, who is his next door neighbor, I would say "cast
> down your bucket where you are"—cast down in making friends in every manly
> way of the people of all races by whom we are surrounded.[45]

He further sought to condone the South's wholesale violation of the civil rights
of African Americans by arguing that "whatever other sins the South may be
called to bear, when it comes to business, pure and simple, it is in the South that
the Negro is given a man's chance in the commercial world." It is ironic that
Washington would make such claims at a time when the practice of reducing

African Americans to perpetual indentured servants was a way of life and lynching them for attempting to exercise their basic civil and human rights was a common thing.[46]

The philosophy that Washington outlined in his speech was nothing new. It was simply a recapitulation of the American thought pattern of "racial adjustment," which had been brewing since the Civil War. Essentially, he argued that the solution to the race problem was for African Americans temporarily to give up three things: (1) political power, (2) insistence on civil rights, and (3) higher education of African American youths.[47] In return for surrendering these basic human and civil rights, Washington proposed to sell African Americans on the notion that the solution to the race problem was the "application of the gospel of wealth" and "material prosperity."[48] He also urged African Americans to place emphasis upon self-help and racial solidarity, moral uplift, and economic development. It seemingly never occurred to Washington that these goals were unattainable as long as African Americans' freedom to acquire property and to seek employment opportunities rested on the goodwill of their adversaries and competitors and not on a principle of law.

The power elite was successful in elevating Washington to the level of national spokesman for African Americans at the Atlanta Exposition. This is evidenced by the fact that Washington was practically unknown when he went to the Exposition. After he left, he was identified by the white media as the "African Americans' leader." The white media, it must be noted, had a tradition of printing news about two types of African Americans: the so-called "good nigger," and the "bad nigger." When the media wrote about the so-called "bad nigger," it was trying to depict the negative image of African Americans; and when it wrote about the so-called "good nigger," it was trying to depict the "ideal type" African Americans. In most cases the latter were the docile or accommodating African Americans, or "Uncle Toms," whom the rest of the African Americans should model their lives after.

The political thrust of Washington's philosophy of racial accommodations was to take the civil rights of African Americans off a principle of law and place them upon the goodwill of their adversaries and competitors who, at that time, opposed any expression of economic, political, social, or educational equality.[49]

The most dynamic step that Washington took to institutionalize the Social Darwinian Theory was when he advised African Americans to forget about higher education and concern themselves with industrial and agricultural education, or "progressive education." The progressive education during that period, at its best, was preparing African Americans for:

skills that were being outmoded by the progress of the Industrial Revolution, and preparing them for lives as small individualistic entrepreneurs at a time when the philosophy of economic individuals was becoming obsolete.[50]

When Washington urged African Americans to forget about higher education, he was not only urging them to forget about thinking altogether, but foreclosing their freedom to enter into mainstream America. His emphasis upon "progressive education" coincided with lawmakers' "steady withdrawal of aid from institutions for higher learning."[51] Shortly after the Civil War, the Peabody Fund was established to aid African Americans' education. As a precondition for receiving funds, African Americans were "expected to conform to the racial policy of the foundation."[52] This policy was designed to shape not only their philosophy of racial adjustment but also their "general social philosophy according to the social philosophy of the northern philanthropic foundation."[53]

During the time when the Peabody Fund was doling out pennies to the African American colleges, Congress was doling out to white colleges "more than a quarter of a billion dollars"[54] in the form of grants and land under the Morrill Act of 1862.[55] The political significance of this act is that it recognized "the principle that every citizen is entitled to receive educational aid from the government and that the common affairs of life are proper subjects with which to educate or to train men."[56] This principle, however, applied only to whites and European immigrants during the period from 1862 to 1920. Education was made available to prevent the culture of poverty from developing among them. African American schools, for the most part, depended largely on donations from whites who insisted that African American students adopt a philosophy of racial adjustment.[57] This policy was overseen by Booker T. Washington.

After he convinced African Americans temporarily to give up their political rights and to place them on the goodwill of their adversaries and competitors, Washington became the unidirectional political link between African Americans and the American power structure nationally. He had quasi-dictatorial power to suppress dissent among those African American leaders who overtly criticized his philosophy as one of accommodation. Although Washington resided in Tuskegee, Alabama, he could still use his quasi-dictatorial power to have a African American fired from a civil service job in New York if that African American "published some disparaging remarks about [his] leadership."[58]

Economically, Washington controlled the purse strings–and the decision-making mechanism–for the majority of those programs designed to improve the status of African Americans. Any program that did not conform to his ideas of racial adjustment did not receive financial support, because the philanthropists who funded these programs would consult Washington to make sure that the recipients of these programs were safe, or conformed to the policy of docility, before they would support them.

Devoid of a system of protection to safeguard their civil rights to an education, African Americans could not increase the relative size of their middle class–that is, increase the number of African Americans lawyers, doctors, and businessmen. Any attempt to do so was undermined by the southern system of injustice and the repressive nature of the plantation system. From the end of the Reconstruction Period to the passage of the civil rights laws of the 1960s, the white man's word was the law in the South, as far as African Americans were concerned, and in many parts of the North. Often, African Americans were forced to take the judgments and opinions of whites as the law of the land. Southern whites felt it to be their moral obligation to punish violently any African American who disputed a white man's word.[59]

Hence, the deprivation of these civil rights that Washington forced African Americans to give up in the 1890s kept them pinned down on the beachheads of the culture of poverty until the culture itself began to develop among them. The culture of property was perpetuated by the principle of intergenerational downward mobility. This cycle was partially broken with the adoption of the 1964 Civil Rights Act and the implementation of affirmative action. Affirmative action, as we shall see in Chapter 8, took the civil rights of African Americans to seek employment opportunities off the goodwill of their competitors and adversaries and placed them on a principle of law.

Structural Conditions of the American South

American South continued in a somewhat modified form, as it were, before the Civil War. The social structure there was a classic example of the feudal system in which the aristocracy (landowners) dominated both the economic and political life of the South, and the lower-class whites (land tenants) and African Americans (mostly sharecroppers) were left to compete for the meager tangible and intangible benefits that were left. The lower-class whites served as a buffer to minimize the conflict between the masses of African Americans and the aristocrats and large landholders.[60]

The conflict that often emerged between the lower-class whites and the African Americans centered around the distribution of tangible and intangible benefits or values, more of the latter than the former. The tangible values centered around the ownership of property, and there was very little conflict here because it was clear that the aristocrats owned the majority of the land.[61] The real conflict emerged in the struggle for the intangible values, which were mani-fested in the control of those social and political institutions that were an inti-mate part of the old caste system of the antebellum South. The whites had come to control these institutions either through their own achievements or through inheritance, more often the latter. When African Americans were emancipated and the carpetbaggers from the North invaded the South during the Recon-struction Period, African Americans began to pose a threat to those intangible values that whites had come to believe to be theirs by birthright—values such as control of the social and political institutions. More important, when African Americans started competing for these positions, they began to destroy the false sense of racial superiority that the lower class whites felt toward African Americans. The lower class whites, for the most part, owned very little land or property. If African Americans were put in the same social status as whites, they would not have anyone to feel superior to in the eyes of their wives and children.[62] Therefore, it was a concerted effort on the part of the antebellum South to design an environment, both politically and economically, governed by race and class.

The practical consequence of these cleavages was that they prevented Af-rican Americans from acquiring the human capital that was indispensable for their competition in the northern industrial society. They were prevented from entering the economic system by law. Race prejudice (attitude) was not enough to keep them from entering the economic system on a competitive basis. There were also specific laws that foreclosed their freedom to take advantage of a wide range of economic activities that would have enabled them to elevate themselves up off the beachheads of the culture of poverty.

By the time African Americans started migrating North, they had fully de-veloped a pattern of dependency. This pattern significantly impeded their rapid adjustment to an urban environment.

The African Americans' Migration

The dominant forces that precipitated the African Americans' migration from the American South were very much like those that uprooted the Euro-pean peasants. Both groups were freed from a feudal system that had kept them tied to the land. The European feudal system differed from the plantation sys-tem in the American South in that the South continued to hold African Ameri-cans in slavery on the plantations through the debt-slavery system.[63]

The forces that broke bonds that held the European peasants to the land were related to the rise of the Industrial Revolution during the seventeenth and the whole of the eighteenth centuries. Industrialization did not evolve in America until the nineteenth century. When it did, it surfaced primarily in the North and did not significantly influence the South. The South's economy was restricted primarily to growing cotton and tobacco. At the height of this economy, it supplied over three-fourths of the world's cotton needs. The South continued to supply the world with cotton up to the turn of the twentieth century, when America began to receive competition from abroad and the manufacturers started shifting to synthetic fibers.[64]

The African American labor supply was indispensable to the United States economy because it was irreplaceable. As mentioned before, in order for a country to develop economically, there has to be a supply of cheap labor available. When industrial development began in America, the majority of African Americans were locked into the institution of slavery. If they had been freed in 1830 and had migrated North to fill the labor demand, it would have severely affected the American economy, both in the North and the South. Cotton was needed by the North as raw material for manufacturing clothing. The northern clothing factories could not have survived without it. To promote northern industries and the southern economy, manufacturers and southern planters cooperatively adopted a policy of social control. African Americans were confined to the South, as we have seen, to support the southern economy, and whites were recruited from abroad for northern industries. The advent of World War I and the passage of the Immigration Act of 1917 significantly curtailed the flow of European labor to America. This curtailment occurred when American industry was at its peak and when European countries depended on America for food and war materials. Northern industries turned for the first time to the untapped labor force in the South.

Northern industries would not have been so successful in recruiting African Americans if the economic conditions of the South had not begun to free African Americans from the land some fifteen years earlier. There were several factors that helped to loosen the bonds that had kept African Americans tied to the plantation since Reconstruction.

Southern crops were suffering from floods and the disasterous effect that the boll weevils had upon the cotton crop. The first crop disaster occurred in 1892, when boll weevils from Mexico attacked cotton in Texas. They spread 160 miles a year, until they had invaded all the southern states except for the Carolinas and Virginia.[65] The boll weevils significantly lowered the profits of the plantation owners. Before the boll weevil invasion, the South produced approximately 400,000 bales of cotton a year; after the invasion, the production of cotton was cut in half. It was estimated that the South lost $250,000 worth of cotton in the first three years of the boll weevil invasion.[66]

With the curtailment in the production of cotton, plantation owners had less money to buy supplies for their tenants. Merchants accustomed to lending money to the plantation owners began to curtail the merchants' line of credit, because the former saw no bright future in the southern staple crop. "This, of course, means financial depression, for the South is a borrowing sector and any limitation to credit there blocked the wheels of industry."[67]

The amount of damage the boll weevils could inflict upon the cotton depended heavily upon the amount of rainfall the crop received. The South experienced its heaviest rainfalls in the summer of 1915, when thousands of African Americans were left destitute. With a curtailment in cotton production and constraint on credit, many plantation owners were reluctant to continue investing in the cotton industry. As a consequence, many African Americans were left homeless and out of work for the first time since the end of Reconstruction, thus creating the southern labor surplus. This occurred at the time when the numbers of industries were in full gear and suffering from a shortage of labor. The industries were forced to turn to the untapped labor of the South for the first time.

When the industries began recruiting the southern labor surplus, they received a labor force with a predominantly agrarian background. They recruited both African Americans and white laborers. Although whites were recruited, the bulk of the labor supply consisted largely of African Americans whose ties to the plantation system had been broken by the effect of the boll weevils.

The most compelling force expediting the African Americans' migration northward was the "Work or Fight" order issued by the War Department during World War I.[68] With this order, the war economy forced the labor unions to suspend their systematic discriminatory policies against hiring African Americans in workshops. For the unions to act to the contrary would have depicted a degree of disloyalty to the war effort. Thus, for the first time labor unions felt external pressure to relax their policy of racial exclusion.[69]

Before the war, African Americans had very little incentive to migrate North, even if they could escape the restrictions of the Black Codes of the South. The labor unions had adopted a policy of racial exclusion–which systematically excluded African Americans from joining their unions. But with the whites going off to war, as a result of a direct response to the Draft Act requiring all males between the ages of 18 and 45 to register, there was a large vacuum left in the labor force, which was filled by African Americans.[70]

As large numbers of African Americans began to abandon the South, the plantation owners became alarmed and tried to curtail the migration by passing strict ordinances designed to constrain the recruiting agents' efforts in facilitating African Americans' migration. In many cases, these agents offered free passage North.[71] Mississippi, Florida, Georgia, and Alabama were the hardest hit by the African Americans' migration. Some of these states required the recruiting agents to post $1,000 licenses or be subjected to 60 days in jail or a $600 fine.[72] But the state of Georgia had one of the stiffest laws designed to discourage recruitment. For instance, the City Council of Macon passed an ordinance requiring license fees of $25,000 and demanded that the labor agent be recommended by ten local ministers, ten manufacturers, and twenty-five businessmen. Notwithstanding these restrictions, it has been estimated that over one million African Americans left the South in 1918.[73]

Contact with the Northern Cities

When African Americans made contact with northern cities, there were more jobs available than people to fill them. The war economy had created greater demands for goods than industries could produce. Unlike the Irish, who had a similar agrarian background, African Americans did not have to rove around the country from city to city seeking employment. They found work at the end of their journey. However, when the country began to shift from a war to a peacetime economy, the situation changed.

During the war, African Americans were fully employed in the economy. However, they did not have a system of protection to safeguard their property rights to employment—that is, protection against arbitrary layoffs and dismissals as did the European immigrants. When white soldiers returned home from the war, African Americans were either fired outright or asked to work for lower wages than whites. Thus, the temporary foothold they had gained in the economy was wiped out during this period and during the Great Depression in the 1930s.[74]

At the close of the war, once again a conflict erupted between African Americans and whites who were competing for the same jobs. The political and social consequences of this conflict resulted in the construction of barriers to foreclose African Americans' freedom to take advantage of a wide range of employment opportunities. These constraints were manifested in the so-called "job ceiling" that had an effect on African Americans' upward employment mobility similar to that of the Black Codes in the South.[75]

The job ceiling prevented African Americans from elevating themselves to the middle-class plateau by their own bootstraps. To their dismay, they found that Booker T. Washington's philosophy of "progressive education" led them directly to a stone wall. Under this system of education, African Americans subscribed tenaciously to the Protestant work ethic—that is, working hard and delaying present gratifications for future ones, just to learn that their skin color was the sole criterion foreclosing their freedom to elevate themselves to the middle-class plateau. In the Black colleges, for example, African Americans acquired skills as artisans and craftsmen (human capital), just to find these occupations were foreclosed to them in the North. They were systematically excluded from joining the unions of their trade. Those African Americans with:

> trades either gave them up and hired out as waiters or laborers, or they became job workmen and floating hands, catching a bit of carpentering here or a little brickwork or plastering there at reduced wages.[76]

Through unionization, whites were able to keep African Americans out of job competition with them. They attempted to derive the same psychological gratification of being better off than African Americans as did the southern whites. The greatest opposition that African Americans encountered in joining labor unions came from the Irish, who entertained anti-African American sentiments because they monopolized the service occupations during the 1840s, 1850s, and 1870s, while the Irish were just a level below them.[77] For instance, it was the Irish who launched the race riot against African Americans before the Civil War.

Unlike the British West Indians, African Americans did not have the protection of the federal government to safeguard their freedom to pursue a wide range of employment opportunities. The African American male was deprived of the freedom of expressing any of the signs of aggressiveness, as had the West Indians. Any attempt to depict such behavior in the North was met with a system of oppression geared to put him back in his so-called "place," as was the case in the South. In the South, for example, the African American male found that the average white citizen had the legal authority to deprive him of his life, liberty, and property rights without due process of law. In the North, he found this task had been relegated to the police. Regardless of whether they were in the North or South, African Americans did not receive a system of protection to safeguard their property rights until the passage of the civil rights laws of the 1960s. These laws were not nearly as effective as the system of protection that foreign subjects received from the federal government, because foreign relations laws are questions of diplomatic relations with foreign countries (see Chapter 10). Any tampering with these policies precipitated immediate intervention by officials from Washington.

The Lack of a Pattern of Entrepreneurship

Unlike the British West Indians, African Americans were unable to develop a class of entrepreneurs among themselves after their migration North because they did not have the necessary human capital to do so. As we have seen, the British West Indians acquired their human capital for entrepreneurship in the West Indies because they did not have a white middle and lower class with which to compete on the islands. However, African Americans had both middle- and lower-class whites to compete with in the South. Therefore, when the African American professionals were confronted with racial discrimination, they did not have the human capital with which to broaden their choice possibilities by starting their own businesses. Consequently, they were subjected to demotion, arbitrary layoffs, and dismissals. Many African American professionals, such as lawyers, teachers, and so on, were forced to seek employment in the post office system.

Because of their lack of experience in management know-how, African Americans were unable to establish businesses in their community to any marketable degree. The majority of the businesses were owned by the West Indians. For example, a survey taken of African American businesses in Harlem in the late 1950s revealed that a high proportion of the African American owned-and-operated businesses were owned by West Indians.[78] There were some successful African American businessmen in Harlem other than in the service businesses, but their numbers were not commensurate with the numbers of successful West Indians.

It could be argued that African Americans were not able to obtain a foothold in business in Harlem because of the competition with the West Indians and whites. But the West Indians were confined to the East Coast (mostly in New York and Boston), and African Americans' poor showing in business is systematic throughout the northern cities. If we look at the African Americans who migrated to Chicago, which had very few West Indians, we see the same picture as in New York.

African Americans who migrated to Chicago were unable to establish competitive businesses with whites, as the West Indians had. As St. Clair Drake and Horace Clayton have pointed out, African Americans in Chicago were highly concentrated in the service businesses before the Big Black Migration. As far back as 1885, there were over 500 enterprises and 27 fields in which African American owned and operated businesses.[79] These businesses were in the service fields, with barber shops and moving and storage establishments forming the majority of the enterprises.

The number of African American owned-and-operated businesses increased in Chicago because the Big Migration created a market for them. Although the number of such enterprises increased during this period, the enterprises themselves were similar to those owned by African Americans in Harlem, namely businesses in which African Americans received little or no competition from whites (see Table 13).

Table 13
Ten Most Numerous Types of Black-Owned Businesses in Chicago, 1938

Type of Business	Number of Units
Beauty parlors	287
Grocery stores	257
Barber shops	207
Tailors, cleaners, and pressers	163
Restaurants	145
Coal and wood dealers	87
Taverns	70
Undertakers	50
Shoe repairing	48
Dressmakers	42
Total	1,356

SOURCE: St. Clair Drake and Horace R. Clayton, *African Americans Metropolis* (New York: Harper and Row, 1962), p. 438.

The most noticeable large African American businesses were the two banks and four insurance companies. They drew the majority of their capital "from within the Negro community to lend money for the purchase of homes."[80]

Social scientists have offered many explanations for why African Americans fared so poorly in business during their initial stage of contact in the northern cities. For example, Drake and Clayton give the following reasons:

(1) difficulty in procuring capital and credit, (2) difficulty in getting adequate training, (3) inability to secure choice locations on the main business street, (4) lack of sufficient patronage to allow them to amass capital and to make improvements, and (5) inability to organize for co-operative effect.[81]

The difficulty of procuring capital and credit brings into consideration the broader question of the problems involved in securing initial capital for establishing new businesses.

One major argument that has been advanced to explain African Americans' lack of success in business is that the lending institutions have systematically discriminated against them.[82] On the surface, this argument seems to have some validity. But a close examination of lending institutions conducted by Alfred R. Oxenfeldt in *The New Firms and Free Enterprise*,[83] reveals that these institutions rarely lend money to small and/or new enterprises, regardless of race. Oxenfeldt further argues that small and new enterprises are financed primarily by owners, their relatives and friends, suppliers or materials and equipment; only slight accommodation is extended to small businesses by banking institutions. Therefore, raising capital to start up new businesses is a problem faced by all groups; they must obtain such funds from other places.

As we have seen, the West Indians, Chinese, and Japanese were able to raise initial capital for business through their traditional rotating credit system. Hence, it seems that the all important variables for a group to succeed in business include first the freedom to interact in a human capital environment where individuals can have the opportunity to acquire managerial skills, and second, developing a process for raising the initial capital.

In short, the chief reason African Americans were unable to escape the slums, as did the European immigrants, was because the government has consistently refused to provide them with a system of protection that safeguarded their freedom to connect themselves to the mother lode of America's income redistribution system. It has historically placed their civil rights to acquire and possess property on the goodwill of their adversaries and competitors. These individuals have acted in the same manner in which Madison predicted that they would in his Federalist papers. They have oppressed the minorities.

Notes

1. See especially Robert Fogal and Stanley Engerman, "The Economics of Slavery," in *The Reinterpretation of America Economic History* (New York: Harper and Row, 1971) pp. 311–341; *Time on the Cross: The Economics of American Negro Slavery*, 2 vols. (Boston: Little, Brown and Company 1974).

2. Nathan Glazer, "A New View of Slavery," *Commentary* 58 (August 1974) 68–72; and *Affirmative Discrimination* (New York: Basic Books, 1975).

3. Herbert G. Gutman, "The World Two Cliometricians Made: A Review-Essay of F + E = T/C," *The Journal of Negro History* 60 (1975): 107. For a critique of the revisionist historians read the entire essay, pp. 53–277.

4. For a discussion of the Madisonian theory of democracy, see Robert A. Dahl, *A Preface to Democratic Theory* (Chicago: The University of Chicago Press, 1956), chapter 1.

5. E. Franklin Frazier, *Black Bourgeoisie* (New York: The Macmillan Company, 1957), p. 114.

6. Exodus 3:35.

7. For a discussion of the American goal values, see Harold Lasswell, *The World Revolution of Our Times* (Stanford: Stanford University Press, 1951).

8. W.E.B. Du Bois, *Black Reconstruction in America* (New York: Russell & Russell 1935), p. 602

9. Edwin E. Slosson, *The America Spirit in Education*, a series of the *Chronicles of America* (New Haven: Yale University Press, 1921), chapter 15.

10. Paul Miliukov, *History of Russia* (New York: Funk & Wagnalls, 1969), p. 10

11. Ibid.

12. See Forest G. Wood, *The Era of Reconstruction* (New York: Thomas Y. Crowell Company, 1975), chapter 1.

13. Du Bois, *Black Reconstruction in America*, p. 601.

14. Ibid., p. 602.

15. Ibid., p. 221

16. Martin Abbott, *The Freedmen's Bureau in South Carolina* (Chapel Hill: University of North Carolina Press, 1967), p. 109.

17. See Arnett G. Lindsay, "The Negro Banking," *Journal of Negro History* 14 (1929): 156-201.

18. Walter L. Fleming, *Documentary History of Reconstruction* (New York: McGraw-Hill Book Company, 1966), Chapter 5.

19. Ibid.

20. Du Bois, *Black Reconstruction in America*, p. 600

21. Matthew Josephson, *The Robber Barons* (New York: Harcourt, Brace & World, Inc., 1962), pp. 177-178.

22. John Hope Franklin, *From Slavery to Freedom: A History of Negro Americans* 4th Edition (New York: Aflfred A. Knopf, Inc., 1974), p. 251.

23. Franklin, *Reconstruction* (Chicago: University of Chicago Press, 1961), p. 34

24. DuBois, *Black Reconstruction in America*, p. 603

25. Ibid.

26. For a discussion of the Black Codes, see Rayford W. Logan, *The Negro in the United States* (Princeton: D. Van Nostrand Company, 1957), pp. 109–110.

27. Fleming, *Documentary History*, chapter 4.

28. Logan, *The Negro in the United States*, p. 110.

29. For a discussion of how brutal the white man was toward African Americans, see Allison Davis et. al., *The Deep South* (Chicago: University of Chicago Press, 1965), chapter 11.

30. For a discussion of how the "Sambo" personality type developed as a result of interacting under absolute authority, see Stanley Elkins, *Slavery* (Chicago: The University of Chicago Press, 1965).

31. Logan, *The Negro in the United States*, p. 110.

32. Ibid.

33. Fleming, *Documentary History*, pp. 259–312.

34. See Harold Lasswell, *The Analysis of Political Behavior: An Empirical Approach* (New York: Oxford University Press, 1947), pp. 195–234.

35. Ibid.

36. Ibid., p. 207.

37. Ibid.

38. Frazier, *Black Bourgeoisie*, chapter 9.

39. George M. Fredrickson, *The Black Image in the White Mind* (New York: Harper & Row, 1971), pp. 97-129.

40. See Thomas F. Gosset, *Race: The History of an Idea in America* (Dallas: SMU Press, 1963), p. 145.

41. Louis L. Knowles and Kenneth Prewitt, *Institutional Racism in America* (Englewood Cliffs, N.J.:Prentice-Hall, 1969), p. 10.

42. Franklin, *From Slavery to Freedom,* pp. 291-292.

43. Ibid.

44. See Du Bois, *The Souls of Black Folk* (Greenwich, Conn.: Fawcett Publications, 1961), chapter 3.

45. Arthur P. Davis and Saunders Redding, eds., *Cavalcade: American Writing from 1760 to the Present* (New York: Houghton Mifflin Company, 1971) pp. 158–161.

46. Davis et al. *The Deep South*, chapter 11.

47. Du Bois, *The Souls of Black Folk*, p. 49.

48. August Meier, *Negro Thought in America: 1880–1915* (Ann Arbor: University of Michigan Press, 1968), p. 100.

49. Gilbert Osofsky, *Harlem: The Making of a Ghetto* (New York: Harper and Row, 1963), p. 164.

50. Meier, *Negro Thought*, p. 93.

51. Du Bois, *The Souls of Black Folk*, p. 49.

52. Frazier, *Black Bourgeoisie*, p. 85.

53. Slosson, *The America Spirit in Education*, p. 226.

54. Ibid., p. 225.

55. Ibid., pp. 232-233.

56. Frazier, *Black Bourgeoisie*, p. 85.

57. Osofsky, *Harlem: The Making of the Ghetto*, p. 164.

58. Davis et al., *The Deep South*, chapter 11.

59. Pierre van de Berghe, "The United States Is a 'Herrenvolk' Democracy," *Nation of Nations: The Ethnic Experience and the Racial Crisis*, ed. Peter I. Rose (New York: Random House, 1972), p. 213.

60. Davis et al., *The Deep South*, chapter 11.

61. See Gunnar Myrdal, *An American Dilemma* (New York: Harper and Row, 1962), chapter 4.

62. This system was used by the Mexicans before and after their independent. As will be demonstrated in chapters 13 and 14, this is one of the major reasons for the impoverished Mexican population.

63. Leon F. Litwack, *North of Slavery* (Chicago: University of Chicago Press, 1961), pp. 64-112.

64. Carter G. Woodson, *A Century of Negro Migration* (New York: Russell and Russell, 1969), p. 171.

65. Ibid.

66. Ibid., p. 172.

67. Thomas A. Bailey, *The American Pageant: A History of the Republic* (Boston: D. C. Heath and Company, 1956), p. 740.

68. See Litwack, *North of Slavery*, for a discussion of the economic repression of African American in the Northern cities, pp. 153-186.

69. Bailey, *The American Pageant*, p. 740.

70. St. Clair Drake and Horace R. Clayton, *Black Metropolis* (New York: Harper and Row, 1962), p. 58.

71. Ibid.

72. Ibid., p. 59.

73. Ibid., pp. 77–98.

74. Ibid.

75. Ibid.

76. Du Bois, *The Philadelphia Negro* (New York: Benjamin Blom, 1967).

77. Oscar Handlin, *Boston's Immigrants* (Cambridge: Harvard University Press, 1959), p. 70.

78. Osofsky, *Harlem: The Making of a Ghetto*, p. 133.

79. Drake and Clayton, *Black Metropolis*, p. 436.

80. Ibid.

81. Ibid., p. 437.

82. Myrdal, *An American Dilemma*, pp. 314-318.

83. Alfred R. Oxenfeldt, *The New Firms and Free Enterprise* (Washington, D. C. : American Council on Public Affairs, 1943), p. 46.

CHAPTER 7

Assessment of Groups' Economic Linkages and Income Inequality

The previous five chapters consist of a critical examination of the structural conditions in groups' homelands and the economic and political linkages they fashioned with the American polity in their early and initial stages of contact. The task of this chapter is to assess the impact of these linkages in the period between 1920 and 1970, in order to determine subsequent group behavior.

The data that have been used in this assessment are drawn from the various U.S. Census reports from 1920 to 1970. Data between 1970 and 1980 are not to be used because during this period various civil rights measures were adopted to improve African Americans', and other minority groups', freedom to acquire and possess property. The political effect of these measures (affirmative action and other measures) was that they temporarily took this freedom off the goodwill of these groups' adversaries and competitors and placed it on a principle of law.

Economic Linkages of European Immigrants, 1920-1970

As demonstrated in previous chapters, European ethnic groups came over and fashioned economic linkages with the American polity. The data in Table 14 indicate that these groups have not deviated significantly from these linkages. These data allow us to trace the occupational rank order for seven white ethnic groups in the period between 1920 and 1970.[1]

The year 1910 marked the beginning of the decline in agriculture as America's dominant occupation. At the beginning of that year, 32.5 percent of the workers in the labor force were engaged in agricultural work.[2] Table 37 in

Table 14

Occupational Mobility of Race and Ethnic Groups, 1920-1970

Years	English	Germans	Irish	Italians	Russians	Norwegians	Swedes
1920	1 Farm.[a] 18.1	Farm. 64.4	Crafts. 18.5	Crafts. 10.2	Crafts. 11.5	Farm. 87.3	Farm. 81.4
	2 Crafts.[b] 13.8	Crafts. 8.1	Farm. 13.5	Mgrs. 2.8	Farm. 4.1	Crafts. 11.3	Crafts. 10.3
	3 Mgrs.[c] 5.6	Mgrs. 2.8	Mgrs. 8.9	Farm. .9	Prof. 3.8	Mgrs. 0.5	Mgrs. 1.3
	4 Prof.[d] 0.8	Prof. .8	Prof. .8	Prof. .7	Mgrs. 2.8	Prof. 0.05	Prof. .09
1950	Crafts. 17.0	Crafts. 16.2	Crafts. 16.3	Crafts. 28.4	Mgrs. 25.5	Farm. 22.4	Crafts. 14.1
	Mgrs. 14.6	Farm. 14.8	Mgrs. 12.4	Mgrs. 11.1	Prof. 15.3	Crafts. 12.3	Mgrs. 13.3
	Prof. 11.2	Mgrs. 12.5	Prof. 9.7	Prof. 6.0	Crafts. 12.0	Mgrs. 11.4	Farm. 13.0
	Farm. 5.7	Prof. 7.3	Farm. 2.8	Farm. 1.1	Farm. 4.9	Prof. 7.5	Prof. 10.3
1960	Crafts. 17.7	Crafts. 23.1	Crafts. 18.6	Crafts. 23.4	Mgrs. 23.3	-	Crafts. 22.9
	Prof. 15.1	Mgrs. 12.7	Prof. 13.3	Mgrs. 11.6	Prof. 20.0	-	Mgrs. 14.8
	Mgrs. 15.0	Farm. 11.7	Mgrs. 12.7	Prof. 9.6	Crafts. 12.0	-	Prof. 13.1
	Farm. 3.2	Prof. 9.8	Farm. 1.5	Farm. 0.8	Farm. 3.5	-	Farm. 9.7
1970	Crafts. 20.5	Crafts. 22.0	Prof. 17.6	Crafts. 23.7	Prof. 25.4	Crafts. 21.5	Crafts. 22.0
	Prof. 19.6	Prof. 14.3	Crafts. 17.5	Mgrs. 13.7	Mgrs. 23.5	Prof. 14.4	Prof. 16.7
	Mgrs. 16.0	Mgrs. 13.4	Mgrs. 15.0	Prof. 12.5	Crafts. 12.0	Mgrs. 14.3	Mgrs. 16.2
	Farm. 2.0	Farm. 8.0	Farm. 0.7	Crafts. 0.6	Farm. 2.4	Farm. 11.5	Farm. 6.7

The percentages in this table were taken from Tables 26, 31, 32, and 33 in the appendix, and they do not represent the total percentage of each group that is engaged in the labor force. For the total occupational percentage for each period, see Tables 26, 31, 32, and 33 in the appendix. Data for Norwegians were not available in 1960.

Notes: These occupational categories (Craftsmen,[a] Professional,[b] Managerial[d]) were selected because they had the greatest percentage of expansion between 1920 and 1970. See E. P. Hutchinson, *Immigrants and Their Children* (New York: John Wiley and Sons, 1956), pp. 197-218. The farming category was selected because it was considered to be the dominant occupation in the 1920s for the Protestants.

the appendix indicates that agriculture constituted the highest percentage (37.6 percent) of all workers engaged in the labor force among this cohort. These data are limited to the extent that they cover only six states (Massachusetts, New York, Pennsylvania, Michigan, Minnesota, and Wisconsin) and do not represent the total population in America for each group. These states were selected by the Immigration Commission, because they had the largest numbers of foreign-born workers employed in the occupational categories selected for this table. The data are not as complete as they are in Tables 31, 32, and 33. However, they are sufficient to give us some indication of the occupational status of groups in 1920.

In Table 14, four occupational categories (professional, managerial, craftsmen, and farming) were selected in an attempt to trace occupational mobility among the seven white ethnic groups represented during the period between 1920 and 1970. The first three categories were selected because they represent the occupational trend between 1920 and 1950.[3] The farming category was selected because it represents the dominant occupation in which the Protestants were engaged in 1920.

The data in Table 14 seem to indicate that the English were maintaining economic linkages similar to those which they fashioned with the American polity during the colonial period. Their occupational rank order in 1920 indicates the following pattern: farming, **18.1** percent; craftsmen, 13.8 percent; managerial, 5.6 percent; and professional, 0.8 percent. The highest percentage of the English were engaged in the coal mine operative category (41 percent).[4] By 1950, however, the Census Bureau had ceased recording this category. The jobs previously included in this category were re-classified and assigned to the craftsmen and operative categories. The coal mine operative category of 1920, therefore, is not a good indicator for making a strong inference about groups' occupational status. For this reason, this category will be ignored when discussing the rest of the groups. |imitation

During the period between 1920 and 1950, there was a shift in occupational services. Agriculture continued to decline as America's dominant occupation. It was replaced by managerial, professional, and craftsmen categories. As the English left the farms, they moved into the craftsmen category (17 percent), and this remained their dominant occupation until 1970. Between the years 1950 and 1960, the English began increasing their percentages in the professional category. This category remained their second occupational preference up to 1970, with craftsmen at 20.5 percent; professional, 19.6 percent; managerial, 16 percent; and farming, 2 percent.

An examination of the economic linkages of immigrants of the 1830s and 1850s will reveal that the occupations they fashioned for themselves in their initial stage of contact followed the same general patterns in 1920, approximately three generations later. As has been demonstrated, the vast majority of Germans moved directly into the interior and settled on farms, while the Irish-Catholics settled in the cities.

In 1920, the Germans had the following occupational order: farming, 64.6 percent; craftsmen, 8.1 percent; managerial, 2.8 percent; and professional, 0.8 percent.[5] Thus, around 1950, as the process of urbanization continued to increase, and numbers of fourth-generation Germans began to enter the labor force, they began to enter the craftsmen category. Their occupational order shifted to the following between 1920 and 1950: craftsmen, 16.2 percent; farming, 14.8 percent; managerial, 12.5 percent; and professional, 7.3 percent. By 1970, the highest percentage of Germans in the labor force was in the craftsmen category (22 percent), followed by professional, 14.3 percent; managerial, 13.4 percent; and farming, 8 percent.

The Irish-Catholics, however, settled in the cities between 1830 and 1860 and were still in the cities in the 1920s. In 1920, for example, 13.5 percent of the Irish were engaged in farming. It must be noted, however, that a large proportion of farmers tabulated here were Scots-Irish rather than the Irish-Catholics. The census did not make a distinction between the two groups. Besides, many of the farmers can be assumed to be Scots-Irish because of the linkages that groups established with the American polity in their initial stage of contact.

The significant aspect of the Irish-Catholics' occupational status is that the occupational categories in which they were concentrated were those traditional urban occupations (municipal jobs) which have been traditionally associated with political patronage. Many of the municipal jobs are classified as managerial in the census. Hence, the Irish had the following occupational rank order in 1920: craftsmen, 18.5 percent; farming, 13.5 percent; managerial, 8.3 percent; professional, 0.8 percent. In 1950, the Irish had the following occupational rank order: craftsmen, 16.3 percent; managerial, 12.4 percent; professional, 9.7 percent; farming, 2.8 percent.

By 1970, the highest percentage of the Irish males were employed in the professional category (17.6 percent) and craftsmen (17.5 percent), followed by managerial (15 percent). The professional and managerial categories in which the Irish were concentrated are closely related to their tradition of pursuing jobs in the public sector. In looking at all of the European ethnic groups in this cohort that were employed in the government bureaucracies in 1970, we find the Irish were mostly represented in the local government agencies (12.6 percent) in comparison to other white males. (The rest of the white males had less than 7.7 percent employed in this category. See Table 41 in the appendix.)

The Scandinavians who immigrated during the 1860s and 1870s followed the same general pattern in adjustment and occupational pursuits as did the Germans. In 1920, the Scandinavians were still highly concentrated in farm-ing. By 1950, they had begun to leave their farms and to move to the cities, if we assume that non-farming occupations are urban occupations.

The Norwegians began to leave the farms at a much slower rate than the Swedes. Around 1950, the occupational rank order of the Norwegians had the following composition: farming, 22.4 percent; craftsmen, 12.3 percent; mana-gerial, 11.4 percent; and professional, 7.5 percent. However, the Swedes' occu-pational rank order was as follows: craftsmen, 14.1 percent; managerial, 13.3 percent; farming, 13 percent; and professional, 10.3 percent.

The data for the Norwegians in the 1960s were not made available in the census. But in the 1970s, the occupational rank order of the Norwegians and the Swedes was basically the same while their percentages differed slightly (see Table 14). There was a higher percentage of Norwegians on farms than Swedes in the 1970s. Between 1960 and 1970, the Swedes began gradually to move out of the managerial category into the professional, thereby placing farm-ing at the bottom of their list of occupational preferences.

The data in Table 33 seem to indicate that the majority of Italian males were concentrated in the craftsmen category. As we shall see in the next chap-ter, the majority of the craftsmen in the northern cities were controlled by labor unions. Therefore, we can reasonably assume that the largest percentage of Italians concentrated in the craftsmen category in 1970 were members of the labor union (see Table 37 in the appendix), and the linkages they fashioned with the American polity in their early stage of contact constituted the same general pattern that they were currently following.

The data in Table 37 in the appendix indicate that Italian males have not pursued government jobs at the same rate as the Irish. This low rate of employ-ment can be accounted for by the principle of intergenerational mobility (i.e., sons following the occupations of their fathers). As we have seen, the Italians did not fashion linkages with the government in their initial stage of contact. Therefore, the Italians' employment in municipal jobs exceeds the average per-centage among this cohort by a mere 1.2 percent (the average percentage, 7.3 percent; the Italians, 8.5 percent). The highest percentage of the Italians in the working class category are either in the self-employed category (11.3 percent) or among the private wage and salary workers (72 percent).[6]

We have already seen that the primary reason the Jews were kicked out of the Russian Empire was that they dominated the trade and commerce indus-tries and, to a certain extent, the liberal professions. In order for the Russians to undergo economic development, they felt it necessary to seize control of these industries–thus displacing the Jews. When they immigrated to America, they pursued many of the same occupations they had held in Russia. As we have seen, the underlying reason that Jews came to dominate these occupations in Europe was because they were looked down upon by the Christians. But in America, these occupations constituted the core of the mother lode of the income redistribution system. Consequently, the Jews were able to catapult themselves upon the middle-class plateau faster than most groups. Although the Jews were heavily employed in the professional and managerial classes, their upward mobility was not realized until after the implementation of the New Deals programs and the liberal policies after WWII, which will be discussed in Chapter 8.

In pursuing occupations in America, the Jews no doubt faced some form of discrimination. However, this discrimination did not operate to foreclose their freedom to acquire property and to take advantage of a wide range of economic opportunities as it did for African Americans. Because of the human capital they brought with them, they were able to offset the effect of discrimination by drawing upon their resources (1) to establish new businesses and (2) to develop educational institutions–thus adding to the economic growth of the country.

Around 1920, the Russian Jews had the following occupational rank order: craftsmen, 11.5 percent; farming, 4.1 percent; professional, 3.8 percent; managerial, 2.8 percent. Table 14 does not give us an adequate picture of the occupational distribution of Russian Jews for 1920. In Table 30 in the appendix, the Russian Jews are shown highly concentrated in the clerical category (25 percent) and the coal mine and operative category (33.9 percent). But the most significant aspect of the Russian Jews' employment is that they constituted the highest percentage among this cohort in the professional category (3.8 percent). The professional category since 1920 has been expanded to cover a wide range of professionals. The figures in the 1950 census seem to present a better picture of the occupational rank order of the Russian Jews. By 1950, the percentage of the Russian Jews in the managerial category had increased from 2.8 percent to 25.5 percent. As we have seen, the managerial, professional, and craftsmen categories had the greatest percentage increase since 1920. The Jews, therefore, had the highest percentage of increase for males in the managerial category. In 1920, craftsmen ranked number one as the Jews' occupational preference listed in Table 14. But by 1950, this craftsmen category had moved to third and remained there into the 1970s. Between 1910 and 1960, the Russian Jews were highly concentrated in the professional and managerial categories, and their percentage in the craftsmen category remained at almost the same percentage point as they had in 1920: 11.5 percent in 1920, and 12 percent in 1970.

The percentage of the Russian Jews employed in government jobs (local, state, and federal) is far below the average for the thirteen groups computed. The highest percentage of Jewish males is concentrated among the private wage and salary workers (66.4 percent) and the self-employed category (20.2 percent). (See Table 41 in the appendix.)

Among the racial ethnic groups, we have the Japanese, Chinese, African Americans, British West Indians, Spanish, and Puerto Ricans. The data on the Spanish and Puerto Ricans are not complete in many instances. As we mentioned earlier, the U.S. Census Bureau lumped all Spanish-speaking immigrants together and did not make a distinction between Puerto Ricans and those who emigrated from Mexico. Therefore, this group is referred to occasionally, but the primary focus is on the Japanese, Chinese, African Americans, and West Indians.

We have seen that the Japanese were able to develop skills as merchants and craftsmen because the structural conditions existing at that time served as a *de facto* system of protection that allowed them the freedom to interact in a human capital environment. When they made contact with the states, they were highly represented in the entrepreneurial and craftsmen categories. We have also seen how they monopolized the green vegetable market on the West Coast before their land was confiscated by the government during World War II. Despite this confiscation, they were still highly concentrated in the farm and farm manager categories (15.3 percent) in the 1950 census.[7] The next most prestigious occupation in which they were concentrated was the craftsmen category (9.7 percent) and managerial (8.6 percent).

The data on the Japanese in the 1950s were not so complete as in the 1960s because, during the former period, they had just been released from the concentration camps. Turning to the data collected in the 1960s, we find that the Japanese had the following occupational rank order: craftsmen, 20.1 percent; professional, 12.6 percent; farming, 12 percent; and managerial, 9.5 percent. Of all the ethnic groups that pursued farming during their initial stages of contact, the Japanese had the highest percentage of males employed in this category in 1960. They were followed by the Germans (11.7 percent) and the Swedes (9.7 percent).[8] By the 1970s, the Japanese occupational rank order had risen to the same level as other ethnic groups despite their oppression here during World War II. Their occupational rank order was as follows: craftsmen, 22.2 percent; professional, 20 percent; managerial, 13.8 percent. In looking at the Class of Workers of the Native Population in Table 41 in the appendix, we see the Japanese are highly concentrated in the private wage and salary workers (63 percent) and self-employed categories (17.3 percent). Hence, the Japanese did not deviate significantly from the occupational linkages they established with the American polity in their early stage of contact.

As we have seen, the British West Indian and Chinese immigration to America was constrained by the Immigration Act of 1917. This act restricted immigration to the skilled and the well-to-do. The Chinese who were able to immigrate to the United States after the Exclusion Act of 1882 were highly skilled and in the professional category.[9] In 1970, the occupational rank order of the Chinese was the following: professional, 27.7 percent; managerial, 14 percent; craftsmen, 10.5 percent.[10] Professionally, the Chinese lead other groups, having the highest percentage for their males concentrated in the professional category (27.7 percent) followed by the Russian Jews (25.4 percent) and the Japanese (20 percent).[11] The percentage of the rest of the ethnic groups employed in the professional category is below 20 percent.

In the working-class category, the West Indians are highly concentrated in local and federal government; 16.6 percent and 11 percent, respectively.[12] Discrimination in the private sector of the economy–that is, foreclosing a wide range of employment opportunities–has driven racial ethnic groups disproportionately to public employment where the rules for hiring, promotion, and layoffs rest on a principle of law. In looking at this sector in Table 41 in the appendix, African Americans, West Indians, Chinese, and Japanese have a higher percentage of males employed in government than the average for all groups. The Mexican or Spanish and the Puerto Ricans are hard to trace because of the method the Census Bureau used in collecting data. But where the ethnic identification is consistent, we can find a pattern of racial minority groups highly concentrated in those government agencies where the decision for hiring and promotion rests on a principle of law.

Educational Attainments

According to the 1970 U.S. Census, the Russian Jews had the highest level of educational attainment–with 12.8 median school years completed, followed by the Chinese with 12.7, and the Japanese with 12.6 (see Table 40). The English and West Indians are equal in the number of school years completed, 12.4, but the English surpass the West Indians if we consider the groups with the highest percentage of four or more years of college education: English, 17.5 percent; and West Indians, 14.8 percent.[13]

An examination of all those groups in this cohort with 17 percent or more of their males employed in the professional category reveals a close correlation between educational attainment and occupational status. For example, all groups with median school years completed of 12.4 or higher have over 17 percent employed in the professional categories: the Russian Jews, Chinese, Japanese, English, and British West Indians. A similar pattern can also be found among the groups concentrated in the craftsmen category with 12.1 or less median school years completed–except for the Japanese, who have 12.6 median school years completed. However, there is a disparity in the educational attainment among the Catholics (Irish and Italians). A closer look at the occupational categories in which these groups are concentrated reveals that 23.7 percent of all Italian males in the labor force were employed in the craftsmen category, while the Irish males were evenly scattered throughout the professional (17.6 percent), managerial (15 percent), clerical (12.3 percent), and craftsmen (17.5 percent) categories (see Table 37). As we mentioned in the Introduction Chapter, selecting religion to measure group behavior will not yield a systematic analysis. The characterization of ethnicity must be based on groups' memories of migration, as Max Weber argued. The differences in the behavior of the Irish-Catholics and the Italians (also Catholics) support Weber's argument.

The craftsmen category does not prescribe the same level of educational attainment as the professional and managerial categories.[14] However, the craftsmen occupations prescribe a higher level of median family income than education. The Italians have a family median income slightly higher than the Irish ($11,857 and $11,776, respectively). It may appear that the differences are inconsequential; but they are highly significant when we take into consideration the size of both groups (Italian families, 1,314,594; Irish families, 423,888). Again, the Italians have a higher percentage of families earning incomes of $10,000 or more: 62.3 percent and 60.3 percent, respectively (see Table 34 in the appendix).

Educationally, the professional and managerial occupations in which the Irish were concentrated were governmental bureaucracies prescribing a higher level of education, but lower income, than the craftsmen occupations. There are slightly more Irish males employed in white-collar occupations (41 percent) than Italian males (33.7 percent). (White-collar occupations consist of professional, managerial, and sales workers. See Table 37.)

The Protestants are also employed in the craftsmen occupational categories, as are the non-Protestants. But there is a disparity in median income. This disparity can be explained when we introduce region as an independent variable. As Table 15 indicates, less than 30.2 percent of all Protestants (English, Swedes, Germans, and Norwegians) studied here are concentrated in the nine standard metropolitan areas. However, all of the non-Protestants–except the Italians–are highly concentrated in the large metropolitan areas in the eastern

Table 15

Population by Nativity, Percentage, and Race for Nine SelectedStandard Metropolitan Areas

	Total and Percent	New York	Chicago	Detroit	Milwaukee
English	1,778,951 (33.1)[a]	130,449 (7.3)	57,964 (3.2)	62,026 (3.5)	17,058 (0.9)
Irish	1,198,844 (50.1)	230,619 (19.2)	72,682 (6.0)	14,920 (1.2)	2,792 (0.2)
Italians	3,232,245 (48.2)	724,897 (22.4)	143,644 (4.4)	66,008 (1.2)	11,639 (0.2)
Polish	1,232,246 (50.1)	248,224 (13.3)	214,863 (11.8)	125,938 (10.5)	34,463 (1.9)
Russians	1,497,733 (54.2)	380,153 (25.7)	76,138 (5.1)	34,003 (2.3)	9,038 (0.6)
Swedes	679,068 (21.3)[a]	21,383 (3.2)	52,934 (7.4)	8,302 (1.2)	4,086 (0.6)
Norwegians	517,406 (18.4)[a]	24,252 (4.7)	22,149 (4.3)	4,165 (0.8)	5,968 (1.1)
Mexicans	1,579,362 (27.2)	5,629 (0.4)	60,255 (3.8)	10,013 (0.6)	3,690 (0.2)
Blacks	22,539,362 (27.2)	1,620,693 (7.2)	1,214,922 (5.3)	748,078 (0.4)	105,467 (0.4)
West Indians	149,157 (68.6)	81,826 (54.8)	2,804 (1.9)	1,395 (0.9)	319 (0.2)
Japanese	273,554 (28.0)	1,936 (1.6)	7,159 (2.6)	1,699 (1.0)	342 (0.1)
Chinese	167,111 (51.5)	21,936 (13.1)	4,295 (2.5)	1,699 (1.0)	320 0.2)
Germans	2,789,070 (29.5)[a]	203,782 (7.3)	166,507 (6.0)	68,871 (2.5)	73,467 (2.6)

	Cleveland	San Francisco	Pittsburgh	Philadelphia	Los Angeles
English	23,029 (1.3)	44,784 (2.5)	40,254 (2.3)	78,070 (4.4)	86,311 (4.8)
Irish	13,669 (1.1)	28,535 (2.3)	20,859 (1.7)	71,795 (6.0)	28,177 (2.3)
Italians	47,488 (1.1)	65,633 (2.0)	93,207 (2.9)	181,973 (5.6)	85,752 (2.6)
Polish	48,180 (1.1)	10,708 (0.6)	54,566 (3.0)	70,491 (3.8)	47,376 (2.6)
Russians	29,200 (1.4)	21,217 (1.4)	18,350 (1.2)	90,551 (6.1)	96,110 (6.4)
Swedes	3,550 (0.5)	16,203 (2.2)	4,148 (0.6)	5,129 (0.7)	29,052 (4.2)
Norwegians	1,169 (0.2)	11,394 (2.2)	611 (0.1)	3,088 (0.6)	19,244 (3.7)
Mexicans	1,084 (0.06)	44,388 (2.8)	1,087 (0.06)	1,131 (0.6)	302,511 (19.1)
Blacks	329,554 (1.5)	323,110 (1.4)	167,112 (0.7)	828,845 (3.6)	745,551 (3.3)
West Indians	644 (0.4)	1,676 (1.1)	643 (0.4)	4,093 (2.7)	4,847 (3.2)
Japanese	664 (0.2)	15,181 (5.5)	343 (0.1)	2,280 (0.8)	44,507 (16.3)
Chinese	844 (0.5)	35,379 (21.1)	596 (0.3)	2,035 (1.2)	15,724 (8.8)
Germans	40,740 (1.5)	46,404 (1.6)	46,300 (1.7)	73,281 (2.6)	88,311 (4.8)

SOURCE: Calculated from: U.S. Bureau of the Census, Census of the Population: 1970, Subject Reports, Final Report PC (2)-1A, *National Origin and Language* (Washington: Government Printing Office, 1973).

[a]Protestants

164

states. The Irish, the Italians, and the Russian Jews are highly concentrated in the New York metropolitan area. The Poles are the only ones who seem to be dispersed throughout the New York, Chicago, and Detroit areas. The Italians, however, are scattered around the eastern states in cities such as Newark, New Jersey, Buffalo, New York, and other surrounding metropolitan areas.

Statistically, the regional and occupational variables seem to explain conclusively the socioeconomic disparity among the Protestants and non-Protestants. They also explain why certain racial groups are doing considerably better than the Protestants and Catholic groups. The West Indians, Japanese, and Chinese are highly represented in those occupational categories that prescribe high incomes. Again, these groups are concentrated in large metropolitan areas or in heavily industrialized states, where the economic structures prescribe a high level of income. For example, 54.8 percent of the West Indians reside in New York, 21.1 percent of the Chinese reside in San Francisco, and 16.3 percent of the Japanese reside in Los Angeles (see Table 15).

The lower percentage of the groups in the latter two cities must not be taken here to represent flaws in my theory. There exist two phenomena operating to support this argument. First, California's economy depends heavily on its defense industries. Under the Davis-Bacon Act, defense contractors are required by law to pay union wages even if the shop is non-union. Second, the peculiarity of the state's geological characteristics (providing a high potential for earthquakes) necessitated the building of numerous suburbs (before the 1970s) that catered predominantly to those workers who fall in the professional, managerial, and craftsmen categories. Hence, although the Chinese and Japanese are scattered throughout the state of California, they are concentrated in those industries that prescribe a high level of income.

Furthermore, the downward mobility of the Protestants and upward mobility of the non-Protestants can also be seen as a shift in the mode of production. When the American economy began to feel the impact of automation, the Germans and Scandinavians were still largely on the farm. The impact of automation was felt more heavily in the industrial states where industries were flourishing. When automation shifted into high gear, the non-Protestants were in those industrial cities and states that benefitted from this shift in economic growth. As automation increased, the standards of living in these industrial states and cities rose more rapidly than they did in the non-industrial states.

The African American and Spanish males, however, are considerably less well-off educationally and economically because they are under-represented in those occupational categories that prescribe high incomes (see Table 17). All of the ethnic groups that have achieved economic security among this cohort have done so because they have established an economic base in the three high-income occupational categories: professional, managerial, and craftsmen. Each of these groups has 43.6 percent or more of their males concentrated in these occupational categories. Only 23.8 percent of African Americans and 33.7 percent of Spanish are concentrated in these same occupational categories. In other words, 76.2 percent of the African American males are concentrated in those occupational categories that do not prescribe high income.

Toward a Theory for Measuring Income Differences

The attempt to explain the chief cause of income differences has preoccupied social scientists since the 1960s. Many arguments have been advanced and models constructed to isolate and identify the independent variables that can best explain this difference with the maximum degree of certainty. As we have seen in the Introduction, Thomas Sowell has identified age, geographic distribution, and fertility as independent variables. These are not independent variables, but merely a citation of statistical incidence. They tell us very little, if anything, about society's income redistribution system.

One of the greatest pitfalls that social scientists fall into when they attempt to measure groups' income differences is that they attempt to lump all white ethnic groups together and compare race—that is, African Americans, whites, and others. Such comparison invariably forces them to assume that race itself—that is, the biological make-up of the groups—has functional economic and political characteristics. Because the assumption is false, the scientists' conclusions are inevitably false, thus adding very little, if anything, to the understanding of the cause of income differentials.

To avoid these pitfalls, this study measures the socioeconomic characteristics of groups on a one-to-one basis. For example, we will compare the total percentage of income above $10,000, the median income for this cohort in the 1970s, with occupational categories.

Using the 1970 U.S. Census data in looking at the wealthiest ethnic groups in this cohort, we can see that the Japanese stand at the top of the totem pole, with 73.6 percent of their families earning incomes of $10,000 or more, followed by the Jews with 71.2 percent, the Poles with 64.5 percent, and the Chinese with 64.3 percent (see Table 16).

As we stated in Chapter 4, many of the immigrants listed as Poles are in fact Jews. The U.S. Census does not make this distinction between Poles and Jews because it is not allowed to ask individuals questions concerning religious affiliation. However, in 1975, Andrew M. Greeley conducted a study of

Table 16
Percentage Distribution of Ethnic Groups with Family Incomes of $10,000 or More, 1970

Ethnic Groups According to Rank Order	Percentages $10,000 or More
Japanese	73.6
Russian Jews	71.2
Poles	64.5
Chinese	64.3
Italians	62.3
Irish	60.3
English	57.5
Swedes	53.1
West Indians	53.1
Norwegians	48.8
Germans	46.1
Spanish	34.7
Blacks	23.3

SOURCE: These percentages are taken from Table 34 in the appendix.

the Polish Catholics. His study showed that they had a median family income of $11,298.[15] The U. S. Census reported their income to be $12,274. This discrepancy in median income suggests that a large percentage of Jews was included among the Poles in the census survey.

There does not appear to be a close correlation between the ethnic groups with the highest economic achievement and those groups with the highest educational attainment. Where median school years completed are compared among this cohort, we get a different rank order than we did in family incomes. At the top of the totem pole, we have the Russian Jews, with 12.8 median school years completed, followed by the Chinese with 12.7 percent, the Japanese with 12.6 percent, and both the English and the British West Indians with 12.4 percent (see Table 40).[16]

The previous data indicate that the racial minorities—except for African Americans and some Hispanics—and the non-Protestant ethnic groups overall are doing much better economically and educationally than the Protestants. There appears to be an economic disparity between the Protestants and the non-Protestants. This disparity was first brought to the attention of students of group mobility by Greeley. He interpreted this disparity as an indication of a reverse in the Protestant work ethic theory, and he saw no obvious reason for its reversal.[17]

What Greeley was looking at in his study was not a reverse of the Protestant work ethic. As we argued in the Introduction Chapter, the Protestant work ethic is not a scientific argument explaining groups' upward mobility on a systematic basis. What Greeley was looking at were the economic linkages that groups had connected between themselves and society's mainstream-income distribution system. As stated in the Introduction Chapter, the mainstream consists of three linkages: trade, commerce, and real estate. We postulated that those groups or individual(s) who connect themselves to all three of these linkages will always have a higher income than those that do not. The data overwhelmingly supports this when we look at the high rate of entrepreneurship of the Asian groups.

Again, the Protestant work ethic is simply a self-victimization argument that social scientists freely use to explain African Americans' lack of success. This is exemplified in the "lack-of-values" argument which they have advanced to explain African Americans' lack of success. The success of the non-Protestants can better help us to understand Max Weber's statement that Protestantism was not responsible for the Protestants' economic success but was a product of it.[18] These Protestants were connected to the three linkages of the mainstream (see Table 17).[19]

Table 17
Occupational Categories Which Prescribe High Group Income, 1970

Groups	Professional	Managerial	Craftsman	Total
Russian Jews	25.4	23.5	12.0	60.9
English	19.6	16.0	20.5	56.1
Japanese	20.0	13.8	22.2	56.0
Swedes	16.7	16.2	22.0	54.9
Chinese	27.7	14.0	10.5	52.2
Poles	15.5	11.5	23.6	50.6
Norwegians	14.4	14.3	21.5	52.2
Irish	17.6	15.0	17.5	50.1
Italians	12.5	13.7	23.7	49.9
Germans	14.3	13.4	22.0	49.7
West Indians	17.3	8.6	16.7	42.6
Hispanics	6.7	5.1	21.9	33.7
Blacks	5.6	3.0	15.2	23.8

SOURCE: Table 37 in the appendix.

This table measures the percentage of group male income above $10,000 (median for 1970) . In Table 16, we rank groups according to their percentage of families earning income above $10,000. In Table 17, we rank them according to their total percentage in the three major occupational categories in which groups are concentrated: professional, managerial, and craftsmen categories.

At the top of the totem pole, we have the Russian Jews with 60.9 percent of their male work force employed in these three categories. They are followed by the English, 56.1 percent; Japanese, 56 percent; Swedes, 54.9 percent; Chinese, 52.2 percent; Poles, 50.6 percent, an so on.

There are several conclusions that can be drawn from Tables 16 and 17. First, all groups with 60 percent of their family earning income of $10,000 or more have over 35 percent of their male work force employed in the professional or craftsmen categories. With the exception of the Russian Jews, Chinese, and Irish, all groups that have over 10 percent of their families earning income above $10,000 have over 20 percent of their male work force concentrated in the craftsmen category. As we shall see in Chapter 8, the craftsmen category prescribes a high level of income because it is highly subsidized by the federal and state governments. Government subsidies include such items as fringe benefits, union scale wages, apprenticeship programs, guaranteed weekly wages, and the mandates of the Davis-Bacon Act—as will be discussed in later chapters.

The professional category also prescribes a high level of income. Both the Russian Jews and Chinese have over 25 percent of their males employed in this category: 25.4 percent, and 27.7 percent, respectively. Both groups have the lowest percentage concentrated in the craftsmen categories: 12 percent and 10.5 percent, respectively.

African Americans and Hispanics have a disproportionately low number of their males employed in all three categories: African Americans have 5.6 percent concentrated in the professional categories, 3 percent in managerial, and 15.2 percent in craftsmen. The Hispanics have 6.7 percent concentrated in the professional, 5.1 percent in managerial, and 21.9 percent in craftsmen categories. Hence, the low income is a function of groups not being concentrated in those occupational categories that prescribe high income.

What the figures in Tables 16 and 17 demonstrate is that occupational categories are the best indicators to explain group income differences. These categories help social scientists to identify the economic linkages which groups have fashioned with the mainstream. The downward mobility of Protestants and the upward mobility of the non-Protestants and some racial minority groups can be explained by the geographic areas and these linkages.

The data in Table 17 indicate that the occupational categories in which ethnic groups are concentrated have a more positive relationship in determining income differences than educational attainment, as has been commonly thought. Therefore, the pattern of downward mobility of the Protestants and the upward mobility among the Catholics and racial minority groups can be understood partly by looking at the occupational categories in which each group is employed. The shift in the American economy from agriculture to industrialization, coupled with the various labor laws, also had a determinative impact on the economic and social status of these groups. As we shall see in the next chapter, there are high levels of government subsidies embedded in the professional and craftsmen categories.

As stated earlier, the Germans and the Scandinavians were still on the farm in the 1950s when automation began to have an impact upon the American economy. Automation had its greatest impact, perhaps, in those industrial states where industries were flourishing. Thus, when automation was shifted into high gear, the non-Protestants were there in the cities to seize control of those economic sectors that were highly subsidized by the federal government and which prescribed high income, as will be demonstrated in the next chapter. As automation increased, the standards of living in these industrial states rose higher than they did in the less industrial states. The Protestants (particularly the Swedes, the Norwegians, the Germans, and the Scots-Irish) had originally settled in those states where industrial development and government subsidies were less pronounced. The English were scattered throughout the industrial and non-industrial states, particularly in the South. Thus, their downward mobility can also be viewed not so much as their having moved downward, but that the other groups have caught up with and surpassed them. As we shall see in the next chapter, the primary cause for this change in mobility is that the American system of income redistribution shifted between the 1940s and 1970s while the Protestants stayed put.

The disparity in the educational attainment between the Catholics—that is, the Irish-Catholics and the Italians—can best be understood if we look at the occupational categories in which each group is concentrated. Of the Italian males, 23.7 percent are employed as craftsmen, while the Irish are evenly scattered in the professional (17.6 percent), managerial (15 percent), clerical (12.3

percent), and craftsmen (17.5 percent) categories. The craftsmen category does not prescribe the same level of education as do the professional and managerial categories. Since many of the professional and managerial jobs are in the public sector or other related bureaucracies, it is obvious why the Irish have higher educational attainments than the Italians. There are slightly more Irish employed in white-collar occupations (professional, 17.6 percent, and managerial, 15 percent) than Italians (professional, 12.5 percent, and managerial, 13.7 percent). Again, the Irish are employed in those occupational categories that have very low positive statistical relationships in determining median family income (management and clerical and kindred workers); it follows then that the occupational categories in which the Irish have established an economic base prescribe a higher level of education than income—the opposite is true for the Italians. The Protestants are also employed in the same craftsmen occupational categories as the non-Protestants, but the difference here is that the former groups are concentrated in non-industrial states, and the latter groups are concentrated in industrial states. There is good reason to believe that if the costs of living in the industrial states were compared with those of the non-industrial states there would be very little difference in the percentage of family income among these groups. This is merely a suggestion, and a full exploration of the subject is beyond the scope of this study.

The underlying reasons why some racial minority groups are doing considerably better than some Protestants and the Catholic groups is that the former groups are concentrated in those occupational categories and geographic areas that prescribe high income.

However, African American and Spanish males are doing considerably less well educationally and economically in the 1970 census, because they are under-represented in those occupational categories that have a determinative impact on income. Over 76 percent of African American males are employed in those occupational categories that have a very low income.

In summary, this chapter has examined the economic linkages that groups fashioned with the American polity between the years 1920 and 1970. It has been revealed that groups maintained the same linkages they established in their initial stages of contact. It has also been demonstrated that income inequality can best be explained by comparing geographic areas in which groups are situated to the economic linkages that groups have fashioned with the American polity. Such a comparison will enable social scientists to obtain a systematic analysis of behavior among groups. It must be noted here that is not a close correlation between educational attainment and income. Education is relevant, insofar as it serves as a ticket to enter those occupational categories that prescribe high income. In the next chapter, we will examine those factors within the occupational categories that prescribe high income.

Notes

1.   In Table 14, there are four occupational categories. At particular times, the seven ethnic groups were more heavily concentrated in one or more of these categories than they were at other times. Therefore, I ranked each category according to the higher percentage of each group's males engaged in each category for that time period. Subsequent reference to these occupations will be stated as "occupational rank order."

2.   See Table 14 for subsequent references to data on occupational rank order.

3.   Edward P. Hutchinson, *Immigrants and Their Children: 1850-1950* (New York: John Wiley and Sons, 1956), pp. 197-218.

4.   See Table 30 in the appendix.

5.   See Table 30 in the appendix for an overall picture of the Germans' occupation distribution.

6.   See Table 42 in the appendix for the data previously cited.

7.   See Table 35 in the appendix.

8.   See Table 36 in the appendix.

9.   Lawrence Guy. Brown, *Immigration* (New York: Longmans, Green and Company, 1933), chapter 14.

10. See Table 37 in the appendix.

11. Ibid.

12. See Table 41 in the appendix.

13. See Table 40 in the appendix.

14. See, for instance, Peter M. Blau and Otis D. Duncan, *The American Occupation* (New York: John Wiley and Sons, 1967), p. 27; Otis D. Duncan, David L. Featherman, and Beverly Duncan, *Socioeconomic Background and Achievement* (New York: Seminar Press, 1972).

15. Andrew M. Greeley, "Ethnicity, Denomination and Inequalities," A Bicentennial Report to the Ford Foundation, Center for the Study of American Pluralism, National Opinion Research Center, Chicago, 1975, p. 88.

16. See Table 40 in the appendix.

17. Greeley, "Ethnicity, Denomination and Inequalities." p. 46.

18. Max Weber, *The Protestant Ethic and the Spirit of Capitalism* (New York: Charles Scribner's Sons, 1958), pp. 35–36.

19. Henri See commented that it was "only because the English have become merchants and traders that London has surpassed Paris in extent and in the number of its citizens: that the English can place 200 warships on the sea and subsidizes allies." Henri See, *Modern Capital* (New York: Adelphi. 1982), p. 87.

CHAPTER 8

Gaining an Economic Foothold in the American Economy: The Late Nineteenth Century Immigrant Groups

This chapter is directed toward answering the underlying question that was raised in Chapter 1: "Why were African Americans unable to escape the slums as did the European immigrants?" This question can best be answered by restating it in the following manner: "How were the European immigrants able to escape the slums?"[1] Whatever explanations we offer here must fit firmly within the framework of the liberal democratic theory and David Easton's schema for systematic research. As we stated in Chapter 1, he argued research that is not tutored by theory "may prove trivial" and "theory unsupported by data, futile."[2] Let us now turn to offering a systematic explanation for the success of the nineteenth century European immigrants and the failure of African Americans. We are going to defer discussing the success of Asians and Mexicans to later chapters. These groups immigrated in large numbers after the passage of the 1964 Civil Rights Act and the adoption of various affirmative action measures. These measures support our general theme that group mobility is highly contingent upon a set of government-issued bootstraps.

The primary reason the European immigrants were able to escape the slums, to hypothesize, was because the government offered them a set of bootstraps that safeguarded their freedom (1) to interact in a human capital environment, and (2) to connect themselves to the mother lode of society's income redistribution system. At the same time, it refused to offer African Americans the same protection. This proposition superimposes all of the traditional arguments advanced thus far. To repeat, students have argued that group success is contingent upon their willingness to accept or to reject the "Protestant work ethic,"[3] their "weak family structure,"[4] "African Americans' inability to delay present gratifications for future ones,"[5] "fertility rates,"[6] "IQ deficiency,"[7] "groups' culture and not discrimination determines who get ahead,"[8] and so on.

These arguments, as we have stated, are micro in nature. What they have in common is a lack of an analysis of group behavior within the framework of the liberal democratic theory, where the focus of analysis is on studying what role the government played in protecting groups' freedom to connect themselves to society's income redistribution system. Embedded in this system is an awesome system of government subsidies in terms of fringe benefits. Let us turn to an examination of the economic linkages that groups have fashioned with the American polity.

Groups' Economic Linkages and Mainstream

One of the major pitfalls in studying group inequality is the tendency of social scientists to compare the behavior of African Americans to that of whites. In order to obtain a systematic analysis of ethnic and groups' socioeconomic status, it is necessary to go beyond simply comparing African Americans' income to that of whites. For example, social scientists usually write that African Americans' income is 60 percent of that of whites'. Such measurement is tantamount to little more than a recitation of statistical incidences. It tells us nothing about how groups are structured within society's income redistribution system. To identify such variables, it is necessary to compare group income on a one-to-one basis among the thirteen race and ethnic groups for a twenty-year period. The figures in Table 18 are an attempt to achieve this goal.

The figures in this table measure the percent increase of groups' income above the median for this cohort. The median income for this cohort was $2,245 in 1950 and $11,374 in 1970 (see Tables 33 and 34 in the appendix). In 1970, the United States Census Bureau used intervals of four digits ($9,999 to $14,999) to compute group income. From this tabulation, we cannot locate the median income of $11,374. Therefore, in Table 18, we selected $10,000 or more as group median income for 1970, and $2,500 or more as group median income for 1950. We then tabulated the percentage of each group with income above this figure. For example, 73.6 percent of the Japanese families in the work force were earning incomes above $10,000 in 1970. They were followed by the Russian Jews, 71.2 percent; Poles, 64.1 percent; and Chinese, 64.3 percent. In 1950 the percentage of Japanese families earning incomes above the median

($2,500) was 18.8 percent. By 1970, that percentage had increased (i.e., percentage of $10,000) to 73.6 percent. Hence, the Japanese experienced a 54.8 percent income increase from their average in 1950.

Table 18
Percentage of Increase in Family Income Above Median, 1950 and 1970

Ethnic Groups	Percentage of Family Income above Median[a]		Perentage Increase above Median from 1950 to 1970
	1950	1970	
Japanese	18.8	73.6	54.8
Chinese	15.8	64.3	48.5
Russian Jews	33.2	71.2	38.0
Italians	27.3	62.3	35.0
Poles	32.0	64.5	32.5
Irish	28.6	60.3	31.7
English	28.5	57.5	29.0
Spanish	9.4	34.7	25.3
Swedes	32.4	53.4	21.0
Norwegians	28.5	48.8	20.3
Blacks	3.4	23.3	19.9
Germans	27.9	46.1	18.2

SOURCE: See Tables 29 and 30 in the appendix.

[a]The median income for the entire cohort was $2,245 in 1950 and $11,347 in 1970. However, the median income for 1970 falls somewhere between $10,000 and $14,999. From $9,999 to $25,000, the U.S. Bureau of the Census used intervals of four thousands and nine thousands. Since it is difficult to locate the median income between $10,000 and $14,999, $10,000 or more is used to compute the percentage above the median for this cohort.

The Most Upward Mobile Group between 1950 and 1970

There have been some questions raised regarding which ethnic group has achieved the highest rate of social upward mobility during the period between 1950 and 1970. This period is significant here, because it epitomizes the era in MP which the New Deal and other liberal income redistribution programs were instituted.[9] Groups that had a system of protection that granted them the freedom to connect themselves to this system showed a marked socioeconomic upward mobility between the years 1950 and 1970. Groups that were excluded showed a marked decline in the same area (see Table 19).

Table 19
The Most Upwardly Mobile Group between 1950 and 1970

Ethnic Groups	Percentages above or below average median[a]	
	1950	1970
Japanese	- 0.9	34.1
Russian Jews	13.5	31.7
Poles	12.3	25.0
Chinese	- 3.9	24.8
Italians	7.6	22.8
Irish	8.9	20.8
English	8.8	18.0
Swedes	12.7	13.9
Norwegians	8.8	9.3
Germans	8.2	6.6
Spanish	-10.3	- 4.8
Blacks	-16.3	-16.2

SOURCES: Tables 33 and 34 in the appendix.

[a]The total percentage of families above the median income for this cohort was 19.7 percent in 1950 and 39.5 percent in 1970.

-Below the median average.

From the data in Table 18, we can see that the most upwardly mobile groups during this period were the Japanese, followed by the Chinese, the Russian Jews, and the Italians. There are two basic reasons for this marked increase in the Japanese and Chinese income percentage during this period. First, they are highly concentrated in those occupational categories that prescribe high income (i.e., professional, managerial, and craftsmen; hereafter, high-income occupational categories. For example, in 1950, 6.4 percent of Japanese males were engaged in the professional category. By 1970, this figure had increased to 20 percent. In the managerial category, the figure was 8.6 percent in 1950 and increased to 13.8 percent by 1970. The largest increase for the Japanese was in the craftsmen category, which increased from 9.7 percent in 1950 to 22.2 percent in 1970 (see Tables 31 and 33 in the appendix).

The Chinese had 6.3 percent of their males concentrated in the professional category in 1950. By 1970, that figure had increased to 27.7 percent. However, they experienced a decline in the percentage of males engaged in the managerial category: from 22.2 percent in 1950 to 14 percent in 1970. As we saw in the last chapter, the managerial category has a very low correlation in determining median income. The Chinese showed a marked increase in the percentage of their males engaging in the craftsmen category: from 3.3 percent in 1950 to 10.2 percent in 1970. Therefore, the high income increase for the Chinese can be explained by their marked increase in the professional and craftsmen categories. Chinese / Japanese

The second reason for the Chinese and Japanese increase in the percentage of families earning income above the median was because they were concentrated in highly industrialized states and cities. As has been demonstrated in the previous chapter, the Japanese and Chinese are highly concentrated in California and other western states. California is included among the highly industrialized states because of its economic expansion after World War II and its defense industries. Again, California happens to be one of those states in which the Scandinavians and Germans did not settle in the 1860s and 1870s. These groups did not migrate to the western states, as did the Irish and Italians, who traditionally followed public work projects.

Table 18 offers further evidence that geographic areas are factors in deter- MP mining income differences. Embedded in these geographic areas are those industries that have built-in income redistribution systems prescribing high income. For example, the Russian Jews have 60.9 percent of their males concentrated in occupational categories that have a strong correlation with high income. However, 25.7 percent of the Russian Jews are concentrated in New York City; followed by Los Angeles at 6.4 percent; Philadelphia at 6.1 percent; and Chicago at 5.1 percent (see Table 15 in Chapter 7).

The West Indians also have a high percentage of their families earning incomes above $10,000, 53.1 percent (see Table 16 in Chapter 7). They are also concentrated in New York City; for example, 54.8 percent of them live in New York City alone. Embedded in the occupational structures in New York City are many professional jobs that prescribe high income and contain a high structure of government subsidies. For instance, the Russian Jews have 25.4 percent of their males concentrated in the professional category and 23.5 percent in the managerial category. By the same token, the West Indians have 17.3 percent and 8.6 percent of their males in the same categories, respectively.

The Chinese have 52.2 percent of their males concentrated in the three high-income occupational categories. They are also concentrated in the most industrialized cities in America, 21.1 percent in San Francisco, and 13.1 percent in New York City. The Japanese are spread throughout the western states (see Table 15 in Chapter 7). Their highest concentration is in Los Angeles, 16.3 percent, and San Francisco, 5.5 percent. However, they are also scattered throughout the state of Washington, which also has a large defense industry.

As will be demonstrated, the mere concentration of groups in the three high-income occupational categories is not within itself a guarantee of high income. As Table 17 in Chapter 7 indicates, 56.1 percent of the English males and 54.9 percent of the Swedes are concentrated in these categories. However, the percentage of these groups' families earning incomes above $10,000 for 1970 was not as high as some of the other racial ethnic groups and the Russian Jews; for example, the number of English families earning incomes above $10,000 equaled 57.5 percent; and the Swedes, 53.4 percent (see Table 18). The English had only 30.2 percent of their group living in the nine metropolitan areas that were compared in this study (see Table 15 in Chapter 7).

. It is obvious from this analysis that the income redistribution systems embedded in these occupational categories can offer a better explanation for groups' income differences than other non-measurable factors such as the Protestant work ethic, fertility rates, age, and so on. An examination of these systems will be the focus of the next section. The groups concentrated in the high-income occupational categories seem to have improved their conditions over the years. For instance, very few African American and Hispanic males were concentrated in the professional and managerial categories in 1970: 8.6 percent and 13.8 percent, respectively. These data strongly indicate that these two groups were being excluded from the income redistribution system at a time when the government was pumping billions of dollars annually into the economy in the form of federal subsidies.

In Table 18, we have seen that all groups within this cohort experienced an increase in the number of families earning incomes above the median between the period of 1950 and 1970. For example, in 1950, 6.9 percent of all African American families engaged in the labor force were earning incomes above the median income for this group during this period. By 1970, this figure had increased to 23.3 percent–with a net gain of 16.4 percent.

If we tabulate the total number of families for this cohort earning incomes above the median for 1950 and 1970, we obtain a better picture of how well African Americans and Hispanics fared in relation to the other groups. For instance, the total figure of families earning incomes above the median ($2,245) in 1950 for this cohort equaled 19.7 percent. In 1970, this number had increased to 39.5 percent–a 19.8 percent increase. In Table 19, we compared each group's median income with the average for both 1950 and 1970. In 1950, median income of the Japanese, African Americans, Chinese, and Hispanics was below the average median for this group. But by 1970, the Japanese and Chinese had caught up with the rest of the group. In fact, the Japanese surpassed the entire group, showing a 31.5 percent increase above the median for this cohort (see Table 19).

The most astonishing finding among this group is the decline in the status of African Americans. Instead of gaining percentage points above the median, they actually lost ground. In 1950, African Americans were 12.8 percentage points below the average. In 1970, they were 18.6 percentage points below this average, thus falling 5.8 percent further behind the rest of the groups in the twenty years since 1950. The relative downward mobility of African Americans seems somewhat ironic when we consider the tremendous amount of literature purporting to show that African Americans are doing considerably better than they were in the 1950s. The data does not support such arguments.

As Table 19 indicates, African Americans, Japanese, Chinese, and Hispanics had incomes below the median in 1950, but the Japanese and Chinese closed this gap by 1970. The Japanese lead this cohort in widening the gap between themselves and the median, while African Americans lost ground. The Hispanics closed the gap slightly, but still fell below the median for this group. The question that emerges here is: What factors can be attributed to African Americans' decline in the percentage of family income below this cohort while the European groups experienced an increase? This question will be addressed in the next section.

The Status of Groups Before Liberalism

In this section, we will offer a systematic explanation to the old-age question as to why the nineteenth-century European immigrants were able to escape the slums and African Americans were not. This question will be answered within the conceptual framework developed in this book. This framework is so important to this area of inquiry that it is worth repeating here. In order for a group to elevate itself to the middle class plateau, it needs two things: *a pair of boots* and *a set of bootstraps*. Without the possession of these two variables, a group will remain pinned down on the beachheads of the culture of poverty by their competitors and adversaries until they develop the culture of poverty. Once developed, it will become a process of intergenerational downward mobility. This group will remain there until there is some form of government intervention.

As stated in the Introduction Chapter, no group has been able to escape the slums without a pair of boots and bootstraps. This theory is strongly supported by the Irish-Catholics' experience. When they came over, the government was offering immigrants a set of bootstraps in the form of land under the Land Grant Act of 1828. Because they had lost their skills for farming, they were unable to take advantage of these opportunities. Consequently, they remained pinned down on the beachheads of the culture of poverty until the adoption of the liberal programs during and after the New Deal.

The factors that kept the late nineteenth-century immigrants pinned down on the beachheads of the culture of poverty was that the government did not offer them a set of bootstraps until the adoption of the liberal programs. These groups include the Russian Jews, Poles, and Italians. Among these groups, the Jews immigrated with the greatest amount of human capital. However, they were not able to escape the slums until the adoption of the liberal programs. Let us turn to an examination of these liberal programs and those factors that kept these groups pinned down on the beachheads of the culture of poverty.

Combination in Restraint of Trade

European benefits

The liberal programs that enabled the European immigrants to escape the slums were (1) the various national labor laws between the years 1930 and 1960, (2) fringe benefits accompanying labor agreements, (3) the Federal Housing Act of 1932 and 1948, (4) and the G.I. Bill. Among these measures, the labor laws were the centerpieces for providing groups a platform to catapult themselves onto the middle-class plateau.

Before the passage of the first national labor laws in 1932, employers kept union workers pinned down on the beachheads of the culture of poverty. They used a legal tool known as _combination in the restraint of trade_, which was prohibited by the Sherman Anti-Trust Act of 1890. This act was originally designed to prevent businesses from forming monopolies for the purpose of restraining trade. But in 1908, the United States Supreme Court ruled, in _Loew v. Lawler_, that this act made "every contract, combination, or conspiracy in restraint of trade illegal," regardless of whether the entities were businesses, farmers, or labor unions.[10] From this year to 1932, employers used the Sherman Anti-Trust Act to undermine the efforts of the unions to organize. For example, whenever unions attempted to organize and strike for better working conditions and higher wages, employers would go to federal court seeking an injunction to thwart the unions' activities.

Because of the standardized "form of pleadings" and "vaguely worded affidavits, injunctions were often issued _ex parte_ and tended to be cast in such broad terms as to include the permitted with the proscribed. While a full hearing on the appropriateness of continuing the injunction would eventually be held, usually this came too late to help the union, whose strike, boycott or other activity had been effectively broken."[11]

With the power of an injunction, employers effectively restricted unions' freedom to organize and blocked their ability to bargain collectively for high wages and better working conditions for their members. Because of the use of injunctions, labor unions experienced a marked decline in membership and strength between World War I and the 1930s, from 5 million members in 1920 to fewer than 3 million in 1933.[12] At the beginning of the depression in the 1930s, the permanent demise of the unions seemed imminent. The unions were unable to protect their members' rights to employment security during this period; consequently, employers were extravagant with their use of injunctions to curb union activities.

In an attempt to get the country out of the depression, Congress passed the Norris-LaGuardia Act of 1932.[13] This act took away the legal weapon that employers had to restrict the growth of unions—that is, it removed the power of the federal courts to issue either temporary or permanent injunctions in labor disputes. But this act did not make a significant improvement in the lot of workers. This improvement did not take place until Congress passed the Wagner Act (National Labor Relations Act) in 1935. Essentially, this act threw the weight of the federal government behind unionism and collective bargaining.

National Labor Relations Act and Bootstraps

The National Labor Relations Act was more than a law governing the relationship between labor and management. It constituted: (1) a system of protection that took union members' rights to employment and economic opportunities off the goodwill of management and placed them upon a principle of law, and (2) a set of bootstraps in the form of high wages and fringe benefits that were subsidized by the federal government.

Before the National Labor Relations Act gave unions the right to collective bargaining, the European ethnic groups who immigrated during the last two decades of the nineteenth century were pinned down on the beachheads of the culture of poverty alongside African Americans. But with collective bargaining, these groups were able to elevate themselves onto the middle-class plateau.

Property Rights to Employment

The political significance of collective bargaining is that it took the decisions concerning wages, hiring, layoffs, and seniority off the goodwill of management and placed it upon a principle of law. This law allowed these decisions to be made jointly by both employers and unions. It also bestowed upon union members property interest rights to their continuous employment. Employers could no longer arbitrarily lay off employees or reduce their wages. With collective bargaining, this decision was subjected to procedural due process, which is a constitutionally protected right.

Under the federal collective bargaining laws, unions had the authority to negotiate property rights and fringe benefits for their members. Among these rights were hours of employment, wage employment guarantees (WEG), supplementary unemployment benefits (SUB), and other conditions of employment. The most significant of these with regard to groups' upward mobility was WEG, which constituted job security. The purpose of this provision was "to ensure employees a specified minimum amount of work or compensation for a predetermined period of time. The existing guarantees ranged from one week to a year or more."[14] The provisions of the WEG varied with different contracts; but, the following clauses exemplify a form of job security that the unions could possibly negotiate for their members: "All employees within the terms of this agreement shall be guaranteed not less than 40 straight time hours of work per week."[15] "Every permanent employee who reports for work regularly every day during the work week will be guaranteed 40 hours of pay for the week."[16] "All regular employees shall be guaranteed a minimum of 36 hours of work or pay in lieu of work per week."[17]

WEG provided workers with not only a secured source of income but also opened up new opportunities for them. One such opportunity was the American system of credit which had previously been closed to this class. Individuals now can use their labor as collateral for a loan from the bank, a choice which had previously been restricted to the propertied class. What induced the banks to allow union workers to use their labor as collateral was the guaranteed system of employment. Workers were no longer subject to layoffs and arbitrary dismissals. For those who defaulted on their loans, lending institutions could now seek a legal garnishment against their wages.

One political significance of WEG is that it broadened individual choice possibilities to accumulate wealth. It allowed an individual to use $10 as leverage to control more than $100 worth of real property that had the potential for appreciating in value over a period of time. This possibility enhanced the individual's capacity to achieve his goal in accumulating wealth, which is one of America's most sacred values.

Accompanying WEG was the supplementary wage benefit (SUB). The purpose of the SUB was to provide weekly supplements to government unemployment benefits to workers in case of layoffs. The amount of SUB varied between states and contracts unions were able to negotiate. However, these benefits ranged from 55 percent to 95 percent of the worker's weekly salary.[18] SUB was financed by the employers through one of the following methods: "individual account fund, single-employer pooled fund, multi-employer pooled fund, and unfunded plans."[19]

The method used to fund SUB is of little political significance to our argument here. What is germane is that under the federal collective bargaining laws these benefits were negotiable as property interest rights to employment, and they could not be arbitrarily and/or capriciously taken away from the employees by management. They were safeguarded through procedural due process.

The overall political significance of WEG and SUB was that they constituted income security. In terms of group mobility, this form of security is more important than high income. With it, the European immigrants were able not only to catapult themselves up off the beachheads of the culture of poverty and onto the middle-class plateau, but also to land themselves and their children in the middle of the mainstream of society's income redistribution system. For example, income security qualifies the individual to take advantage of a wide range of other economic benefits that significantly enhance a group's upward mobility, such as good credit ratings, low group insurance, group discounts, and easier qualification for conventional loans. Without job security, these benefits are more likely improbable.

Job Security and Upward Mobility

It has often been argued that European groups left the beachheads of the culture of poverty because of their adherence to the Protestant work ethic. The corollary to this is the racist argument that the primary reason African Americans have not left the beachheads of the culture of poverty (slums) is that they are too lazy to work. Or, as Nathan Glazer has implied, they are there by choice.[20]

European immigrants, to repeat, did not make it to the middle-class plateau because of their hard work, but because they had the full blessing of the federal government to negotiate income security for their members by: (1) enlarging

MP

job opportunities, (2) controlling access to jobs, and (3) providing supplementary income for workers out of work. The latter has already been discussed.

Enlarging Job Opportunities and Mobility

Enlarging job opportunities for members of their own group was a practice that was widely used by European immigrants after the passage of the NLRA. This process can explain groups' mobility better than the Protestant work ethic theory. Through enlarging job opportunities, groups' mobility is characterized more by horizontal mobility than by vertical. Before continuing, an explanation of the various forms of group mobility is in order.

Pitirim Sorokin, who was a pioneer student in this area, constructed a model that divided group mobility into two schemas: *horizontal* and *vertical*. Horizontal social mobility explains how individuals move from one social group to another on the same social stratum. Vertical social mobility describes how individuals descend and ascend from one social stratum to another in a society.[21] Sorokin developed this model in 1927, and "modern analysis has not gone far beyond"[22] his accomplishment.

Modern students have interpreted groups' mobility as being predominantly vertical in America. This is evident in Joseph A. Kahl's study on intergenerational mobility. He attempted to measure the importance of technological change on social mobility by comparing the changes in occupational standings of sons to their fathers for the period from 1920 to 1950.[23]

For conceptual clarity in this study, groups' upward mobility can be divided into a dichotomy of *ascriptive-based means* of success (vertical mobility) and *prescriptive-based means* of success (horizontal mobility). This clarity is necessary here, because of the many unsystematic arguments in the literature which attempt to explain group upward mobility (see the beginning of this chapter).

Students of ethnic and racial inequality write about groups' upward mobility, but they do not take care to make a distinction between vertical and horizontal mobility. In many instances, they select horizontal mobility as that unit of analysis. This mode of analysis can account for the persistent support for those arguments that are not supported by data.

MP

Ascriptive-based means of success are characterized by how an individual is able to "make it" to the middle class, despite the disadvantaged circumstances of his birth, and the many obstacles facing his group or race. From this prospective, one can find evidence of individuals overcoming these disadvantages and excelling in life. This has no respect to race, sex, national origin, or religion.

Take for example, Madame C. J. Walker of Indianapolis, one of America's self-made female millionaires. Before World War I, she had become a millionaire by developing a line of cosmetics and a method of straightening African American women's hair.

In 1954, George E. Johnson had a burning desire to start his own business. Using his skills as a chemist, he developed a series of cosmetic products that were designed to meet the changing lifestyles of African Americans of the 1950s and 60s. This changing lifestyle was brought on by the cultural revolution of the 1950s and 60s. When African Americans started wearing "Afros," George and a friend, who was a barber, decided to go into business. Johnson went to his bank where he was acquainted with the manager, who was white, and applied for a loan to start his business. The banker flatly turned him down. After discussing his frustration with his friend, they drove to another branch of the same bank and applied for a loan for the same amount. But this time, he requested a loan to take his wife on a vacation. Within ten minutes, the loan was approved.

In 1963, *Ebony* Magazine featured an article on A.G. Gaston of Birmingham, Alabama. This is the same city where members of the Ku Klux Klan bombed a black church killing seven young girls who were attending Sunday school. Yet, amidst this hostile environment, Gaston was able to establish several businesses which made him one of the wealthiest African Americans in America.

The list of successful African Americans who elevated themselves to the middle-class plateau through the *ascriptive-means based success* is extensive. It serves no purpose to catalog them here. The most important factor here is that the conditions in that environment did not foreclose their freedom to elevate themselves to a higher socioeconomic status. But the majority of African Americans in these communities remained pinned down on the beachhead of the culture of poverty.

The term *prescriptive-based* upward mobility can best be described as horizontal mobility. This form of mobility can be divided into two categories: *primordial attachment* and *intergenerational mobility*. The term "primordial attachment" is used here to describe the system of employment that is based on individuals obtaining employment based on kinship ties. This system operates on the principle of an individual having someone on the inside to vouch for him. The person could be his father, brother, uncle, or cousin. On the professional level, this person can be a member of the same fraternity, or an alumni from the same university. This is the system the European immigrants used extensively to catapult themselves onto the middle-class plateau.

MP   The term "intergenerational mobility" describes the process that families used to ensure that their offspring remained on the social and economic status which they were born. As demonstrated in Chapter 3, this was one of the major reasons why the European immigrants left Europe and came to America. They were trying to avoid the humiliation of being pushed off the middle-class plateau.

MP   The principle of intergenerational mobility does not necessarily mean that the son follows the same occupation as his father, but that he pursues a skilled or professional occupation that is equal to or better than his father. The economic expansion in America which started in the 1890s and continued through the 1940s augmented the principle of intergenerational mobility. During this period, there was a mechanization of the factories and an increase in urban populations. These two phenomena produced a new class of workers (i.e., service workers). Between 1920 and 1930, the census figures indicate that the service industries grew approximately 66 percent, whereas workers in the productive industries grew about only 26 percent.[24] As Merrell Lynd noted in his study, the percentage of "service workers were becoming more professionalized through time; there were more schoolteachers, more social workers, more dental hygienists."[25] Joseph Kahl further noted in his study of 1953 that the mechanization of industries also created a new class of wealthy manufacturers, bankers, and managers of national corporations. This group "sent their children to local college as a matter of course."[26]

The whole of the change in mechanization of industries and urban concentration significantly constrained the upward mobility of managers within the rank. Instead of selecting managers from the rank, industries–to a large extent, bureaucracies–sought managers from the new middle class that were trained in college as technicians and administrators. This new class was able to perpetuate and promulgate itself by sending its children to college. They were able to do so because they had the financial means. As will be demonstrated later in this chapter, the only students who attended college were those whose parents had the means to do so. It was not until the adoption of the G.I. Bill that this process changed.

Although it can be applied to the professional class, the term *primordial attachment* best explains the upward mobility of blue-collar and union workers. This concept describes how the European immigrants of the late nineteenth century were able to catapult themselves onto the middle-class plateau after the passage of NLRA. The various groups seized control of certain sectors of the economy through the means of collective bargaining and established rules and regulations that protected jobs for themselves and their offsprings. They parceled out jobs via primordial attachment; that is, individuals obtained jobs in their sector not on the basis of merit and qualifications, but through whom the applicant knew. Through primordial attachment, the group could prevent other groups from obtaining jobs in the sector that they controlled.

With collective bargaining giving them the right to participate in establishing rules and procedures for recruitment, the European immigrants were able to create an environment whereby fathers could virtually guarantee jobs for their sons at their respective places of employment. When jobs were not available, they created them through the process of *enlarging job opportunities.*

The notion of enlarging job opportunities did not just appear on the scene after the national labor law was passed. This law simply strengthened the hands of the unions to utilize this method. Essentially, enlargement of job opportunities resulted from unions restricting the outputs of production–that is, making work last. As part of their conditions of work, the unions would negotiate the minimum as the "maximum, impressing upon its members that to produce more would throw someone out of a job."[27] The unions were further able to enlarge job opportunities through job classifications and jurisdiction. For example, in a theater the unions would require the employer to hire separate workers to handle the curtains, property, or lights. If the theater was not unionized, all of these tasks could be handled by one person.[28] Hence, the process of job enlargement undermines the argument that the European immigrants made it because of hard work or their adherence to the Protestant work ethic. Hard work proved to be more of a disadvantage in collective bargaining than an advantage.

A combination of job enlargement and primordial attachment were practices that unions used to control access to employment until the election of President Ronald Reagan. This process was slightly altered by affirmative action, but it received its demise when President Reagan launched a protracted war on labor. He started attacking unions in 1981 when he issued the union an ultimatum: return to work within forty-eight hours or you are fired. Never in the history of labor had a President issue such an ultimatum. Therefore, the union leaders did not take him seriously. When they did not return to work, he fired them.

The second assault on unionism occurred when President Reagan eliminated the bulk of the funds for apprenticeship programs that were controlled by the unions. Reagan eliminated these programs with a host of other programs that he deemed to be social programs. The repercussion that these cuts had on the status of union workers was that it truncated the father's ability to guarantee his son a job down in the plant where he worked.

Priority Rights to Jobs

Priority rights to jobs were another method European groups used to maintain their standing on the middle-class plateau. This method consisted of equal division of labor and seniority. Both concepts are basically the same; the major difference is the sequence of operation. Equal division of labor occurs when work is persistently irregular. When the work is slow employees are laid off according to seniority. But the burden of layoffs is shared with all workers, not concentrated with a few. Seniority comes into play in a reverse manner when the work load increases. That is, the last to be laid off are the first to be rehired.

Seniority also gives workers preference to new and high-paying jobs. Whenever a new position is made available, a senior person bidding for the position has preference for the job even if he is not the best qualified for it.

In short, a combination of enlargement of job opportunities, primordial attachment, priority rights to jobs, and intergenerational mobility, all of which were supported directly or indirectly by the federal government, can explain how white ethnic groups were able to catapult themselves onto the middle-class plateau. After they made it to the plateau, they began to establish rules and procedures to foreclose African Americans' and Puerto Ricans' freedom to elevate themselves to the same plateau, thus keeping them pinned down on the beachheads of the culture of poverty until the implementation of affirmative action. The following section will be a discussion of these practices.

What Happened to African Americans?

After discussing the success of European immigrants, social scientists—and commentators alike—usually raise the following two questions: What happened to African Americans? Why did they not join the unions like the European groups? These questions can best be answered within the framework of the liberal democratic theory. African Americans were unable to escape the slums, because they were pinned down on the beachheads of the culture of poverty by their competitors and adversaries. This power to exclude them constituted the tyranny of majoritarian rule. As James Madison perceptively noted in his Federalists papers, as long as the rights of any group rests on the goodwill of the ruling class, they will always be subjected to the severe deprivation by the tyranny of majoritarian rule. This was practically the status of African Americans from the close of the Civil War up to the adoption of the civil rights measures of the 1960s.

It is not necessary to identify the groups that kept African Americans pinned down on the beachheads of the culture of poverty. Suffice it to say that within the framework of the liberal democratic theory, they did not have a system of protection to safeguard their freedom to connect themselves to the mainstream of society's income redistribution system. As this writer has maintained, groups will always remain in such condition until there is some form of government intervention.

The Government's Refusal to Protect African Americans

This section will consist of an analysis of some of the roles that the federal government played in oppressing African Americans. Such analysis is very important to our major argument, because of the persistent attempt by critics of racial inequality to shift the blame of the present-day conditions of African Americans to factors other than the failure of the government to adopt positive measures to protect their freedom to take advantage of life opportunities. As we have seen in Chapter 6, various social sciences have attempted to place this blame on the institutions of slavery or a master class that no longer exist.[29] Or they have attempted to offer an apology of "benign neglect" as Daniel P. Moynihan asserted in 1972. But the present-day conditions of African Americans is a function of (1) the unions' long-standing policy of racial exclusion, (2) the government's refusal to include an anti-discrimination clause in NLRA, (3) the legal authority that NLRA gave the unions to have African Americans fired from their jobs to make room for whites, and (4) dramatic increases in the amount of federally subsidized programs that benefitted unions and white workers.

The period between 1935 and 1968 marked the period in which the government adopted a series of measures that significantly improved the standards of living for most workers. President Franklin D. Roosevelt referred to these measures as the "Second Bill of Rights." Politically, these measures were tantamount to being a government *bonanza giveaway*–which significantly improved the socioeconomic status of whites. This *bonanza* included such measures as subsidized housings, job training programs, federal aid to education, and a host of other fringe benefits that unions could negotiate as part of their collective bargaining agreements. African Americans were largely excluded from benefitting from this bonanza giveaway by either a *de facto* or a *de jure* policy of racial exclusion.

The political philosophy that underlies this policy of racial exclusion was a combination of the racial doctrines of *romantic racialism* and *Social Darwin-*

ism. To repeat, these doctrines maintain that (1) African Americans are biologically inferior to whites, and (2) they should always maintain a socioeconomic status in society inferior to that of whites either by fact or law. In order to validate this argument, special measures had to be undertaken to constrain African Americans' ability to raise their standards of living equal to that of whites. The only way that this policy could be carried out was to adopt measures, either *de facto* or *de jure*, to foreclose their freedom to connect themselves to the mainstream of society's income redistribution system. Evidence of the existence of these racial doctrines during this period can be found in the intense resistance whites had toward the concept of racial equality. The operative effect of this resistance was to ensure that facts conform to theory. As will be demonstrated in a later chapter, African Americans were able to raise their standards of living significantly after the adoption of affirmative action.

An understanding of the political philosophy that underlies a policy of racial exclusion is of paramount importance to the understanding the failure of African Americans to leave the beachheads of the culture of poverty before the 1970s. Their competitors and adversaries influenced the government to adopt positive measures to exclude them from benefitting from the Second Bill of Rights measures. They did this not so much out of racial bias–although such bias did play a major role–but out of their own self-interest. Within the framework of the liberal democratic theory, groups do not have a legal nor a moral obligation to look out for the interests of their competitors and adversaries. This is the duty and the responsibility of the national government, which is an inherent part of the "social contract." According to the political philosophy of John Locke, this social contract places a duty and a responsibility on the government to adopt positive laws to safeguard groups right to an orderly means of subsistence. The failure to do so would constitute a breach of this contract, which inadvertently will force men back to their original state of nature, which is the natural state of war.[30] This was one of the underlying reasons why policymakers adopted this giveaway bonanza policy. They were afraid that this large pool of unemployed white workers during the Great Depression would revolt. To eliminate this possibility, they adopted this giveaway bonanza policy, but African Americans were excluded from benefitting from this policy because of the unions' policy of racial exclusion.

This policy of racial exclusion was adopted by the unions following the close of the Civil War; it remained in effect until government intervened during the Richard Nixon Administration. In their efforts to seek a conservative approach to civil rights in the early 1970s, the Republicans adopted an affirmative action program which was called the "Philadelphia Plan." Before the adoption this plan, African Americans' rights to take advantage of a wide range of occupations in the area of artisans and craftsmen were foreclosed by unions' policy of racial exclusion (see the section on apprenticeship). The failure of the government to step in and provide them with a system of protection against this political tyranny before the passage of NLRA constituted a *de facto* policy of exclusion. After its passage, it constituted *de jure* policy of exclusion, because the government in effect gave the unions legal authority to exclude them.

The Rejection of an Anti-Discrimination Clause

When the NLRA was being debated in Congress, African American leadership foresaw the political repercussions of this act.[31] Members of the National Association for the Advancement of Colored People (NAACP) and the National Urban League lobbied hard to get Congress to attach an anti-discrimination clause to this bill.[32] The purpose of this clause was to deny any union the right to collective bargaining if it had a policy of racial discrimination. Senator Robert Wagner, who sponsored the bill, had this clause written into the original draft. But the American Federation of Labor (AFL), which was dominated by the late nineteenth-century immigrants, exerted its power in Congress and had the clause removed from the bill. Thus, the fight over the bill boiled down to two African Americans' advocate organizations that were both weak in resources and small in numbers in terms of potential voters, and the powerful AFL, which was strong in all these areas. Even President Franklin D. Roosevelt, with his charismatic leadership, was unable or unwilling to withstand the pressure from the powerful leadership of AFL. Thus, from the passage of the NLRA to the implementation of the various civil rights laws, the unions not only had the power to deny African Americans their liberty interest right to pursue a higher standard of living, but also were able to do so with the full blessing of the federal government.

The power to exclude African Americans from the labor market had both economic and social implications. Socially, the unions had the power to elevate or to reduce individuals' socioeconomic status in society. As far as African Americans were concerned, it significantly restrained their growth and development. This practice of exclusion ensured whites that African Americans would never achieve a social status equal to theirs. In order to get a clearer understanding of the effect of this policy between the period of 1930s and 1970s, let us turn to an analysis of the power that the NRLA conferred upon the unions.

First, the NLRA conferred upon unions the exclusive right to collective bargaining within their respective units. Second, it gave them the power to authoritatively allocate property and interest rights to their members on the basis of rights and privileges by law. The right to acquire skills as craftsmen and artisans became a property right under this law because it was a contract. By giving unions such exclusive power, NLRA also gave them the power to exclude others. Third, it provided unions with the political linkages to connect themselves to both the political system—where they could significantly influence public policy—and the mainstream of society's income redistribution system by which they could accumulate wealth over a period of time. The political impact of this process is that it allowed the principle of intergenerational mobility to come into play whereby union members could guarantee that their siblings maintained or improve their social status. Fourth, it enabled the unions to set wages by law, which were previously determined by the free market system. Finally, it gave the unions the legal authority to engage in a process of job encroachment and displacement of African Americans.

Job Encroachment and Displacement

The process of job encroachment and displacement was one of the most frequently and widely used tools that unions had at their disposal to keep African Americans oppressed. Since these processes played a major role in constraining their growth and development, they need to be discussed separately.

Job Displacement

When the economy was flourishing, African Americans could find jobs in non-union shops. But as soon as there was a recession, the unions were in a position legally to move into non-union shops and use their exclusive bargaining power to force employers to dismiss African Americans and hire whites in their place.

The unions used this process to foreclose a wide range of employment opportunities for African Americans from 1935 until the government intervened in the 1970s. For instance, the Brotherhood of Electrical Workers in Long Island City, New York, decided in the 1930s to expand its jurisdiction over the electrical supply shops that had employed several dozen African Americans. With a policy of racial exclusion, the Brotherhood Union moved in and organized these shops. Their first order of business was to force the employers to dismiss all African Americans. This practice was not confined only to New York but was carried out throughout the country. In St. Louis, for instance, employers found to their dismay that they could not employ even one skilled African American to build the $2 million Homer Philip's Hospital in the heart of the African American community. When the General Tile Company of St. Louis attempted to hire one highly trained African American worker as a tile setter, all of the AFL's workers walked off their jobs and held up construction for two months,[33] thus causing the employer to suffer irrevocable economic loss. This strike had a ripple effect upon the employment status of African Americans throughout the country, particularly in the northern cities. It touched the central nervous system of the business world and forced many employers to think twice before they employed African Americans in any job where they had to compete with whites. For instance, the building committee of the St. Louis Board of Education refused to hire African Americans to perform maintenance work on the seventeen schools in the African American community out of fear of the white workers suddenly turning up sick or having to take off from work to take care of personal business. The political significance of these maintenance jobs was that they paid the "prevailing" union wages, which were covered by the Davis-Bacon Act (discussed later in this Chapter).

Before the passage of the NLRA, jobs in the building service areas were traditionally filled by African Americans; however, when the Building Service Union was formed in the 1930s, it began to organize hotels, restaurants, and office buildings. Once these entities were unionized, white groups forced employers to discharge all African American waiters, elevator operators, and other service workers and to hire whites. There were a number of instances in which the AFL moved into an open shop, such as the Wehr Steel Foundry of Milwaukee, organized the workers, and made one "blanket demand": fire all of your African Americans.[34] The power of the unions to make "blanket demands" on companies to fire African Americans lasted for ten years–from 1937 to 1947.

The Taft-Hartley Act of 1947 stripped the unions of the power to make "blanket demands" on employers. By this time, the practice had taken its toll in reducing the numbers of skilled African American workers in society between 1935 and 1970. The unions were adamant in using the power they obtained from NLRA to foreclose African Americans' freedom to pursue skilled occupations. In 1963, Myrna Bain conducted a study of organized labor and African Americans. She found the unions to be extravagant in their use of collective bargaining to push African Americans out of high-paying and skilled jobs. She wrote:

> When the International Brotherhood of Electrical Workers became the collective bargaining agent at the Bauer Electric Company in Hartford, Connecticut, in the late forties, the union demanded and got the removal of all Negro electri-

cians from their jobs. The excuse was advanced that, since their union contract specified "white only," they could not and would not change this to provide continued employment for the Negroes who were at the plant before the union was recognized. Similar cases can be found in the Boilermakers' Union and the International Association of Machinists at the Boeing Aircraft Company in Seattle.[35]

From the latter part of the 1940s to the mid-1950s, the competition over recruiting members by the AFL and the Congress of Industrial Organization (CIO) offered African Americans a temporary *de facto* system of protection to compete freely in skilled occupations. The CIO emerged as a strong competitor for the AFL. The CIO was able to grow fast because it recruited workers, skilled and unskilled alike, who were already on the job, including African Americans. However, the AFL used the cardinal principle of exclusive jurisdiction to recruit only skilled workers.

The AFL soon recognized that the CIO's method of recruitment was to build a strong union, both in numbers and financially. This strength was derived from the fact that unions were able to bargain for the right to have union members pay their union dues through payroll deduction instead of coming down to the union hall at Thursday night meetings to pay to do so. This gave the union leadership more time to concentrate on organizing. If left unchecked, the AFL feared that the CIO would eventually drive them out of business. To undermine the CIO's strength, the AFL altered its policy of racial exclusion and began recruiting African American workers.[36]

Although the CIO recruited African Americans, its members did not accept them on an equal basis with whites. They were confined to low-paying jobs and prohibited from participating in the upgrading system. In addition, it restricted their opportunities for upward mobility by keeping a separate seniority roster[37] and isolating them into segregated locales, both in the South and the North. For example, in the North, white workers walked off their jobs when the CIO attempted to upgrade African Americans and assign them to what had traditionally been considered "white men's jobs." Thus, from the end of World War II up to the merger of the AFL and CIO in 1956, African Americans' promotion and employment were related highly to competition between these two unions for membership. In the South, for instance, the CIO lost several bargaining units to the AFL, largely because of their racial policies. However, the AFL lost several areas to the CIO in the North for the same reason.[38]

The competition between the AFL and CIO in recruiting African American members ended in 1956 when these two unions merged, thus stripping them of their *de facto* system of protection that this system inadvertently provided. Consequently, from this date up to the implementation of the Philadelphia Plan in the 1970s, the relative numbers of skilled African Americans began to decline markedly relative to that of whites.

The unions were able to keep the number of skilled African Americans at a significantly low number by its systems of seniority and primordial attachment. The latter system eliminated African Americans from entering skilled occupations by its method of recruitment. Skilled jobs were parceled out to individuals on the basis of kinship ties. Since African Americans had previously been excluded from skilled jobs, they were automatically excluded from the recruitment process.

The seniority system worked to the detriment of upward mobility and employment of African Americans. For example, during periods of prosperity, this system allowed African Americans to enter the labor market on the lower strata of the economic ladder. Whenever a recession set in, the seniority system came into play and workers were laid off according to seniority; this automatically forced African Americans to give up their low-paying jobs to whites.

Federal Subsidies and Bootstraps

As the data indicates in the tables in this chapter, all of the ethnic groups in this cohort, except African Americans and Puerto Ricans, were able to escape the slums. They were able to elevate themselves to the middle-class plateau, not by hard work and their acceptance of dirty and low-paying jobs, but by the system of protection and the various federally subsidized programs (bootstraps). We have already discussed how the collective bargaining laws connected the late nineteenth century immigrant groups to the mainstream of society's income redistribution system, and how these groups used these laws to foreclose African Americans' freedom to compete with them on a level playing field. One law which was enacted during the 1930s and had an equal or greater impact in constraining the upward mobility of African Americans was the Davis-Bacon Act. An analysis of this act will shed some light on why African Americans experience downward mobility from this period up to the implementation of affirmative action.

The Davis-Bacon Act of 1931

The Davis-Bacon Act was passed in 1931 and required federal construction contractors to pay their workers "prevailing wages."[39] On the surface, this law seems to be free of any racial bias; but a close examination will reveal that its very essence partakes on various elements of the politics of racial exclusion. It was a job encroachment strategy concocted by the unions' leadership to solicit the government's help to carry out their will of oppression against African Americans. The operative effect of this act was to foreclose African Americans' freedom to take advantage of employment opportunities at the government-funded public projects.

The genesis of the Davis-Bacon Act can be traced back to 1927, when a contractor from Alabama won a contract to build a Veteran's Hospital in Long Island, New York. He had been in the construction business for many years in the South; during which time, he was able to assemble a large crew of skilled construction workers. Since the South remained non-unionized during this period, many of his skilled workers were African Americans, whom he brought to New York with him.

The union workers were appalled when they saw that the crew consisted of African American construction workers. To them, this represented racial equality because African Americans were doing the same skilled occupations as whites. This caused them to experience psychological discomfort, because it was destroying the foundation on which their false sense of racial superiority rested. Their sense of racial superiority was a remnant of the Social Darwinism movement of the 1880s and 90s. The only way that this false sense of racial superiority could be sustained was to make facts conform to theory. The mere presence of African American construction workers on government-funded projects undermined this doctrine. Consequently, union leaders started complaining to their congressmen that African Americans were taking over the "white man's jobs." They found Rep. Robert Bacon to be sympathetic to their cause. He introduced H.R. 17069 in the House. This bill required "Contractors and Subcontracts Engaged in Public Works of the United States to Comply with State Laws Relating to Hours of Labor and Wages of Employment as State Public Works."[40] This was the beginning of a protracted war that the unions launched to solicit the aid of the government's help to foreclose African Americans' freedom to compete with whites for skilled jobs on federally funded projects.

Over the next four years, Rep. Bacon introduced more than thirteen bills to establish regulations for labor on federal public projects. Eventually, he was able to persuade Sen. James J. Davis to join him in sponsoring the Davis-Bacon Act of 1931. This act was a wage determining law which established the level of wages for all federal funded programs by law and not by the free market.

The purpose of the unions in sponsoring this bill was to eliminate African Americans' competition in government-funded projects with whites. There was an influx of African American construction workers migrating from the South during this period. Contractors preferred hiring them over whites because they were hard workers, much like the case with the current Mexican migrant workers.

Because the South was practically non-unionized, there was no policy to foreclose African Americans' freedom to do construction work. In fact, the construction industry was the biggest area of employment for African Americans other than agriculture. They were not barred from doing skilled construction work. For example, according to the U.S. Census Bureau of 1940, there were approximately 435,000 unskilled construction workers in the United States. African Americans made up 19 percent of the workers nationwide. In the South, there were approximately 89,060 construction workers. African Americans comprised 45 percent of this number. As for skilled carpenters, they comprised 16 percent of the carpenters in the South.[41]

African American construction workers and carpenters started migrating North during the "Big Black Migration" during and after World War I. Around the 1930s, they had gained a foothold in the construction industry in the non-South. Acquiring jobs as construction workers and skilled craftsmen and artisans was a quantum leap in socioeconomic status for African Americans. Migrating from a southern environment where hard work and low pay was a way of life, African Americans carried these skills and habits with them wherever they migrated. Contractors preferred hiring them over whites because their productivity was significantly higher. This precipitated resentment from whites.

The beginning of the 1930s marked a period in which this country was deeply enmeshed in a severe depression. Here, contractors were recruiting and hiring African American construction workers from the South, while union workers remained unemployed in the North. The continuous employment of African American construction workers had begun to destroy whites' false sense of racial superiority. Consequently, the unions began to pressure their Congressmen to adopt positive laws to foreclose African Americans' freedom to compete with whites on an equal footing. Their complaint was that African Americans were taking the white men's jobs.

In order to satisfy the demands of the unions, policymakers felt it was necessary to adopt positive laws to tilt the playing field in favor of white union workers. Rep. Bacon and Sen. Davis introduced the Davis-Bacon Act. When this bill was being debated in Congress, the intent of the bill was expressed by several politicians. For example, Rep. Clayton Allgood, who supported the bill, complained about cheap African American labor that was "in competition with white labor throughout the country."[42] Based on the various remarks in the Congressional Records of 1931, there were strong sentiments among congressmen against allowing African Americans to compete on a level playing field with white workers. The sentiments were overwhelmingly in favor of adopting positive laws to eliminate African Americans' competition.

Evidence that Congress wanted to bar African American construction workers from federally funded projects cannot be found in the Davis-Bacon Act itself. It is to be found in the implementation of the act. At first, the act required that all federally funded construction projects in excess of $5, 000 must pay their workers "prevailing wages." This meant the union's scale wages. Many subcontractors were hiring African American workers because of their reputation as hard workers. To contractors, this meant higher profits on their contracts. This practice upset the union leadership. They felt that the Davis-Bacon Act did not go far enough in protecting union members jobs. Consequently, they started lobbying Congress to amend the Davis-Bacon Act to lower the minimum contract from $5000 to $2000. Since the unions had great influence in the Department of Labor, the amendment to this act meant that virtually all wages would be paid at "prevailing wages."

The operative effect of this new regulation was that it allowed the unions to solicit the aid of the federal government to support their will of depression by foreclosing African Americans' freedom to seek employment on federally funded projects. Contractors were confronted with a new economic reality. Since the law requires them to pay "prevailing wages" in areas where it was at least 30 percent unionized, they had no economic incentives to hire African American construction workers over whites. It became economically advantageous to recruit workers through the unions, which had a built-in recruitment system. This had a devastating impact upon the employment status of African Americans in the construction industry. The doors of opportunities were closed to both skilled and unskilled African American workers alike. Hence, the federal government had designed a system of racial exclusion in order to guarantee whites whatever jobs that were available on public projects.

When World War II broke out, the economic status of African Americans took a nose dive in the construction industry. To meet the needs of the war efforts, the government passed various laws to fund war industry projects. The unions immediately stepped in to ensure that the racial doctrine of romantic racialism remained intact. The AFL lobbied the various federal agencies to sign "stabilization agreements."[43] These agreements guaranteed closed shops to all unions' affiliates of the Building Construction Trade Department of AFL. Closed shops automatically disqualified all African Americans from working on war industry projects because they were not allowed to join unions.

Locked out of the economically lucrative war industry, African American leaders started complaining. Here, America was fighting a war abroad to guarantee freedom and democracy, but it was denying its own citizens the freedom to compete for work on federally funded war industry projects on the homefront. H. Philip Randolph, an African American union leader, started organizing a protest movement in which he threatened to march upon Washington with an army of 50,000 protesters. This was an embarrassment to America. To avoid such embarrassment, President Roosevelt issued an executive order outlawing the formation of the stabilization agreements. This executive order temporarily opened up the doors in the defense industry for African Americans.

To enforce this executive order, Congress established the Fair Employment Practice Committee (FEPC). This committee proved to be ineffective in eliminating racial exclusion in the defense industry. However, it was effective in eliminating the signing of stabilization agreements that the unions used to guarantee the exclusion of African Americans. However, at the close of the war, it became less and less effective in eliminating racial exclusion in federally funded projects. Its ineffectiveness allowed the forces of the Davis-Bacon Act to come into full play to foreclose job opportunities for African Americans on government-funded projects. African Americans were barred on all fronts of public work projects. Neither skilled nor unskilled workers could obtain work on government-funded projects. Whenever an employer attempted to hire African American construction workers, the unions would suddenly stage a work stoppage protest. This practice was a tool that they used to keep African Americans out of government-funded projects from the close of World War II to the mid-1960s. For example, unions staged stoppage on construction projects such as the New York City Terminal Market in 1964, the Cleveland Municipal Mall in 1966, and the U.S. Mint of Philadelphia in 1968.[44] This type of discrimination took place despite the prohibition against discrimination provided by Titles 6 and 7 of the 1964 Civil Rights Act. It continued until the Nixon Administration intervened with the Philadelphia Plan.

The political role that the Davis-Bacon Act played in creating racial inequality cannot be overemphasized. It allowed wages to be determined not by the free market, but by law. It artificially raised workers' income higher than that earned in the manufacturing and nonagricultural industries. For example, for the year 1969-1970, workers' income in the manufacturing industry increased about 5.3 percent. In the construction industry, it increased 9.2 percent.[45] Because there was no anti-discriminatory clause to protect African Americans from racial exclusion, the unions foreclosed their freedom to raise their standards of living. The extent to which the unions were able to exclude African Americans without interference has been well-documented by Herbert Northrup, in *Organized Labor and the Negro*,[46] and Ray Marshall, in *The Negro and Organized Labor*.[47] This exclusion took its toll upon the socioeco-

nomic status of African Americans between 1941 and 1964, despite efforts of
the executive branch to combat such efforts.

As mentioned previously, the government first started attacking the union's
policy of racial exclusion during World War II. In addition to the effort of
President Roosevelt, other presidents attempted to combat this practice by establishing various committees: President Truman established the Committee
on Government Contract Compliance; Dwight Eisenhower, the Presidential
Committee on Government Contracts (PCGC); and John F. Kennedy and
Lyndon B. Johnson, the Committee on Equal Employment Opportunity (EEO).[48]

These commissions served no more than investigative functions. Between
1951 and 1956, the PCGC investigated only complaints of discrimination against
African Americans, except in one instance where a complaint was filed by a
Hispanic against the railroad. The following passage summarizes some of the
charges that the PCGC investigated:

> The specific charges included denial of membership to Negroes, thereby forc-
> ing companies to discharge them; refusal by a company to hire a Negro be-
> cause he could not get in the union; restricting Negroes to certain departments
> and excluding them from apprenticeship training programs; violation of se-
> niority rights; providing in the contract for separate lines of progression for
> Negroes and whites; failure of a union to protest seniority violations; refusal to
> file charges against the company for failing to promote or hire Negroes in
> categories other than laborers and janitors. Also, a construction local was ac-
> cused of rejecting an agreement with international union representatives which
> provided that eight or ten Negroes would be employed on a project; the result
> was that Negroes were denied work on the project.[49]

All of these previously charges, collectively, took their toll upon the status
of African Americans between the period of 1930 and 1969. After 1969, the
federal government intervened with its affirmative action policy. During this
period, there were two major factors constraining African Americans' upward
mobility. There was the Davis-Bacon Act and the unions' policy of racial exclusion, both of which were legally supported by the federal government. But
the one that had the most detrimental impact on job upward mobility was the
unions' refusal to admit African Americans.

When the PCGC commissions charged the unions with racial discrimination, the unions not only admitted that they discriminated against African Americans, but also defended their right to do so. They went so far as to include
discriminatory clauses in their contracts. Thus, inadvertently throwing the force
of federal law behind their will foreclosed African Americans' freedom to job
upward mobility. For example, African Americans in Philadelphia charged a

company and union with "blocking their promotion to higher jobs; the company said it would promote ... [African Americans] if the union would agree."[50] The union flatly refused to adhere to the agreement. They argued that the FEPC did not have the legal authority to force them to allow the company to promote African Americans.

Since there were no anti-discriminatory laws in employment, the incident in Philadelphia was duplicated, if not multiplied, throughout America during the period between 1940 and 1970. Companies that attempted to hire African Americans in union shops were forced to dismiss them when the unions refused to admit them. When the FEPC found a local plumbers' union guilty of discrimination in Chicago, its officials argued that it was the prerogative of a union to discriminate.[51]

The National Apprenticeship Act of 1937

The National Apprenticeship Act of 1937 was–and still is today to a large extent–a major contributor to the creation of racial inequality. This law institutionalized a national apprenticeship program which provided opportunities for many men and women to aquire skills as artisans and craftsmen. It gave the Secretary of Labor the authority to:

> . . . . formulate and promote the furtherance of labor standards necessary to safeguard the welfare of apprentices, to extend in the application of such standards and by encouraging the inclusion thereof in contracts of apprenticeship, to bring together employers and labor for the formulation of programs of apprenticeship, to cooperate with State agencies engaged in the formulation and promotion of standards of apprenticeship, and to cooperate with the Secretary of Education in accordance with section 17 of title 20.[52]

The clause which contributed to racial inequality was "to bring together employers and labor for the formulation of programs of apprenticeship." With their policy of racial exclusion, the mere inclusion of labor in developing these programs automatically meant the exclusion of African Americans. Unions' participation required the exclusion of African Americans, because they had racial exclusion provisions written into their constitutions. Thus, the Apprenticeship Act placed the federal government center stage in promoting racial inequality. It was supporting the growth and development of the late nineteenth century immigrants while at the same time aiding and abetting in constraining the growth and development of African Americans.

The political repercussions that these constraints had upon the growth and development of African Americans cannot be explained away as a process of "benign neglect," as Moynihan has asserted. Critics have persistently attributed their lack of success to some defect in their character or biological makeup. On the other hand, they have attempted to attribute the success of European immigrants to hard work and the internalization of the Protestant work ethic. An analysis of this act offers strong evidence to the contrary. For example, prior to the adoption of this law, there were approximately 17,300 individuals registered as apprentices. Under this system, an individual who wished to learn a trade such as a brick mason would have had to approach a journeyman and ask him to sponsor him as an apprentice. He would then work for him for four years, during which time, the apprentice would pay the journeyman to allow him to work for him. At the end of the training period, the apprentice would be certified as a journeyman.

Under the old system of apprenticeship, very few individuals could afford to pay for the training. For example, before the federal government adopted this program, there were less than 16,000 persons signed up as apprentices nationwide. After the adoption of the apprenticeship act, this number increased markedly. For example, the number of "apprentices in training in registered programs increased from 17,300 on January 1, 1941, to 40,171 on January 1, 1945, 131,217 on January 1, 1947, and to 230,832 at the beginning of 1950."[53] Between 1950 and 1962, the number decreased to 151,490 for a variety of reasons. One reason was that there already existed a large number of trained individuals. Second, there was a recession between 1955 and 1962. Between 1962 and 1964, this number increased to 156,000.[54]

The political significance of the apprenticeship program was that it was paid for by the federal government. The government reimbursed job instructor fees, paid for instructional supplies, provided consultation and advice on training problems, assisted in developing training programs, recruited job applicants, and arranged for area-wide training programs.[55] In 1962, the apprenticeship program cost the federal government $4 million annually. By 1964, this amount had increased to $5 million.[56]

The benefits that the apprenticeship program provides have changed over the years in form but its substance remained constant. The following excerpt is a current description of the benefits that this program offers:

> Not only will you learn new skills, but you'll get paid to do it. Under the Federal guidelines, apprentices are employees who earn as they learn. Pay is on an increasing scale, based on the typical hourly wage for the occupation you chose

to enter. You'll receive "raises" as you satisfactorily progress through the training, until your wage reaches 85 to 90 percent of the rate for your occupation.

After successful completion, you'll receive an Apprenticeship Completion Certificate, which earns you nationwide recognition as a qualified journeywoman or journeyman (skilled worker). It is one of the oldest and most-portable industry credentials, which makes you eligible to work anywhere you can land a job for which you qualify.

You might even earn credits toward an Associate Degree, depending on the program you join.[57]

Figure 1 consists of a list of the most popular apprenticeship programs that are subsidized by the federal government.

Figure 1
24 Most Popular Apprenticeship Programs

1. Electrician	13. Construction Craft
2. Carpenter	14. Painters (Construction)
3. Pipe Fitter (Construction)	15. Tool and Die Maker
4. Plumber	16. Machinists
5. Electrician (Maintenance)	17. Electricians (Aircraft)
6. Sheet Metal Worker	18. Millwrights
7. Electronics Mechanic	19. Boiler Maker
8. Structural-Steel Worker	20. Correction Officer
9. Bricklayers (Construction)	21. Cook (Any Industry)
10. Roofers	22. Telecommunication Technician
11. Operating Engineer	23. Power Plant Operator
12. Maintenance Mechanic	24. Cook (Hotel and Restaurant)

SOURCE: U.S. Department of Labor's Employment and Training Administration. See website for a more comprehensive list of occupations.

The second political significance of the apprenticeship programs is that they developed the individual's mind. It enabled the individual to master some form of technology. This is one of the cultural values that is glorified in the American society. The mastery of such technology gives the individual a sense of self-worth and respect in society. The lack of the acquisition of some form of technology is automatically interpreted in the American society as biologically inferior, a stereotypical image that has been attached to African Americans.

In addition to apprenticeship programs, there were other government subsidized programs from which the European immigrants benefitted. These programs were intertwined within the three occupational categories that prescribed high income–that is, professional, managerial, and craftsmen. The level of federally subsidized programs had increased dramatically by 1972.

The twenty-four most popular programs listed in Figure 1 are the most popular programs in which an individual can enroll if he/she is a member of the union, according to the Departmental Labor Employment and Training Administration:[58]

In 1972, Senator William Proximire held a hearing on the economics of federal subsidy programs. At this hearing, it was discovered that federal subsidy programs constituted $63 billion of the total federal budgets. This figure does not include "welfare payments, old age benefit payments" and free government services.[59] It includes programs that are fed through the private markets to stimulate economic activities.

In short, this section has offered strong evidence to reject two major arguments advanced by the critics of civil rights. First, the late nineteenth century European immigrants became skilled artisans and craftsmen as a result of strong family values and hard work. They acquired these skills because the government subsidized their training. Finally, it rejects the argument that the reason that African Americans did not acquire these skills was because they were either too lazy to work or genetically inferior. They did not acquire these skills because their freedom to do so was foreclosed by both their adversaries and the federal government.

NOTES

1.   It is commonly thought that the European immigrants made it to the middle-class plateau by accepting dirty and low-paying jobs, adhering to the Protestant work ethic, and working hard. Social scientists too often overlook the role played by government in assisting these immigrant groups.

2.   David Easton, *A Framework for Political Analysis* (Englewood Cliff, N. J.: Prentice-Hall, Inc., 1965), p. 7.

3.   See Andrew M. Greeley and William C. McCready, *Ethnicity in the United States* (New York: John Wiley & Sons, 1974), chapter 2.

4.   Daniel P. Moynihan, *The Negro Family* (Washington, D.C.: Department of Labor, Policy Planning and Research 1965).

5.   Edward C. Banfield, *The Unheavenly City* (Boston: Little, Brown and Company, 1968), chapter 3.

6. Thomas Sowell, *Markets and Minorities* (Boston: Basic Books, 1981), chapter 1.

7. Arthur R. Jensen, "How Can We Boost IQ and Scholastic Achievement?" *Harvard Educational Review* 39 (Winter 1969): 1–123.

8. Sowell, "Culture–Not Discrimination–Decides Who Gets Ahead." *U.S. News & World Report 91* (October 12, 1981): 74–75.

9. For a discussion of the economic philosophy behind the New Deal programs, see John Kenneth Galbraith, *The Affluent Society* (Boston: Houghton Mifflin Company, 1969), chapter 8.

10. *Loew v. Lawler*, 208 U.S. 274 (1908); 52 L.ed. 488.

11. Douglas L. Leslie, *Labor Law* (St. Paul, Minn.: West Publishing Company, 1979), p. 4.

12. E. Edward Herman and Alfred Kuhn, *Collective Bargaining and Labor Relations* (Englewood Cliffs, N.J.: Prentice-Hall, 1981), p. 18.

13. This was the first federal law designed to protect labor; it is known as the Anti-Injunction Act.

14. *Supplemental Unemployment Benefit Plans and Wage Employment Guarantees* (June 1965), Bulletin 145-3 (Washington, D.C.: United States Department of Labor, Bureau of Labor Statistics).

15. Herman and Kuhn, *Collective Bargaining,* p. 405.

16. Ibid.

17. Ibid., p. 407.

18. *Jobs? or Jobless Pay? The Real Issue Behind the New Guaranteed Wage Proposals* (Washington, D.C.: Chamber of Commerce of the United States, 1954).

19. This was the first federal law designed to protect labor; it is known as the Anti-Injunction Act.

20. Nathan Glazer, "Blacks and Ethnic Groups: The Difference, and the Political Difference It Makes," *Social Problems* 18 (1971): 444-461.

21. Pitirim A. Sorokin, *Social and Cultural Mobility* (New York: Free Press, 1959).

22. Celia S. Heller, ed., *Structural Social Inequality* (London: Macmillan and Company, 1969), pp. 251-257.

23. Joseph A. Kahl, *The American Class Structure* (New York: Holt, Rinehart and Winston, 1961), p. 310.

24. Kahl, *The American Class Structure,* p. 59.

25. Herman and Kuhn, *Collective Bargaining,* p. 405.

26. Ibid.

27. Ibid., p. 440.

28. Stanley B. Mathewson, *Restriction of Output Among Unorganized Workers* (New York: Viking Press, 1969), p. 173.

29. See Chapter 6.

30. John Locke, *"Of the Dissolution of Government," The Two Treatises of Government.*

31.   *Apprenticeship Past and Present,* United States Department of Labor, Manpower Administration, Bureau of Apprenticeship and Training (Washington: Government Printing Office, 1964).

32.   See Raymond Walters, "Closed Shop and White Shop: The Negro Response to Collective Bargaining, 1933-1935," in *Black Labor in America*, Milton Contor, ed. (Westport Conn: Negro Universities Press, 1969).

33.   Frank W. McCulloch, *The National Labor Relations Board* (New York: Praeger Publisher, 1974).

34.   Walters, "Closed Shop and White Shop," p. 143.

35.   Myrna Bain, "Organized Labor and the Negro Worker," *National Review* (June 4, 1963), p. 455.

36.   Horace R. Clayton and George S. Mitchell, *Black Workers and the Unions* (College Park, Md.: McGrath Publishing Co., 1969), chapter 11.

37.   Ray Marshall, *The Negro and Organized Labor* (New York: John Wiley and Sons, 1965), p. 45.

38.   Ibid., p. 56.

39.   The Davis-Bacon Act is still applicable today. Although it has been amended since 1931, its general description remains the same. The following is a description of those laws: TITLE 40, CHAPTER 3, Sec. 276a. - Rate of wages for laborers and mechanics (a) The advertised specifications for every contract in excess of $2,000, to which the United States or the District of Columbia is a party, for construction, alteration, and/or repair, including painting and decorating, of public buildings or public works of the United States or the District of Columbia within the geographical limits of the States of the Union or the District of Columbia, and which requires or involves the employment of mechanics and/or laborers shall contain a provision stating the minimum wages to be paid various classes of laborers and mechanics which shall be based upon the wages that will be determined by the Secretary of Labor to be prevailing for the corresponding classes of laborers and mechanics employed on projects of a character similar to the contract work in the city, town, village, or other civil subdivision of the State in which the work is to be performed, or in the District of Columbia if the work is to be performed there; and every contract based upon these specifications shall contain a stipulation that the contractor or his subcontractor shall pay all mechanics and laborers employed directly upon the site of the work, unconditionally and not less often than once a week, and without subsequent deduction or rebate on any account, the full amounts accrued at time of payment, computed at wage rates not less than those stated in the advertised specifications, regardless of any contractual relationship which may be alleged to exist between the contractor or subcontractor and such laborers and mechanics, and that the scale of wages to be paid shall be posted by the contractor in a prominent and easily accessible place at the site of the work; and the further stipulation that there may be withheld from the contractor so much of accrued payments as may be considered necessary by the contracting officer to pay to laborers and mechanics employed by the contractor or any subcontractor on the work the difference between the rates of wages required by the contract to be paid laborers and mechanics on the work

and the rates of wages received by such laborers and mechanics and not refunded to the contractor, subcontractors, or their agents.

40.   For a full discussion of this Act, see U.S. Congress. House Committee on Labor. Hearing on H. R. 17069, 69 Congress, Sess. Feb. 28, 1927.

41.   Mark W. Kruman, "Quotas for Blacks: The Public Works Administration and the Black Construction Worker," *Labor History* 16, Winter 1975, p. 38.

42.   See the remarks of Representative Allgood in Congressional Record, Feb. 28, 1931, p. 16,513.

43.   For a discussion of these tactics, see Richard C. Weaver, *Negro Labor: A National Problem* (Port Washington, NY: Kennikat Press, 1948), p. 10.

44.   This conflict became the basis for the Nixon Administration to adopt the Philadelphia Plan. The issues center around this plan is beyond the scope of this chapter. The important point here is that this marked the first time the federal government was able to effectively attack the union of policy of racial exclusion.

45.   Congress of the United States, Joint Economic Committee, *The Economics of Federal Subsidy Programs* (Washington, D.C.: Government Printing Office, 1972), p. 165.

46.   Herbert Northrup, *Organized Union and the Negro* (New York: Harper, 1944), chapter 1.

47.   Ray Marshall, *The Negro and Organized Labor* (New York: John Wiley and Sons, 1965), chapters 2 and 3.

48.   Ibid., p. 219.

49.   Ibid., p. 221.

50.   Summer H. Slichter, James J. Healy, and E. Robert Livernash, *The Impact of Collective Bargaining on Management* (Washington, D. C. : The Brookings Institute, 1960), p. 69.

51.   Ibid., p. 215

52.   Section 50. "Promotion of Labor Standards of Apprenticeship," The National Apprenticeship Act (50 Stat. 664; 29 U. S. C. 50).

53.   *Appendix: The Budget of the United States Government* (Washington. D.C.: Government Printng Offfie, 1962), p. 603.

54.   *Appendix: The Budget of the United States Government* (Washington. D.C.: Government Printing Offfie, 1962), p. 603.

55.   United States Department of Labor. Bureau of Apprenticeship and Training, Manpower Administration. "Apprenticeship Program," 1963

56.   *Appendix: The Budget of the United States Government* (Washington. D.C.: Government Printing Office, 1962), p. 603

57.   Section 50. "Promotion of Labor Standards of Apprenticeship," The National Apprenticeship Act (50 Stat. 664; 29 U. S. C. 50).

58.   See the U.S. Department of Label's Employment and Training Administration website for a more comprehensive list of occupations.

59.   Congress of the United States, Joint Economics Committee. The Economic Committee, The Economic of Federal Subsidy Program, p. 4.

CHAPTER 9

How the Late Nineteenth Century European Immigrants Escaped the Slums

As mentioned in Chapter 1, social scientists have attributed the success of the late nineteenth century immigrant groups' ability to escape the slums to hard work, strong family structures, and values. It will be demonstrated in this chapter that these are dependent variables. These groups did not escape the slums until the government intervened and provided them with the means and opportunities to do so. At the same time, it adopted positive laws to specifically exclude African Americans from taking advantage of these opportunities. To a large extent, some of these laws are still in operation.

First, let us briefly review the dependent variables that social scientists have typically identified to explain the failure of African Americans to escape the slums. The major methodological problem that this writer finds with these variables is that they at best serve as blinders that prevent social scientists from identifying those independent variables that promote and constrain groups' capacity to escape the slums. To support their arguments, social scientists too often resort to (1) making various generalizations about the variables that enabled groups to escape the slums, and (2) attempting to support their arguments by marshaling forward a voluminous amount of data. On the surface, this data seems to have a strong statistical cause and effect relation. But, once these arguments are submitted to systematic scrutiny, they tend to break down. Take, for example, the following excerpt that was taken from an article written by Dennis Kinder and Donald Sears, entitled, "Prejudice and Politics: Symbolic Racism." This excerpt epitomizes the typical arguments made to justify racial inequality. They wrote:

Symbolic racism represents a form of resistance to change in the racial status quo based on moral feelings that blacks violate such traditional American values as individualism and self-reliance, the work ethic, obedience, and discipline. Whites may feel that people should be rewarded on their merits, which in turn should be based on hard work and diligent service. Hence symbolic racism should find its most vociferous expression on political issues that involve "unfair" government assistance to blacks: welfare ("welfare cheaters could find work if they tried"); "reverse discrimination" and racial quotas ("blacks should not be given status they have not earned"); "forced" busing ("whites have worked hard for their neighborhoods, and for their neighborhood schools"); or "free" abortions for the poor (if blacks behave morally, they would not need abortions.")[1]

From their extreme manifestation, these arguments are convincing. What is missing are the independent variables (government intervention) that can best account for white groups' success in escaping the slums. Since the thrust of this book is to offer a systematic explanation of the cause of group inequality (i.e., an explanation free of internal contradictions), a brief historical analysis of the American housing policy is in order. Such an analysis is critical in offering a systematic explanation as to how groups were able to escape the slums. As mentioned earlier, social scientists have persistently focused on the social aspects of groups' behavior in leaving the slums but left untouched the physical.

Before groups can escape the slums, it must be noted, they must have (1) the financial means to do so, and (2) a place to go. We have seen in the previous chapter that groups began to acquire the means to escape the slums the after the government adopted various positive measures to provide job security for workers in the 1930s and '40s. These measures significantly improved the standards of living of this class. What is missing from the literature is a discussion of the cause and effect relationship between groups leaving the slums and their moving to the suburbs. Writers have focused on racial attitudes and white flight. They have practically overlooked the previously mentioned economic variables as the basic cause of white flight. Before we can answer the question of suburbanization, we first need a brief historical analysis of the American housing policy.

The American Housing Policy

Oscar Handlin, a historian, offers a historical analysis of the housing policy in New York City which we will summarize here.[2] His description offers clues as to how housing was developed in other American cities. Cities have traditionally adopted a Master Plan for providing housing for its residents. One of the major components of this plan was the trickle-down theory. This theory holds that new housing was to be built on the outskirts of town for the middle class by the private sector. As the city population grew as a result of an influx of newcomers, new housing was to be built far out on the outskirts of town for the middle class. This class would move into this housing, and the moderate middle class would move into the housing vacated by the middle class. The newcomers would then move into the old housing vacated by the moderate middle class. Once the housing spread so far from the center of town, then housing would be built in the inner city for the upper-middle class, and the process would start all over again. The various urban renewal projects of the 1950s and the construction of high-rise condominiums of the 1960s and afterward offer credence to this theory.

The trickle-down theory, which was adopted in the early 1800s, worked relatively well until the large influx of immigrants in the 1830s. This new wave of immigrants placed greater demands on housing that the trickle-down theory could not meet. This precipitated real estate agents to start a process of converting old single-family homes into two-to-three family units. As the demands for housing continued to grow, real estate agents started converting warehouses into housing[3] and crowding immigrants into them.

One of the negative impacts of the policy of housing conversion was that it created socially undesirable conditions among populations that were not conducive to their growth and development. For example, the first wave of immigrants that settled and created slums in the inner cities was the Irish-Catholics. But as we have seen, their conditions were attributed to their lack of the necessary human capital to take advantage of life opportunities. They did not start escaping the slums until the 1950s, when the government started pumping billions of dollars ino the housing industry to provide decent housing. This was the beginning of suburbanization.

The Origin of Suburbanization

The process of suburbanization in America has many facets, all of which are not germane to our study. The focus here is to identify those independent variables that can best explain how the late nineteenth century immigrants were able to escape the slums. This movement can be traced back to the construction of Levitt's ranch style homes in New York City, which later became known as Levittown. Since Levittown had such a dramatic impact on American housing policy and racial discrimination, a brief discussion of its role is in order.

Levittown was built on the heels of The Federal Housing Act of 1949 by Levitt and Sons. This company was formed by Abraham Levitt, a lawyer and the son of a Jewish Rabbi immigrant from Russia. As a lawyer, Abraham started out representing real estate clients. Around 1925, he "accepted 100 lots in Rockville Centre from a bankrupt client"[4] and started a career in developing housing. He later formed the Levitt and Sons construction company (with his two sons, Alfred and Williams) and started the mass construction of low-cost housing.

Levitt and Sons first acquired their experience in mass producing low-cost housing when they won a contract with the military to build housing for the Navy in Norfolk, Virginia in 1942. However, Levitt and Sons had started building houses in 1929 under the trickle-down theory. Under this theory, three-fourth of the housing built during this period was marketed to the top one-third of the affluent populations. This was a period in which the upper class income increased rapidly and at the same time there was a drastic decrease in the economic status of the lower class. Political leaders were of the opinion that wealth would eventually trickle-down to the poor. During the Great Depression, the housing situations in the cities throughout America grew progressively worse.

The upper-middle class, which had benefitted from the housing boom of the 1920s, suddenly found their home mortgages in default. The bankers and real estate industries appealed to the federal government for help in order to prevent the virtual extinction of the housing market. The government responded by providing long-term home mortgages financing under the Federal Home Bank Act of 1932. This act was designed to help the upper class hold on to their homes; but the impact of the Great Depression undermined the intent of this law. Record number of foreclosures continued to persist as a result of the high rate of unemployment.

This act was not designed to help the late nineteenth century immigrants to escape the slums. As mentioned earlier, some social scientists have claimed that these groups had escaped the slums earlier through hard work and internalization of the Protestant work ethic. They were trapped deeply in the slums at the beginning of the Great Depression. Many of them were among the ranks of the homeless. The constant increase in the number of homeless prompted not only policymakers to reconsider America's longstanding policy that providing housing was exclusively the responsibility of the private sector through the trickle-down theory but also the real estate and building industries to wane their opposition to the government's financing of public housing.

To address the problem of homelessness, Congress passed the Wagner- Segal Act in 1937, which created the United States Housing Authority. The purpose of this bill was to demolish slum housings and to replace them with public housings. Special provisions were written into this bill to ensure that the number of public housing built would be matched by an equal removal of the number of substandard housing from the market to ensure that public housing does not drive down the prices of housing in the private sector. The operative effect of this policy was to limit the number of individuals to escape the slums so that the trickle-down theory could remain intact.

At the close of World War II, the housing situation became progressively worse. There was a large influx of migrants (African Americans and whites) who were leaving the farms and moving to the cities to man the war industries. Policymakers began to recognize the shortcomings of the trickle-down theory. This sentiment can best be summarized by Sen. Robert Taft (Republican of Ohio) who strongly supported public housing. During a Senate Committee hearing, he stated: "I believe that the Government must see that every family has a minimum standard of decent shelter. . . . The hand-me down theory works, but it works to provide indecent housing to those who get it on the last hand-down. . . . We cannot pour in all the assistance from the top, and that it is all private industry can do, or be expected to do. I think we must also attack the problem from the bottom . . . "[5]

Prior to the introduction of the Housing Act of 1949, Congress had passed a series of acts designed to provide decent housing for the general public.[6] But the one that contributed significantly to the late nineteenth century immigrants' escaping the slums was this Act. It provided a ticket for the descendants of this group to escape the slums. Evidence to this effect can be found in the preamble of the Act, which was read by President Truman when he signed this bill into law:

> The Congress declares that the general welfare and security of the Nation and the health and living standards of its people require housing production and related community development sufficient to remedy the serious housing shortage, the elimination of substandard and other inadequate housing through the clearance of slums and blighted areas, and the realization as soon as feasible of the goal of a decent home and a suitable living environment for every American family, thus contributing to the development and redevelopment of communities and to the advancement of the growth, wealth, and security of the Nation. —*Preamble of the 1949 Housing Act.*

Signing this bill into law marked the first twist from the policy of providing for the upper-middle class. For example, the National Housing Act of 1934 provided for low interest and long-term mortgages for the upper class. It insured mortgages up to 80 percent of the financing at 5 percent interest. The whole of this act was to support the principle of the trickle-down theory. But the Housing Act of 1948 provided the framework to deviate from the trickle-down theory and started the process of suburbanization.

Around 1948, Levitt and Sons had created a model for mass producing low-cost housing. They had acquired such experience when they obtained a government contract to build housing for the Navy in Norfolk, Virginia, in 1942. In 1947, they built the Cape Cod project "on 7.3 square miles of land near what was then called Island Trees in Nassau County."[7] This was an old potato field that was later converted into Levittown.

Levitt and Sons were able to mass produce low-cost, single-family homes through their new cost-cutting measures and revolutionary architectural design. There were three methods which they employed. First, they built four-and-a-half bedroom houses on 25-by-90 foot slabs. Next, they eliminated the basement and car garage, replacing the latter with a car porch. Finally, they moved the kitchen from the back to the front and furnished it with full kitchen appliances, including a Bendix washer. Levitt first rented these Cape Cod houses for $60–65 per month with option to buy after a year for $7,500.[8]

When President Truman introduced the Federal Housing Act of 1949, he stated that the purpose of this act was to keep the cost of housing less than $10,000.[9] Levitt and Sons immediately saw how they could make a handsome profit by mass producing low-cost housing with federally subsidized mortgages. In 1949, they started building their ranch style homes in Hempstead with the same style as Cape Cod with the four-and-a-half bedrooms.[10] However, the size of these homes was 50 square feet larger than the Cape Cod homes. They came with a kitchen full of appliances, which included a Bendix washer, G.E. refrigerator, and the stove, ". . . pre-assembled white metal Tracy cabinets" which "were not just trendy—even the White House kitchen had them—but faster and cheaper to install than wooden cabinets, which had to be measured, painted, sanded and painted again."[11] These homes could be purchased for $7,990 with "zero" down payment and a monthly mortgage payment of $58.

It is no doubt that the Housing Act of 1948 became the vehicle by which the sons of the late nineteenth century immigrants were able to escape the slums. The Levitt Ranch style homes became the model for the nation at a time of prosperity and the rapid technological changes. People were looking for a new style of life, and the Levittown Ranch homes provided opportunity for East Coast residents to import California so-called "good life"–which consisted of a beautiful ranch style home in a relaxed environment.[12] The Highway Act of 1958 significantly augmented the pace of suburbanization by making it easier for residents to work in the city and commute to the suburbs.

The political significance of Levittown Ranch style homes is that they became the national model for building homes in the suburbs. One social repercussion that these new communities created was a caste system based first on class, and then, race. Except for the limited numbers of GI's, the persons who qualified to move into these new homes were the young upwardly mobile families. The mere fact that home mortgages were subsidized by the government gave builders throughout America economic incentives to build homes in the suburbs based on income.

The variables that promoted and sustained the caste system were the schools built in these communities. The schools operated to segregate populations by the classes. Take, for example, California. Builders built homes for families earning upper middle-class, middle-class, and moderate middle-class incomes. The curriculums of these schools in these communities were designed to prepare students to attend the University of California system, which caters to predominantly middle-class students. The curriculums in the moderate middle-class and lower middle-class were designed to prepare students to attend the state and community college systems. This social structure made it extremely hard for an individual to break out of this social system, despite the social scientists' claims that American had a liberal and democratic educational system.

Levittown also became the model for the national policy on racial discrimination. Levitt specifically excluded Jews and African Americans. Racial discrimination was not just based on whites' attitudes, but on a public policy. William Levitt was undoubtedly influential in formulating the FHA policy. By the late 1940s, he was well connected politically. He was able to persuade not only the Hempstead Town Board to change its housing policy so he could build his ranch style homes, but also Congress in writing the Federal Housing Act of 1947[13] so that he could do the same. One provision that was written into the administration of the FHA was the clause that stated "racial homogeneity" was necessary for the economic stability of the community.[14] The political connections that Levitt had formed at this time offers evidence that he was influential in formulating the policy of racial discrimination in housing. He had already established such policy in his construction of homes for the affluent population in the Cape Cod Project. He excluded African Americans and Jews.

Although Levitt himself was Jewish, he discriminated against Jews. His publicist, Paul Townsend, later said that he rationalized this "policy as an unfortunate cost of doing business" and that he went along with the real estate-agents' "gentlemen's agreement" not to sell to Jews.[15] But his refusal to sell to African Americans in the Levittown project was related to his experience in Brooklyn when a middle class African American lawyer moved next door to him. His family moved to Long Island in fear of a decline in property value.

Levitt's practice of excluding African Americans from his Levittown development became the model for America's policy on racial discrimination in housing that lasted until it was outlawed by the Federal Fair Housing Act of 1968. Long before the 1940s, real estate agents throughout America had adopted a policy of racial discrimination in housing. They saw how they could profit from such policy. They employed the government in helping them to carry out their scheme of racial exclusion by including a "restrictive covenant" clause into the buyer's contract not to sell to an African American. If African Americans, by chance, could purchase a home in this area, the other homeowners could go to court and seek an injunction to legally force African Americans to vacate their newly acquired property. Although the practice of restrictive covenants was struck down by the U.S. Supreme Court in 1948,[16] Levitt continued to practice racial discrimination throughout the 1950s and '60s, despite the passage of the Civil Rights Act of 1964.[17] African Americans did not gain any legal relief from discrimination in housing until the passage of the Federal Fair Housing Act of 1968. Thus, they were legally trapped in the ghettoes. Regardless of how hard they worked, they could not escape the slums like whites who were being subsidized by the government.

The political significance of examining Levitt's policy of racial exclusion is that it demonstrates how Levitt was able to solicit the help of the federal government in denying an entire population one of America's most sacred values, home ownership and the subsequent accumulation of wealth. As discussed in the Introduction Chapter, the ownership of real estate is the most stable and reliable way that an individual can accumulate wealth. The accumulation of wealth leads to power, prestige, and the promotion of self-esteem. Whenever the government participates in a scheme to deny an entire group the freedom to acquire wealth, it is also inadvertently supporting a policy that operates to strip that group of its self-esteem.

There are four major means of accumulating wealth in America through the ownership of a home in the suburbs. First, there is the equity built into the house as the individual pays his monthly mortgage. Second, there is the tax credit that the government offers as a reward for buying a home. Third, there is the equity buildup as a result of inflation, which increases the value of a house.

Finally, there is the subsidized mortgage by the federal government. Added together, these benefits constituted the government's *bonanza giveaways* that we discussed in the previous chapter.

There were many types of mortgages that the federal government adopted in the 1940s that played a significant role in assisting the late nineteenth century immigrants to escape the slums: the G.I. Bill and the Federal Housing Act (FHA). Both of these laws insured the down payment of a loan for a house. Take, for example, a $7,990 house before the adoption of FHA. Banks required prospective home buyers to pay a 20 percent down payment to insure the cost of the loan. The purpose of the down payment is to cover administrative cost in the event that the house is forced into foreclosure. With a federally insured mortgage, this down payment was guaranteed by the federal government, consequently, encouraging banks to loosen some of their strict requirements for granting loans to prospective home buyers.

The houses in Levittown, which could be purchased for $7,990 with "zero" down payment, gradually increased in value over the years. The majority of these homes were bought by young families. By the end of the 1960s, the values of these homes had skyrocketed to $162,600.[18] The political significance of this increase is that home buyers of the early 1950s now had enough equity built up in their homes to send their children to prestigious colleges and universities. In other words, they were able to activate the *principle of intergenerational mobility*. Without money, their children would have been forced to attend state or community colleges, thus reducing the possibility of families to activate the principle of intergenerational mobility.

In short, the discussion of the American housing policy coupled with the Levittown model for racial discrimination offers strong evidence that groups do not escape the slums without some form of government help.

The Creation and Maintenance of the Ghettoes

The first official explanation for the creation of the American Black ghettoes was offered in the Kerner Commission Report of 1965. Writers theorized that the ghettoes were created by white racism, and white racism was maintaining it.[19] In an attempt to refute this argument, critics advanced the argument that the causes of the ghetto can be attributed to African Americans' biologically inferior inheritance.[20] They managed to marshal forward a voluminous amount of data that appears to show a close correlation between African Americans' socioeconomic status and their IQs.[21] What is missing from these analyses is a description of those institutional arrangements that operated to fore-

KA oppression

close African Americans' freedom to escape the slums. These institutional arrangements can be identified by examining the policy and practice of the (1) real estate, (2) unions, (3) insurance industries, and (4). banking.

Real Estate Industry

When African Americans left the cotton fields of the South and started migrating to the urban areas (the Big Black Migration), the real estate industry had already established an economic model for creating slums. As we have seen, they developed this model during the immigration of the Irish-Catholics in the 1830s and '40s, as a result of the housing shortage. When African Americans arrived in the cities, they walked into a process that was already in the making. The primary reason for this housing shortage was the American housing policy (i.e., the trickle-down theory). This policy proved to be in effective in providing adequate housing for the masses. To address the problem of inadequate housing, real estate agents crowded populations into the existent housing by converting single family housing into multiple family dwellings. Single family homes were converted to house two to three families. Accompanying crowded houses were the various contagious diseases, violence, and other social deviant behaviors,[22] which had become an increasing problem during the Big Black Migration. This was one of the problems that policymakers were trying to address when they passed the Federal Home Loan Bank Act of 1932.

At the beginning of 1933, the annual housing starts in the United States had dropped as low as 93,000 units.[23] These houses were marketed for the top one-third of the population. *low income homes* The persistent and constant growth of the homeless population prompted Congress to address the problems of housing for the poor. At first, there was stiff opposition from the home building and real estate industries. They feared that the federal government's efforts to produce more public housing would undermine their profits as slum landlords. Consequently, they heavily lobbied Congress to influence the formation of the housing law in order to reduce this competition. They insisted on writing special provisions into the housing laws to ensure that the number of public housing built would match the number of slum houses demolished. The purpose of this provision was to ensure that the supply of public housing would not drive down the costs charged by slum landlords.

Another strategy that the real estate and building industries undertook to control the production of public housing was to write provisions into the housing law to limit access to government funds to build public housing. These provisions were so stiff, that they drove the cost of constructing public housing so high that only large-scale construction firms could afford to build them. This provision required that public housings units were to be "built of reinforced concrete frame construction, concrete piers, foundations, concrete floor and roof slabs, concrete columns, filled in with tile block, and exterior and walls with plaster on metal lath interior partitions."[24] Another provision was to place the construction and administration of public housing under local control. This was done to ensure the real estate industry that they could continue to profit from slum housing.

[margin note: public housing laws]

The Role of the Unions in the Creation of Slums

The role that the unions played in creating slums can be found in their policy of racial exclusion, as discussed in Chapter 8, and licensing laws. The fields of carpentry, plumbing, electricity, and plastering were all under the control of the AFL. Their policy of racial exclusion within itself did not contribute to the creation of slums. It can be found in local government policy on issuing licensing and permit laws in repairs of homes. *[margin note: MP unions / contribution to slums]*

In order to do any repairs on a house, the repairer must get a building permit from the licensing commission, usually comprised of three political appointees. By law, one member of this commission must be a union member. The purpose here was to make sure that permits were issued only to contractors who were union members.

The policy of restricting building permits only to union members operated to foreclose African Americans' freedom not only to get permits to do repairs on their own homes, but also to keep up their neighborhoods. Any repairs done on a house must be approved by the city code inspector. As mentioned previously, a lot of African Americans skilled as brick masons migrated North during the Big Black Migration. They could not legally use these skills because they were barred from joining the unions. *[margin note: AA]*

The constraints placed upon African Americans in keeping up their neighborhoods lay in the fact that all repairs to housing had to be approved by a city inspector. If any African American carpenter attempted to make repairs on his home without a permit, he was subjected to a fine in the amount of $50 per violation. In addition to this fine, the city would require him to hire a union carpenter to come out to inspect the repairs and bring them up to building codes. If the project required two days of work, the union carpenter would come out and sit down on the job doing nothing for two days. The African

American carpenter would have to pay him union wages by the hour for sitting down and doing nothing.

The discriminatory policy of denying African American artisans and craftsmen permits to do repairs on homes provided a pattern for urban decay, which eventually led to slum creation. Hence, this pattern of slum development in African American communities continued until the late 1950s. This problem was compounded as a result of the unions preventing young African Americans from joining the apprenticeship programs. As discussed in Chapter 8, these jobs were designated as the "white man's jobs."

The low-paying jobs to which African Americans were restricted barely paid them enough for their subsistence. This left them with very little money to pay a union craftsman to make the repairs on their homes that they themselves could do better. Consequently, they were not only stripped of any incentive to make repairs on their homes but also the means to do so. Those who were fortunate enough to acquire the necessary funds to pay the union to do repairs would choose to move out of the neighborhood to better housing that was being abandoned by "white flight" to the suburbs. Thus, the trickle down theory as it applied to low-income African Americans was a recipe for urban decay.

Redlining by the Insurance Industry

At the head of the line in creating ghettos was the insurance industry with a policy of redlining communities based on demographics. Historically, this policy has been at the heart of the creation of slums and ghettoes. This policy can be traced back to the 1930s when Congress adopted its first housing policy. This policy was not seriously examined until the 1960s when investigators of the Kerner Commmission on Civil Disorders were trying to ascertain the causes of the African Americans' rioting during that time.

The writer of the Kerner Report noted that the insurance industry's practice of redlining African Americans' communities was a major contributing factor to the creation of slums. But a close examination of redlining will shed some light on the political dynamics that this policy plays in the creation and perpetuation of slums. Before continuing, a description of the role that insurance plays in the real estate industry is needed.

Insurance provides the homeowner a package of protection against unforeseeable disasters. This package offers the homeowner protection against damage of his property, "liability or legal responsibility for any injuries and property damage"[25] to his home, or injuries that members of his family cause to other people. Without such protection, not only will the homeowner be left out on a limb, but also the banks that financed the home. Consequently, the banks adopted a policy of refusing to finance homes in the geographical area where insurance companies had redlined. The policy of redlining was in effect when Congress adopted FHA.

When the federal government started subsidizing mortgages in the suburbs, it inadvertently became involved in creating slums. From the 1950s throughout the 1960s, the federal government financed an average of 1.5 million home mortgages per year.[26] At the same time, Congress limited the construction of public housing units to 810,000 for a six-year period, from 1950 to 1956. This limitation provided the framework for creating and perpetuating slums and, subsequently, the social unrest of the 1960s.

In 1968, the Kerner Commission cited a report issued in 1967 by the National Advisory Panel on Insurance in Riot-Affected Areas. The panel found:

> There is a serious lack of property insurance in the core areas of our nation's city. For a number of years, many urban residents and businessmen have been unable to purchase the insurance protection they need. Now, riots and threat of riots are aggravating the problem to an intolerable degree. Immediate steps must be taken to make insurance available to responsible persons in all areas of our cities.[27]

This panel's recommendations fell on deaf ears because of the structural conditions of society which shield the insurance industry from federal influence. This industry is regulated by state governments which give the insurance industry a freehand to practice redlining without federal interference. Attempts were made to bring this industry under the antitrust laws. As soon as the U.S. Supreme Court ruled that the insurance industry was covered under these laws, Congress immediately passed the McCarran-Ferguson Act, which exempted the insurance industry from the antitrust laws. This act states:

> The business of insurance, and every person engaged therein, shall be subject to laws of the several States which relate to the regulation to taxation of such business.[28]

The insurance industry is the most powerful entity in American society. This act was passed before Congress enacted FHA, which provided the vehicle for white flight. The refusal to write insurance in integrated neighborhoods became the driving force that promoted segregation and subsequent deterioration of neighborhoods. Social scientists have traditionally interpreted "white flight" as a function of racial attitudes. However, the driving force behind this flight has always been the lack of protection against the investment in their property.

Once the insurance company draws a redline around an integrated neighborhood, it activates the self-fulfilling prophecy that neighborhood deterioration will always follow the integration of neighborhoods. This prophecy becomes true as a result of the banks falling in line with the insurance industry's redlining policy. The banks have no protection on their investments; consequently, they start denying conventional loans to communities that are predominantly African American or integrated, thus providing the basis for urban decay.

Banking: Urban Decay and the Practice of Redlining

Urban decay does not occur overnight. It is a cumulative process that results from the real estate, insurance, and banking institutions' practices of not making home improvement loans to residents in low income or racially mixed neighborhoods. This practice is known as *redlining*. It does not particularly single out African Americans alone. It applies to everyone who lives in a neighborhood where the redline has been drawn. Whites who live in this neighborhood are also affected, thus reducing their incentive to remain there after the line has been drawn. However, redlining has its greatest disparity impact upon African Americans, because it significantly reduces their choice possibilities of obtaining decent and affordable housing.

The origin of redlining can be traced back to a study published by Homer Hoyt at the University of Chicago in 1933. After the passage of the Federal Home Loan Bank Act of 1932, he was hired by the federal government to develop underwriting criteria for home loans. He compiled a list of ethnic groups whom he considered to be a "good credit risk." He ranked them from 1 to 10, with African Americans being second to the last; Mexicans were ranked number 10.[29] This became the official list for the American Institute of Real Estate Appraisers.[30]

The American Institute of Appraisers used Hoyt's list to warn "appraisers of the harm to property values cause by the 'infiltration of inharmonious racial groups.'"[31] This warning appeared in the McMichael's Appraising Manual as late as 1975.[32] The so called "credit risk list" was subsequently institutionalized by the real estate and banking industries. Since the real estate agents are the advanced guards in maintaining racially harmonious neighborhoods, the National Association of Realtors developed codes of behavior for their agents. These codes restricted agents from selling homes in white neighborhoods to

African Americans. These restrictions were designed to replace the "restrictive covenants" that were declared unconstitutional by the U.S. Supreme Court in 1948.[33] The real estate industry continued to practice racial discrimination in housing, even after the passage of the Fair Housing Act of 1968. It took a lawsuit by the U.S. Justice Department to force the real estate and banking industries to remove these racial restrictions in 1977.

As discussed previously, the banking, real estate, and insurance industries have always exploited low income neighborhoods. The incentive for doing so was to maximize their profits. One of the major repercussions of redlining is that it allows room for emergence of unregulated subprime lenders. These groups usually take on the name of mortgage companies.

The subprime lenders pride themselves on being able to help "high risk" customers. They offer loans at a higher interest rate than conventional institutions. As late as 1988, twenty years after the passage of the Fair Housing Act, the banking and real estate industries were still practicing redlining. In a series of articles ran in 1988 by the *Atlanta-Journal Constitution*, its investigative reporters found that 96 percent of African Americans home buyers obtained their home loans from unregulated mortgage companies in Fulton County, Georgia.[34]

In practicing redlining, individuals are not judged on their own responsiveness and records of paying off their loans, but on their race. The *Atlanta-Journal Constitutional* ran several articles depicting the difficulties that African Americans experienced in getting a homeowner loan to do repairs on their homes. The list is long on examples of such practices, and there is no need to repeat them here. However, there was one article, with which most African Americans are familiar, that illustrates the disparity impact that redlining has in constraining African Americans from keeping up their communities.

Since the theme of this book is to demonstrate that upward mobility is highly contingent upon individual freedom to acquire and possess property, an analysis of the impact of redlining cannot be overemphasized. The *Atlanta-Journal Constitution's* articles shed some light on the how redlining foreclosed African Americans' freedom to acquire property. This practice is not restricted to low income African American communities. For example, the *Atlanta-Journal Constitution* ran an article, entitled "Fulton Michael Lomax: If I Can't Get a Loan, What Black Person Can?" Lomax was the chairman of the Fulton County Commission. When he decided to run for mayor of Atlanta, he approached the various banks for political contributions. He received contributions from all of them. But when he tried to get a home improvement loan to build a guest house in the middle class neighborhood in which he lived, he was rejected. The banks asked him why he wanted to build in "that neighborhood."

The newspaper article also cited the trials and tribulations that another African American had in getting a loan to repair the roof of his home. This was a 56-year-old retired railroad worker who wanted to get a $5,000 home improvement loan to replace the roof of his home. He applied at the bank where he had been banking for the last ten years; it turned him down. He subsequently turned to an unregulated mortgage company. The company lent him the $5,000 that he needed. Instead of granting him a loan at the conventional rate of 15 percent, the Company charged him 18 percent, plus $3,180 in the discount points and other add-ons. The discount points are used by lending companies to bring down the percentage point of the loan, which in turn would reduce the borrower's monthly payment. The cost of these discount points is added onto the total loan payback.

A close examination of the impact of the discount points will shed some light on the dynamics that this practice has for perpetuating the deterioration of African American communities. If the banks had not adopted a policy of redlining, this retired railroad worker would have been able to get a conventional loan at 15 percent, with a ten-year payback period. The interest and principal of such loans would have cost him $11,764.82. But his loan from the mortgage company, with all of the add-ons, drove up his interest rate to 27.1 percent. Over a period of ten years, the total cost of his loan was $30,722.30.[35] Although this article is anecdotal, it clearly illustrates the impact that redlining has on African American communities throughout America. Such practice guarantees the creation and perpetuation of slums. In the final analysis, critics have persistently attributed such failure to African Americans' biological inferiority[36] instead of the redlining practices utilized by the banking, real estate, and insurance industries to maximize their profit.

Economic Incentives for Redlining

Although its effects lead to racial oppression, the underlying factor for the persistent practice of redlining by the industries is economic. These industries learned as early as 1932 that they could maximize their profits through the manipulation of the real estate market by redlining and promoting racial hysteria. Ninety some odds years later, they are still engaged in this practice despite the numerous laws passed by Congress and decisions rendered by the courts to curb this practice.

In the 1970s, these industries found that they could further maximize their profits by the high turnover rate of homeownership in middle-class white neighborhoods. In examining the report of the Federal Financial Institution Examination Counsel, researchers of the *Atlanta-Journal Constitution* found that the loan defaults rate in middle-class African American communities was significantly lower than they were in middle-class white neighborhoods. For example, they found that the Citizens Trust Bank, which was African American owned, had a lower rate of loan defaults than the six largest banks that refused to lend money for housing in African Americans communities.[37] If these facts are true, then what are the underlying reasons for the lending institutions' persistent practice of redlining the African American communities? There are two obvious reasons: racism and economics.

Racism: The term racism as used here must not be mistaken with the term race bigotry where individuals or groups typically use the "N" word. Instead, this it is to be understood here as describing those practices and policies that the lending industries use that operate to foreclose African Americans' freedom to connect themselves to one of the main arteries of America's income redistribution system. This form of race prejudice stems from what Pierre van de Berghe called "competitive prejudice," which is typically found in a highly competitive and industrialized society.[38] It is intensified when whites see African Americans competing on an equal footing for those "consensually desired resources."[39]

As mentioned in the Chapter 1, homeownership is the linchpin to achieving the American dream. This is the main vehicle for American families to accumulate wealth and to promote those basic social values, which society has accused African Americans of consciously rejecting.[40] These values include social upward mobility, individual responsibility, and curbing crimes in African American communities. Various writers have attempted to attribute the lack of African Americans' success in acquiring these values to their lack of innate ability.[41] But, as we have demonstrated, upward mobility is a function of the freedom and the assistance that the government provides for a group to acquire and to posses property. Homeownership allows families to borrow money to send their children to college, to take vacations, for retirement, and for a host of other things. More importantly, it becomes the basis for the transferring of intergenerational wealth. Through interactions and personal interviews with African American middle-class families, this writer has found numerous families that were able to bequest millions of dollars to their children as a result of having the freedom to purchase real estate in the suburbs after the passage of the Federal Fair Housing Act of 1968.

Despite the anti-discrimination law, the lending industries found other ways to maximize their profits through redlining. First, they found the turnover rate in the African American communities to be significantly lower than it is in middle-class white neighborhoods. When African Americans move into a middle-class community, they tend to remain there until their retirement or death. This practice reduces the potential profits. By contrast, they found that they could significantly increase their profits by concentrating on the high turn-over rate in middle-class white neighborhoods. The *Atlanta-Journal Constitu-tion* researchers found evidence to this effect when they analyzed "the real estate records of all home sales in 1986 in 16 of the 64 neighborhoods" in DeKalb County, Georgia.[42] They found that economic incentive was the driv-ing force that can best explain the disparity in home financing. Banks made their money by promoting variable instead of fixed-interest rate loans. In addi-tion, money is made from a variety of fees, which include loan originator fees, closing costs, points, homeowners' insurance, and "junk fees." The latter fees include such items as document preparations, credit checks, attorney fee, credit report, and processing fee, and so on. These fees are unnecessary and could be eliminated.[43]

A variable rate loan, first of all, starts out with a lower interest rate, with adjustable intervals of one, three, or five years. The lending industries make their money on these loans by charging interest points that must be paid upfront. Each point is 1 percent of the total loan. Take, for example, in the Atlanta area where the *Constitution* researchers found that the major banks do not make loans in African American neighborhoods. One explanation given for their refusal to make loans in African American communities was the loan process. Banks typically make loans brought to them by the loan originators, the sales-people who drum up loans. Most of these individuals in the Atlanta area are white. They tend to work where they can make the most profit with the least amount of paperwork. This is where the unintentional discriminatory effect comes into play.

Let us assume the legitimacy of the lending institutions' argument for refus-ing to grant loans to African American communities in the Atlanta area to as-certain their profit margin. The *Constitution* researchers use the figures of $50,000 for homes in the African American communities and $100,000 in middle-class white communities. The time and paperwork to process a loan in both neighborhoods are exactly the same. The difference occurs in the amount of profits made on each loan.

If the points for both loans were 3.5 percent, the lender would make $3,500 on a $100,000 loan in a white community and only $1,750 on a $50,000 loan made in African American community. The incentive to discriminate is further enhanced by the fact that a variable rate loan will allow the banks to make the same profit on points by refinancing or reselling the property within five years. By contrast, because the value of homes and the turnover rate in the African American community is lower than they are in white communities, lenders have to make two loans in the former communities in order to make the same profit that they would make in the latter communities.

In order to maximize their profit in African American communities, banks have established subprime lending institutions such as mortgage companies to serve these communities. These companies are not regulated by the federal government; therefore, they are free to charge higher interest rates than the conventional institutions and to tack on higher "junk fees." The latter fees are used by lenders to entice borrowers to apply for loans. The amount of money that lenders discount in the application fee is thrown into the closing cost in the form of "junk fees" to make up the difference.

The role that the government plays in promoting racial inequality in housing is not apparent. Its role comes into play when we examine the tax breaks given on loan points. These points are 100 percent deductible. Let us assume that Homebuyer A, who is white, and Homebuyer B, who is an African American, are both public employees for the city of Atlanta and earning an annual salary of the $50,000 each. Homebuyer A bought a $100,000 home in a white neighborhood and Homebuyer B bought a $50,000 home in the African American neighborhood. Both homebuyers are allowed to deduct their mortgage from their income tax. The differences will come into play when the discount points reduce their income tax rate. For tax purpose, Homebuyer A income tax rate will be reduced to $47,500, while Homebuyers B tax rate will be reduced only to $48,250. Homebuyers A's tax liability will further be reduced because of his higher mortgage payments, which are also 100 percent deductible for the first five years.

The Problem in Controlling Redlining

Despite the various attempts made by the federal government, it has been unsuccessful in eliminating the practice of redlining. The problem lies in the structural arrangements of the laws covering the banking and insurance industries. As mentioned earlier, Congress removed the control of the insurance industry from the reach of the long arms of the federal government. In doing so, it inadvertently restricted its authority to control the banking and insurance industries' practice of redlining. The banks are caught in a Catch-22 situation. They will not make a loan in a predominantly African American neighborhood unless the property is insured. Insurance companies will not insure properties in African American neighborhoods. Without insurance, banks do not have any protection for their investments.

Despite the lack of authority over the insurance industry, the federal government has enacted the following measures in an attempt to control redlining: the Fair Housing Act of 1968; the Equal Credit Opportunity Act (ECOA) of 1974; the Home Mortgage Disclosure Act (HMDA) of 1975; and the Community Reinvestment Act (CRA) of 1977. All of these measures have been ineffective in eliminating the practice of redlining, primarily because the term "racial discrimination" is not easy to establish in the area of lending.

Gary A. Dymski has summarized the various attempts made by the courts and Congress to define the term racial discrimination in lending. He summarized these definitions into the following categories:

Overt discrimination – refusing to initiate a transaction with a person of color.

Disparate treatment –screening minorities more harshly than whites in the application process, or subjecting minority applicants to different application processes.

Disparate impact –conducting commercial practices that disproportionately harm racial minorities without being justified by a legitimate business need.[44]

These variables are interrelated. They generate a market process that operates to foreclose African Americans' access to economic resources. Within the context of these variables, lending institutions can offer a legitimate justification for not lending to African Americans loans to buy homes or to make improvements in their communities.

On the surface, HMDA seems to be a very promising measure to combat redlining. It requires banks to disclose their geographic distribution of their residential mortgage loans. Census tracts were used to determine the extent of redlining. However, research has shown that HMDA does not offer an adequate remedy in combatting the practice of redlining. Fourteen years after its passage, Congress amended this act to require lenders to report key variables such as race, gender, and the applicants' income. Seven years later, the new reporting requirements indicated that 40 percent of African Americans and 29.5 percent of Hispanics' loan applications were rejected. However, this data indicates that color was not the primary factor in granting loans. The Asians' denial rate was equal to or, in some instance, less than that of whites, which was 20 percent.

The metropolitan areas in which researchers examined the practice of redlining were Boston and Atlanta. Alicia Munell (et. al.) used various variables in an attempt to isolate race as a factor in denying an applicant a loan. Once all of the variables were taken into account, they found that "minority applicants with the same economic and property characteristics as white applicants experienced a denial rate of 17 percent rather than the actual white denial rate of 11 percent."[45]

Another study completed by the Federal Institutions Examination Council in nineteen large metropolitan areas examined the rate in which applicants were denied loans based on race and ethnicity. In all of these areas, it found that African Americans' rejection rates were the highest. This denial rate was without respect to class among African Americans. At the highest income level of the survey, they were turned down more frequently than other groups. For example, "the denial rates in the group were 8.5% for Anglos, 11.2% for Asians, 12.8% for American Indians, 15% for Latinos and 21.4% for" African Americans (see Table 20).

Table 20
Mortgage Rejection Rates by Race and Ethnic Group for 19 Large Metropolitan Areas During 1990

Metro Area	Asian	Black	Latino	Anglo
Atlanta	11.1	26.5	13.6	10.5
Baltimore	7.3	15.6	10.1	7.5
Boston	15.4	34.9	21.2	11.0
Chicago	10.4	23.6	12.1	7.3
Dallas	9.3	25.6	19.8	10.7
Detroit	9.1	23.7	14.2	9.7
Houston	13.3	33.0	25.7	12.6
Los Angeles	13.2	19.8	16.3	12.8
Miami	16.9	22.9	17.8	16.0
Minneapolis	6.4	19.9	8.0	6.1
New York	17.3	29.4	25.3	15.0
Oakland	11.6	16.5	13.3	9.6
Philadelphia	12.1	25.0	21.0	8.3
Phoenix	12.8	30.0	25.2	14.4
Pittsburgh	12.2	31.0	13.9	12.0
St. Louis	9.0	31.8	13.5	12.1
San Diego	11.2	17.8	15.1	9.8
Seattle	11.6	18.3	16.8	10.7
Washington, D.C.	8.7	14.4	8.9	6.3

SOURCE: *Los Angeles Time* (October 22, 1991), pt A, p. 25. This report was compiled by the Federal Financial Institutions Examination Council and analyzed by the Federal Reserve Bank of Boston.

The passage of CRA was an attempt by Congress to force the lending institutions to reinvest in the areas that they serve. A study conducted by researchers of the *Atlanta-Journal Constitution* revealed the ineffectiveness of this law. They examined the U.S. government record in grading the 17,000 banks, saving and loans' performance in granting loans in the communities that they serve, as required by CRA. Across the nation, they found that the government has passed 98 percent of these institutions as meeting the requirements of CRA. In evaluating the record of CRA, Senator Proxmire, chairman of the Senate Banking Committee, commented: "I wish I had a grade teacher like that when I was in school. . . And I asked myself, how is it that so many neighborhoods are continuing to fail, while so many lending institutions are continuing to pass."[46]

In addition to the annual exam, CRA requires regulators to examine the lending pattern of banks when they seek to open up a new branch or seek to acquire another. Over a ten-year period, the researchers at the *Atlanta-Journal Constitution* found that regulators only denied 8 of the 50,000 applications as a result of their poor performance record in serving low income communities.

In short, the driving force behind the creation of the slums is economic. It is a combination of the efforts by the banking, insurance, and real estate industries influencing the formation of public housing laws to maximize their profits. They took special care to make sure that the construction of decent public housing did not undermine their profits in maintaining slum housing. In other words, these industries were the driving force behind creating and maintaining slums. They will continue to do so until another system is constructed to discourage the creation of slums.

European Immigrants Tickets out of the Slums

So far, we have demonstrated that the partisan arguments that European immigrants were able to escape the slums and pulled themselves up onto the middle-class plateau by their own bootstraps, the strong family structure, and hard work are not supported by historical data. To elevate itself to the middle-class plateau, a group needs a change not only in its geographic location but also a change in its socioeconomic status. The latter requires a college education. To accomplish this goal, a group needs two tickets: (1) a ticket to move to the suburbs, and a ticket to aquire an education. The federal government issued the European immigrants these two tickets: the FHA laws and the G.I. Bill for education.

Before FHA

The role that the FHA played in the European immigrants' upward mobility cannot be fully understood until we examine the structural conditions of the ghetto before its implementation. This bill was passed in 1949 and its implementations began in the early 1950s. At this time, the European immigrants were trapped into the ghettoes by the American policy on housing (i.e., the trickle-down theory). This policy was not providing adequate housing for the masses. Evidence to support this contention can be found in the literature on rent strikes.

Thanks to the latitudinal study by Ronald Lawson and Mark Naison, we have a sufficient amount of data to examine the structural conditions that constrained the European immigrants' capacity to escape the slums. These authors studied the history of the tenant-landlord relationship during the latter part of the nineteenth century and up to the 1990s in New York City.

Their research team employed "detailed research from a range of primary sources—Yiddish language newspapers, participant interviews, and tenant council minutes."[47] They examined "the social basis of the tenant movement" and described the "context and significance of the movement at the grass roots level." Their study was "part of the history of American Judaism, radicalism, and working-class protest."[48] The scientific significance of this study to the basic argument of this book is that it strongly supports the argument that stronger family structure is not an independent variable that can explain group upward mobility, and groups do escape the slums without some form of government help. As mentioned in the introduction chapter, the Jews have a reputation for having a strong family structure and family values. Yet, they were pinned down on the beachhead of the culture of poverty for approximately three generations (i.e., from the 1880s to the 1950s).

What the Lawson research team found was a struggle between tenants and landlords where the latter had an upper hand. The first large rent strike took place in the Lower East Side of New York, which was predominately occupied by Jewish immigrants of the late 1880s and 90s. There was a severe shortage in rental housing and the landlords, who themselves were Jewish, took advantage of this situation and increased the rent from 20 to 30 percent.[49] This uncontrolled rent had its most profound effect upon the socioeconomic status of the Jews. These tenants consisted of seasonal garment workers and small businessmen. Their rent swallowed up approximately one-third of the breadwinner's income, which was 60 cents a day. His rent increased "from

$8.50 to $13 a month." [50] Accompanying this rent increase was a decline in services and maintenance of the buildings. Any tenant who lodged a complaint about these conditions was "liable to summary evictions."[51]

This uncontrolled rent, coupled with seasonal work and low wages, renders the strong family structure and hard work arguments null and void. Even if groups wanted to escape the slums, they could not because they had neither the means nor the resources to do so. As we have seen in Chapter 8, the set of bootstraps (the right to collective bargaining) that the government provided allowed these groups (1) to get a foothold in the American economy, (2) job security, and (3) to raise their standards of living. It does not require the marshaling forward of a voluminous amount of data to support the argument that landlords increased their rent in proportion to the increase in the standards of living of their tenants. The economic incentives were there.

It was not until after the passage of the FHA that the European immigrants of the late nineteenth century began to escape the slums. The implementation of this law began in the 1950s and lasted throughout the 1960s. The impact of this policy was not evaluated until 1970 by William Tabb in his book, entitled *The Political Economy of the Ghetto.*[52]

The Impact of the G.I. Bill

It is without question that the gateway to social upward mobility is through education. Although an individual can earn a middle-class income, he/she is not considered to be middle class until having acquired a college education. Such education signifies that the individual has undergone, or is in the process of undergoing, a social transformation. It is his interaction in a middle-class environment where he learns the skills for rational thinking and adopting middle-class social and cultural values for assimilation and acculturation.[53]

The notion of assimilation and acculturation have been the driving force in Western culture that has introduced individuals to desire an education. In America, this has been the dominant driving force that has promoted individuals' for a desire college education. Unfortunately, education has always been in the reach of the privileged few in America until the government intervened to democratize the education system.

Literature on social upward mobility is inundated with studies purporting to show that group upward mobility can be attributed to groups' internalization of certain cultural values such as hard work, strong family values, and their desire to assimilate into mainstream America. What is missing from these studies is a systematic analysis of those environmental conditions that make it possible for individuals to acquire a college education to move up the social ladder. Here, the focus must be directed not toward social values, but conditions that constrain and promote groups' choice possibilities, or opportunities, to move up the social ladder.

Before a group can move up the social economic ladder, to hypothesize, the conditions in their environment must be conducive to their upward mobility. There is no need to marshal forward a voluminous amount of data to support this argument. We only need to examine some of those variables social scientists have most frequently identified as the cause of group upward mobility. The one that is used most frequent is strong family values.

In examining the role that strong family values play in group upward mobility, we need to identify a group that has a reputation for a strong family structure and values. As will be demonstrated in Chapter 10, there is no concrete definition of a strong family structure other than a nuclear family. This family structure can be found among poor people. But for this section, we are going to focus on a group that has a reputation for having strong family values and structure to ascertain how these values helped them to overcome the conditions in their environment and supported their upward mobility. Here, we have the Russian Jews.

If any group could have made it to the middle class based on strong family values, it would have been the Jews. They immigrated to America in large numbers during the 1880s and '90s, and settled in the lower tenements of the cities, better known as the ghettoes. Despite their values for hard work and strong family structures, they remained pinned down on the beachhead of the culture of poverty for more than three generations.

An example of the plight of the poor worldwide can be found in the collection of essays compiled by Robert A. Wood in 1895. The article in this book that is germane to our study is the one that was written by Jacob A. Riis, entitled "The Children of the Poor."[54] He offers one of the best summarizations of the Jews' values toward education in their initial stage of contact with the American polity in the following paragraph.

> The poorest Hebrew knows–the poorer he is, the better he knows it–that knowledge is power, and how well as the means of getting on in the world that has spurned him so long, is what his soul yearns for. He lets no opportunity slip to obtain it. Day- and night-schools are crowded with his children, who run rapidly and with ease. Every synagogue, every second rear tenement or dark back-yard, has its school and its school-master, with his scourge to intercept those who might otherwise escape.[55]

Despite strong values placed on education, the Jews were unable to acquire a college education in large numbers before the passage of the G.I. Bill in 1944. As the previously passage illustrates, they had the yearning for a college degree, but not the means to achieve it. Until the federal government stepped in and offered them a set of bootstraps during the New Deal Era, a college education remained virtually a figment of their imagination. It was the G.I. Bill that enabled them to translate their desire for a college education into a reality.

The Jews, perhaps, benefited from the G.I. Bill more than any other single ethnic group, not because any special favors were granted to them by the government, but because of the large percentage of them who served in the Armed Forces during World War II. Their high percentage was not necessarily a reflection of their patriotism as it was their desire to fight Hitler's regime, which was persecuting their families and ancestors in Germany. When they returned home after the war, the government had already provided them with a vehicle by which they could easily achieve their goal of acquiring a college education (i.e., the G.I. Bill).

The importance of the G.I. Bill in explaining group upward mobility cannot be underestimated. Historians have unequivocally agreed that the G.I. Bill was one of the most significant pieces of legislation passed by Congress in terms of social upward mobility. This bill had many impacts upon American society from the 1950s to present day.

First, the G.I. Bill made a college education available to more than 15 million veterans. It significantly increased the rate of social upward mobility in America. Prior to the passage of this bill, college education was basically reserved for the affluent and upperclass populations. The cost of tuition was the greatest barrier blocking group upward mobility. Take, for example, the tuition at Brownsville Junior College of Texas in 1941. Its tuition was $126 per year. This figure was reduced from the price it was in 1926 before the start of the Great Depression.[56]

Second, the G.I. Bill opened a floodgate to the colleges and universities throughout America. Enrollment increased approximately 7.8 million: 2,230,000 in college, 3,480,000 in other schools, 1,400,000 in on job training, and 690,000 in farm training.[57] In 1947, veterans accounted for one half of college enrollment. The colleges and universities were not equipped to accommodate such a large influx of students. Their capacity was limited to serving the upper class and a few less affluent students on scholarships. But this new influx of students came with money that increased the universities' budgets. With this increase, they could now hire more faculty members and build new facilities to meet the demands of student enrollment. At first, many colleges and universities had to construct prefabricated buildings and Quonset huts for classrooms and convert military barracks into dormitories. In addition, they were forced to make accommodations for married students. Having been away from their loved ones for the duration of the war, many veterans were eager to get married after they returned, which many of them did. They still wanted to take advantage of the G.I. Bill by acquiring a college education. To accommodate them, the universities and college converted trailers into housing.

The third impact that the G.I. Bill had upon the colleges and universities was to force them to change their curriculums. Prior to the G.I. Bill, the curriculums of the colleges were focused on the liberal arts. But the veterans demanded more practical education such as degrees in engineering and business, and so on. This change in curriculums significantly bolstered the American economic growth and development during the 1950s. The world was undergoing rapid technological changes during this period. This new technology required skilled workers, which the G.I. Bill helped provide. Although this bill helped increase the number of engineers in America, it proved to be inadequate around 1957 when Russia launched Sputnik into space. To rectify this shortage, Congress passed the National Defense Education Act in 1958.

The fourth significant impact that the G.I. Bill had upon the American society can be found not so much in the fact that it brought higher education within the reach of the lower class, but it enabled veterans to activate the principle of intergenerational mobility among their class. The G.I. Bill made it possible for them to interact in an environment that socialized them to internalize the value of a college education. In turn, they were able to transmit these values to their children. Many veterans grew up during the Great Depression and had vivid memories of the horrible struggles that their parents had in trying to provide their family with a means of subsistence. They wanted to make sure that their children were spared such horrible experiences; consequently, they undertook special measures to make sure that their children received a better education than they had, particularly in the form of a college degree.

The fifth impact that the G.I. Bill had upon the American society is that it forced states to increase the number of colleges and universities. For example, the influx of veterans enabled the state of New York to establish its state University system, known as the SUNY system. Other states followed the same pattern. Around the 1960s, college expansions continued to accommodate the "baby boomers."

The sixth significant impact that the G.I. Bill had upon higher education is that it forced institutions to strengthen their curriculums. When the veterans started invading the college campuses, the critics of this program made similar arguments that critics of affirmative action made in the 1960s (i.e., this program would weaken academic standards). But instead of weakening the standards, the G.I. Bill actually forced the colleges and universities to strengthen their curriculums by demanding practical programs leading to degrees in the new fields of technology. Academically, these programs were more demanding than the liberal arts' curriculums that the colleges and universities had before the veterans arrived. The veterans were best suited for these programs because of their maturity and self-discipline acquired as a result of serving in the armed forces. Furthermore, they were not interested in the parties and joining the social clubs on campus which preoccupied the affluent class students. They wanted to get their degree before their G.I. benefits ran out.

Finally, the G.I. Bill produced many of our current prominent political leaders and professions. The following leaders are beneficiaries of the G.I. Bill:

> . . . George Bush and Gerald R. Ford; Vice President Albert Gore, Jr.; Chief Justice William H. Rehnquist and Justice John Paul Stevens, both of the Supreme Court; Secretary of State Warren M. Christopher; journalists David Brinkley and John Chancellor; actors Clint Eastwood, Paul Newman, and Jason Robards, Jr.; and former Dallas Cowboys football coach Tom Landry.[58]

In addition to these, a host of other individuals were listed in a documentary narrated by Cliff Robertson, entitled "The G.I. Bill: The Law that Changed America."[59] This video featured interviews with movie stars such as Tony Curtis, Harry Belafonte, Walter Mathau, and a host of other stars. For politics, it identified Senator Bob Dole. For education, most of the prominent professors in their late '60s. All of these individuals were in agreement. "They would have never gone to college if it was not for the G.I. Bill."

In short, the overall thrust of this chapter has been directed toward demonstrating that the variables that Kinder and Sears have identified as independent are, in fact, dependent variables. Groups have been able to escape the slums not by the cultural values that they have internalized but by the support that the government provided to assist their flight to the suburbs and moving up the social economic ladder. It offers strong evidence to the basic argument of this book, which is that groups cannot escape the slums without a set of boots and bootstraps. The Jews had internalized all of these cultural values, but the structural conditions in their communities prevented them from escaping the slums until the 1950s.

Notes

1. Dennis R. Kinder and Donal O. Sears, "Prejudice and Politics: Symbolic Racism versus Racial Threats to the Good Life." *Journal of Personality and Social Psychology,* 40, (1981): 414-431.

2.   Oscar Handlin, *The Newcomers: Negroes and Puerto Ricans in a Changing Metropolis* (Cambridge, Massachusetts: Harvard Press, 1959), Chapter 2.

3.   Ibid., p.14.

4.   ·Charlie Zehran, "The Dream Builder," http://www.lihistory.com/specsec/hslevpro.htm, p. 5.

5.   This quote was cited in the website of the City of Houston, http://www.texashousing.org/txLHIS/phdebate/introl.html.

6.   For example, the Federal Home Loan Bank Act of 1932, The Resettlement and Administration Act of 1935, the United States Housing Act of 1937, the National Housing Act Amendments of 1938, the Servicemen's Readjustment Act of 1944 (G.I), the Housing Act of 1948, and the Housing Act of 1949.

7.   Zehren, p. 1.

8.   Geoffrey Mohen, "Growing Pains," http://www.lihistory. Com/specsec/hslevtwo.htm.

9.   Michele Ingrassia, "The House That Levitt Built," http://www.lihistory.com/specsec/hslevpro.htm, p. 1 of 4.

10.   Zehran, p. 8.

11.   Ingrassa, p. 4.

12.   Ingrassia, p. 2.

13.   Zehren, p. 9.

14.   William F. Tabb, *The Political Economy of the Ghetto* (New York: W.W. Norton & Company,1970)

15.   Zehren, p.7.

16.   *Shelly v. Kreamer*, 334 U.S. 343 (1948).

17.   Zehran, p. 3.

18.   Mohen, "Growing Pains," http://www.lihistory. Com/specsec/hslevtwo.htm.

19.   See Chapter 2 of The Kerner Report, *Report of the National Advisory Commission on Civil Disorder* (Washington: Government Printing Office, 1968).

20.   Edward C. Banfield, *The Unheavenly City* (Boston: Little Brown and Company, 1968), p. 48. After severe criticism, Banfield struck this argument from his book. But the thrust of his argument remains.

21.   See Arthur Jensen, *Genetics and Education* (New York: Harper & Row, 1972). Jensen was a strong advocate of racial inferiority.

22.   Handlin, p. 16.

23.   Barry G. Jacobs et.al. *Guide to Federal Housing Programs* (Washington, D.C.: The Bureau of Affairs, Inc., 1986), p. 8.

24.   Stephen Fox, "The past: United States Housing Act of 1937 Political compromise shapes public housing," http://www.texashousing.org/txLIHIS/phdebate/past6.html.

25.   "What Is in a Standard Homewners Insurance Policy," Insurance Information Institute, Inc., www.iii.org/individuals/homei/hbasics/whatisin.

26.   See "63 Years of Federal Action in Housing and Urban Development," *HUD Cityscape: A Journal of Policy Development and Research*, 1 No. 3 (September 1995), pp. vi-ix.

27.   Kerner Report, p. 360.

28. 15 U.S.C. sec. 1012.

29. "The Color of Money," *Atlanta-Constitution Journal*, May 1, 1988, p. A1.

30. Ibid.

31. Ibid.

32. Bill Dedman, "Southside Treated Like Banks' Stepchild? Blacks May Shun Some-Loan Lender Because They're Shunned First, Critics Say," *The Atlanta Journal-Constitution*, May 2, 1988, A1.

33. *Shelly v. Kreamer*, 334 U.S. 343 (1948).

34. Dedman, "A Tale of Two Neighborhoods, One Black and One White," *Atlanta-Journal Constitutional*, May 1, 1988, A14.

35. Ibid.

36. Banfield, p.48.

37. Dedman, "The Color of Money," *Atlanta-Journal Constitution,* May 1, 1988, p. A1.

38. See Pierre van de Berghe, Chapter 2.

39. Louis Kriesberg, *Social Conflict* (Englewood Cliffs, N. J.: Prentice-Hall, 1973), p.39.

40. See Kinder and Sears, "Symbolic Racism."

41. This argument was first advanced by Daniel P. Moynihan in 1965 and his report on the black family. This argument resurged in the 1980s by the conservatives in an attempt to undermine the legitimacy of affirmative action.

42. Dedman, "A Tale of Two Neighborhoods, One Black and One White," *Atlanta Journal-Constitution,* May 1, 1988, A1.

43. Buyer Agents Realty," www.buyeragentsrealty.com/homebuyer_tips-mortgages-lender_junk_fee.htm.

44. Gary A. Dymski, "Why Does Race Matter in Housing and Credit Market?" in *The Frontiers of Research on Discrimination* (Kluwer Academic) edited by Patrick L. Mason and Rhonda Williams.http://iml.umkc.edu/econ/AFEE/Dymski Race HousingCredit.html.

45. Alicia H. Munnell, Lynn E. Browne, James McEneaney, and Geoffrey Tootell, Mortgage Lending in Boston: interpreting HMDA Data. Working Paper No. 92-7. (Boston: Federal Reserve Bank of Boston, 1992), p.2.

46. Dedman, "Regulators Say 90 Percent Obey," *Atlanta Journal-Constitution,* May 3, 1988, A1.

47. Ronald Lawson and Mark Naison, *The Tenant Movement in New York City, 1904-1984* (New Brunswick, NJ: Rutgers University Press, 1986).

48. Ibid.

49. Jenna Weissman Jaselit, "The Landlord as Czar Pre-War I Tenant Activity," in *The Tenant Movement in New York.*

50. Lawson and Naison, p. 1.

51. See Lawson and Naison, Introduction Chapter.

52. See Tabb, *Political Economy of the Black Ghetto*, Chapters 1 and 2.

53.   For a discussion on assimilation and acculturation see Milton Gordon, *Assimilation in American Life: The Role of Race, Religion, and National Origins* (New York: Oxford University Press, 1964).

54.   Jacob A. Riis, "The Children of the Poor," in *The Poor in Great Cities,* ed. Robert A. Woods (New York: Garrett Press, Inc., 1970).

55.   Ibid., pp. 102-103.

56.   "World War II: A Difficult Time for the Junior College," The University of Texas at Brownsville and Southmost College, http://pubs.utb.edu/anniversary/world_war_ii.htm

57.   "History of the G.I.Bill," http://www.gibill.va.gov/education/GI_Bill.htm

58.   "Government Agencies and Programs," http://www.wld.com/conbus/weal/wgibill.htm

59.   PBS Home Video, B3620. Produced by Thirteen/WNET in New York and Film Odyssey Inc. 1997.

CHAPTER 10

The Politics of Poverty and the Self-Victimization Argument

Throughout America's history, there have always been individuals who have ended up in the ranks of the poor and poverty stricken. Historically, benevolent organizations have been formed to help the less fortunate and questions have been raised as to what is the basic cause of individuals falling into the ranks of the misfortunes. Throughout the years, there have been many theories advanced to explain why. Once deducted to their logical conclusion, they seem to have some of the basic elements of the Protestant theology (i.e., the self-victimization argument). The genesis of this argument is that the reason why persons are poor is that God is punishing them for their sin. The only thing that they have to do is to repent, amend their ways, and ask God for forgiveness, and they would be blessed like everyone else.

Over the years, the same arguments have been secularized to explain the cause of group inequality. Instead of attributing the conditions of the poor to their sins, the effort has too often been directed toward some form of self-victimization. Poverty is accepted as proof of a personal or group inadequacy instead of some form of social injustice. Such argument is calculated (1) to engender into the consciousness of poor people a sense of guilt and self-depreciation,[1] and (2) to rid the broader society of any guilt or responsibility for the cause of poverty. For example, the first ethnic group to fall victim to being blamed for causing their own poverty was the Irish-Catholics, who immigrated in 1830s. The explanation that writers gave for their poverty was that God was punishing them for being Catholics. The only thing that they needed to do was to convert to Protestantism.

Placing the blame of poverty on the backs of victims themselves became a convenient tool for social scientists to use—in the 1960s and afterward—to explain the cause of poverty found among minority groups, in general, and African Americans, in particular. The major shortcoming of any self-victimization theory is that it too often fails to withstand systematic scrutiny and is thus devoid of any scientific import. As stated earlier, theories can be internally consistent and empirically accurate, but in order to be scientific, they must withstand systematic scrutiny. A systematic theory, as David Easton has reminded us, must be comparative in nature and supportive by historical data. To better understand the cause of poverty, researchers need to construct a conceptual framework capable of conducting a macro-analysis. This analysis must (1) state the objective conditions under which poverty is more likely to occur, (2) be comparative in nature, (3) withstand systematic scrutiny, and (4) be supportive by historical data.

In the absence of a systematic comparative framework, the best that a researcher can expect to obtain from any analysis of the cause of poverty is the collection of data. Such an analysis is bound to be laden with numerous internal contradictions and statistics incidents. For example, researchers have persistently identified strong family structures and values as independent variables that can best explain group upward mobility. But in order for this argument to hold true, it has to withstand systematic scrutiny. Specifically, it has to hold true for all immigrant groups that have escape the slums in America. If one group can be found that has a reputation for a strong family structure when they made contact with the American polity and remained on the beachhead of the culture of poverty for a prolonged period before escaping the slums, then the family structure argument is invalid. As we have seen, the Russian Jews fell into this category, and they remained impoverished for approximately three generations. The practice of self-victimization is not exclusively an American phenomenon; it is part of the Western cultural value system.[2] Let us now turn to an analysis of the self-victimization arguments that were advanced from the 1960s and forward to ascertain whether they can withstand systematic scrutiny.

Poverty and the Self-Victimization Arguments

The first major self-victimization argument of the 1960s was advanced by Daniel P. Moynihan. Although some have argued that self-victimization was not his original intent, the bulk of his argument hinges on it. In an attempt to drum up support for President Lyndon B. Johnson's "Great Society" program, Moynihan conducted a survey of the socioeconomic status of the African American family and found an unusually high rate of single female head of the family.[3] He subsequently mistakenly concluded that this was the primary cause of African Americans' lack of socioeconomic success. Since this report, critics of civil rights and social programs have been cranking out numerous articles and books purporting to support this position.

The effort to place the blame for African Americans' lack of economic success on their backs escalated in the latter part of the 1970s and through the 1980s and 1990s. The effort was led by a group of African American conservatives. As stated in Chapter 1, Thomas Sowell was a forerunner among this group, followed by Walter Williams, Julius Wilson, Glenn Lowry, and Shelby Steele.

Among this group, Wilson's writings contain the most credulous argument in support of the self-victimization argument. In *The Declining Significance of Race*, he advanced the illusory argument that race was declining as a significant barrier to African Americans' opportunities for advancement. He was followed by Sowell (who wrote six books during this period), Walter Williams, Nathan Glazer (who is white), Glenn Lowry, and Shelby Steele.[4] These authors' writings had one thing in common: they rejected the role of government intervention as an independent variable in groups' economic growth and development. They argued, either explicitly or implicitly, that a group's growth and development can be attributed more to self-initiatives than governmental intervention. The opposite of this argument is that the reason African Americans have not achieved economic success is because of their lack of self-initiative.

Objective Conditions for Poverty

What Wilson and other writers have failed to recognize is that there is a set of objective conditions under which this type of behavior will always exist. From this perspective, we can turn to the philosophies of Thomas Hobbes and John Locke. Both of these philosophers directly or indirectly described patterns of social deviant behavior as a group forced into the natural state of war. This notion of the natural state of war was first advanced by Hobbes. He argued that this state "consistieth not in the actual fighting; but in the known deposition thereto, during all times there is no assurance to the contrary."[5] Historically, the state of war has occurred for a group in a society whenever the government failed to adopt positive laws (bootstraps) to safeguard their rights to an orderly means of subsistence. Adopting such laws, Locke maintained, is the duty and responsibility of the Commonwealth (the government). The government must do this by adopting positive laws.[6] The failure to do so, he argued, will force man to resort back to his original state of nature (i.e., the natural state of war).[7]

As has been demonstrated throughout this book, whenever the government failed to adopt positive laws (bootstraps) to protect a group's freedom to connect themselves to the mainstream of society's income redistribution system, this group was pinned down on the beachheads of the culture of poverty by its adversaries and competitors. They remained there until the government intervened. With this analysis, we are now in a position to state a proposition when a given society can expect a pattern of social deviant behavior to develop among any given population.

Social deviant behaviors, to hypothesize, can always be expected whenever the government fails to adopt positive laws to protect members of a group's freedom to connect themselves to the mainstream of society's income redistribution system.[8] Once developed, the culture of poverty has an extraordinary propensity for intergenerational downward mobility. Such downward mobility will continue until the government intervenes and adopts positive laws to brake this pattern. Therefore, social deviant behaviors such as a high rate of crimes, violence, black-on-black crimes, gang warfare, teenage pregnancy, high rates of prisons, chronic unemployment, underemployment (i.e., are nothing more than symptoms of a population that has been forced into a natural state of war). In this state, this type of group behavior can be expected and predicted with a relatively high degree of accuracy (i.e., members are going to do whatever they see fit for the preservation of their nature). This behavior, it must be noted here, is without respect to race. It is characteristic of any population that has reached this state. A historical comparative analysis of groups' experience in America will lend credence to this argument.

The Irish-Catholics and Poverty

The immigrant groups who were first to be pinned down on the beachheads of the culture of poverty were the Irish-Catholics and a few Germans. These groups, who immigrated between the 1830s and 1850s, broke the traditional immigration pattern of moving directly to the interior and settling on farms. Instead, they congregated in the cities and remained there despite concerted efforts by private benevolent organizations, such as the Association for Improving the Conditions of the Poor to lure them to the interior.[9]

The Land Grant Act of 1829 served as a set of bootstraps to ensure immigrant groups the opportunity to gain a foothold in the economy. As stated in Chapter 1, in order for a group to make it to the middle-class plateau collectively, it needs both a pair of boots and a set of bootstraps. The government provided the Irish-Catholics with a set of bootstraps; however, they were unable to take advantage of these opportunities because they had lost their skills (human capital) for farming. They also lacked other marketable skills such as artisans and craftsmen; therefore, they were forced to seek jobs as common laborers—which was on the lower level of the totem pole. At this level, groups' behavioral patterns can be expected to be socially deviant. This was precisely what happened to the Irish-Catholics and the Germans who settled in the cities during this period. They faced problems similar to the ones that African Americans and Hispanics are experiencing today (i.e., a shortage of housing and skilled jobs).

[handwritten margin note: Irish similar to AA.]

We have discussed the politics of housing in Chapter 9. To repeat, crowded housing has been accompanied by a high rate of contagious diseases such as typhus, typhoid fever, cholera, and tuberculosis. The Irish experienced a disproportionate amount of these diseases during the period between the 1830s and 1850s.[10] Accompanying these diseases was a high rate of crimes and pauperism (see Table 21).

Table 21
Social Disorganization in New York City, 1855

Ethnic Groups	Population Number	Percent	Relief granted, 1854-1860 Percent	Arrests for Crimes, 1859 Percent
United States	303,731	48	14.2	23
England, Scotland, and Wales	32,135	5	4.5	7
Ireland	175,775	28	69.0	55
Germany	95,986	15	10.8	10
All others	22,287	4	1.5	5
Total	629,914	100	100	100

SOURCE: Kate H. Claghorn, "The Foreign Immigrant in New York City," in United States Industrial Commission, *Reports on Immigration*, 42 vols. (Washington, D.C.: Government Printing Office, 1901), 15: 442-94.

As the table indicates, the Germans experienced less social disorganization than the Irish. It was demonstrated in Chapter 3 that the Germans who settled in the cities were predominantly craftsmen and artisans, with a few common laborers. Data in this table offers strong evidence that a group's possession of skills will serve as a deterrent to its being thrown into a state of social disorganization. The Germans constituted 15 percent of the population,

[handwritten margin note: MP skills equal but's trap in itself.]

but only 10.8 percent of those on relief, and committed only 10 percent of the crimes; their percentage did not exceed the percentage of the population.

It is worth noting here that a large percentage of the Germans who settled in New York City were, in fact, Jews. But as Kate H. Claghorn has perceptively noted, the Jews "withstood the physical influences of the tenements most remarkably"[11] and did not experience a high rate of social disorganization. However, another breed of Germans settled in New York besides craftsmen and artisans. These were the Germans who were uprooted in their homeland for a generation or so and had adopted the culture of poverty.[12] They were frequently referred to as ragpickers or "chiffonniers" who many thought were importations from Paris, London, and other cities.

> These were at that time to be found in considerable numbers plying their occupations along streets, overturning the heaps of rubbish and filth in search of bits of paper, etc., or scraps of food thrown out of houses as garbage, which they either carry home to recook or eat on the spot.[13]

Dr. John H. Criscom, a city inspector of New York City, argued that this group was very frugal and that by their "habits of economic and constant application to their wretched business enabled nearly all, sooner or later, to accumulate sufficient funds to enable them to migrate west."[14]

The English, Scotch, and Welsh constituted 5 percent of the population and 4.5 percent of those on relief, but they exceeded their percentage of crimes–7 percent. This high percentage of crimes can probably be explained in part by England's practice of deporting a large number of her undesirable people to the United States during this period and by the fact that many of the states had laws which restricted undesirable people–except for New York and Pennsylvania.[15]

For all practical purposes, it can be said that the Irish-Catholics constituted the bulk of the unskilled laborers in the urban areas in the 1850s. They were the ones left behind to fill the demand for unskilled labor in the factories and on public work projects–which thrived on the cheapness of labor and chronic layoffs. In addition, they were confined to other low paying jobs such as "porter, sweepers . . . and their wives and children went into services."[16]

As Table 20 indicates, the Irish-Catholics constituted 28 percent of the population of New York City, 69 percent of those on relief, and 55 percent of the crimes. Some of the categories in which they had a high crime rate were for drunkenness and disorderly conduct, in which they constituted 58.8 percent of those convicted in New York City courts in 1859. The next highest category was vagrancy, in which they constituted 21 percent of those convicted.[17]

The social disorganization that the Irish-Catholics experienced in their initial stage of contact remained with them until the government issued them a pair of boots and a set of bootstraps–which were a part of the New Deal programs. These measures include labor laws, various subsidized job-training programs, and housing mortgages–which were discussed in Chapter 8. These were affirmative measures that catapulted the Irish up off the beachheads of the culture of poverty onto the middle-class plateau during the period between 1940 and 1960. As we have seen, African Americans and dark-skinned Puerto Ricans were purposefully excluded from participating in this process by their competitors and adversaries. Therefore, the social deviant variables found among these groups are similar to the ones found among the Irish in the initial stage of contact with the American polity. They are a function of the national government's failure to adopt positive measures to include them into the mainstream of society's income redistribution system.

In short, this historical comparative analysis demonstrates that group social disorganization is a function of government action, either *de jure* or *de facto*. However, it will not dispel the false argument that strong family structure is an independent variable in groups' success–as the conservatives have argued. Let us now turn to a historical comparative analysis of groups' family structures to determine the internal inconsistencies of this argument.

The Moynihan Report: Family Structure vs. Structural Conditions

When Moynihan identified the high rate of single-female head of family as the fundamental cause of the low economic status of the African American community, he was overlooking the structural conditions that support a two-parent family. The frame of reference that underlies his type of research forced him to seek validation of the self-victimization argument. For example, he argued that the high rate of single-parent families found among African Americans could be attributed to the "high rate of divorce, separation, and desertion"[18] on the part of the African American males. He attempted to validate this argument by comparing African American families to those of whites. He stated that the "white family has achieved a high degree of stability and is maintaining that stability."[19] Implied in this statement is that African American males are unwilling to accept their moral responsibilities of taking care of their families, or they lacked the innate ability to acquire the social values necessary to establish and maintain a stable family structure.

To support his argument, Moynihan compared the educational attainment of the African American males and females. He produced statistics to show the African American females traditionally have achieved a higher level of education than their male counterparts. He attributed this disparity to the fact that the African American females have demonstrated themselves to be better students than the African American males.[20]

Educational attainments, matriarchal family structures, and low socioeconomic status, are nothing more than symptoms of a group that has been forced into a natural state of war. In this state, this type of behavioral pattern, to repeat, can be expected. Members of this group are going to do whatever they see fit for the preservation of their nature, as will be demonstrated later in this chapter.

The major shortcoming of Moynihan's theory for the cause of the single-female head of family is that he failed to state the structural conditions under which society can expect this form of behavior to exist. Unfortunately, his announcement became the framework for evaluating the cause of ethnic and racial inequality. This framework is so pervasive in the literature that it has impeded analysts' ability to develop a conceptual framework by which the cause of racial inequality found among groups can be objectively evaluated. Consequently, analysts are at a loss in stating the objective conditions under which one can expect a pattern of single-parent family structures to develop among groups. Let us now turn to constructing such a framework.

Social scientists can expect to find a pattern of matriarchal family structures, to hypothesize, under conditions where females are made economically independent of males. There are two instances where this condition can be found: the middle-class and lower-class. Let us turn to an examination of a historical analysis of the old structural conditions that have the white family structure together prior to Moynihan's study.

The Structural Conditions for Stable Middle-Class Family Structure

The causes for stable family structure that Moynihan found among whites can be traced back to the structural conditions in Europe before the beginning of the Industrial Revolution. Here, the family structure was resting on the premise of communal stability, which tied the family and the land together in a tenacious and unyielding knot.[21] Marriage in Europe during the whole of the eighteenth and nineteenth centuries rested on economic considerations. It was not a freedom of expression or a privilege resting on the premise of individual passion. Nor was it something that a boy and a girl could come together to make passionate deliberations about:

> matters of such importance could not be left to the whim of individuals; they rested instead in the hands of experienced, often of professionals, match-makers who could conduct negotiations with decorum and ceremony, who could guarantee the fitness of the contracting families and the comparable in rank of the individuals involved.[22]

Thus, the economics of land in a marriage contract was so important that very little, if any, consideration was given to individual passion. Land was the only productive good that gave individuals respect in European society.[23] Therefore, high consideration was given to the possible economic contribution that the girl could give to the preservation of the land. WHITE ↑

The marriage of the elder son, therefore, played a protagonistic role in determining the subsequent social status of the whole family. When the newly married bride came to live with her father-in-law, she had to bring with her a dowry that had to be commensurate to the family social status. This dowry, in many cases, was given to the brother of the elder son because the former could not, by law, inherit the land. The purpose of the dowry was to ensure him the same standard of living to which he was accustomed. In some instances, part of the dowry was given to the sister, in the hope that she might be able to marry someone compatible to, or higher than, her family social status. A large dowry increased the possibility of her marrying someone of a higher social status than her family.[24]

It was the obligation of the elder son, upon his father's retirement or death, to maintain the family status on the same social level as his father. To allow the family to slip from this level meant a social disgrace to the whole family because they would be kicked out of their social class.[25]

Therefore, the family became a functional economic unit of the village that revolved around the husband and wife. The vows that the boy and girl took during the marriage ceremony were clearly defined. The woman vowed to love and obey, and the man vowed to love and protect. Hence, the man was at the head of the household. He controlled all of the goods, made all of the critical decisions, and sometimes all of the routine ones. He was given full control of the property, which he could dispose of at his discretion, but he was bound to a moral compulsion to keep the land intact in honor of his father and for the future of his children. To lose the land meant loss of respect.[26] The woman's place was in the home, and her major concern was with the domestic affairs (i.e., making provisions for food, clothing).

Common-law marriage during the whole of the eighteenth century and part of the nineteenth century was practically absent from the European experience. The reason for such absence was not a matter of moral conduct, but economic. A couple came together through the process of matrimony and stayed together until "death do us part." Divorce and having children out of wedlock were constrained by the structural conditions of the village. For a girl to get a divorce or to have children out of wedlock would place a burden upon the state.[27] As the land became scarce and indivisible, many young men postponed marriage until a piece of land became available or refrained from getting married altogether because the land was the bond that held the family together.[28] Without land, there was no means to support a family.

When the European peasants began to immigrate to America, the concept of the whole family working together as a unit had been internalized into their value system.[29] The woman's role in the home was defined as raising children and concerning herself with domestic affairs. The long-term political and economic implication of this practice is that it reduced many of the middle-class white women to becoming totally economically dependent upon the white males for their livelihood. The more the males were able to raise their standards of living, the more defined the white woman's role was in the home. The social significance here is that, if a man could provide for his family without his wife having to work, it not only symbolized success in the eyes of his neighbors, but also represented an assertion of his manhood.

Another practice that helped reduce the white woman to becoming totally dependent upon the male economically was the concept of "white womanhood." This concept can be traced to the Old South where southern whites used it as a psychological justification for the cruel and the inhuman treatment of more than six million African Americans.[30] As the time progressed, the concept of the white woman was eventually internalized into the American value system in which the white woman accepted her sterile role that her husband insisted that she play. As a consequence, "she became a doll, ornament, like a beautiful painting on a wall that is admired and given lip service by everyone but which is actually loved by no one."[31]

The practice of defining the middle-class white woman's role in the home was not separate from the economic system. Before the Civil Rights movement of the 1960s, there were very few jobs in the labor market which the middle-class white woman could hold that paid a salary large enough to support a single-parent family. The only types of jobs that were available to women were relegated to the moderate- and lower-class white females in the capacity of a secretary, nurse, school teacher, and a few other related jobs that could closely be associated with femininity.

The majority of these jobs, except for nursing and school teaching, did not pay a large enough salary for a single-female-headed family to live in middle-class neighborhoods. The housing market there was designed to discourage single family living. Unlike the lower-class African American female, a middle-class white female could not survive on welfare in a middle-class neighborhood before the 1970s. Nor could she move to a lower class neighborhood. The social pressure of the middle class precluded this possibility. This social pressure also had a determinative impact upon the number of females having children out of wedlock. If the single female wanted to exercise her freedom of expression to have a baby, the economic conditions in her environment prohibited it.

Another social pressure that contributed to the stability of the middle-class family structure was the expectation of the female. She was expected to go to college, not necessarily to get an education, but to find a husband. Once she landed the right guy, she could look forward to pursuing a career as housewife where she was expected to be a "good wife"–which included raising the children and taking care of domestic affairs.

It follows then that the bonds that had held the white family structure together until the mid 1960s were the structural arrangements in the middle-class white society. This stable family structure began to fall apart in the early part of the 1970s when the women's liberation movement began agitating for women's rights. One of the major political and economic repercussions that this movement had on the white family structure was that it removed the female's dependence on the male.

First, there was the no-fault divorce law that started in California: many other states followed suit. Before 1969, divorce laws were written in such a way to discourage males from seeking a divorce. In the typical divorce settlement, the woman was almost assured to be awarded all of the community property, custody of the children, child support, and alimony. After the no-fault divorce law was passed, the settlement in a divorce case was not certain. Some men began to turn the divorce laws into a two-edge sword effect. Instead of the judge awarding the woman custody of the children, some judges awarded the children to the father and forced females to pay child support and alimony. This practice encourages divorces among middle-class Americans.

The other factor that contributed to the weakening of the middle-class family was the anti-sex discrimination laws in housing, which were part of the Federal Fair Housing Act of 1968. This law made it easier for a single-parent head of household to rent an apartment in middle-class neighborhoods. Before this law was enacted, many landlords refused outright to rent apartments to middle-class white females with children. The reason for this practice was two-fold. First, it was hard for a single woman to pay her rent on time. Second, if a woman got behind in her rent, it was hard for landlords to evict her. Landlords found it extremely hard to convince judges to issue an eviction order against a white single mother. A single mother could live in an apartment any where from six months to a year without paying rent. Hence, the inability to rent an apartment discouraged middle- and lower-class females from seeking a divorce.

In short, the stable family structure among whites remained constant until the 1970s. This stability was not resting on moral sentiments but structural and economic arrangements. The women's liberation movement altered these ar-rangements whereby a white female can support a family without being eco-nomically dependent on the white male. Consequently, the white family struc-ture that Moynihan had asserted was maintaining its stability based on moral principles, began to crumble in the 1970s. This crumbling was a repercussion of the various anti-sex laws passed during this period, which inevitably made the female economically independent of the male. Now, let us turn to a histori-cal analysis of those conditions that promote family instability among lower class populations in general and African Americans in particular.

Lower-Class and Single-Parent Family Structures

A comparative historical analysis of four ethnic and racial groups in America will help us to isolate and identify the independent variable that causes single-parent family structures. Here, we are going to compare the experiences of African Americans, Jews, Puerto Ricans, and Italians. These groups–except for African Americans–had a reputation for strong family structures before mi-grating to America.

The pattern of single-female head of families that Moynihan found among African American was a function of the structural conditions that the national government has historically failed to adopt positive measures to safeguard their rights to acquire and possess property. Consequently, this population, at vari-ous times in history, has been forced into a natural state of war whereby they were forced to do whatever they saw fit to preserve their nature. Developing a pattern of single-parent families was just one of the responses to their condi-tions. A historical analysis of those public policies that contributed to the de-velopment of single-female head of the African American family lend cre-dence to this argument. These policies were (1) the Black Codes, (2) the practice of emasculating the African American males during and after slavery, (3) the strategies the African American families adopted to protect their daughters, (4) discrimination in housing, and (5) the "man-in-the–house" rule.

The Impact of the Black Codes on the Family Structure

As we have seen in the previous chapter, the Black Codes were designed to keep African Americans tied to the soil after Reconstruction. These codes had a determinative impact in maintaining a pattern of family instability. By restricting African Americans to predominantly unskilled and common labor jobs, it prevented them from establishing an economic foundation on which to build a stable family. Economic security gave the free African American families their institutional character during slavery.[32] There were large numbers of free African Americans who lived outside of the plantation. They were able to establish a stable family structure because of the economic security they gained through the ownership of land:

> The progressive stabilization of Negro family life continued throughout the nineteenth century and during the first decade of the twentieth. This process was associated with a gradual increase in home and land ownership and has involved the intermarriage of the stable elements among the descendants of free Negroes with the two more ambitious and successful freedmen with a background of slavery.[33]

There are, however, other forces which can be attributed to the development of a stable family among African Americans after emancipation; however, they did not have as a great impact as those that had the right to acquire and possess property.

Emasculating the African American Male

The origin of the African American single-parent family structure can be traced to the institution of slavery, which stripped the African American man of his fatherhood and destroyed the patriarchal family structure that they had developed in Africa. E. Franklin Frazier describes the African family structure in the following manner:

His wife and children gathered around him, and served him with as much
respect as the best drilled domestic serve their masters; and if it was a fete day
or Sunday, his sons-in-law and daughters did not fail to be present, and bring
him some small gifts. They formed a circle about him, and conversed with him
while he was eating. When he had finished, his pipe was brought to him, and
then he bade them to eat. They paid him their reverences, and passed into
another room, where they all ate together with their mother.[34]

The African Americans' patriarchal family structure as it was known in Africa had to be destroyed in America in order to institutionalize slavery. Slave
masters found it increasingly hard to control the slaves socially with resem-
blance of a patriarchal family structure. Secondly, since African Americans
were considered to be commodities, any effort to establish a stable family structure among the slaves would have been detrimental to the economic interest of
slave owners. Therefore, for these reasons:

only the mother-child bond continually resisted the disruptive effect of the economic interests that dictated the sale of fathers away from their families. Not
only did the practice of selling away fathers leave the mother as the prime authority in the household but whenever the black male was present, he was not
allowed to play the norm masculine role in the American culture.[35]

The African American woman's role was more important on the plantation
than the male's, for she formed the direct linkages between the African American family and the slave master. All of the food and clothing were issued to the
slave woman. The male, unless he was a house slave, was not allowed to go
near the big white house during slavery. He was, for all practical purposes, a
defenseless and emasculated man who could not protect his wife from being
violated by the slave masters.[36]

Strategies for Protecting the Daughter

Raping African American women during and after slavery was a common
thing for the white man. Although emancipation destroyed the institution of
slavery, it did not destroy the white man's "animalistic attraction"of African
American women.[37] In order to continue the practice of raping the African
American woman without interference, it was necessary for the white man to
continue emasculating the African American man. Too often, a beautiful and
attractive African American daughter of a sharecropper was always susceptible

to being raped by plantation owners. When the daughter reached the age of thirteen or fourteen, the plantation owner would demand that she come to the big house to help "Mrs. Ann," his wife, in the kitchen. For a single African American girl to work in a white man's kitchen was synonymous with being his mistress.[38] Since African Americans were stripped of their property rights, they had no legal recourse, because the white's word was the law of the land as far as African Americans were concerned.[39] African American families responded to these conditions by developing an internal mechanism to protect their daughters.

The most common practice adopted to protect the daughter from being raped by whites was to keep her out of the labor market as long as possible. The lower-class African American families adopted the practice of encouraging their daughters to get married at an early age.[40] The inevitable consequence of this practice was that it set a pattern of early marriage which had the propensity for a high fertility rate among the lower class African Americans. Studies have shown that this pattern of early marriage is still widely practiced among low-class African American families that live in the non-South.[41]

The middle-class African American families developed a pattern of keeping their daughters in school as long as possible, even at the expense of their sons. Whenever a family was confronted with the decision as to whether to send the daughter or the son to college, they would almost always send the daughter.[42] Furthermore, before the late 1960s, the African American male was discriminated against so pervasively in the labor market, that the African American woman could not depend on him for her livelihood—as the white woman could the white male. Therefore, the only reliable security that the middle-class African American family had for their daughter was to train her to become self-supporting. As a result, African Americans developed a pattern of producing more educated females than males. Moynihan and other scholars have taken this as evidence that African American females "are better students than their male counterparts."[43]

The use of education as an independent variable in evaluating family structure is simply a reenforcement of the long-adopted policy to emasculate the African American male. As demonstrated in Chapter 7, educational attainment is prescribed by those occupational categories in which groups are concentrated. For example, Protestant females, except for the English, have educational attainments higher than their male counterparts.[44] Each one of these groups has more than 18 percent of it females employed in the professional categories—which prescribes a high level of education.[45]

The low educational attainment among African American males is closely associated with their low percentage of representation in those occupational categories that prescribe a high level of education. Before the adoption of affirmative action policy in the early 1970s, the African American males found that their education was of little value in climbing up the economic ladder. They have too often gone to college just to find that they could only get jobs as waiters, porters, and janitors.[46] As a consequence, the African American family developed a pattern of placing a lower premium upon their son's performance in school than their daughter's. The daughter was encouraged to stay in school, while the son was encouraged to drop out and get a job to help the family financially.

Thus, if the African American son dropped out of school and entered the labor market, he was only subjected to the exploitation of the economic system. But if the daughter dropped out, she was subjected to both the exploitation of the economic system and rape by the white man, if she lived on the farm, or forced into prostitution, if she lived in the cities. The latter two were the greatest concerns of the African American family from emancipation up to the adoption of affirmative action.

Protecting the African American female from being raped was one of the major concerns that John Howard Griffin found among African American families when he toured the South in the 1960s, posing as an African American man. He found that the African American woman was still involuntarily subjected to the white man's lust as she was during slavery. In his book, *Black Like Me*, he reported a conversation that he had with his white employer:

> He told me how all of the white men in the region crave colored girls. He said he hired a lot of them both for housework and in his business. "And I guarantee you, I've had it in every one of them before they ever get on the payroll"
> "Surely some refuse," I suggested cautiously.
>   "Not if they want to eat–or feed their kids," he snorted.
> "If they don't put out, they don't get the job."[47]

This practice over generations had long-term political and sociological implications for the African American family. Parents began to respond to these structural conditions not as individuals but collectively as a subsystem. They developed behavioral patterns that were contradictory to the American value system. The latter prescribe the male to be the one to go to college because he was supposed to be the breadwinner in society. But the African American families did the opposite. Instead of sending the male to college, the family would send the female. This contradiction in values served to perpetuate the single-parent family structure and low economic status among African Americans.

When the Big Black Migration began during World War I, it appeared to offer the African American family another means of protection for their daughter. If she did not get married and the family was unable to send her to college, they would send her North to live with some relatives as soon as she reached the age of sixteen or seventeen, sometimes earlier.

However, the white man's lust for the African American woman was not confined to the South, but it was also pervasive in the North. Therefore, sending their daughters from the South to the North gave African American families an apparent increased sense of protection for their daughter. For they only extricated her from the mouths of the tigers to place her in the mouths of the lions. She was still confronted with the sexual myths. Calvin C. Hernton noted in 1965 that:

> To some degree, however microscopic, all white men in America, save a few, carry in their perception of Negro females a dark sexual urge that borders on the vulgar. The lewd concept of Negro sexhood is not exclusively a personal attitude. It is a part of the American ideology towards Negroes in general. Few whites, no matter how liberal or unprejudiced they may be, can escape it.[48]

Thus, when African Americans migrated from the South, they were not able to break the pattern of pushing the daughter ahead at the expense of the son. For the middle-class African American family, the end result meant an increase in the number of educated females as opposed to the males. This practice can explain in part the recent study that indicates a decline in the number of African American male students enrolling in college while the females showing a slight increase.

On the other hand, the African American lower-class families behaved differently than the middle class. The methods that they developed to protect their daughters resulted in developing a pattern of having children out of wedlock. The typical family too often condoned their daughter in this instance instead of condemning her. The reason being that in many of the urban areas the daughter could easily get on welfare and receive the economic security that she could not receive otherwise. Getting on welfare reduces her chances of being forced into prostitution—one of the African American families' major concerns.

Discrimination in Housing

The ownership of property, it must be noted, is the cement that holds a family together. Therefore, in conducting a historical analysis of a group's family structure, the role of the government in assisting groups to obtain decent housing should always be the basic unit of analysis. As discussed in Chapter 9, the Jews were exploited by slum landlords up to the 1950s. This exploitation was made possible because of the housing shortage created and maintained by the trickle-down theory. In some instances, a Jewish family of eight was crowded into three rooms "without a bathroom and sharing the toilet with three neighbors."[49] To worsen their living conditions, rent was sometimes raised every month. Coupled with this raise in rent was the charging of an additional fifty cents per child. Under these conditions, the Jews felt that they "lived and worked for the landlords."[50] Although the Jews staged numerous rent strikes, they did not get any formal release from rent exploitation until the implementation of FHA in the 1950s. This law increased the amount available housing, which in turn broadened their choice possibilities for housing.

Although the Jews were exploited by slum landlords, this exploitation did not have a detrimental impact on their family structure, so far as producing single-female head of families. In fact, it contributed to their family stability, because it reduced the female's choice possibilities for housing. It was not until the implementation of the housing and anti-sex discrimination laws in the 1970s that housing started to have a detrimental impact upon the Jewish family structure; it broadened the Jewish female choice possibilities for obtaining housing independent of a spouse.

But FHA had the opposite effect upon the African American family struc-ture. Instead of broadening opportunities for them, it foreclosed their freedom to take advantage of this bonanza giveaway by law. It explicitly excluded them from participating in this program. As discussed in Chapter 9, the federal gov-ernment adopted a policy of racial exclusion. The following provision was written into the law:

> racial homogeneity was essential to a neighborhood financial stability. It there-fore placed higher valuations on property in neighborhoods that were white than in those that were mixed. This policy served as a powerful inducement to segregation.[51]

The political significance of this policy is that it was designed to aid white families in realizing their goals in becoming homeowners, and at the same time, discouraging African American families from realizing the same goal. Under FHA racial policy, whites could move into a new home with no down payment. On the other hand, African Americans were restricted to buying the old home vacated by whites at an interest rate as high as 10 percent or more.[52]

Economically, this discriminatory practice significantly reduced African Americans' purchasing power. Their income was significantly less than that of whites, but they had to pay more of their income for housing. As we have seen in the previous chapter, the same house that whites moved into with no down payment in the 1950s had increased in value to approximately $166,000 in the later part of the 1960s. Here, the federal government was subsidizing the stability of the white family structure while at the same time promoting instability of the same for African Americans.

The close correlations between governmental policy on housing and family instability cannot be overemphasized. It is the key to understanding the differences in African American cultural values and mainstream America. The American basic cultural values such as accumulation of property, individual responsibility, being work-oriented, delaying present gratifications for future ones, the Protestant work ethic, education, and so on, all depend on the individual family having the freedom to purchase a decent home. Without a home, a group's ability to internalize these values will become a remote possibility. With a home, a family is able to take the growing child through a process of learning individual responsibility, for example, assigning the son chores around the house such as keeping the lawn mowed and clean, taking out the garbage. The female's chores usually consist of helping her mother do domestic work in the house. These choices represent the beginning of a process to instill into the growing child a sense of personal responsibility.

Throughout the children's growing life, they learn from their parents responsive behavioral patterns. They soon learn that the destruction of household goods is a "no-no," and when an item is accidentally broken, their parents are going to convey to them a message that the broken item is going to cost money to get fixed or replaced. Repetition of this practice over the years instills into the growing child a sense of personal responsibility. But if the parents are renters, their expression of disapproval of a broken item does not have the same intensity.

The value of personal responsibility that the growing child learns at home is carried over to adulthood, where he/she becomes a responsive and productive citizen in society–and not a part of the penal system. Acquiring this value depends largely upon the parents' freedom to purchase a decent home. When the government assists the family in achieving this goal, it is inadvertently helping the family to impose upon the growing child a sense of personal responsibility. This is precisely what the federal government has been doing for white families since the passage of the Federal Housing Act of 1949. On the other hand, it has refused to do the same for African Americans. The Federal Fair Housing Act of 1968 prohibits racial discrimination in housing; however, it was not enough to eliminate the practice of discrimination in housing for African Americans, as we have seen in the previous chapter.

Man-in-the-House Rule

Perhaps, the most important factor that promoted family instability among lower class African American was the provisions of the Aid For Dependent Children Act (AFDC) of 1935. This act was originally designed to provide assistance for widows and orphans. The provision of this act that significantly affected the African American family was the "man-in-the-house" rule. In essence, this rule stated that as long as a man was in the house, the mother and her children could not receive welfare assistance. The African American man traditionally has held a precarious position in the labor market. Traditionally, he has been the last hired during periods of prosperity and the first fired during periods of austerity. When fired during the latter period, he had no means by which he could provide the bare necessities for his family (i.e., food, clothing, and shelter). Unemployed with no means of subsistence, the only alternative left open is to seek welfare assistance. He could not seek welfare assistance because of the "man-in-the-house"rule. Many African American families responded to this rule by having the man hide out whenever the welfare agent visited their home. But welfare agencies in many cities became aware of this practice and began staking agents outside the recipients' homes in the middle of the night to ascertain whether a man was actually living in the house. If a man was found living in the home, the family was taken off the welfare roll, regardless whether the man was working or not.

The African American male, therefore, was left with two alternatives: allow his family to starve because of a moral compulsion to keep the family together, or leave the house so that his wife and children could receive welfare assistance. Out of humanitarian reasons, he would opt to take the latter alternative. Abandoning the family was not strictly an African American phenomenon. White males did the same, but data of this type of behavior among whites are very seldom collected.

Spying on welfare recipients forced the lower-class African American family to adapt new behavioral patterns to survive in the urban environment. Welfare, in effect, made the lower-class African American woman economically independent of the African American male. When it became evident to the wife that her husband could not find a job, she would push him out of the house in order to qualify for welfare assistance for herself and her children. This practice continued until 1968 when the United States Supreme Court struck down this rule, which applied to eighteen states.[53]

There were, however, some states that did not have the "man-in-the-house" rule. Instead, they had a policy which discouraged the male from working after his family started receiving aid:

> If a father of a family who was on welfare got a job, most of what he earned was deducted from his family welfare payments. In effect, he may have been taxed up to 100 percent of his family earnings. So he faced a hard choice: Quit his job or abandon his family?[54]

In short, the pattern of the single-parent families that is found among African Americans was caused by the various governmental policies, either *de facto* or *de jure*, that defined and limited their choice possibilities over generations. These conditions caused African Americans to adopt behavioral patterns that are inconsistent with middle-class Americans. These behavioral patterns could be expected to develop among any population that is forced into a natural state of war.

Social Disorganization Among the Jews, Italians, and Puerto Ricans

Regardless of the strength of a group's family structure when migrating to a highly developed capitalistic society, there are certain structural conditions that tend to promote social disorganization among them in their initial stage of contact. The Jews, Italians, and Puerto Ricans had a reputation for having a strong family structure before immigrating to America. Yet, the Jews and Puerto Ricans experienced a higher level of social disorganization than the Italians. An analysis of this group will shed some light on this disparity.

The Jews

The Jews achieved economic success in America at a much faster rate than other ethnic groups. Their success has been attributed to their strong family structure. Yet, at the peak of their immigration from Europe, their strong family structure was not able to prevent the high rate of prostitution found among them during the period of 1880 to 1901. They constituted the highest percentage of females convicted in disorderly houses and soliciting cases in the night court of New York during this period. Out of the 581 females convicted, the Jews constituted 225, or 38.7 percent of the total; followed by the French, 154 or 26.5 percent (see Table 23). In commenting on the immoral practice during this period, the Immigration Commission stated that it seems probable that the percentage of French women who practiced prostitution before arrival in this country is decidedly larger than the percentage of Hebrews who engaged in that business before coming. Apparently the ability of the Jewish procurers (madams) and pimps to seduce young girls into this type of life in this country was greater than that of the French, and perhaps on the whole more profitable than the plan of importing women who were already familiar with this life.[55]

Both the French and Jews had a reign of prostitution in Europe and in the United States during this period. They recruited young innocent girls from Europe by promising them wages four to ten times as much as they were receiving in Poland, Romania, and elsewhere. Both females and males recruited young, innocent girls for immoral purposes. "To the innocent girl the woman procurer offered one the inducement of work, and usually work of menial nature, though at higher pay than that to which the girl had been accustomed to at home."[56]

During the period studied in the Table 22, Jewish females were more vulnerable to be forced into prostitution than other groups. Because of the rent exploitation and low wages (50 cent or less a day), a single female found it extremely hard to survive without a close nuclear or extended family ties. Widows with children were the most vulnerable. This led the Jewish leaders to push for the passage of the various "white slavery laws." These laws prohibited the transporting of women across state lines for the purpose of prostitution.

The Italians

The Italians who immigrated to the United States during the same period as the Jews constituted twice as many immigrants as the Jews, but had an unusually lower proportion of prostitutes than the Jews. Out of the total convicted prostitutes during this period, the Italian females constituted only 31 prostitutes–5 percent of the total (see Table 22). It would appear on the surface that the Italians should have had a much higher rate of prostitution given the agrarian background from which they immigrated. This was one of the arguments that the social scientists made about the high rate of prostitution among the Irish during the 1830s. But among the Italian immigrants, there was a significantly higher proportion of males than female immigrants. For the North Italians, there were 78 percent males and 21 percent females. On the other hand, there were 78 percent males and 21.4 females from South Italy. With a shortage of

Table 22

The Number of Women Convicted for Prostitution in New York High Court During the Period 1870-1901 by Ethnic Groups

Ethnic Groups	1901	1900	1890-1899	1880-1889	1870-1879	Not Reported	Total
African, Negro	-	-	1	-	-	-	1
Canadian, French	-	-	-	-	-	-	1
Croatian	-	-	-	-	-	-	1
Danish	-	-	-	-	-	-	2
Dutch	1	-	-	-	-	-	2
English	2	1	3	3	-	1	19
Danish	-	-	-	-	-	-	1
Flemish	2	-	-	1	-	1	6
French	14	11	14	6	1	6	154
German	10	3	31	3	-	5	69
Hebrew	28	31	63	8	-	20	225
Irish	2	1	8	4	-	7	29
Italian, North	-	1	2	-	-	-	5
Italian, South	1	3	5	4	-	2	26
Magyar	-	1	1	-	-	-	9
Mexican	-	-	3	-	-	-	3
Polish	-	1	4	11	-	1	10
Scandinavian	-	-	2	-	-	-	9
Scotch	-	-	1	2	-	1	4
Slovak	-	-	-	-	-	-	1
Spanish	1	-	-	-	-	-	3
Swedish	-	-	-	-	-	-	1
Total	61	53	138	32	1	44	581

SOURCE: *Importation and Harboring of Women for Immoral Purposes*, 37:64.

Italian females, there were very few single females who had to enter the labor market and be subjected to sexual and economic exploitation as were African American females. Furthermore, the Italians were sensitive to the latter type of exploitation, and they developed a pattern of keeping their females out of the labor market whenever possible, because the men felt that the women could easily be lured into vices.[57] The figures in the 1970 U.S. Census seem to lend credence to this claim. The Italian females have the lowest percentage (9.7 percent) among the white ethnic groups among this cohort pursuing an occupation in the professional category. I am assuming here that an occupation in this category is indicative of a female desire to become a career woman because this category has a high statistical relationship in determining high income.

The Puerto Ricans and Disorganization

One of the major advantages of looking at the Puerto Ricans' experience is that it allows us to examine the impact that race and religion play in a group's stability. The Puerto Ricans are predominantly Catholics. The ethos of this religion condemns divorces, yet, marriages were not able to withstand the stresses and strains placed on the Puerto Ricans as a result of their being forced into the natural state of war when they migrated to urban America.

On the island, the Puerto Ricans had developed extremely strong family bonds. Their family structure was fashioned in the Spanish tradition in which the primary family was redefined to cover all those who were living in the same house: "not only the father, mother, children, but also aunts and uncles, cousins and grandparents, nieces and nephews."[58] They did not restrict the definition of the primary family to those who were related by blood as typical of Western Europe. For the Puerto Ricans, all those who were living under the same roof were considered members of the nuclear family.[59]

One of the major reasons why the Puerto Ricans made the extension of the nuclear family structure was because of the unusual and extraordinary degree of loyalty they displayed toward their children. In Puerto Rico, it is commonly said that "there is a large number of orphans but there are no orphanages."[60] Again, the same claim was made about the Jews in Europe during the nineteenth century (i.e., "the Jews had no beggars").[61] What is at play here is that both groups had developed internal institutions to take care of their orphans and the needy.

Statistically, in 1946, the illegitimate rate in Puerto Rico was significantly higher than the mainland. But a close examination of this illegitimate rate will reveal that a large percentage of this rate is accounted for by the census tabulating all those children who were born out of consensual marriages to a large extent. According to the 1946 census, consensual marriages accounted for 50 percent of the non-skilled workers and 25 percent of the skilled workers.[62] The primary cause of the high rate of consensual marriage practice was not a product of immorality on the part of the Puerto Ricans but economic and social conditions of the island.

Economically, the cost involved in getting married in the church, and any other type of legal marriage, was out of the reach of many people who lived in the rural communities of Puerto Rico:

> Especially in an isolated rural community, a church marriage is very expensive, since it involves a marriage fee, a trip into town, a ceremony which requires at least a bridal gown in white–the symbol of the virgin–as well as the costly incidentals which usually accompanied celebrations in Spanish countries. It is less trouble for many people simply to live together, and common-law marriage may be as stable as legal ones.[63]

The high rate of illegitimacy which was found in Puerto Rico in 1949 was not indicative of the degree of sexual freedom on the part of the females. Unlike the Puerto Rican males who were allowed a high degree of personal freedom, the girls were highly supervised, especially in upper- and middle-class families. In these families, the girls are protected by chaperons. They were not allowed to come in close contact with non-family men unless they were accompanied by a chaperon.

Within their culture, a girl was expected to maintain her virginity until she was married. If she lost it, she also lost her chances of getting married legally.[64] If the news of a girl losing her virginity was made public, the only type of marriage that she could hope to have in Puerto Rico was a consensual one.[65]

The concept of the girl's maintaining her virginity until marriage was also applied to consensual marriages. When a boy and a girl came together through a consensual marriage, the girl was supposed to behave in the same manner as if she had a legal one: "adultery on the part of a woman strongly disapproved of. A husband may be warned by his neighbors of his wife's misbehavior, and he was expected to do something about it."[66]

When the Puerto Ricans began to migrate to New York City, they transplanted the value of consensual marriage to the mainland. While in Puerto Rico there was pressure from society for the man to maintain the unit of a consensual marriage, the structural conditions in the mainland destroyed the fabric that held this marriage together. Increasingly, the Puerto Ricans found that a consensual marriage was more of a liability than an asset. The liability became apparent when the Puerto Ricans began to seek tangible welfare benefits in New York City.

Without proof of legal marriage, many low-income Puerto Ricans were denied access to low-income rental housing which was owned and operated by the city. Professionals took it upon themselves to deny low-income family welfare benefits simply because they did not have any proof of a legal marriage.[67] This rule precipitated a pattern of single-parent families among the Puerto Ricans. For example, a Puerto Rican woman commented that she would not hesitate to leave her husband "if necessary, to get an apartment in a city housing development for herself and her children."[68]

Seeking welfare assistance also added to the deterioration of the Puerto Rican family structure. The "man-in-the-house" rule which was responsible for the radical deterioration of the lower income African American families also played a dominant role in promoting family instability among the Puerto Ricans. If a Puerto Rican man could not have a job or could not earn enough money to provide for his family on his income, the structural arrangements in New York City encouraged the Puerto Rican woman, as it did the African American woman, to push him out of the house so that she and her children could receive welfare assistance.[69] In many cases, the man who felt a moral obligation to stay with his family which was receiving welfare, despite the fact that such living symbolized a loss of his manhood, would pretend to leave the house while actually "staying around but hiding out when the Welfare Department Inspector comes."[70]

Another factor that added to the deterioration of the Puerto Rican family structure was the fact that a female could find employment much easier than the male and, thereby, become economically independent of him.[71] It was a disgrace in the Puerto Rican culture for the woman to support a man. But the structural conditions in New York began to destroy these cultural values. In many cases, the female left her family with her husband in Puerto Rico and came to New York to seek employment. As was demonstrated in Chapter 5, the Puerto Rican females could find work much more easily in the garment factories in New York because of their skills in needlework.

The Catholic religion has been thought to play a dominant role in family stability. This argument has been made in reference to the stable family structure of European immigrants. A stable family has been noted among the Irish, Italians, and Poles. However, it has been hard to isolate Catholicism from economic security. Our examination of the Puerto Ricans seems to have overcome this obstacle, and it has been demonstrated that family stability is closely related to economic security (i.e., a set of bootstraps).

In summary, the thrust of this chapter was to marshal forward data from a historical and comparative nature to demonstrate that social disorganization is a function of the structural conditions in society. A group's social deviant behaviors are symptoms of its being forced into a natural state of war. In this state, social deviant behavior can be expected.

Notes

1.   For a discussion of this concept, see Robert Merton, *Social Theory and Social Structure: Toward the Codification of Theory and Research* (Glencoe, Ill., 1994), pp. 125-150.

2.   For a discussion of this cultural value, see John Hodge, et al., *The Cultural Bases for Racism and Group Oppression* (Berkeley: Two Rider Press, 1972); Winthrop Jordan, *White Over Black: Attitudes Toward The Negro, 1550-1812* (Chapel: University of North Carolina Press, 1968).

3.   Daniel P. Moynihan, *The Negro Family* (Washington, D.C.: The United States Department of Labor Policy Planning and Research, 1965), p. 5.

4.   Nathan Glazer, *Affirmative Discrimination* (New York: Basic Books, 1975); Shelby Steele, *The Content of Our Character: A New Vision of Race in America* (New York: HarperCollins Publishers, 1990); William Julius Wilson, *Declining Significance of Race* (Chicago: University of Chicago Press, 1978).

5.   Frederick J. E. Woodbridge, *Hobbes Sections* (New York: Charles Scribner's Sons, 1958), p. 258.

6.   *Two Treatises of Government*, Section 2.50.

7.   John Locke, *Two Treatises of Government*, Section, 2.222.

8.   See Chapter 1 for a definition of this term.

9.   Kate Claghorn, "The Foreign Immigrant in New York City," United States Industrial Commission, *Reports on Immigration*, 42 Vols., Washington, D.C.: Government Printing Office, 1901) 15: pp. 462–63.

10.   Claghorn, pp. 462-63.

11.   Ibid., p. 478.

12.   Oscar Lewis, *La Vida* (New York: Random House, 1965), pp. xii-xiii.

13.   Claghorn, p. 461.

14.   Ibid., p. 462

15.   Lawrence Guy Brown, *Immigration* (New York: Longmans, Green and Company, 1933), pp. 73–132.

16.   Handlin, *The Newcomers*, p. 12.

17.   See Table 42 in the Appendix A.

18.   Moynihan, p. 5.

19.   Ibid.

20.   Ibid., p. 3

21.   Handlin, *The Uprooted* (Boston: Little, Brown and Company, 1951), p. 12.

22.   Ibid., p. 13

23.   Ibid., p. 20.

24.   See William Thomas and Florian Znanieck, *Polish Peasant in Europe and America* (New York: Alfred A. Knopf, 1927), pp. 106–28.

25.   Handlin, *The Uprooted*, pp. 24–36.

26.   Ibid.

27. "The whole family structure rested on the premise of stability, on the assumption that there would be no radical change in the amount of available land, in the size of the population, or in the net of relationships that held the village together." Handlin, *The Uprooted*, p. 13.

28. Ibid.

29. Ernst, p. 66.

30. For a discussion of the concept of the "white womanhood" and the inhuman treatment of blacks, see W. J. Cash, *The Mind of the South* (New York: Vintage Books, 1960).

31. Calvin C. Hernton, *Sex and Racism in America* (New York: Grove Press, 1965), p. 18.

32. E. Franklin Frazier, "The Negro Family in America," in *On Race Relations*, ed. G. Franklin Edwards (Chicago: University of Chicago Press, 1968), p. 190.

33. Ibid., pp. 201–202.

34. Frazier, p. 7.

35. Robert Staples, "The Myth of the Black Matriarchy," in *Race Relations*, ed. Edgar G. Epps (Cambridge: Winthrop Publishers, 1973), p. 180.

36. See John W. Blassingame, *The Slave Community* (New York: Oxford University Press, 1972), pp. 88–89.

37. Hernton, p. 16.

38. This was a common practice in Alabama in the 1950s in Barbara County where the author grew up.

39. Allison Davis, Burleigh B. Gardener, Mary R. Gardener, *Deep South* (Chicago: (University of Chicago Press, 1965), p. 45.

40. See Thomas R. Pettigrew, *A Profile of the Negro American* (Princeton, N.J.: D. Van Nostran, 1964).

41. Whitney Young, *To Be Equal* (New York: McGraw-Hill, 1964), p. 25.

42. Young, p. 25.

43. Moynihan, p. 31.

44. See Tables 42 and 43 the Appendix.

45. See Table 37 in Appendix.

46. DuBois, Chapter. 12.

47. John Howard Griffin, *Black Like Me* (New York: Signet, 1963), p. 100.

48. Hernton, p. 95.

49. Janna Weissman Joselit, "The Landlord Czar Pre-World War I Tennant Activity," in Tanent Movement in New York City, ed., Ronald Lawson and Mark Naison (New Brunswick, NJ: Rutgers University Press, 1988).

50. Ibid.

51. William K. Tabb, *The Political Economy of the Black Ghetto* (New York: W. W. Norton and Company, 1970), p. 16.

52. See Moynihan's discussion of the AFDC program, pp. 12–14.Carmichael and Hamilton, p. 22. National Commission on Urban Problem, "The City as It Is and as It

Might Be," in *Urban Studies*, ed. Louis K. Loewenstein (New York: The Free Press, 1971), p. 83.

53. Numerous cases have arisen regarding welfare agents searching the homes of welfare recipients to ascertain whether a man was in the house. See for example, *Camra v. Municipal Court*, 387 U.S. 523 (1967), and *Wyman v. James*, 400 U.S. 309 (1971).

54. National Commission on Urban Problem, "The City as It Is and as It Might Be," in *Urban Studies*, ed. Louis K. Loewenstein (New York: The Free Press, 1971), p. 83.

55. Reports of the Immigration Commission, *Importation and Harboring Women for Immoral Purposes*, 42 vols. (Washington, 0.C.: Government Printing Office, 1911), 37:64-65.

56. Ibid., p. 66.

57. This was one of the major arguments that was made by Frank J. Cavaioli in his paper, "Comparative Elements, Italian-American," delivered at the Fourth Annual Conference on Minority Studies, April 28 to May 1, 1976.

58. See Table 40 in the Appendix.

59. Mills and Senior, p. 8.

60. Ibid., p. 95.

61. Clarence Senior, *Strangers and Neighbors* (New York: Columbia University Press, 1952), p.101.

62. Abrahams, p. 307.

63. Mills and Senior, p. 8.

64. Ibid., p. 10.

65. Elena Padilla, *Up from Puerto Rico* (New York: Columbia University Press, 1958), p. 190.

66. Ibid., pp. 190–194.

67. Ibid., p. 101.

68. Ibid.

69. Ibid.

70. Ibid.

71. Mills and Senior.

CHAPTER 11

Model Minorities: The Politics of Their Success

In the early 1980s, numerous articles concerning the relative success of Asian Americans started appearing in newspapers and magazines. Bob H. Suzuki, a Japanese sociologist, wrote that these articles were "proclaiming that Asians are 'Outwhiting the Whites,' explaining 'Why Asians Are Going to the Head of the Class,' and touting 'triumph of Asian Americans.'"[1] The negative stereotypes that America had traditionally used to characterize Asians had given way to the image of a population whose family income and educational attainment were moving, as it were, to the head of the American social class.

Social scientists–and commentators alike–started focusing on the Asians in wake of the national attention given the urban riots and unrest among African Americans. The cause of this unrest was white racism, so stated the Kerner Commission. The question that eventually simmered to the top was this: If Asian groups can succeed in America's competitive society, then why not African-Americans? Implied in this question is the racial inferiority argument that was advanced by Arthur Jensen in the latter part of the 1960s.

In the early 1980s, the racial inferiority argument was escalated. This escalation came at a time when the Reagan Administration made a decision to use the instrumentalities of the federal government to block the civil rights advancement of African Americans. Officials of his administration were quick to point out that racism was not the cause of African Americans' low socioeconomic status. Look at the Asians! Racism did not impede their success. We cannot see why African Americans could not do the same. Consequently, critics of affirmative action and civil rights started parading the Asians in the press as the "model minority." This group includes the Chinese, Japanese, Filipinos, Koreans, Vietnamese, Asian Indians, Hmong, Laotians, Cambodians, and Thais.

The fact that the Asian groups can move into African Americans' communities, revitalize them, and put afoot new and thriving businesses seems, on its face, to lend credence to the "deficit model."[2] But a close examination of these groups' experiences in America will reveal that their success is consistent with the conceptual framework developed in this study.

MP This chapter will be restricted to studying the "model minority" experiences in America and the various measures that the government undertook to incorporate them (i.e., to Americanize them) into the mainstream of society's income redistribution system. This study will be divided into two sections—the socioeconomic status of the Asian groups that migrated before 1974 and the Southeast Asian Refugees.

The Socioeconomic Status of
Asians Before 1975

Civil rights critics are correct in their argument that race by itself does not impede group success. Groups, to hypothesize, can overcome the effect of racial discrimination if they are granted the freedom to acquire and possess property. Therefore, it is the amount of human capital that groups bring with them coupled with the system of protection that the national government offers them in their initial stage of contact that will determine the differential rate in growth and development among groups. For the "model minority," their relative success can be attributed to the four following factors: (1) immigration laws, (2) the pair of boots that they bring with them, (3) the set of bootstraps that the American government issued them in their initial stage of contact (i.e., to Americanize them), and (4) their cooperative cultural value system).

Immigration Laws

Among the reasons listed previously, the immigration laws have had, perhaps, the greatest impact in determining the success of the Asians in America.[3] Acknowledging the impact that these laws have in determining groups' success in America cannot be overemphasized. They restrict analysts' mode analysis. Instead of starting out studying poor and poverty-stricken populations, the immigrant laws force analysts to start studying the characteristics of non-impoverished and well-to-do individuals. This principle applies to all immigrants, including the British West Indians and Africans as well. Although these groups are of the same race as African Americans, they are not found among the ranks of the poor and poverty-stricken. For example, recent studies have shown that the British West Indians demonstrate a great capacity for entrepreneurship as early as the 1920s.[4] On the other hand, African-Americans have had a less impressive record. The reasons for this differential behavior have been documented in Chapters 5, 6, and 8.

As was demonstrated in Chapter 5, the Chinese immigration to America was curtailed by the Chinese Exclusion Act of 1882. The reason was twofold. First, the labor demand created by the gold rush and the railroad in the nineteenth century had declined, and white Americans wanted to eliminate their competition with them. Second, because of their race, it was thought that they were unassimilable into the "melting pot."[5] These factors led Congress to enact laws to restriction their immigration for a ten-year period. This law was renewed several times up to 1924. In this year, Congress adopted a quota law on immigration for European countries, but it excluded all members of the yellow or Mongolian race–including the Japanese and Chinese. Consequently, the members of these groups that immigrated to America after this period were subjected the restrictions of the immigration laws (i.e., the exclusion of impoverished individuals).

It is worth noting here that, until 1882, the national government did little more than count the immigrant populations and attempted to regulate living conditions on ships.[6] From this period onward, it gradually began undertaking positive measures to limit the migration of the undesirables and poverty strickened individuals. For example, it adopted a policy to prevent the immigration of:

> paupers, polygamists, and victims of certain diseases . . . epileptics, prostitutes, professional beggars, anarchists, violent revolutionaries, and assassins were added to the list two year later. In 1907, tuberculars, imbeciles, and those with a record of moral turpitude were also banned.[7]

The Immigration Act of 1917 significantly reduced the illiteracy rate among immigrants. Before this law was enacted, this rate among some of the European immigrants was as high as 50 percent. This percentage began to decrease significantly after 1917; however, the figures never reached zero because of the provisions to allow individuals who are trying to escape political and religious persecution, as was the case with some of the Vietnamese immigrants. In contrast, the migration of African Americans from the South and the Puerto Ricans, was not affected by the immigration laws. The illiterate, impoverished, and unskilled were always allowed to migrate along with the skilled and literate individuals.

When the Asians started immigrating to America, on the other hand, their migration was restricted to the potentially upwardly mobile individuals. For example, when the Japanese started immigrating to America in significant numbers in 1891,[8] the federal government had already started regulating immigration. Their immigration continued throughout the first quarter of the present century. As we have seen, the reason for their immigration was not to avoid poverty or political persecution as many of the European immigrants did but to acquire human capital so that the Empire of Japan could be strong.[9] Therefore, at the offset, the Japanese immigration was characterized by a group of individuals who had a propensity for upward mobility.

Although the Chinese and Japanese experienced some form of racial discrimination, they were not subjected to the same systematic form of racial repression as African Americans, particularly the racial doctrines of *romantic racialism* and *Social Darwinism*. Both of these doctrines operated to place African Americans into a position of inferiority to whites both by law and by fact. The mere perception that a group is inferior to the dominant class is not enough in itself. Society has to undertake positive measures to repress this group by making facts conform with theory. Evidence to support this contention can be found in the various stereotypical images that the dominant class has formed toward these groups.

In examining the stereotypes of groups, it is necessary to keep in mind the various studies conducted on this subject before the New Deal Era, in which the national government became involved in redistributing wealth. The political significance of government involvement in the economy is that the various programs adopted during this period operated to assist groups to realize American goal values (i.e., income, safety, and deference).[10] These are the traditional values that analysts use to evaluate individual and groups' success in America. Whenever a group does not internalize these values, they are hated by the general public, according to Dennis R. Kinder and Donald O. Sears. They called this form of hatred *symbolic racism*.

They described symbolic racism as a sociocultural theory of prejudice "which emphasizes abstract, moralistic resentments of blacks, presumably traceable to preadult socialization."[11] Through the process of socialization, they maintained, "children and adolescents acquire prejudices along with other values and attitudes that are normative in their social environments."[12] The values that are germane to this study are the traditional American moral ones "embodied in the Protestant Ethic."[13]

Kinder and Sears argued that whites resent African Americans, not because of their race, but because they have violated "such traditional American values as individualism and self-reliance, the work ethic, obedience, and disci-

Table 23

Characteristics Most Commonly Used by 100 Princeton Students in 1952

Chinese		Japanese		Negroes	
Characteristic	Number of Respondents Agreeing	Characteristic	Number of Respondents Agreeing	Characteristics	Number of Respondents Agreeing
Superstitious	34	Intelligent	45	Superstitious	84
Sly	29	Industrious	43	Lazy	75
Conservative	29	Progressive	24	Happy-go-lucky	38
Tradition-loving	26	Shrewd	22	Ignorant	38
Loyal to family ties	22	Sly	20	Musical	26
Industrious	18	Quiet	19	Ostentatious	26
Meditative	18	Imitative	17	Very religious	24
Reserved	17	Alert	16	Stupid	22
Very religious	15	Suave	16	Physically dirty	17
Ignorant	15	Neat	16	Naive	14
Deceitful	14	Treacherous	13	Slovenly	13
Quiet	13	Aggressive	13	Unreliable	12

SOURCE: Stanley Lieberson, *A Piece of the Pie: Blacks and White Immigrants Since 1880* (Berkeley: University of California, 1980), 366, citing Daniel Katz and Kenneth W. Braly, "Verbal Stereotypes and Racial Prejudice." In *Readings in Social Psychology*, 2nd rev. ed., edited by Guy E. Swanson, Theodore M. Newcomb, and Eugene L. Hartley (New York: Henry Holt, 1952), pp. 67–73.

conform or get out

pline."[14] Whites believe that individuals should be rewarded based on whether they have internalized these values.

Evidence that African Americans were victims of symbolic racism can be found in a study conducted by Daniel Katz and Kenneth W. Braly as early as 1930. In an attempt to assess whites' attitudes toward African Americans, Chinese, and Japanese, Katz and Braly asked 100 undergraduates at Princeton University to characterize these groups. Table 23 contains the outcome of the survey.

The students did not evaluate African Americans as having any of America's favorable traditional values. Seventy-five percent of them thought that they were lazy, 38 percent thought they were ignorant, and 22 percent thought they were stupid. On the other hand, 43 percent of the students thought that the Japanese had internalized the work ethic (industrious), and 45 percent of them thought they were intelligent, in comparison to 22 percent who thought African Americans were stupid. For the Chinese, 18 percent thought they were industrious, and only 15 percent thought they were ignorant. Overall, the 100 undergraduates surveyed thought African Americans had lesser of the traditional values among this cohort.

The political significance of Katz and Braly's study in explaining the relative success of the "model minority" is that these groups were practically isolated from institutionalized repression in America. The individuals among these groups that would have depicted the negative characteristics attributed to African Americans in Table 23 were prevented from immigrating by law. Hence, the Asian ethnic groups were in a position to profit from many of the benefits that the government doled out during the period between 1930 and 1964 (i.e., a period before the enactment of the civil rights laws). Their liberty to take advantage of these benefits was not foreclosed by the tyranny of racism. On the other hand, African Americans' liberty to do the same was. These restrictions remained until the passage of the civil right laws in 1964 and afterward.

Asian v.s AA no conform

In order to be effective, racial repression must be institutionalized for at least two generations. Take, for example, the Japanese. When they were placed into the internment camps during World War II, they were stripped of their physical capital. Although this policy was discriminatory, it did not constitute systematic repression but temporary inconvenience. This is not an endorsement or justification for the injustice done to the Japanese, but to point out the differences between racial discrimination—which is sporadic and thus poses a temporary inconvenience to a group—and systematic racial repression—which forecloses a group's liberty to take advantage of a wide range of educational and economic opportunities that society has to offer. African Americans were a victim of the latter.

The Japanese were never stripped of their human capital, which, to recapitulate, is necessary for a group to be able to compete on an equal footing with their competitors and adversaries in a competitive society. For example, Table 33, in the Appendix, shows the income for the thirteen race and ethnic groups studied in this book. Their median income in 1950 was $2,245. The percentage of families with income above the median for this cohort was 19.7. The Japanese had 18.8 percent of their families with income above the median, a difference of -.9 below the average. However, the Japanese had far excelled this cohort in 1970 in terms of the number of families with income above the median: the cohort, 39.5 percent of the families with income above $10,000; Japanese, 73.6 percent. The Chinese were likewise, with 64.3 percent above the median income.

Education and the Process of Socialization:
A Comparison of the "Model Minority"
and African Americans

In studying the cause for the differences in group behavior, analysts have the tendency to wipe the slate clean and start their mode of analysis with groups' present-day experiences, as was pointed out in Chapter 1. Consequently, they ignore the influences that the economic, political, and social institutions have had in shaping their behavior. This is particularly true for education. Before making a scientific statement about a group's social behavior, an analyst must take care to examine such a statement within the framework of "socialization theories. These theories will allow us to examine the role that the government has placed in safeguarding these groups' right to acquire a quality education. Table 24 shows the differences in educational attainment among African-Americans, Chinese, and Japanese during the period between 1950 and 1970. For instance, during the period between 1950 and 1960, the national government played a minus role in allocating educational opportunities. In the 1960s, however, it became deeply involved.

Before government involvement, the Chinese showed a marked increase in their educational attainment during this period: increased from 8.4 percent in 1950 to 11.7 percent in 1960. The Japanese attainment remained constant. African-Americans, on the other hand, lagged far behind this cohort during this period: 6.6 percent in 1950, 8.3 percent in 1960, and 9.3 percent in 197 (see Table 24).

Table 24
Racial Groups' Educational Attainment, 1950, 1960, 1970

Groups	1950	1960	1970
African Americans	6.6	8.3	9.3
Chinese	8.4	11.7	12.7
Japanese	12.2	12.2	12.6

SOURCE: Tables 38, 39, and 40 in the Appendix.

In 1950, 9.1 percent of the Chinese males earned seven years or more education, compared to 7.7 percent for the Japanese, and 1.5 percent for African Americans. Both the Chinese and Japanese educational attainments in this category were higher than the average for the cohort in this study (see Table 38 in the Appendix).

In 1965, James Colemen offered further evidence that Chinese and Japanese freedom to take advantage of a wide range of educational opportunities was not repressed by the tyranny of racism. He found that the Asian students scored the highest among this cohort on the nonverbal tests in the first grade: Asians, 56 percent; whites, 54.1 percent; and African Americans, 43.4 percent. On the verbal test, Asians scored 51.6 percent, African Americans; 45.4 percent; and whites, 53.2 percent.

In the twelfth grade, the Asians scored 51.6 percent on the nonverbal test and 49.6 percent on the verbal. African Americans scored 40.9 percent, and whites scored 52.1.[15] In almost every category in which the students were tested, the Asian students' scores approximated those of whites. Their success can be partially attributed to the fact that educational opportunities have always been opened to them. African Americans, on the other hand, scored constantly lower than the Asians in every category. This can be attributed to the policy of racial repression (i.e., racial segregation solely for the purpose of education).

It is worth noting here that the Asian groups were never segregated for the purpose of education as was the case with African Americans. This is true regardless of whether they were attending K–12 schools or colleges and universities. For example, those Asian groups who lived in the South during the period of legal segregation were not forced to attend segregated schools, although they might have lived in an African American community. The government classified them as whites and treated them accordingly. They had access to the best education that society had to offer in the region in which they lived. The educational success of the Chinese and Japanese during this period is, within itself, evidence that the government did not adopt a policy of racial repression toward them. Let us now turn to a brief discussion of the education policy that America has historically adopted for African Americans.

Education and Repression of African Americans

Shortly after emancipation, America adopted a public policy of racial repression (i.e., *romantic racialism*, for the newly freed slaves). This policy of subordination was carried out by the various philanthropic foundations established by the northern capitalists whose interest in the South was not to promote racial equality but to eliminate racial conflicts so that they could invest in its development. As mentioned in Chapter 6, the first fund to be established to this end was the Peabody Fund, in 1867, by George Peabody. At the onset, the trustees of this fund made it clear that they were not interested in racial equality. For example, in 1971, it stipulated that "when white and colored teachers were receiving the same salaries, Negro schools should receive only two-thirds the allotment made to white schools."[16]

There were several funds established to support the African American education between the period of 1867 and 1917: some died and others survived.[17] Those that survived were the ones that supported a policy of racial repression. This repression, to repeat, was carried out with the aid of Booker T. Washington with his program of industrial education. Washington influenced philantrophists to channel their funds to those schools that emphasized industrial education instead of higher education. As a result, those schools that did not have industrial education as their primary objective soon died out.

The political significance of the policy of industrial education was that it defined the social status of African Americans from its inception until the passage of the 1964 Civil Rights Act. "The emphasis of this education was supposed to be on the 'heart and the hand' rather than the head because southern white people did not want the Negro's head to be educated."[18] The force to repress African Americans through education was very pronounced. For example, E. Franklin Frazier commented once that he was chastised by the Director of Academic Department at Tuskegee Institute for walking across campus with books under his arms. The director feared some white passing through the campus might get the impression that the institute had shifted its emphasis from training the African American student's heart and hand to developing his mind.[19]

There are many famous court cases that can be marshalled forward to further support the contention of institutionalized repression of African Americans, starting with the *Gaines* case to the famous *Brown* decision.[20] The impact on these cases has been discussed elsewhere, and there is no need to rehearse it here.[21] Suffice to say that a comparison of the educational attainment of the "model minority" and African Americans is a misnomer. The former group has always had the freedom to take advantage of a wide range of educational opportunities while the latter was restricted to segregated schools for the purpose of subordination and repression.

Model Minorities and Their Cooperative Value System

Since the 1960s, social scientists have been somewhat baffled in their attempt to offer a scientific explanation for the success of Asian-Americans in education. As mentioned in Chapter 5, Harry H. L Kitano attempted to describe the success of Japanese Americans as "white Anglo-Saxon Protestants" who were covered with a yellow skin.[22] He attributed their success to their ability to acculturate and to internalize America's cultural values and goals. But a close examination of their culture will reveal that their success in the field of education can be attributed more to their *cooperative value system* than their desire to acculturate American values.

Because this writer has long sought a scientific explanation for the high academic performance of Asian Americans, he asked his students in his cultural diversity classes to write term papers on their ethnic group's cultural value toward education. One general theme that he found among Asian students was the emphasis that they placed on their *cooperative value system*. They adhere to this system not because they want to impress white America but because each member of the groups evaluates himself in relation to his group rather than society. On any given campus, for example, in California, one can observe Asian students huddled together studying as a group: sharing and comparing notes.

One advantage the cooperative value system gives the Asian students is that it helps them to operationalize their course of study. Take, for example, a course in calculus. Through their cooperative value system, the Asian students collect as many syllabi and returned tests as they possibly can of professors who teach this course. Over several semesters, they are able to collect enough materials to be able to predict the questions that any given professor will give on an exam. The students learn very quickly that regardless of who is teaching this course, there are only so many questions that can be asked, for example, about the properties of a perfect square.

The practice of operationalizing professors' courses is widespread. For example, once the Asian students operationalize professor "X's" calculus course, they will encourage their classmates to take his class. The process is duplicated in other courses. Hence, by pairing students with instructors, the Asian students have been able to reduce the errors in their course of study, thus showing a remarkable rate of academic success.

It must be noted here that the practice of operationalizing a professor's course is not to be misconstrued as cheating. This practice is nothing new on American college and university campuses. The fraternities and sororities have been practicing this for years. For example, it is known fact that many of the traditional Greek organizations have kept copies of professors' old exams on file. The major difference between the Greek organizations' practice of cooperative studying that of Asians is that the latter group is able to practice it on a broader scale than the former. A student does not have to be initiated into his race; he is born into it. Whereas the Greek organizations require initiation before one can join.

Another advantage that the cooperative value system gives Asian students over their white counterparts is the practice of taking advantage of supplementary education. For example, in the early 1980s, the state of California started tightening its admission requirements for the University of California and the California State University systems. They raised the SAT score and increased the course requirements for admission. In order to prepare students for college admissions, many school districts started offering advanced placement courses in those subjects that the college and university systems required for admission. Asian students are heavily enrolled in these courses. In some schools, they constitute a majority of the students enrolled in these courses. This majority, it must be noted here, does not come at the expense of excluding other students. Their educational achievement is attributed not just to the fact that their parents place a higher value on education than the general population, but because their culture has come to perceive careers in math and the sciences to be more financially stable. These subjects, it most be noted, use a universal language. Therefore, it does not matter whether an Asian student is American or foreign born. Mastering these subjects will give the average student a competitive edge over his or her classmates.

Another reason for these students' success is that so many of their high school teachers counsel them to "go into math and sciences that many [Asian] students develop the fear that they may fail in other fields."[23] As one student noted, Asian students are "discouraged from going into creative fields like art and acting because" they are not "seen as free thinking or extroverted."[24] This complaint is just the opposite of the ones made by African American students; they are discouraged from taking courses in math and sciences.

Asian students also perform well on standardized tests. The practice they use to give themselves an edge over their counterparts in scoring well on standardized tests is to take special classes, or advanced classes during the summer. For example, a non-profit organization called Pegasus Program Inc., located in California, offers academic programs during the summer at various cites throughout California. They are designed "to enhance and supplement the public/private education of students."[25] Among the programs it offers is a five-week program called "Pegasus Project for the Academically Talented," (PPAT). This is a program which consists of "high level math, writing, physical and biological sciences, Latin, study skills, leadership, debates, Japanese, and engineering."[26] At the end of the five weeks, students are expected to be prepared to return to their schools in the "fall with strong independent learning and study habits necessary for high achievement and grade point average."[27]

In 1988, for example, Pegasus offered a PPAT program at the University of California at Irvine. This writer visited one of its classes and found that approximately 98 percent of the students taking the courses were Asians. This program is open to everyone who qualifies; however, it costs over $600 dollars per student. It is just that the Asian families value this program enough to pay the fees. The benefits that students receive for enrolling in supplementary education programs are skills to enhance their chances to improve their academic performances and to score high on standardized tests.

In short, stereotyping Asian ethnic groups as a "model minority" in respect to academic overachievers is no misnomer. The problem lies in the reason for their success. They succeed not because they have a great desire to internalize the American cultural values, but because of their cooperative value system that is peculiar to their culture. African Americans, on the other hand, have internalized the same value system as white America (i.e., individualism).

Bootstraps for Southeast Asian Refugees

There are many ways in which one can describe the bootstraps that the government offered the Southeast Asian refugees to assist them in getting adjusted to American polity in their initial stage of contact. But because they have been held up as the "model minority," a clear distinction between the bootstraps that the government offered them and the ones it offered African Americans during the same period is in order, (i.e., between 1970 and 1990).

The bootstraps that the government offered African Americans were sugarcoated with vinegar, while the ones offered Southeast Asians were sugarcoated with honey. As the saying goes: "One can catch more flies with one drop of honey than he could with a gallon of vinegar." A set of bootstraps sugarcoated with honey places a sweet taste into the mouths of employers. They consist of the various economic incentives that the federal government offers private agencies and state and local governments to participate in the refugee resettlement programs. The primary goal of these programs was twofold: (1) to get the refugees employed as soon as possible and (2) to promote economic self-sufficiency among them.

A set of bootstraps sugarcoated with vinegar, on the other hand, places a bitter taste into the mouths of employers. They consist of affirmative action laws that offer the apparent threat of penalties for employers who fail to comply with federal guidelines. To initiate such penalties, a lawsuit has to be filed either by private individuals or a government agency on behalf of a group. Either way, it is a long, drawn out process in which a plaintiff very seldom wins; whenever he does, his victory is usually realized over a period of five to ten years. In short, affirmative action offers few, if any, incentives for local governments and private employers to employ African Americans.

The distinction between the two sets of bootstraps is important in understanding the relative success of the Southeast Asians and the failure of African Americans during the time period between 1970 and 1980. The Asians' economic growth and development were nourished by both government actions and efforts by voluntary agencies (volags). On the other hand, African Americans' growth and development have been hamstrung by the federal government during the same period: first, by the United States Supreme Court in the *Bakke* decision, which significantly undermined affirmative action; secondly, by the Justice Department under both Presidents Reagan and Bush's Administrations. Let us now turn to an historical analysis of the bootstraps that the government has established for immigrants and refugees.

The Origin of Bootstraps for Refugees

The government has had a longstanding policy of offering refugees a set of bootstraps that are sugarcoated with honey in their initial stage of contact with the American polity. This policy was adopted during the colonial period, which was discussed in Chapter 2. However, the bulk of these services were sponsored by private groups on a voluntary basis up to World War II. Afterward, these private efforts were institutionalized (i.e., clothed with government subsidies and protections). The government adopted affirmative measures to assist refugees in getting adjusted to the American polity "within a 90 day period"[28] after making contact. These measures include the following:

> Displaced Persons Act of 1948, the Refugee Relief Act of 1953, the Refugee-Escapee Act of 1957, the Hungarian Refugee Program of 1957, the Refugee Fair Share Act of 1960, the Cuban Refugee Program, and the Indochinese Refugee Assistance Program."[29]

The refugee programs are highly structured. They are managed by the Bureau for Refugee Programs, which is housed in the State Department. The Bureau contracts with volags to participate in the cooperative agreement programs for the resettlement and placement of refugees. It manages the success of these programs through its request for proposals. Each volag is required to stipulate in its proposal specific steps as to how it plans to direct refugees "towards employment as quickly as possible"[30] and to promote self-sufficiency among them. Each volag must also demonstrate in its proposal its success record in this area. For example, in 1983, three volags submitted proposals to the Bureau for Refugee Programs to participate in the resettlement and placement programs: Iowa Refugee Service Center, Lutheran Council in the USA, and U.S. Catholic Conference. Among these volags, the Lutheran Council in USA has one of the most elaborate and successful programs in terms of resettling and replacing refugees. A brief discussion of its structure and operation will shed some light on the "model minority" success.

The Lutheran Council in USA has been assisting immigrants in getting adjusted to the American polity since the eighth century. The first program was started by Henry Muhlenberg, the German Benevolent Society of Pennsylvania. This society was a ministry of the Lutheran Church to assist new arrivals. Over the years, the church developed its ministry into a highly effective organization. It has participated in the resettling of immigrants from the eighth century to the present.

To carry out its function, the Lutheran Council established the Lutheran Immigration on Refugee Services (LIRS). This agency developed a three-tiered delivery system which operates on the local, regional, and national levels. The locals function as grass-root organizations. They are responsible for providing the "core services" for the resettlement and placement programs. Since 1975, LIRS has encouraged over 6,000 local congregations to sponsor refugees, "many of them repeatedly."[31] The sponsors assist refugees to assimilate "in the community and provide contacts for employment."[32]

During the ninety-day period in which the program lasts, friendships are developed among the sponsors and refugees which lasts much longer. The role that the sponsors play in assisting refugees in getting adjusted to the American polity cannot be overemphasized. They serve as mediators who mediate the complex between the private life of the refugees and the large, and sometimes alienating, social and economic institutions in a strange land. By intervening in their private lives, the sponsors serve as a link of trust between the refugees and these large institutions. They interpret the complexity of the institutional settings to the refugees on the one hand and their unique behavior to these institutions. In short, sponsors serve as mentors and role models for many of the refugees.

The second-tiered system of LIRS operates on the regional level. At this level, LIRS has "Regional Consultants and their resettlement staff workers" that are "employed by Lutheran social service agencies."[33] The role of the Regional Consultants is to ensure that "all core services mandated by LIRS' cooperative agreement with the Department of State are provided, and in an effective and efficient way. In so doing, the Regional Consultants also provide a variety of support services to the local sponsor."[34] The Regional Consultants also assist the local sponsors by coordinating and "holding consultative meetings with local and state government officials and resettlement forums."[35]

The third-tiered system of LIRS operates on the national level. The primary role of this system is program management. It oversees the regional and local management. This includes:

> ensuring appropriate local sponsorship; coordinating reception services at ports of entry and final destination; seeing that tracking and monitoring requirements are met; providing technical assistance in such areas as job development, English as a second language tutor training and administration of volunteer networks; collecting travel loans issued by the Intergovernmental Committee on Migration (ICM); providing situation-specific grants or loans to refugees; and in general, helping the local sponsor extend resources as far as possible.[36]

The political significance of the LIRS three-tiered system is that it is permanently located in the Lutheran Church governmental structure. Members of the local congregations participate in the program, not so much because of a mandate by the federal government, but because they look upon such an endeavor as part of their Christian duty. More importantly, members of this congregation are employed in private corporations and governmental institutions on the local, regional, and national level. By operation, many of them are in decisionmaking positions where they can easily influence their employers to participate in the refugee resettlement program by providing jobs and other services.

Funds for Refugee Programs

Although volags' participation in the refugee programs is voluntary, their services are not free. The federal government awards them a "fixed per capita grant of $525 for non-European refugees and $365 for European refugees"[37] (i.e., bootstraps sugarcoated with honey). In addition, the federal government provides separate funds for other programs such as:

> 1) the state/local share of AFDC, Medicaid, SSI and General Assistance during a refugee's first 36 months, and administrative costs associated with these programs; 2) preventive health programs, at a 40 % increase; and 3) the voluntary agency matching grant programs.[38]

The per capita grant was designed to allow states wide flexibility in helping refugees to achieve self-sufficiency in a short period of time. The typical federal guidelines that place restrictions on domestic programs were relaxed. In testifying before the Subcommittee on Immigration and Refugee Policy, James N. Purcell, stated:

> [s]tates will be able to take initiative uninhibited by the standardization problems involved in nation-wide rulemaking. My office and the Office of Refugee Resettlement are firmly committed to working with the States to help the states to succeed.[39]

Volags' Success in Job Placements

Volags have been very effective in placing refugees in employment within the ninety-day period mandated by law. Studies have shown that refugees are more successful in finding jobs through informal networks and volags than they do through the formal job services.[40] For example, the institute for social research (IRS) found that:

half of the sample of recent Southeast Asian arrivals had found their employment through personal contacts (friends, relatives or own activities) and another 14 percent through American sponsors and local churches; only 29 percent attributed job placements to formal employment services and resettlement agencies.[41]

The political variable that can best account for the refugees' early employment, as it seems, are the incentives that the government offers private businesses to hire refugees.[42] Incentives come in various forms. For example, businesses are given tax credit for employing refugees and funds for training them. These methods depart markedly from the way in which the government has traditionally treated African Americans.

Employment Rate for the Refugees

The rate of employment for the refugees is impressionistic. Under the Refugee Act, a refugee is required to actively seek work, and once found, must accept it. This policy resulted in over "55 percent of the overall Southeast Asian refugees over the age of 16" being "employed or actively seeking work" within a ninety-day period.[43]

The employment rate of the refugees seems to be stable. They are not victims of the "revolving-door phenomenon" as is the case with African Americans. The latter group has long complained that they have been the last hired and the first fired. Studies have shown that refugees' employment rate stabilizes within a six-month period and gradually increases over the years. For example, the employment rate of the 1975 refugees was higher than the rate for the overall population: Southeast Asian refugees, 76 percent; the general population, 64 percent. Four years later, the refugees' employment was 76 percent, while the general population was 64.5 percent (see Table 25).

The type of employment that the refuges are engaged in is not as important as the fact that they are employed immediately upon their contact with the American polity. Employment connects them to the mainstream of the society income redistribution system, which is, to recapitulate, indispensable for individuals within a group to be able to take advantage of the many opportunities that society has to offer.

Furthermore, embedded in this system are fringe benefits that help these groups from succumbing to the culture of poverty. A study by ISR found that over 75 percent of the refugees employed full-time had jobs that paid benefits such as paid vacation, medical and dental insurance, and retirement pensions.[44]

Table 25
Employment Status of Southeast Asian Refugees: 1981 to 1984

Year of	Labor Force Participation				Unemployment			
	1981	1982	1983	1984	1981	1982	1983	1984
1984	—	—	—	30.0	—	—	—	41.0
1983	—	—	20.7	41.6	—	—	65.0	35.6
1982	—	25.2	40.9	45.4	—	62.5	30.4	12.5
1981	22.8	41.5	46.5	51.4	45.2	40.7	16.8	16.4
1980	52.8	51.3	55.3	54.5	27.1	32.1	21.1	11.6
1979	49.2	60.2	60.5	60.1	8.1	19.3	17.6	9.8
1978	48.8	67.6	68.2	66.2	5.0	19.0	19.7	2.6
196-7	70.7	74.3	79.5	76.1	3.5	2.4	17.2	4.6
1975	76.0	72.1	69.7	67.6	6.4	12.9	12.1	6.3
U.S. Rates*	64.0	64.1	64.1	64.6	7.5	9.9	8.4	7.0

SOURCE: Susan S. Forbes, "Adaptation and Integration of Recent Refugees to the United States."
*October unadjusted figures from the Bureau of Labor Statistics. Department of Labor.
**Proportion of original sample of 2,700 successfully located and interviewed, by year of entry. The total number interviewed, 1,244.

Bootstraps in the Area of Job Training

The high rate of employment found among the Southeast Asian refugees can be attributed not to the fact that they found these jobs by looking in the wanted ads–as the critics of civil rights suggested to African Americans–but to the positive steps that the government undertook to incorporate them into various federally funded job training programs.

There are several job training programs that the government sponsored over the last sixty years that operated to incorporate groups into the mainstream. In each program, it has taken positive steps to include immigrants and refugees into these programs, but flatly refused to do the same for African Americans. As demonstrated in Chapter 8, African Americans were purposefully excluded from the National Apprenticeship Program solely because of their race. These programs were the centerpiece for incorporating young men into skilled occupations. Jobs, it must be noted, not only defend individuals' social status in society but also their self-worth. A policy that operates to deny members of a group the liberty to compete for skilled occupations because of their race is also a policy that promotes the false perception of racial inferiority of that group.

The next program adopted was the Manpower Development and Training Act of 1962. This act provided "classrooms and on-the-job training for persons with an established work history who had lost their job through no fault of their own."[45] African Americans were not included in this program. Their freedom to participate was foreclosed by "the job ceiling policy" that America had adopted toward them.[46]

The third program adopted was the Economic Opportunity Act of 1964. This program was not restricted exclusively to skilled job training. African Americans participated in these programs; however, many of these programs were designed to train persons for dead-end jobs. This was also true for the Comprehensive Employment Training Act of 1972.

The program that had teeth in terms of getting persons employed in the labor force was the Job Training Partnership Act of 1982 (JTPA). This act provided for "classroom skill training, on-the-job training, remedial education, and English as a second language."[47] These programs were adopted, it must be noted here, under the Reagan Administration, where federal officials were undertaking positive steps to block the civil rights of African Americans and, at the same time, taking positive steps to incorporate Asian Refugees into the mainstream. For example, a cooperative agreement was established between the National Governors' Association and the Office of Refugee Resettlement to:

> secure for refugees a level of participation in training and placement programs under JTPA on basis of equity and proportionality to the refugee number in the universe of need in each state, and in each sub-state Service Delivery Area."[48]

In short, the federal government extended its strong arm to help the Asian refugees to become Americanized and, at the same time, declared a war on the civil rights of African Americans, which had the operative effect of foreclosing the liberty of their youths to enter the mainstream.

Displacement of African Americans

In an attempt to make the refugees employed and self-sufficient as soon as possible, the federal government inadvertently pitted them against AfricanAmericans. The resettlement program was directed toward placing the refugees in the localities where there was a high concentration of African Americans: Houston, Los Angeles, Boston, Seattle, Washington, and Chicago.[49] In each locality, African Americans had a high rate of unemployment. In 1982, for example, the unemployment rate for the refugees ranged from "24.9 percent in Houston to 56.9 percent in Seattle."[50] But as Table 25 indicates, the unemployment rate of the refugees was lower than that of the general population in 1984.

In localities with poor economies, the refugees' employment rate was achieved at the expense of African Americans. A study by the Social Research Institute noted that tension over jobs developed between Vietnamese and African Americans when the latter group "accused the refugees of displacing them from jobs, housings, and services. New Orleans has a chronic high unemployment; Black unemployment is usually about 20 percent."[51] At one large company in Louisiana, African Americans charged that over 300 African Americans were fired and replaced with Vietnamese. They argued that this practice was being duplicated in other localities where the refugees were resettled.

Another area in which African Americans were displaced by the refugees was in business. The *Sentinel*, an African American newspaper in Los Angeles, ran a series of articles in 1984 detailing how Asian businesses displaced African American businesses. This is particularly acute in areas of service station dealerships. In early 1970, for example, African Americans dominated this market in Los Angeles. After the 1975 refugees arrived, the number of African American dealerships dropped dramatically.

The major complaint that African Americans leveled against the Asians is that their competition is "unfair." One practice that the Asians use is multifamilies living in one house. As one African American truck driver observed, "they move one in, and within a week's time, they've got ten of them living in one room."[52] African Americans cannot utilize this practice, because city ordinances prohibit overcrowding, but the refugees are allowed to do so because they are protected under the Refugee Act.

Another complaint that African Americans have leveled against the Asian businesspersons is that "Asian Americans must be getting special assistance of some sort that is not available to other minority groups."[53] This suspicion seems to be a common sentiment among African Americans. It can be best summarized by a comment made by an African American small store owner. He says, "I know that they get some kind of breaks, because I have seen it." Time and again African Americans who are investigating these complaints would be "told in whispered tone of federal programs, easy bank loans, special benefits of all sort."[54] In some instances, Asians are given a signature loan of $25,000. This amount is just enough to compete in low-income communities where African Americans are concentrated, but not enough to compete in white communities.

The fact that the federal government has a policy of making the refugees self-sufficient as quickly as possible lends credence to African Americans' suspicions. For example, the Office of Refugee and Resettlement Programs places heavy emphasis upon community and economic development initiatives. In its request for proposals, the Bureau for Refugee Programs mandates that volags include in their proposals evidence of a well-established program to "bring community groups together with the business sector to foster refugee enterprises."[55] In order to achieve this goal, special breaks are inevitable (i.e., the issuance of a set of bootstraps that are sugarcoated with honey).

Economic Development and Capital Development Skills

Notwithstanding the fact that Asian business persons are given special breaks by the federal government, they possessed a set of skills that African Americans do not have (i.e., capital development skills). These are the skills that groups bring with them when they immigrate. Capital development skills consist of managerial know-how and knowledge of the economic system. For example, knowledge of how to raise capital to start a business is more important than having capital itself. As was demonstrated in Chapter 5, the Asians and West Indians utilized the rotating credit system to raise capital to start businesses. The Southeast Asians also utilized this system very effectively to raise capital.[56]

The Southeast Asian business persons had these skills when they immigrated. Therefore, the government only had to issue them a set of bootstraps in order for them to put afoot successful businesses. The Asians' propensity for pursuing entrepreneurship was documented by a study conducted by the Institute for Social Research. It found that significant numbers of the refugees were moving into self-employment. Reginald P. Baker and David S. North found that the number of 1975 refugees engaged in self-employment increased over time. This increase was followed by a decrease of Social Security income.[57]

The fact that the refugees were moving toward self-employment is evident in that they had capital development skills when they made contact with the American polity. One tactic that they utilized in helping themselves to become self-employed is the use of "cash economy." Refugees soon learned that they can accumulate wealth much faster by engaging in cash economy than they could by being employed in "core sector jobs."[58] This writer has found this to be a general practice not only among the Southeast Asians but also the Persians and Arabs.[59] As mentioned earlier, this writer, in an attempt to learn more about the recent immigrants' culture, asked students in his cultural diversity classes to write a term paper on their ethnic background. One task he asked them to was to explain the methods that their group uses to compete in the American competitive society. The Persian students, for example, indicated that many of the men would get a degree in business or engineering. Regardless of which degree obtained, their ultimate goal was to become self-employed. The rationale behind this thrust is that they have learned that a person can accumulate more wealth in a "cash economy" in one year than he could in five years in "core sector jobs." For example, a yearly income of $25,000 in a cash economy equals $35,000 or more in a core service job. The major difference is that the standard deductions such as Social Security, state and federal income taxes, so on, are not taken out of a self-employed person's salary.

Another reason that the refugees seek self-employment is social. Refugees feel that they will be accepted by the American public much faster as a business person than they will as a service employee. They view business as a vehicle to accumulate wealth, which can be translated into power and prestige.

In short, the politics of the model minority success is a function of (1) immigration laws that restricted immigration to those individuals that have the propensity for upward mobility, (2) the human capital that they bring with them, (3) the set of bootstraps that the federal government issues them in their initial stage of contact, and (4) their cooperative value system.

Notes

1. Bob H. Suzuki, *Change* (November/December 1989), p. 13.
2. The deficit model is consistent with the weak family structure argument.
3. As we mentioned in Chapter 1, the immigration laws restrict immigration to those individuals over the age of sixteen who are educated and skilled and prevent the poor and poverty-stricken individuals from immigrating.
4. Reynolds Farley and Walter Allen, *The Color Line and the Quality of Life in America* (New York: Oxford University Press, 1987), p. 362–407.
5. Although the notion of the "melting pot" has not been coined at this time, its basic premise was conceptualized by the dominant culture.
6. *A Piece of the Pie: Blacks and White Immigrants Since 1880* (Berkeley: University of California, 1980), p. 207.
7. Ibid.
8. See Table 9 in Chapter 5.
9. See Chapter 5.

9. See Chapter 5.

10.   Harold D. Lasswell, *The World Revolution of Our Time: A Framework for Basic Policy Research* (Stanford: Stanford University Press, 1951).

11.   "Prejudice Politics: Symbolic Racism Versus Racial Threats to the Good Life," *Journal of Personality and Social Psychology,* Vol. 40. No. 3, p. 414.

12.   J. Owens Smith and Carl Jackson, *Race and Ethnicity: A Study of Intracultural Socialization Patterns* (Dubuque: Kendall/Hunt Publishing Company, 1989), p. 266.

13.   Sears and Kinder, 1971; Sears and McConahay, 1973; McConahay and Hough, 1972).

14.   Smith and Jackson, p. 267

15.   James Coleman et al., "Equality of Educational Opportunity," in *Urban Studies: An Introductory Reader*, ed Louis K. Loewenstein (New York: Collier-Macmillan Limited, 1971), pp. 229-269.

16.   E. Franklin Frazier, *Black Bourgeoisie* (New York: The Macmillan Company, 1957), p. 72.

17.   Ibid., pp. 60-61.

18.   Ibid., p. 63.

19.   Ibid., p. 203.

20.   *Brown v. Board of Education of Topeka*, 347 U.S. 483 (1954).

21.   J. Owens Smith, Mitchell F. Rice, and Woodrow Jones, Jr., *Blacks and American Government: Politics, Policy and Social Change*, 2nd ed. (Dubuque, Iowa: Kendall/ Hunt Publishing, 1991), see Chapters 3 and 4.

22.   *Japanese Americans: The Evolution of a Subculture* (Englewood Cliffs, N.J.: Prentice-Hall, 1969), p. 3.

23.   Jennifer Toth, "Asian-Americans Find Being Ethnic 'Model' Has Downside," *Los Angeles Times,* May 21, 1991, Section A. p. 4.

24.   Ibid.

25.   "Pegasus Programs '88: Challenging Minds to Succeed," *Pegasus Programs,* Inc., 2900 Bristol, Suite B-306, Costa Mesa, CA 92626, p. 3.

26.   Ibid.

27.   Ibid.

28.   Susan S. Forbes, "Adaptation and Integration of Recent Refugees to the United States," hearing before the *Subcommittee on Immigration and Refugee Policy,* August 1985, pp. 649-696.

29.   Ibid., p. 653.

30.   Ibid., p. 93.

31   Ibid.

32.   Lutheran Council in the USA, insertion in "Adaptation and Integration of Recent Refugees to the United States, " by Susan S. Forbes, August 1985, p. 442.

33.   Ibid.

34.   Ibid.

35.   Ibid.

36.   Ibid., pp. 442-443.

38. Purcell, p. 35.
39. Ibid.
40. Forbes, p. 665.
41. Ibid.
42. Purcell, p. 37.
43. Forbes, p. 657.
44. Forbes, p. 659.
45. "The Refugee Resettlement Program and the Job Training Partnership Act: Some Mutual Opportunities," *Subcommittee on Immigration and Refugee Policy* to consider reauthorization of refugee admission and resettlement programs under the Refugee Act of 1980, p. 281.
46. St. Clair Drake and Horce R. Clayton, *Black Metropolis* (New York: Harper and Row, 1962).
47. Ibid., p. 260.
48. Ibid., p. 246.
49   Forbes, p. 657-658.
50. Ibid., p. 658.
51. Ibid., p. 682.
52. Karl Zinsmeister, "Bittersweet Success," *Reason*, vol. 19, No. 5 (October 1987), p. 24.
53. Ibid.
54. Ibid.
55. Purcell, p. 36.
56   T. Chotigeeat, Phillip W. Balsmeier, and Thomas O. Stanley, "Fueling Asian Immigrants' Entrepreneurship: A Source of Capital," *Journal of Small Business Management* (July 1991): 50–60.
57. Forbes, p. 659.
58. Ibid.
59. This is one of the general themes that I found in the term papers that these students write for my cultural diversity classes.

CHAPTER 12

The Methodological Problems in Lumping All Hispanic and Latino Populations Together

Studying the Hispanic populations in America poses several methodological problems. First, they are not a homogeneous population and were not considered to be a racial minority group until the implementation of affirmative action. In fact, the U.S. government did not recognize them as a racial minority group until after the 1980s. From 1848 to 1980, the Census Bureau counted them as white–thus avoiding saddling them with the disability of race. Yet, the media keeps referring to them as minorities as though they are a homogenous group. This all-in-one classification has hamstrung social scientists' ability to construct a model by which to evaluate their socioeconomic behavior on a systematic basis. To overcome this shortcoming, let us start by analyzing how the government defined Hispanics.

The term "Hispanic" is used by the U.S. Census Bureau to refer to all Spanish-speaking populations. These populations include the Puerto Ricans, Cubans, Dominicans, Mexicans, Mexican Americans and Central and South Americans, and Spaniards. According to the 2000 U.S. Census, the Hispanic populations comprise 11.4 percent of the American populations, and they are becoming the fastest growing minority group in the country. If this trend continues, they are expected to replace African Americans as the largest minority group. The increase trend of this population is not as important as it is for social scientists to be able to conduct a systematic comparative analysis of their socioeconomic status after their arrival in America. Prior to the 1980s, there was not a sufficient amount of data collected on Spanish-speaking populations to conduct a systematic analysis of their behavior. In 2000, the Census Bureau attempted to rectify this problem by conducting a comprehensive survey of their socioeconomic behavior. It reported that this population is the fastest growing minority group in America. They have surpassed African Americans, it says, as the largest minority group. To arrive at this conclusion, the Census Bureau lumped all Spanish-speaking group together and classified them as a single ethnic minority groups based solely on their language. In doing so, it departed markedly from its historical method of classifying ethnicity within the framework of Max Weber's definition of the term ethnicity. Weber argued that ethnicity (nation) cannot be defined on the basis of language, but by (1) groups' "memories of a common political destiny with other nations,"[1] and (2) groups' "sentiment of solidarity in the face of other groups."[2] These immigrants came from twenty-nine different countries with different political destinies. The Census Bureau's departure from the Weberian definition has posed a serious problem for social scientists to make scientific explanations about these groups' socioeconomic behavior. As this writer has maintained, such an analysis cannot be adequately made without first examining those conditions of groups' homelands that caused them to emigrate.

There are many flaws in the Census Bureau's departing from Weberian methodology of classifying ethnic groups. The source of these flaws can be found in its survey questionnaire. This survey asked individuals to check one of the following five questions listed in Figure 1.

From this survey, the Census Bureau was able to identify 35 million individuals having Hispanic origin. Out of this number, 58.5 percent were Mexicans, 9.6 percent Puerto Ricans, 3.5 percent Cubans, 4.8 percent Central Americans, 3.8 percent South Americans, 0.3 percent Spaniards, 17.3 percent of All other Hispanic or Latino, and 2.2 percent Dominican Republicans (see Table 26).

Figure 2.

Reproduction of the Question on
Hispanic Origin From Census 2000

5. Is this person Spanish/ Hispanic/ Latino? Mark ☐ the
    "No" box if not Spanish /Hispanic /Latino.

☐ **No,** not Spanish / Hispanic / Latino   ☐ Yes, Puerto Rican
☐ Yes, Mexican, Mexican Am., Chicano   ☐ Yes, Cuban
☐ Yes, other Spanish / Hispanic / Latino   ☐ *Print group.*

SOURCE: U.S. Census Bureau, Census 2000 questionnaire.

What the Census Bureau overlooked is that Latin American countries comprise of the entire western hemisphere South of the United States. These countries were developed from colonies of Spain, Portugal, and France. By categorizing these groups as a single minority, the Census Bureau overlooked the fact that all these groups are not all nonwhite. Even for those that are nonwhite, America has not saddled them with the disability of race as it has done African Americans. This fact was pointed out in the *San Antonio School District v. Rodriguez* case by the U.S. Supreme Court in 1972. It found that the Hispanics had "none of the traditional indicia of suspectness: the class is not saddled with such disabilities, or subjected to such a history of purposeful unequal treatment, or relegated to such a position of political powerlessness as to command extraordinary protection from the majoritarian political process."[3] Therefore, by lumping all groups of Hispanic origin together and calling them a single minority, the Census Bureau has arbitrarily made them a "suspect" class without the government's having saddled them with the disability of race.

Historically, the government has treated immigrants from these countries as whites. This policy was adopted in 1848 when the United States signed the Treaty of Guadalupe Hidalgo at the close of the Mexican American War, as we will see in Chapter 13. Hence, including Spanish-speaking populations into the protective class simply because of their language seriously undermines the government effort to address the persistent abject poverty among those historically racial minority groups that America has saddled with the disability of race (i.e., African Americans and Native Americans). More important, this classification overlooks the mode of immigration.

The Native Americans were already here when the Anglo-Saxons arrived. They were conquered and subordinated, placed on a reservation, and subordinated to an inferior status. African Americans derived their subordinate status from the fact that they were placed in chains, brought over here involuntarily, and enslaved for 200 years. After slavery, they were subordinate to an inferior status by a set of institutionalized laws. Both groups were ascribed a minority status.

Historically, the term minority was first used to provide a system of protection for the minority of property owners (white) against the tyranny of the majoritarian rule. Over the period of history, this problem was solved by constructing various devices of checks and balances in our system of government.[4]

The issue of the Native Americans was addressed through time by extermination, placing them on a reservation and considering them as a nation, or providing provisions for their assimilation into the mainstream society—once they left the reservation. But it was the African descendants' problems that America has never fully addressed. Before and after the Civil War, America has employed various means to dehumanize them and to "stamp a feeling of natural inferiority" into their minds. To achieve this goal, it established a "legalized system of racial segregation" which operated to stigmatize them "as unfit for human association, and every type of propaganda was employed" to prove that they are "morally degenerate and intellectually incapable of being educated."[5] This remained the hegemonic policy for the treatment of African Americans up to the adoption of the various civil rights measures in the 1960s and '70s.

Historically, African Americans have been the victims of racism (i.e., the politics of exclusion). Prior to the 1960s, America has offered various excuses and justifications as to why it could not solve the so-called "race problem." But at the close of the 1950s and throughout the 1960s, a new day was ushered in. During this period, a variety of public policies were adopted to address this problem. The operative effect of these policies was to establish safeguards to protect African Americans' freedom to connect themselves to the mainstream of society's income redistribution system. To achieve this goal, America had to establish legal status for them in order to protect their rights to secure adequate socioeconomic advancement against the tyranny of the majoritarian rule. Critics immediately started devising schemes of oppression to undermine these policies. One such scheme was to increase the number of groups classified as minority in order to reduce the resources committed to address African Americans' socioeconomic problems. This is a form of *insidious racism*.[6]

The usage of language to classify Spanish-speaking immigrants as a single minority is another one of the critics' schemes of oppression. It further exacerbates African Americans' problems. Methodologically, this method of classification will operate to hamstring social scientists' ability to conduct a systematic analysis of these groups' socioeconomic behavior.

As mentioned in the Introduction Chapter, scientific research must be systematic—that is, "research untutored by the theory may prove trivial, and theory unsupportable by data, futile."[7] The usage of language to identify ethnicity will render the tool of systematic analysis useless. Let us turn to an examination of some of the major pitfalls of such an approach.

The first pitfall of the Census Bureau's attempt to lump all Spanish-speaking groups together as a single minority is that this method is devoid of scientific methodology. It has none of the Weberian criteria for identifying ethnicity. The source of the Census Bureau's departure from the Weberian methodology can be traced back to Directive No. 15 issued by the Office of Management and Budget in 1997. This directive was designed to "provide consistent and comparable data on race and ethnicity throughout the Federal government for an array of statistical and administrative programs."[8] The end result was just the opposite. This directive defines race and ethnicity as follows:

a. **American Indian or Alaskan Native.** A person having origins in any of the original peoples of North America, and who maintains cultural identification through tribal affiliation or community recognition.

b. **Asian or Pacific Islander**. A person having origins in any of the original peoples of the Far East, Southeast Asia, the Indian subcontinent, or the Pacific Islands. This area includes, for example, China, India, Japan, Korea, the Philippine Islands, and Samoa.

c. **Black.** A person having origins in any of the black racial groups of Africa.

d. **Hispanic.** A person of Mexican, Puerto Rican, Cuban, Central or South American or other Spanish culture or origin, regardless of race.

e. **White.** A person having origins in any of the original peoples of Europe, North Africa, or the Middle East.

With the exception of India, there is no apparent problem with the classification of the Asian and Pacific Islanders. The value system of the immigrants from India is significantly different from the rest of the Pacific Islanders. Although the Pacific Islanders immigrate from various Asian countries, their skin color is homogeneous. Among the Asian groups, the Filipinos' socioeconomic status differs from the rest of the Asians. Because of their small numbers in America and the restrictions that the immigration laws place on their entrance into America, this classification does not pose serious problems for social scientists to conduct systematic analysis of their behavior.

The second pitfall with the Census Bureau's lumping Latinos and Hispanics together is that these groups have very little commonality except for their language, which varies from country to country. As far as race is concerned, Latin American countries have a variety of races. As we will see in the next chapter, for example, colonial Mexico had five races: Creoles (white), Mestizo (a mixture of Spanish and Aztec Indians), mulattos (black and white), Zombos (Black and Native Americans), and the Peninsulares (white leaders from Spain).

With the exception of the Peninsulares, all of these groups remained in Mexico after it received its independence from Spain in 1821. However, over the years, the population in the Latin American countries became less and less nonwhite. Increasingly, the color of white became more desirable because it represented not only class status but also the acceptable form of beauty, which is an extension of the Elizabethan propaganda campaign of the sixteenth century.

According to the *CIA-The World Factbook of 2002*[9] (hereinafter Report) the Spanish-speaking countries with the largest number of immigrants/migrants to American had a majority of Mestizo/white population. The political significance of these figures is that prior to the adoption of affirmative action policy the American government has classified and treated them as white citizens. As we will see in the next two chapters, the problem that these groups are confronting in the United States is one of class status instead of racial discrimination. Also we will see in Chapter 14, the Mexicans were spared of the type of *invidious racial discrimination* that African Americans experienced as a result of the Mexican government intervening to demand that they be given a system of protection. This system of protection was similar to the one that the British West Indians received from the British government.

The notion that the problem of the Hispanic immigrants is one of class–and not race–cannot be overemphasized. This was demonstrated in our discussion of the Asians and British West Indians' experience in America. Race within itself does not constrain groups' socioeconomic growth and development. What constrains such growth and development is their lack of the necessary human capital to compete on a level playing field when they make contact with the American polity. Our discussion of the Irish-Catholics reveals that race within itself does not guarantee a group's success. They remained impoverished for more than five generations and only began to overcome this difficulty after government intervention.

The Hispanics are not a minority group that the government has historically saddled with the disability of race. They are basically white. For example, the Cubans make up 3.5 percent (1,241,685) of the Spanish-speaking population. The Report indicates that 37 percent of the Cuban population is white, 51 percent are mulattos, 11 percent blacks, and 1 percent Chinese. The Puerto Ricans make up 9.6 percent (3,406,128) of the Spanish-speaking population in the United States. The Report indicates that the Puerto Rico population is 80.5 percent white, 8 percent black, 0.4 percent Amerindian, 0.2 percent Asian, and 10 percent mixed and other. The Colombians make up 1.3 percent (470, 684) of the Spanish-speaking immigrants. The composition of the Colombian populations (470,684) is as follows: 20 percent whites, 28 percent Mestizo, 14 percent Black, 3 percent mixed Black-Amerindian, and 1 percent Amerindian.

The Mexicans make up 58.5 percent (20,640,711) of the Spanish-speaking population in the 2000 count (see Table 26). The composition of the Mexico population is as follows: 60 percent Mestizo, 30 Amerindians, 9 percent white, and 1 percent others. The Ecuadorians make up 0.7 percent (260, 559) of the immigrants. The composition of their population is as follows: 65 percent Mestizo, 25 percent Amerindians, 7 percent Spanish, and 7 percent Blacks.[10]

The composition of the rest of the immigrants from the Spanish-speaking countries has similar population makeup. The most important fact is that the largest percentage of these populations is either Mestizo or white. The political significance of this composition is that the American government has historically treated them as white, thus avoiding saddling them with the disability of race.

Treating the Spanish-speaking population as white is not just a cultural practice. It is a public policy that was adopted in 1848 at the signing of the Treaty of Guadalupe Hidalgo at the close of the Spanish-American war. As we will see in Chapter 12, the American government granted the Mexicans full citizenship with all of the rights and privileges that were granted to whites. But nine years later, it told African Americans that they had no rights that whites were bound to respect and that they were unfit to associate with whites.

The notion that African Americans were unfit to associate with whites was not just a matter of racial attitudes. It was institutionalized into the fabric of the American system of government. As mentioned previously, the attempt was directed toward dehumanizing them and to "stamp a feeling of natural inferiority" into their minds. This policy became the basis for ascribing them minority status. The Hispanics, on the other hand, were never ascribed such status. This was evidenced by the way in which they were treated during World War II. They were integrated into the major branches of the armed forces with other whites. On the other hand, special units were created for African Americans in both World Wars I and II. Because their skin color approximated whites, Hispanics were more acceptable in all of the branches of the Armed Forces. Even the Japanese were not as acceptable as the Hispanics. Special units were also created for them to serve in during World War II.

The Census Bureau reported 3,040,499 immigrants from Central and South America (see Table 26). As we have seen in Chapter 4, a large number of Italians (white) emigrated to this area in the 1880s and '90s. The immigrants from these countries make up more than 3 million of the Latino immigrants which the census bureau have identified as minorities. According to *CIA-The World Factbook of 2002*, the population of Chile (which make up 68,849 of the immigrants) is 95 percent white, 3 percent Amerindians, and 2 percent other. The Argentinean (100,000) population makeup is 95 percent white and 3 per-

Table 26
Hispanic Population by Type, 2000
(For information on confidentiality protection, nonsampling error, and definitions, see
www.census.gov/prod/cen2000/doc/sf1.pdf)

Subject	Number	Percent
HISPANIC OR LATINO ORIGIN		
Total population	281,421,906	100.0
Hispanic or Latino (of any race)	35,305,818	12.5
Not Hispanic or Latino	246,116,088	87.5
HISPANIC OR LATINO BY TYPE		
Hispanic or Latino (of any race)	35,305,818	100.0
Mexican	20,640,711	58.5
Puerto Rican	3,406,178	9.6
Cuban	1,241,685	3.5
Other Hispanic or Latino	10,017,244	28.4
Dominican (Dominican Republic)	764,945	2.2
Central American (excludes Mexican)	1,686,937	4.8
Costa Rican	68,588	0.2
Guatemalan	372,487	1.1
Honduran	217,569	0.6
Nicaraguan	177,684	0.5
Panamanian	91,723	0.3
Salvadoran	655,165	1.9
Other Central American	103,721	0.3
South American	1,353,562	3.8
Argentinean	100,864	0.3
Bolivian	42,068	0.1
Chilean	68,849	0.2
Colombian	470,684	1.3
Ecuadorian	260,559	0.7
Paraguayan	8,769	0.0
Peruvian	233,926	0.7
Uruguayan	18,804	0.1
Venezuelan	91,507	0.3
Other South American	57,532	0.2
Spaniard	100,135	0.3
All other Hispanic or Latino	6,111,665	17.3
Checkbox only, other Hispanic	1,733,274	4.9
Write-in Spanish	686,004	1.9
Write-in Hispanic	2,454,529	7.0
Write-in Latino	450,769	1.3
Not elsewhere classified	787,089	2.2

SOURCE: U.S. Census Bureau, Census 2000 Summary File 1.

cent nonwhite. In addition, there were more than 6 million Latinos who fell into the "All other Hispanics or Latinos" category of the Census Bureau 2000 survey.

The fifth flaw in the Census Bureau methodology of lumping all Hispanic origin groups together as a single minority group is that it does not take race into account. As we will see in the next chapter, there were five major groups in the Spanish colonies: the *Peninsulares* (white leaders born in Spain) *creoles* (children in the colonies born of European descent), the *Mestizos* (a mixture of Europe and Native Americans), the *mulattos* (black and white), and the *Zombos* (Black and Native Americans). After the decline of the Spanish Empire, the creoles became the ruling class that controlled the mode of production (both land and industry). By operation, this class was white and mostly educated and in the middle class. This is particularly true in Central and South America. By lumping them together as Hispanic origin and identifying them as a minority, the Census Bureau has arbitrarily given them a minority status without actually having been saddled with the disability of race.

The sixth flaw in the Census Bureau's Hispanic origin methodology is that it hamstrings analysts' capacity to conduct systematic analyses of their subsequent socioeconomic status in America. It will hide the two most important independent variables for measuring group upward mobility: educational attainment and skills. As we have seen in studying the European groups, group mobility is highly contingent upon the amount of skills and the level of education (human capital) that a group possesses when they make contact with the American polity. These variables determine groups' income. Ignoring them will give a distorted picture of their subsequent socioeconomic success. For example, Colombians (South Americans) are included in the Hispanic origin groups. In comparison to Mexico, the Republic of Columbia has a population of 40,803,000 with a 70 to 80 percent literacy rate. The majority of the Central and South Americans immigrate through the legal process, and the immigration law prevents the illiterate population from immigrating. For example, out of the 1,685 Central and South Americans surveyed for the educational attainment index, 64 percent of them were high school graduates or higher and 18 percent held a bachelor's or higher degree compared to the 4,981 Mexicans' 49.7 percent high school graduate and 7.1 percent bachelor's degree or higher. The figures for those individuals counted in "Other Spanish/Hispanic/Latino" category are even more impressive. Out of the 801 surveyed, 71.1 percent are high school graduate or higher and 15 percent have a bachelor's degree or higher. Income wise, 31.2 percent of "Other Spanish/Hispanic/Latino" and 29.4 percent of the Central and South Americans had income of $50,000 dollars or more compared to 22.8 percent of the Mexicans (see Table 29 in Chapter 14).

The seventh flaw in the Census Bureau's Hispanic origin methodology is that it gives a distorted picture when assessing the relative success of Hispanic groups after they arrive in America. This methodology has the propensity to mislead analysts to overlook one of the most important variables (i.e., the immigration law which restricts immigration to the skilled and literate population). These laws affect Central and South American immigrants more than they do immigrants from Mexico. The majority of the former groups immigrate through the legal channels whereas the latter cross the border illegally. Such immigration has a determinative impact on the socioeconomic composition of the immigrants. It makes it extremely hard for analysts to make a true assessment of the relative success of the Mexican population. Many of the Hispanics counted in the social index as having acquired skills and educational attainment are actually those Hispanic immigrants that were already in the middle class before they immigrated to America. Whereas, the immigrants that cross the borders from Mexico (migrant workers) are predominately in the lower class, and in many instances, have a lower level of literacy. As demonstrated, the income and educational attainment of the Mexicans are significantly lower than Central and South Americans.

Assessing the business success of Mexicans is even harder than assessing their socioeconomic status. Regardless of the origin of immigrants, success in business depends largely on the entrepreneurial skills that groups bring with them. This is without respect to race or ethnicity. We have already seen the success of Jews in business compared to the Irish-Catholics and the British West Indians compared to African Americans.

The eighth flaw in the Census Bureaus' classifying the Latinos as the fastest growing minority group in the United States is that it is inconsistent in identifying nonwhites as a minority group. There is very little, if any, compatible differences in the skin color of the Mestizo Mexicans and the Mideastern immigrants that the government has classified as white. In the classrooms in California, for example, the only way an instructor can distinguish Hispanic students from Mideastern students is by the spelling of their names. If skin color is the criterion for classifying groups as minority, these groups should also be included. As it is, they do not qualify to receive financial assistance from the programs designated as minority programs.

The importance of using scientific methods in classifying ethnicity cannot be overemphasized. The independent variables that can best explain the differentiation in groups' mobility are (1) the conditions of life in groups' homeland, and (2) the immigration laws, which restrict immigration to the educated and well-to-do populations. As we have seen, these variables have a determinative impact in the socioeconomic makeup of immigrants. These variables, however, do not apply to all of the Mexican immigrants who make up 58 percent of the Latino populations, because a large percentage of these immigrants immigrate without official papers, thus bypassing the restrictions of the immigration laws.

For example, the immigrants coming from South America immigrate through the official channels. More than 78 percent of these groups have a high school education and some skills compared to only 47 percent of the Mexicans. As will be demonstrated in the next two chapters, the Mexicans emigrated from a less developed country than the rest of the Latino groups.

The ninth flaw in the Census Bureau's classifying all Latin Americans as a single minority is that it will always allow individuals to become a convenient minority. That is, maintaining their status as white when it is advantageous and switching over to minority status for the sole purpose of receiving those government benefits that were created to secure adequate advancement for the racial minority that has been saddled with the disability of race by society. The political repercussion of such classification is that it constitutes a public policy that increases the pool of applicants seeking a limited amount of government resources without increasing the pot of these resources. By operation, the group with the largest number will always end up getting the lion's share of these resources whether they need them or not. Within its extreme manifestation, this policy promotes a sophisticated form of *insidious* racial discrimination. The status of nonwhite does not automatically give a group a minority status. As was noted by the U.S. Supreme Court in the *Rodriguez* case, such status requires a group to have been saddled with the disability of race. The U.S. government has not saddled any of the populations of Latin America with the disability of race. In fact, this issue was resolved at the signing of the Treaty of Guadalupe Hidalgo when it granted citizens in these countries all the rights and privileges as white citizens. Furthermore, the status of being nonwhite does not automatically constrain a group's upward mobility in the American society. This is evidenced in our discussion of the relative success of the Asians and the British West Indians in America. On the other hand, the status of "white" does not guarantee a group success either, as we have seen with our discussion of the Irish-Catholics.

The flaw in identifying all Hispanics as minority is more pronounced in the area of business. For example, the total populations of the Hispanics are as follows: the Cubans, 3.5; Mexicans and Mexican-Americans, 58.5; Puerto Ricans, 9.6: Spaniard 0.3; Hispanic Latin Americans, 8.6. But when we consider the business sale's receipts per member for these groups, the Small Business Administration reports the following: Spaniards, $159,775; Cubans, $21,439; Latin Americans, $13,503; Mexicans, $3,569; and Puerto Ricans, $2,201.[11] The figures further support our argument that all Hispanics have not been saddled with the disability of race and are not suffering from the class disadvantage. These groups were in the middle class when they immigrated; therefore, it serves no public good in assigning them a minority status (i.e., a suspect class).

What is missing in this analysis is the impact that the immigration laws had on screening the immigrants. These laws favor those immigrants with entrepreneurial skills over those without such skills. This is where the Asians and British West Indians come out on top in business compared to other minority groups. A large percentage of their immigrants come over with entrepreneur skills. Based on our analysis of the Irish-Catholics and African Americans, it can easily be assumed that what can account for the success of the Latin American Hispanic entrepreneurs from Central and South America is that they had these entrepreneurial skills when they immigrated.

In short, by characterizing all Latinos as Hispanics based on their language instead of their common political destiny, the Census Bureau has given a distorted picture of the actual numbers of Hispanics in terms of being the fastest growing minority group in America. Its methodology makes no distinction between whites and nonwhites. This allows immigrants to claim the status of white for the purpose of enjoying the rights and privileges of white citizenship, and at the same time, to claim minority status for the purpose of receiving those benefits established to secure adequate advancement for those minority groups that have been saddled with the disability of race.

In order to get a clearer understanding of the Hispanic origin groups' experiences in America, the next two chapters will examine their behavior within our framework. The next chapter consists of an examination of Mexico's colonial period. The purpose is to ascertain why Mexico did not develop like other countries during this period. The next chapter will focus on the conditions in Mexico that constrained their growth and development and the reasons for their immigration to America.

Notes

1. E. Franklin Frazier, *The Black Bourgeoise* (New York: Collier-MacMillan, 1957), p. 173.
2. Ibid., p. 173.
3. *San Antonio School District V. Rodriguez,* 411 U.S. 1 (1973).
4. Robert Dahl, *A Preference for Democratic Theory* (Chicago: The University of Chicago Press, 1957), pp. 11-15.
5. Ibid., p. 172.

6. See the chapter, entitled "Summary and Conclusion," for an explanation of this term and a discussion of methods used to undermine these policies.

7. David Easton, *A Framework for Political Analysis* (Englewood Cliffs, N. J.: Prentice-Hall, 1965), p. 7.

8. *Standards for the Classification of Federal That on Raise and Ethnicity,* Office of Management and Budget, Federal Register 7/9/97, Part II. Pages 36873-36946.

9. *CIA-The World Factbook of 2002.*

10. Ibid.

11. *Minorities in Business, 2001*, U.S. Small Business Administration Office of Adovacy, Table 10, November 2001.

CHAPTER 13

Hispanics and Colonial Mexico

Since the Census Bureau has classified all Spanish-speaking populations as "minority," which is based on the presupposition that the American government has inflicted some harm upon them to constrain their growth and development, an analysis of the Mexicans and Mexican Americans' colonial experience is in order to add conceptual clarity and empirical accuracy to this area of inquiry. This analysis will be conducted within our conceptual framework which posits that social scientists can best understand groups' current socioeconomic status in America: (1) by beginning their mode of analysis with those structural conditions in groups' homelands, (2) by tracing their migration to America, and (3) by examining those political and economic linkages that they fashioned with the American polity in their initial stage of contact. These linkages, as this writer has maintained, will have a determinative impact upon their subsequent behavior. From this perspective, we must begin our mode of analysis of the Mexicans' experience, not with Mexico but with early Spain.

Early Spain

During the fifteenth century, Spain began to reach her golden age. Changes began to take place in 1469, when King Ferdinand and Queen Isabella married, thus uniting the kingdoms of Aragon (Northeast Spain) and Castille (North and Central Spain). These rulers held a similar philosophy, which was to strengthen the royal authority of Spain.[1] One of the first measures that they undertook toward this effort was to curtail the power of the nobles. They viewed this group as having usurped too many of the functions and privileges of the crown. They persuaded Pope Sixtus IV to issue a papal bull (a decree) to empower them with the authority to appoint three inquisitors. The function of these inquisitors was to root out the heretics and other offenders of the Catholic

Church. The crown used this power as a political tool not only to control the power of the nobles but also to achieve total religious conformity. There were two groups that the crown viewed as of a thorn in their sides: the Moors and the Jews.[2]

In 1492, Ferdinand conquered Granada, a Moorish kingdom in South Spain. This conquest brought to an end of 800 years of domination and warfare between the Moors and the Spaniards. The two problems that the Moors posed to the Spanish were their merchant class and their religion. When the crown started enforcing its policy of absolute conformity to Catholicism, the Moors began to practice *moriscos* (i.e., they publicly confessed converting to Catholicism but secretly practiced their Islamic faith). The Spanish had the same problem with the Jews. The Jews were referred to as *conversos*. They were largely merchants and had amassed a considerable amount of wealth and influence in Spain. To reduce this influence, the Spanish crown expelled 70,000 to 180,000 of them.[3]

During the same year that the Spanish expelled the Moors and Jews, Columbus persuaded the crown to finance his adventure to seek a new route to Asia. Three months after setting sail from Spain, he landed in America, thus establishing communications with the new world. This discovery became the catalyst for elevating Spain to her highest point in world power. From this point onward, Spain began to expand its empire, conquering countries such as Tripoli, Oran, Navarre, and North America. Among these conquests, North America is the country that is germane to our study of the socioeconomic status of Mexican Americans.

Colonial Mexico

The Spanish first settled and established colonies on various islands in the West Indies. The first colony was established in Cuba by Diego Velázquez. He landed there with 300 soldiers in 1511. After three months of intensive fighting, he conquered the natives on the island, established a colony, and began robbing the island of its raw materials. The crown appointed him governor over all of the West Indies' islands. In 1518, he learned of the powerful and wealthy Native American empire called the Aztec Empire. In 1519, he dispatched an expedition of 600 men led by Herman Cortés to explore this rich empire. When Cortés first landed on the Gulf Coast, he encountered various hostile Native tribes which he engaged in battle. He first battled with the Tlaxcalan people. After two weeks of battles, the Tlaxcalans suffered heavy casualties and surrendered. They later agreed to join forces with Cortés' expedition to fight the Aztec Empire, with which they had long struggled.

In 1519, a combined force of 4000 Spaniards and the Tlaxcalans began to march upon the Aztec Empire. They first subdued the city of Cholula and began exploring the road to the Aztec capital. The Aztec leader, Montezuma, heard of the Spaniard invaders and decided not to fight them because he had dreamed that the god Quetzalcoatl would come to take over the rule of Mexico.[4] He met Cortés outside of the city. After greeting each other, Montezuma led Cortés and his expedition into the city. Montezuma allowed Cortés to establish headquarters in the city and gave him permission to freely roam the city. Cortés found large caches of gold and other treasuries in the Aztec storehouses.

Fearing that Montezuma would eventually drive him and his expedition out of the city, Cortés seized Montezuma and held him hostage. He attempted to use similar techniques of conversion as did the inquisitor–that is, he attempted to force Montezuma to pledge allegiance to the crown of Spain (Charles I). As a ransom, Cortés demanded from the Aztecs an enormous amount of gold and jewels.

With Montezuma in captivity, Cortés started devising strategies to conquer the entire Aztec region. Before executing his plan, he learned that Gov. Velazquez of Cuba had dispatched an expedition to Mexico to arrest and return him to Cuba. After receiving word of Gov. Velazquez' orders, Cortés left 200 of his men in the city of Tenochtitlan under the command of Pedro de Alvarado and went to confront the expedition sent by Gov. Velazquez. He launched a surprise attack at night on the expedition, captured the leader, and persuaded the rest of the expedition to join his army.

While Cortés was away, Alvarado instituted a number of harsh measures in Tenochtitlan against the Aztecs which precipitated them to revolt. First, he and his men launched a surprise attack up on a group of Aztecs who were performing a religious ceremony. In the process, they killed hundreds of worshippers. This slaughter outraged the Aztecs and precipitated a revolt. They launched a counter attack against the Spaniards and recaptured the building that they had occupied, including the one in which they were holding their leader, Montezuma.

The revolt was well underway when Cortés returned with his men and more than 3000 Tlaxcalan allies. The Aztecs allowed them to enter the city to join Alvarado, but as soon as they entered, the Aztecs surrounded them and attacked. Montezuma, still under the impression that the Spaniards were sent by the god Quetzelcoatl, attempted to quiet the revolt. The Aztecs stoned him and he died three days later. In the meantime, Cortés saw that the only option of survival for himself and his men was to retreat from the city by night. On June 30, 1520, he ordered his men to start the retreat which ran through the night.

This night was known as the Noche Triste ("Sad Night"). As the Spaniards attempted to retreat, the Aztecs chased and attacked them on both sides. In the process of this retreat, over half of the Spanish troops were killed and the canoes and treasures that they had collected were lost. The survivors reassembled in Tlaxcalan to recuperate.

Around May 1521, Cortés had reorganized his army in Tlaxcalan with reinforcements and equipment from Veracruz. He immediately started attacking the outposts and settlements surrounding the Aztec capital of Tenochtitlan. He ordered his army to surround the city and bombarded the Aztecs with artilleries daily for four months, during which time, the Aztecs' food and water supplies were cut off. Starvation and diseases ravaged the city. On August 13, 1521, the Spanish soldiers captured the Aztec leader and the city fell. After the battle, more than 40,000 Aztecs' decomposing bodies littered the streets and bloated the lake and canals. Thus, the prosperous and great Aztec Empire had fallen.

The fall of the city of Tenochtitlan marked the beginning of the colonization of New Spain. The Spaniards immediately established a government with viceroys in charge and started expanding their colonalization of North and South America. The colonists recognized the political and economic significance of the location of Tenochtitlan. They renamed it Mexico City. Because of its strategic location, the city became the metropolis from which Spain launched its plan to expand its Empire in North America.

The Role of the Catholic Church in New Spain

At the offset, the Catholic Church began to play a major role in shaping and formulating Spaniards' policy of colonization in New Spain. With its power of inquisition, the church established a policy of converting the Native Americans to Christianity. The inquisition policy left no room for religious intolerance and individual freedom, as it was later practiced in the New England colonies. The inquisitors sought complete conformity with Catholicism. Those who were caught practicing a religious faith contrary to the church doctrines were tried and punished.

The church became a political tool by which the Spanish crown controlled New Spain. It sponsored missions throughout New Spain for the purpose of assimilating the natives into the Spanish culture. The crown controlled the church by maintaining its royal patronages. This gave the crown the authority to select clerics and collect tithes (10 percent of a person's income). Since Spain was operating under a system of mercantilism, tithes proved to be very prosperous for the church.

The mandatory donation to the church sustained the finance of the missions, which, in turn, allowed them to serve as a conduit to spread the Spanish language and culture. The missions established schools, taught the natives the Spanish language, and built hospitals to heel the sick, elderly, and mentally disturbed. In addition, the church became the financial institution which lent money to merchants to establish businesses and sponsored capital ventures that purported to promote the economic growth and development of the church.

The clerics, coupled with the powerful inquisition, became very powerful politically throughout the colonies. They were the teachers in primary and secondary schools as well as the universities. Since educational institutions are agents of social control and socialization, this gave the church increased control over the lives of the colonists and natives. As the Spanish established missions throughout its colonies, its effort to convert native Americans to Christianity intensified. The Native Americans were brought into the missions for conversions. Socially, this effort proved to have had a disastrous effect upon the natives. First, the intermingling with the Spanish precipitated a drastic decline in the native population as a result of the diseases such as the smallpox and measles, which were unknown to the natives up to this time. Because their biological system did not have the resistance to these diseases, the native population was drastically decimated. Some estimated that their population declined from 25,000,000 in 1519 to about 1,000,000 in 1620.[5]

As a result of this population decline, Cortés imported African slaves into New Spain to work the mines and cane fields. The slaves were imported for two basic reasons: first, there was a drastic decline in the native populations as a result of the diseases, as mentioned previously. Secondly, as we mentioned in Chapter 2, Native American men were warriors and would rather die as a warrior than live as a slave. Over the course of the Spanish colonial period, it was estimated that more than 200,000 slaves were imported into the colonies.[6] Consequently, intermingling and interracial marriage produced the mulattos and Zombos in New Spain.

The Spanish occupation, coupled with the drastic declined in the native populations, led to an increase in intermingling and intermarrying of the Spanish within the colonies. The practice of intermarriage was promoted by the church policy against cohabitation and having children out of wedlock. Individuals who violated this doctrine were subject to excommunication. This policy led to the emergence of five different populations in the Mexico territory: the Mestizos (a mixture of Europe and Native Americans), the mulattos (black and white), Zombos (Black and Native Americans), Criollos (children in the colonies born of European descent), and Peninsulares (white leaders born in Spain). Among these groups, the Mestizos grew most rapidly and to be the largest. Unlike

Protestants, the Spanish Catholics had not internalized the Manichaean doctrine (which associated the color of black with evil) when they arrived.[7] This doctrine prevented the Protestants from intermarrying with the Africans in the American colonies regardless of whether they were free or slaves. Many of the colonies had laws restricting whites from marrying Africans.[8] It was not until the 1960s that state laws prohibiting interracial marriage was declared unconstitutional.[9]

Social Class Status: As the time progressed, a class distinction began to emerge. Race became an indicator of social class which was drawn strictly along racial lines. At the top of the social ladder were the peninsulares who were sent to the colonies by the Spanish government to hold high political offices in both the church and government. This group remained small. Below them were the creoles (white Spaniards of European descent) who were born in the colonies. They were never given the rank, power, and prestige similar to that of the peninsulares. Below the creoles were the mestizos, followed by the Native Americans and the African slaves.

The creoles resented the privileged status given to the peninsulares. Over the years, this resentment became one of the bases for the Mexicans to fight for their Independence. There was very little social upward mobility among the natives of Mexico as a result of the structural conditions of society, which will be discussed. Whatever mobility there was, it was not based strictly along racial lines as it was in the American South. Individuals with mixed racial background could also climb the socioeconomic ladder the same as the creoles by petitioning the crown for the status as whiteness, for a fee. However, there was very little upward mobility among the natives during the colonial period as a result of the structural conditions which kept them economically prostrated and impoverished, which will be discussed later in this chapter.

The Origin of the Mexicans' Lower Socioeconomic Status

Today's low socioeconomic status of the Mexicans can be traced back to the land tenure policy adopted during this period. This policy can account for their failure to grow and develop during and after the colonial period. As has been argued throughout this book, a group's upward mobility is highly contingent upon the freedom that individuals have within a group to acquire and possess property, either *de facto* or *de jure*.

Starting from their re-conquest of Spain from the Moors' domination, the Spanish adopted a policy of rewarding large land grants to soldiers who participated in its conquests. This policy was continued during the colonial period in Mexico. In 1513, the crown issued a *cédula* (certificate) to establish standards for granting land to soldiers who helped in the conquest. These land grants were divided into two categories: *peonias* and *caballerias*. The peones (infantry) were granted approximately 30 to 50 acres of land to build their homes and to farm and to raise sheep or cattle. The *calaballerias* (mounted troops) were granted between 700 to 1000 acres of land for the same. For the investors, the crown granted them *encomiendas*.[10] The latter, it must be noted, was the catalyst for constraining the growth and development of the Mexicans.

The policy of granting investors *encomiendas* were developed as a way to repay them for the money they put up to fund adventures. According to this system, a group of investors would solicit the king to lend his name to an adventure; in return, he was rewarded sovereignty over all land conquered and the rights to taxation and all the gold and silver captured. The private investors and conquerors, in return, were granted encomiendas. Although these land grants were issued in all areas conquered by the Spanish, we are only concerned with the ones granted in Mexico.

An *encomienda* "consisted of an allotment of a certain number of villages and carried with it the right to collect tribute and to extract personal services (labor in the field and household, etc.) from Indians living in the district."[11] In addition, there was the r*epartimiento,*[12] which was a drafted labor system that required the natives to work forty-five days a year for the owners, the *encomienderos*. Operationally, this system reduced natives within this district to serfs;[13] it was too often abused. Instead of working forty-five days a year, the natives were forced to work twelve hours a day year round and, in many instances, were cheated out of their pay. This system of labor became so abusive that the crown issued a decree abolishing it in the early eighteenth century; however, it received such stiff resistence that it remained in tact until the close of the century.[14]

The *encomienderos* served similar functions as the lords of the feudal system. Their responsibility was to look after the affairs of the natives and convert them to Christianity. At first, the encomienderos were soldiers who fought in the conquest of Mexico. As the conquerors began to settle in, the Spanish crown began to send over the peninsulares, who were well educated and trained in the legal profession, to look after its interest, which was to extract raw materials such as gold and silver from the colonies.

Around 1575, the Spanish crown had divided Mexico into 827 encomiendas: 507 were granted to individuals, and 320 were held by the crown.[15] The number of encomiendas began to decline round the 1720s, because they had become economically unproductive.[16] New Spain had long been plagued by a

lack of population growth. As mentioned previously, there was a drastic decline in the native population as a result of the diseases and unhealthy working
conditions in the forced labor camps.

The encomiendas were held together by the Law of Succession of 1536.[17]
Originally, the large landholdings were subject to revoke at the pleasure of the
crown, or whenever the encomiendado died. The encomiendados petitioned
the king to extend their titles to the encomiendas for the entire life of the owner
and his wife and children. First, it was two generations. Eventually, it was
extended to five generations. During this process, some of the encomiendados'
line of the heirs became extinct, and the land was reverted back to the crown.

The numbers of encomiendas began to decline toward the end of the seventeenth century. First, many of these encomiendas were returned to the king for
a lack of heirs. Secondly, many were confiscated by the crown for some illegal
activities. Between the period of 1520 and 1550, the number of encomiendas
and had declined from 934 to approximately 50.[18] As the Spanish crown dis-
continued the encomienda system, the Mexicans switched to the hacienda system.

The Origin of the Hacienda

The term hacienda has various meanings from its inception. But the most
common usage of this term in the eighteenth century was to describe a large
land estate.[19] The owner of a hacienda was called "haciendado." He was a
make over of the encomiendado. Instead of being from the upper class Spaniards, he was of Mexican origin predominantly from the creoles, although some
mestizos also owned haciendas.

The haciendas were carved out of the encomiendas. Where the latter consisted of various townships and districts, the division of the haciendas varied in
size. Carving up these encomiendas was an attempt by the crown to solve the
struggle for land ownership that started in the 1750s. This struggle ended when
the crown stepped in and passed the Possession Act of 1767. This act empow-
ered the Royal Commissioner to settle the land dispute. He achieved this objective by dividing the land up in the four categories: *primitive settlers, old settlers, recent settlers*, and *capitán*.[20]

The primitive settlers who had been in the colony for more than six years
were to be granted two leagues of pasture land and twelve *caballerias* for agricultural purposes, a total of 10,306 acres. The old settlers and their families
who had resided in the colony less than six years were granted two leagues of
pasture land and twelve *caballerias* for agricultural purposes, a total of 9,606

acres of land. The recent settlers who had immigrated within the last two years received two leagues for pasture and none for farming, a total of 8,806 acres of land. The *capitán*, who was in charge of the garrison, was given twice as much land as the first settlers, 20,712 acres.[21]

The social and economic structures of the hacienda system were a modified form of the encomienda system. Their mere sizes made it easy to maintain the old system of entailed estate where workers were forced to work for the haciendados. The major difference was the size. Whereas the latter landholding extended over villages, towns, and districts, the land holding for the hacienda consisted of large landholding. The exact size of these properties is hard to determine because the Mexicans' method of accountings for the land ownership was never accurate before the twentieth century. But McBride estimated that there were approximately 300 haciendas which contained "at least 25,000 acres each; 116 have not less than 62,500 acres; 51 have approximately 75,000 acres; while 11 are believed to have 250,000 acres a piece."[22] Very seldom did a hacienda consist of less than 2,500 acres.

Structurally, the haciendas contained at least 1000 inhabitants. They constituted a self-contained community where all of those basic necessities of life could be found on location. The customary accessory such as the church, school, the store, and machinery shop, a post office, and in some instances, hospitals were, also on location.

The population of the haciendas was permanent. There was very little room for social upward mobility. The owners of the haciendas did not live on the premises. They were the wealthy class who lived in the capital or some other large city. The average haciendado left the management of his hacienda up to an administrador. Under the latter, that was a group of foremen, the peons and their families, the priest, storekeepers, accountants, shepherds, and cattlemen.

The owners of the haciendas did not depend on these enterprises to generate income, but to use them as leverage for a mortgage and for prestige and their character as ancestral estate. As we shall see, the owners of the haciendas in the territory acquired by America had a hard time holding onto their properties.

Socially, the haciendados carried a degree of prestige. The status of a haciendado was determined by the size of his estate. This automatically placed the economically secure against the economically insecure. Every opportunity that presented itself, the economically secure would acquire, legally or illegally, the haciendas of the economically insecure haciendados. The poor record keeping method adopted by the colonial government made it easy for the economically secure to defraud the economically insecure out of the titles to their land. This practice inevitably led to a reconcentration of large landholdings in the hands of a few, which was the catalyst for perpetuating poverty of the lower class.

The economics of the hacienda system were similar to that of the encomienda in substance if not in form. While the latter system tied the natives to the land by a decree of the Spanish crown (*repartimiento*), the hacienda system tied them to the land through a form of debt slavery, similar to the sharecropping system that African Americans were subjected to in the American South. It can be said with little exaggeration that the peónage system that the American South adopted for African Americans after the Civil War was a carbon copy of the Spanish system because the latter predated the former.

The Mexican peóns were issued rations and other provisions on credit. In many instances, they were allotted a small plot of land to grow corn and other vegetables for their subsistence. In return, they were required to work for the haciendado from sun up to sundown, seven days a week. The scant wages they received were paid not in hard currency but in the form of a certificate which was redeemable at the hacienda store. This system limited the average peón's choice possibilities of shopping at the store in the village where he could have possibly bought the same items at a significantly lower price.

For all practical purposes, the hacienda was a system of slavery without the brutality and the horrible conditions to which African slaves were subjected in the American South. Instead of being shackled to the haciendas by chains, the peóns were tied with a system of perpetual indebtedness (i.e., the debts of the parents were passed down to their children). Unlike the African slaves who received some assistance from liberal whites to escape slavery through the underground railroad system, the Mexican peóns had neither assistance nor a place to which they could escape. Besides, such a system was not looked down on in the Mexican society as being morally wrong and contrary to the Scripture as it was for the system of slavery in America. Even if a peón managed to escape his horrible working conditions, there was no place that he could run. There was a set of laws on the books which prohibited anyone from hiring an indebted peón.[23]

One of the political and economic repercussions of the hacienda system was that it prevented peóns from connecting themselves to the mainstream of society's income redistribution system. He could not own land, which is one of the basic conditions for the accumulation of wealth. He was, however, allowed to live on the hacienda rent free and was granted a small plot of land to cultivate for his own use. In case of a crop failure, he was extended credit at the store to hold him over during hard times.

There are many other aspects of the structures of the haciendas that contributed to the constraint of the socioeconomic growth and development of the

Mexicans which need not be rehearsed here. Suffice to say that these constraints are consistent with the major argument of this study–that is, groups cannot grow and develop in society without positive laws adopted to protect their freedom to connect themselves with the mainstream of society's income redistribution system.

Ranchos

The term Rancho has had various meanings throughout the Mexican history to describe the ownership of land with less acreage than 2,500 acres was a Rancho.[24] The owners of these ranchos were called *rancheros*.[25] Unlike the haciendados, the rancheros work their farm themselves.

Racially, the rancheros were predominantly mestizos. Socially, although they were of Indian blood, they distanced themselves from the Indians because they looked down on the latter as inferior to them. They seldom, if at all, intermarried with the Indians. By practicing intermarrying among themselves over periods of time, they were able to create a social class centered around the ownership of ranchos.[26]

Unlike the haciendas, the Rancho system did not operate to constrain the socioeconomic development of the Mexicans. The rancheros were not subjected to the system of debt slavery as was the case with the peóns on the haciendas. The workers on the ranchos were family members. Very seldom did a ranchero employ laborers. Whenever one ranchero needed extra help, he could depend on assistance from some neighboring rancheros on a quid pro quo basis. There was, however, room for upward mobility for the offsprings of rancheros, but too often; this possibility was precluded by the unstable government of Mexico after the revolution for independence.

In short, the discussion of the policy of land tenure from the colonial period up to the Mexican independence shed light on some of the constraints which precluded the individual Mexican social upward mobility. These constraints became the catalyst for the revolts between the period of 1810 and 1815.

The Decline of the Spanish Empire

One of the major factors which led to the decline in the Spanish empire, perhaps, was the Seven Year War, where European countries were fighting for control of Germany and the supremacy of North America and India. Spain had suffered a number of military defeats in Europe. In an attempt to improve its defense, the crown sought to strengthen its military defense, which called for money that it did not have. To raise these funds, the crown raised taxes and instituted what is known as the *Bourbon Reform*.[27]

The Bourbon Reform was designed to eliminate the corruptions in the colonies and change the method of collecting taxes and increasing them. These tax changes were expensive which received little sympathy from the colonists. First, it attempted to limit the authority of the Catholic Church. The Jesuits had amassed a tremendous amount of power, wealth, and land. This gave them a tremendous amount of influence in determining affairs in the colonies. The crown viewed this influence as political rivalry and resistance to its reform policy. They felt that it had to be curbed. In 1767, the Spanish crown undertook the drastic step of seizing both the Jesuits' land and economic assets of the church. This seizure provoked anger among both the colonists and the Jesuits. It became the catalyst that mobilized the sentiments for the movement toward independence. Confiscating the church property induced the clerics to join this movement that had long been entertained by the creoles. The latter group welcomed this alliance, because they had long resented the class distinction that the crown had created in the authoritative distribution of property and power.

Around 1796, the British Navy had gained supremacy of the Atlanta Sea and largely cut off Spain's trade with the Americas. This blockade was in effect for approximately ten years. During which time, the economic conditions in Spain turned for the worse. New Spain shifted its trades to Britain and the newly formed United States. To further worsen conditions, Napoleon forced Spain to return the Louisiana territory to France in 1800. In 1803, it sold this territory to the United States (the Louisiana Purchase) for $15 million. This territory covered the following states: Arkansas, Colorado, Iowa, Kansas, Louisiana, Missouri, Minnesota, Montana, Nebraska, North Dakota, South Dakota, Oklahoma, and Wyoming. The forced relinquishment of the Louisiana territory further bolstered the sentiment among the colonists to seek Mexico's independence.

The Quest for the Independence of Mexico

The sentiments for the independence of Mexico were brewing among the intellectuals in Mexico during the latter parts of the eighteenth century. This group consisted of the Jesuits and the creoles. Like the North American intellectuals such as James Madison and Thomas Jefferson, they had read literature of the writers of the enlightenment movement which advocated challenging the privilege, social, and political structure of Europe, particularly the monarch formal government. When Napoleon I captured Spain in 1808, the creoles began to pressure the viceroys for a share of the power. This irritated the peninsulares who had a higher status than the creoles. This dispute and resentment eventually led to the Insurgent movement which started in 1810 and plagued the country for eleven years. A brief discussion of the political actors of this movement will shed some light of the problems that constrained the Mexicans from growth and development in the twentieth century.

The Insurgent Movement and
The Hidalgo Revolt

The first revolt against the crown in Mexico was led by Father Hidalgo who was a part of the traditional Creole patriotism. During the eighteenth century, the Creole Jesuits joined the European Enlightenment movement. As this group began to gain influence in both the church and politics, it became annoying to the Bourbon Kings. The kings attempted to curb their influence by expelling them from the Spanish dominion in 1769.[28] One of the issues that the Jesuits had long advocated was freeing Mexico of Spain's economic exploitation.

As Spain attempted to recover from the effect of the Seven Year War and French occupation, it adopted various laws; one such law, which significantly affected the status of the Creole Jesuits, was the adoption of the *Consolidacion de Vales Reales* of 1804.[29] Under this law, the authorities placed a lien on Hidalgo's haciendas and his family as demands of the payment of debts. His debts resulted in his poor management of money and his habits of being lackadaisical in paying his debts. The demands for payments of his debts not only pushed Hidalgo to the edge of bankruptcy but also placed grave psychological hardships upon his family. His brother, Manuel, had a nervous breakdown and died in 1809.

The death of his brother influenced Hidalgo to launch the revolutionary movement for Mexico independence. His struggle ended in 1811 when he was defeated and executed. After his execution, Jose Maria Morelos, who was part of the Hidalgo's army, took up the struggle.

Morelos

Unlike Hidalgo, Morelos was a mestizo. He had divorced himself from the loyalty to Spain when Napoleon invaded Spain in 1808. After Hidalgo's execution on July 30, 1811, Morelos stepped forward to take the reins of the insurrection. He had studied under Hidalgo at the Colegio de San Nicolás. Unlike Hidalgo, he had profound religious faith, coupled with economic necessity of the priesthood. After his ordination, he was assigned to minister the villages of the hot country of Michoacán. This area was not favored to the government because of the lack of economically generating enterprises. The government did not pay Morelos a salary as it did the other priests. He had to rely on the money that he collected in tithes and offerings in church for his subsistence.

Unsupported by the government, Morelos was able to turn this disadvantage into an advantage. He was forced to build his own church by inducing the villagers (the Cestes, Indians, and mestizos) to help him. He had a passion for helping uplift impoverished populations. He felt that one of the major missions of the priesthood was to address not only the spiritual well-being of his congregation but also their material well-being. Although he was profoundly committed to the doctrine of the Catholic Church, he disagreed with its doctrine of fornication. He fathered various children with women of his congregation.[30]

When he learned that Hidalgo had taken up arms against the crown, Morelos agreed to accept the responsibility to form a revolution in South. The South was less developed than northern Mexico. It did not have the mining and agriculture industries to sustain it. It was inhabited by Indian groups and large caste settlements (African descendants) and fewer mestizos and Creoles.

Unlike Hidalgo, Morelos had a greater sense of military strategy and organization as a result of his studying the *Military Instructions* of Prussia's Frederick the Great. Based on Frederick's instructions, he was able to make prudent decisions in selecting his lieutenants and maintaining a sense of order that Hidalgo did not have. With his army, Morelos was able to capture city after city. He did not make the same mistake as did Hidalgo (i.e., robbing the people of the villages). He made it clear to his lieutenants that the purpose of the revolution was to free Mexico from Spain and to strive for equality among the people. This ideology can account for his success throughout his three years of insurgency.

Morelos incorporated elements of the political philosophies of the Enlightenment Movements which were designed to bring about socially equality (i.e., combining economic, political, and social proposals in his struggle). For him, the revolution was more then a matter of arms and politics. It was part of his Christian mission. His struggle was more attractive to Blacks than the Indians. As mentioned, these groups were tied to the haciendas by debt slavery. They were assigned to a legal status of inferiority. Morelos promised them relief if they joined his struggle.

Morelos had bad memories of the social inequality among the impoverished Blacks and Indians, Creoles and affluent Spaniards. He did not want his movement to be characterized as a class struggle as was the case with Hidalgo. He wanted to include all groups with the exception of Spaniards who were of a higher class than the rest. More important, he wanted so desperately to abolish class distinctions. After he captured Oaxaca in 1812, he attempted to achieve this objective by issuing an order to abolish distinctions between populations, and everyone was considered to be an American.[31]

In 1813, Morelos convoked the Congress of Chilpancingo and declared Mexico Independence. In convening the Congress, he had hoped that the group would form a government which incorporated some of the principles of equality as had the French Revolution, and a system of representation and separation of the three branches of government as the American colonists had done. He also wished for the group to incorporate the same noble ideas as the Americans—such as freedom of expression and civil liberties.

When it came to the freedom of religion, he parted company. Morelos wanted Mexico to be a Roman Catholic republic. Equally important, he wanted to restore the Church's exemption and privileges that the Bourbon Kings had stripped away when they came to power in the eigthteenth century. Morelos failed to see the contradiction in the egalitarian principles that he so desperately sought and the absolute authority of the church. This authority would always preempt the noble ideals of civil liberty and freedom. The freedom of expression presupposes an individual's freedom to question the absolute authority of the church. The penalty for questioning the church authority was severe and sometimes resulted in excommunication. This principle marked the distinction between the noble ideal of freedom of expression in America and Mexico. When a person was expelled from the church in America, there were other churches which he could join. But in Mexico, there was only one, the Catholic.

Morelos' downfall came when he placed his military service at the hands of the Congress of Chilpancingo. The Congress was made up of lawyers from the creole class, who were by operation of a higher class than Morelos and his followers (i.e., the castes, Indians, and the mestizos). Morelos did not comprehend the class distinction that existed in Mexico based on skin color. He assumed that this class distinction would disappear with his decree abolishing this distinction.

Instead of pursuing a policy of a classless society, members of Congress immediately started to concoct strategies not only to wrestle the power away from Morelos but also to get rid of him altogether. After drafting the final constitution in 1814, Morelos engaged in a battle with the crown soldiers led by Agustín de Iturbide in which his troops were defeated. Morelos managed to escape but eventually was captured. Numerous charges were brought against him during his trial, including heresy. The leaders of the church (predominantly creoles) were in the forefront in bringing charges against him. He was condemned to be defrocked and executed. And in 1821, after Mexico won it its Independence, Morelos was executed.

Iturbide

After the execution of Morelos, Austin de Iturbide came to power and proclaimed Mexican independence in 1821. Unlike Morelos, he came from a rich family of creoles.[32] He received his military training at the cadet of the Valladolid Regiment of Provincial Infantry. His opposition to the insurgent movement led by Hidalgo and Morelos resulted in his family favorable position with the Spanish crown.

Iturbide had developed a strong dispassion for the insurgents. He fought them with excess anger and freely executed both the insurgent soldiers and civilians without giving them the final rites, which was customary of the Catholic Church. He blamed the Insurgents for destroying the country and the deaths of thousands. More important, he blamed them for promoting racial hatred.[33]

One of the insurgents that was a thorn in Iturbide's side was Vincente Guerrero. Iturbide met with him and persuaded him to join forces to conspire against the crown. They signed the so-called *Pain of Iguala* in February 1821, which paved the way for the Mexican Independence. In August of that same year, Iturbide and Guerrero's forces were able to defeat the Spanish Army near Mexico City. The last viceroy resigned and the *Treaty of Cordaba* was signed, thus ending Spanish colonial power of what had been called New Spain.

On September 27, 1821, Iturbide was able to unite the factions in Mexico under the *Plan de Iguala*.[34] This plan called for the unified army of the two factions and the guarantees of the three functional principles. First, the unity of all ethnic and social groups was to take place. Second, the exclusive rights and privileges of the Church, which the Bourbon crown had stripped it of, were to be restored. Finally, Mexico was to become absolutely separate from Spain, although Iturbide wanted to maintain political ties. By maintaining these ties, he had hoped that the Spanish government would send them a Bourbon prince to reside. But Spain not only refused to send them a prince but also to recognize their independence. This refusal prompted the Mexican Congress to anoint and elect Iturbide as the constitutional temporal of Mexico.[35]

During Iturbide's first ten months in office, he inherited a bankrupt country. The infrastructure of the economic system had been destroyed by the various internal struggles since 1810. Its cultural development had come to a standstill. The country's attempt to borrow money from abroad was met with little or no success. It was deeply in debt. Not only did the European countries turned a deaf ear to the plea for financial assistance but also did the Vatican.

The problem that Iturbide faced was similar to the one that Morelos had faced earlier: rivalry with Congress. The latter were constantly trying to usurp the power of the presidency. At the core of this struggle was the distribution of land which was in the crown possession. This struggle ended when Iturbide dissolved the Congress and appointed a junta, Antonio Lopez de Santa Anna. He was a royalist and a brigadier general from the city of Veracruz. He came out of an environment known for its wealth and moral easygoing. Santa Anna himself was known as a womanizer and a gambler, who had a love for cockfighting and forging commercial documents.[36]

The appointment of Santa Ana as junta proved to be one of Iturbide's greatest mistakes. After assuming power, one of the first steps that Santa Ana undertook was to pronounce against Iturbide and his "absolutism." Iturbide did not attempt to stop him, although he could have with his army. Instead, he reinstated the old Congress, and abdicated the presidency. On March 19, 1823, he was ridiculed by Congress and exiled.

Congress deemed Iturbide to be a "traitor," "a tyrant," and condemned him to death if he were to return to Mexico. Unaware of this condemnation, Iturbide travelled to Italy where he started writing his memoirs. Toward the end of 1823, he received news of a possible reconquest of Mexico by Spain, but he was not aware of the political impracticality of such a rumor. Even if the rumor was true, it could not become a reality because of the Monroe Doctrine of 1823, which prohibited foreign nations from establishing colonies on the North American Hemisphere. On July 19, 1824, Iturbide returned to Mexico and was arrested and executed shortly thereafter.

In the same year Iturbide was executed, Mexico adopted its first Constitution, which was modelled after the United States—a representative Congress and a judiciary. Unlike the United States, the framers of the Mexican Constitution did not address the issue of how to control factions. Consequently, factions began to emerge in the early stage of its independence. The factions that caused the downfall of the Mexican government were the various masonic lodges. The rivalries among these groups practically hamstrung the operation of a democratic government in Mexico. Decisions were made not in the legislative body where issues could be freely debated, but behind closed doors in the lodge's meetings. This practice automatically stripped the Mexican government of one of its most essential components of a free society (i.e., the free press). In debating the role of a free press in the United States, Thomas Jefferson said that if he had a choice between a free press and a free government, he would always choose the former. In the United States, history has proven him to be correct. As a result of factions, the Mexican government was unstable. It elected eleventh presidents between the period of 1824 and 1833. The last president elected before the Mexican-American War was Santa Anna who dissolved the Congress.

President Santa Anna

After Santa Anna was enthroned as president in 1833, he realized that his heart was set on his profession—being a professional soldier. Although he was a strewed politician insofar as being manipulative in affairs behind the scene, he had no heart for the administration of the daily affairs of government. He found such a task boring and, in some instance, he feared it. He once stated that he was not a politician and did not like the career. He found it boring and only brought enmities and worries. He loved being a professional soldier which he saw as an honorable profession. He, along with other soldiers, could not bring himself to become preoccupied with constructing a peaceful state where affairs were administered by institutions. Instead, they longed for the mantra of military glory.

The one aspect of the administration of the daily government that Santa Anna found the most boring was mediating the conflict among the various factions, which had emerged from the former decade. This was a duty that he had to perform as president. He employed every tactic to avoid it. In fact, when he was inaugurated as president in 1833, he stayed at his hacienda, Manga de Clavo, claiming illness. As the new president, he left the administration of government up to his vice president, Dr. Valentine Frariás. Instead of working to establish a sound political and economic base in Mexico, Santa Anna preoccupied himself with "gambling, womanizing, cockfighting, delivering speeches, flattering, and forging commercial documents."[37] These activities diverted his attention from the pressing affairs of the country, such as reducing the national debts and establishing international trades.

For the first thirty years after its independence, Mexico was known as a country of revolution. During this period, the country experienced fifty regimes, vacillating back-and-forth from a republic to a central federalist government. During that time, they elected thirty-seven presidents, "the average term being about seven and a half months."[38] Santa Anna occupied this office of the presidency eleven times. During the first thirty years of its independence, Mexico was unable to establish neither a stable government nor an economy. A brief examination of its economic status is in order.

The Economic Conditions of the
New Republic of Mexico

The New Republic of Mexico was originally plagued with internal conflicts. The country had neither the human resources nor the physical capital to rule the country efficiently. The tax revenue dropped drastically because the revolutionists had no plan for the post-revolutionary war. Distrust among leaders was rampant. Conditions in Mexico were not conducive for self government as they were in the North American colonies the previous century. Wealth and power were concentrated in the hands of a few elites.

The elite class was divided into two groups: the conservatives and liberals. The conservatives came from the ranks of the church leaders, the owner of the haciendas, the creoles, and military applications. They favored a strong centralized government so that they could maintain their power positions. The liberals, on the other hand, wanted a decentralized government with a series of federation of states. More important, they wanted social reforms whereby the power of the Catholic Church could be curtailed and a more liberalized education system would be sponsored by the government instead of the church.

The conflict in the development of the new government became the basis for conflicts in Mexico. The liberals who first gained control of the government established Vicente Guerrero as president. Within a year, he was assassinated by the forces led by the conservatives. Following Guerrero's assassination, there were series of revolutions in Mexico until Santa Anna was elected in 1833, as will be discussed. But political instability plagued this country for the rest of the century. There were two major factors that contributed to this unrest: socioeconomic status and the lack of an adequate land reform policy.

The Socioeconomic Status of Mexico
Prior to Its Independence

The economy of Mexico on the eve of its independence was in a state of stagnation. It was plagued with many problems. First, unlike the United States when it severed its ties with its mother country, Mexico did not have trade relations with other nations. Its domestic economy was plagued by its geological makeup. The productive farmland was located in the Central Plateau which was bordered by the Atlantic Ocean on one side and the Pacific Ocean on the other. Access to this plan was hampered by the rugged mountain ranges on both sides. Without the development of roads or railways, the Mexicans' ability to develop an adequate commerce industry became difficult.

The second factor that hampered the growth and development of the Mexican economy was the structure of the numerous haciendas. As mentioned previously, these were large land holdings in which, in some instances, one family owned as much as 11,626,850 acres of land.[39] In contrast, the United States restricted landownership to 80 acres of land per family, or to what John Locke has said, as much as one can make use of.[40] One of the political repercussions of large landownership is that it breeds poverty among the nation's populations. It leaves little room for individuals to become industrious, as has been demonstrated with the encomienda and hacienda systems.

The third factor that constrained the industrial growth of the Mexicans was the Spanish colonial policy. The Spanish crowns closely regulated the industry in Mexico to prevent the Mexicans from competing with its mother country. This left very little room for the Mexicans to develop a class of merchants. As mentioned in Chapter 1, in order for a group to grow and develop, its members must have the freedom to acquire and possess the necessary property (human and physical) to compete successfully in a competitive market. The Spanish crown stripped the Mexican of this ability.

The fourth factor that plagued Mexico was the lack of the development of a viable manufacturing and merchant class. The Spanish merchants had long constrained this development by its policy of importing almost all of its luxury goods from abroad. They, in turn, would export these goods to the merchants in their colonies. Such restrictions over periods of time had a devastating impact in constraining the development of a merchant class. Such a class, it must be noted, is developed and maintained through the principle of intergenerational mobility.

The fifth factor that constrained the Mexicans' growth and development was the restrictions that the Spanish crown placed on the colonists from manufacturing fine goods. For example, the Mexicans started processing silk during the sixteenth century. But the Spanish merchants stepped in and blocked their production because of the competition it posed with the inexpensive silk that they were importing from China.

Finally, there was the forced labor systems of the encomienda and the hacienda, as mentioned. Forced labor, by operation, offers little, if any, incentive for populations to acquire the necessary property (human and physical capital) for individual growth and development. However, the natives were able to establish industries which manufactured coarse clothing and textile mills during the sixteenth and seventeenth centuries.[41] But these industries were run in a "sweatshop" fashion where the mistreatment of workers was a common practice. In many instances, workers were placed behind locked doors where they were crowded into small quarters at night and were allowed to see their families only on Sundays. Such crowded living conditions always make a population susceptible to diseases. This, in part, can account for the drastic decease in the native population as earlier.

The Lack of an Adequate Land Reform Policy

The failure of the Mexican Congress to adopt an adequate land reform policy after their independence contributed significantly to the country's instability. Historically, one of the major prerequisites for establishing a stable democratic state in any nation has always been a land reform policy which distributed land to the masses. Such reform policy was one of the major reasons why the United States was so successful in establishing a stable society after its Revolution. This policy abolished the feudalistic system of quitrents, confiscated the large estates of the Royalists, divided them up into small plots of 80 acres, and sold them to individual farmers at a nominal price. Politically, this policy tied the farmers to the land and provided, what Thomas Jefferson called, the backbone of democracy. Farmers who owned their land are highly unlikely to revolt unless the security of their land is threatening, as was the case with the Shey's rebellion.

Since large landholding constrains groups' growth and development, the land grant tenure of colonial Mexico, which was granted encomiendas and haciendas, was the catalyst that constrained the Mexicans' socioeconomic growth and development. As we seen, this system placed 97 percent of the land in the hands of one percent of the population, thus precluding the possibility of individuals' socioeconomic growth and development.

The Mexicans, however, did adopt a land policy after the revolution, but it was not directed toward ensuring stability in the country. Instead, it was an attempt to colonize the unpopulated land in the northeast territory, namely Texas. This policy was first initiated by the Spaniards in an attempt to curb the spread of the Americans and French westward. Because of the political disruptions that Spain encountered during the early nineteenth century, it abandoned this policy. After its independence, the Mexican Congress took up this matter again. Before discussing these laws, let us take a look at the socioeconomic conditions of Mexico immediately after gaining its independence in order to identify those conditions that contributed to this instability.

Attempt to Curb Immigration in Texas

We have seen in Chapter 3 that the Louisiana Purchase created the opportunity for the Americans to expand its territory westward. The Land Grant Acts of 1800 and 1828 provided the economic incentive for people to populate this area. At the same time, there was a large influx of immigrants from Ireland and Germany during this period, as demonstrated in Chapter 3. Economic conditions in Germany were in a state of constant deterioration. As farmers were being uprooted from their land, the notion of emigrating to America became more attractive. The available land within the Louisiana territory was quickly occupied. The vast unoccupied land in the Texas territory became attractive to these immigrants and Americans. Since the Mexican government was unable to populate the land nor adequately protect it, these groups started squatting on the land. The Mexican government undertook various measures to curb this squatting, but they did not have the resources nor the manpower to do so.

The dispute over the land continued until the *Treaty of Adams-Onis* was signed by Spain on October 22, 1819 and ratified in October 24, 1819. This treaty settled the dispute by fixing the boundary of the Louisiana Purchase. It did not, however, completely lay to rest Spain's fear of America's expansion into the Texas territory. Their concerns lay not so much on Americans' influx as with the internal dissension that was taking place in Texas. The citizens became increasingly disenchanted with the royal government. The Spanish authorities sensed that a movement for independence was in the winds. Consequently, they appointed Manuel Maria Salcedo as governor of Texas. Instead of quashing the movement, which lasted for eleven years, his appointment did more to promote it.

Spain's Attempt to Curb the Influx
of Immigrant in Texas

After the Louisiana Purchase, Spain became concerned about the American expansion into the Texas territory and its declining economic conditions. Spanish Texas had become the new Spain's northwestern frontier. Around 1808, Anglos had started squatting in Texas. In an attempt to curb this influx of immigrants, the crown appointed Manuel Maria Salcedo as governor of Texas, and attempted to promote the settlement of Texas with Spanish citizens from Mexico. This plan proved to be unproductive because of the lack of people to populate the area.

In 1803, the permanent population of Texas was less than 5,000, including the squatters' settlements. All of the missions that the Franciscans had established were closed with the exception of two. This represented a failure of the Catholic Church and state to colonize Texas through peaceful means. The Native Americans in this region were unconvinced that the Spanish god was superior to theirs.

The total population of New Spain averaged six inhabitants per six square miles. Texas, on the other hand, had only two inhabitants per six square miles. This was less than California with its Baja desert. This left an opened plane in the New Spain northwestern frontier. Altogether, Texas had approximately 5000 inhabitants settled in the territory.

As early as 1783, the Spanish crown began to worry about the vast territory of Texas, which was rich in farmland. If left undeveloped, it would eventually be lost to other world nations seeking to expand their territory. First, the Spaniards adopted a policy of recruiting immigrants from Britain, France, and other European countries to settle in Texas. What hampered this policy was that the Spanish still had intact their policy of Inquisition. This policy was basically contradictory in terms for Spain to achieve its objective. They were recruiting people that had been conditioned by the Enlightenment movement which subscribed to the principle of individualism and freedom of religion. Yet, this recruitment drive required the immigrants to convert to Catholicism as a condition for settlement. This policy within itself made the immigrants from the newly formed United States undesirable. This nation was founded on religious freedom and individualism. The Spanish crown felt that land grants, economic freedom, and freedom of religion would preclude the possibility of settlers from America to pledge allegiance to the Spanish crown. Consequently, the officials at the headquarters of Chihuahua sent an order to the governor of Texas, ordering him to scrutinize closely all persons from the United States and all foreigners without proper papers.

The Republic of Texas and the Mexican-American War

Other than economics, the problem that faced the Republic of Mexico was the large unpopulated land in the northeast territory. Around 1810, the Mexican population was approximately six million. Four-fifths of these individuals were nonwhite and lower class which consisted of mestizos, Blacks, and Indians.[42] As mentioned previously, the entire population in Texas was approximately 5000. In an attempt to correct this problem, the Mexican government adopted a series of colonization laws in 1823, 1824, and 1825. These laws created an empresario system. This system differed from their encomienda system which required forced slave labor. For example, Article 3 of the Colonization Law Decree of 1823 spelled out the duties and responsibilities of the empersarios. These were individuals who contracted with the Mexican authorities to recruit a minimum of 200 families to settle in Texas. Because of the lack of advanced payments, they had to finance their own ventures. Once they recruited and settled the prescribed number of families, they were compensated "five leagues of range land (22,142 acres) and five cultivable labors (886 acres) of farm land, for every 100 families up to the maximum of 100 families."[43] There were no penalties for the empersarios if they failed to fulfill their contracts within the prescribed time period. The only exception was that if an empersario failed to settle 100 families in his colony, the land would revert back to the government.

The colonization law also required the immigrants to be productive persons and of high moral standards and married. For those who were unmarried, this law offered them citizenship if they married Mexicans. This perhaps was an attempt to make up for the shortage of male population lost in the war.

The colonization law offered preferences to Mexican citizens and soldiers. There were many problems associated with this policy. First, Mexico had experienced a shortage of male populations as a result of the Insurgent moments which lasted for more than eleven years. This movement took its toll in reducing the male population, particularly the Creoles and Spanish. Many males were executed after being captured in the war. For example, Hidalgo executed many prisoners of war.[44] The execution of this class of citizens left Mexico largely with the peons who were basically slaves. As mentioned previously, the system of slavery precluded them from acquiring the necessary human capital for social upward mobility. Their experience was similar to that of the Irish-Catholics who immigrated to America without the necessary human capital to take advantage of the opportunities that the government had to offer.

With the lack of citizens to populate the land, the Mexican government relied on the empersario system to fill the void. The first person to sign such a contract with the Mexican government was Stephen Austin in 1821. His father, Moses, had already negotiated a similar contract with the Spanish crown, but died before he was able to carry out his plan for colonization. On his sickbed, he got his son Stephen to promise to carry out his dream of establishing a colony in Texas.

In 1821, Stephen kept his promise to his father and settled 300 families in Texas whom he recruited from Missouri, Tennessee, and Arkansas. His recruitment was aided by the economic conditions in America (i.e., the failure of the banks). The colonization laws were the beginning of the Mexican problems. It became an open invitation for foreigners and non-Catholics to immigrate into the country with the expectation that the settlers, who were predominately Protestants, would abandon their religious belief, which was a lifelong socialization experience, in exchange for another religion which they had been taught from childhood to despise and to reject. In other words, the Mexican colonization laws opened the doors for an influx of religious hypocrites, individuals who would falsely profess their loyalty to the Catholic Church for the purpose of obtaining land and, at the same time, maintain their Protestants' faith.

After Austin succeeded in fulfilling the terms of his contract, other adventurers sought similar contracts. Between the period of 1825 and 1835, the authority of Texas signed twenty-four such contracts with empersarios. In total, these empersarios imported 7,591 families. If we assume that the average number of families per farm was at least 5.2, then it can be estimated that the empersario system was responsible for recruiting more than 35,000 people to the state during this period. This, within itself, placed the non-Mexican population in the majority who were endowed with the democratic value of majority rule.[45]

One of the driving forces behind the successful Texas immigration was cheap land. Families who had lost their farms in America, as a result of the collapse of the banks, could now seek a new lease on life by immigrating to Texas where they could obtain a larger farm for less than the price they could purchase in America. Under the Land Grant Act of 1828, for example, the size of a farm in the United States was limited to 80 acres per family at a price of $1.25 an acre. In Texas, a male 21 years and over could purchase "640 acres for himself, 320 acres for his wife, 160 acres for each child and . . . an additional 80 acres for each slave he brought with him."[46]

This in flux of immigrants immediately began to cause problems for the Mexican government. It expected these groups to assimilate into the Mexican culture by learning the Spanish language and converting to the Roman Catholic religion. Their failure to show signs of assimilation prompted the Mexican government to undertake certain measures to make this happen. The first problem that they attempted to address was the importation of a large number into the state. In 1830, the Mexicans outlawed slavery, but this did not stop the immigrants from bringing slaves into the state. Many of the immigrants came from the southern slave states. To enforce its policy on prohibition of slavery, the Mexican government sent a small numbers of troops to block the importation of slaves. These troops proved to be inadequate to curb the importation of slaves.

The forces that were pushing the importation of slaves in Texas were the advocates of manifest destiny. The philosophy of these groups was that America was to rule North America if not the whole world. The slave owners began to view Texas as an opportunity to expand slavery. They started pressuring the United States government to purchase Texas for the purpose of incorporating it into the union. In comparison to other land in the United States, Texas was virgin land suitable for agriculture, particularly cotton.

With the increase in the importation of slaves, the Mexican government undertook further measures to curb this importation. In 1830, it suspended the colonization law. It subsequently stationed a small number of troops in the state to enforce its abolition of slavery in its constitution of 1824. At the time, slavery had been abolished in Mexico, except for Texas and a few other states. The state legislature of Coahuila and Texas had prohibited slavery in Article 13 in its constitution. This article reads:

> In the state no person should be a slave after this Constitution is published in
> the capital of each district, and six months thereafter, neither will the introduc-
> tion of slaves be permitted under any pretext.

Because of the internal conflict among the officials in the Mexican government, a revolution began and the troops in the colony had to be withdrawn. The new settlers in Texas seized upon this opportunity to carry out their will to spread slavery throughout the colony. Consequently, they joined the parties in Mexico that were opposing the government, with the expectation that they could win concession with the new party for a further importation of slavery.

When the revolution was over, Santa Anna emerged as the new president. One of the first measures that he undertook to curb the importation of slavery was to abolish the Constitution of 1824. He was of the opinion that the Mexicans were too immature to be ruled by a free government. He felt that dictation and despotism were the only means to bring about stability in the country.

When Santa Anna abolished the Constitution, the settlers became worried that their property would be lost. They received support from the slave holders and the land speculators in New York. These elites began to pressure the American government either to purchase Texas outright or to win it by war. By abolishing the Constitution, Santa Anna violated one of the sacred principles of the liberal democratic theory. Locke wrote that when the state violates the trust of the people, then they have a right to revolt. In fact, one of the Mexican leaders,

Lorenzo de Zavala, who opposed to Santa Anna's action, pointed this out the settlers, and urged them to declare Texas' independence. The Texans followed his advice and elected David Burnet as president.

This declaration touched off the war for Texas' independence. To curb this insurrection, Santa Anna was called upon to suppress it. In the winter 1833, he assembled an army of 6,000 soldiers and started marching north through rough terrains until he reached the outskirts of San Antonio. There, he found a group of Texans who had taken refuge in the old Franciscan mission, known as the Alamo. The accounts of what happened at the Alamo have been told many times in textbooks and movies and there is no need to repeat it here. Suffice to say that Santa Anna surrounded the mission with his army of 6000 soldiers and defeated the Texans inside the Alamo. Every one of the Texans was either killed during the battle or executed thereafter.

The capture of the Alamo did not solve the problem that the Santa Anna and the Mexicans had hoped. He was very adamant about preventing foreigners from settling on Mexican territory. He considered all foreigners on Mexico land with arms to be pirates and, therefore, should be punished according to the national law of piracy, which was execution. This sentiment was carried out several weeks later when a Mexican general captured 365 armed Texans in the small town of Golaid. Santa Anna sent an order to the general to execute all of the soldiers. He reluctantly carried out this order.

Instead of serving as a deterrent for foreigners to settle in Texas, the brutal execution at the Alamo and Golaid served to mobilize anti-Mexican sentiment in America. Supplies and men started pouring in to support the Texan's exposition, which was headed by Sam Houston. The advocates of Manifest Destiny began to intensify their campaign for the capture of Mexico. With additional men and supplies, Houston became more confident that he could succeed in defeating Santa Anna. On the afternoon of April 21, he caught Santa Anna and his army off guard at the river of San Jacinto and attacked them. Santa Anna's army was defeated. However, he managed to escape but was captured by one of Houston's patrols two days later.[47]

As a prisoner of war, Santa Anna was forced to sign two treaties with the Texan authorities. First, he agreed never to take up arms against the Texans again. Secondly, all hostilities toward the Texans were to cease. Third, he was to convince the Mexican army to withdrawn below the Rio Grande River. Finally, all prisoners of war in equal numbers were to be exchanged. In return for these agreements, Santa Anna was to be free to return to Mexico to convince the Mexican government to accept these treaties. The Mexican Congress rejected these treaties and, subsequently, passed a law which made all future treaties made by a Mexican President in captivity null and void.

Between the period of 1836 and 1845, Texas remained an independent state. The Mexican government made no attempt to remove the Texans from its territory because of its internal conflicts. During this period of independence, Texas was in a political dilemma. The Texans wanted to retain their status as an independent republic, but they did not have the resources to withstand an attack by the superior force of the Mexican army. On the other hand, they wanted to be annexed to the United States, but the question of slavery was an issue. If Texas were to be annexed, it would have had to come into the union as a slave state, thus upsetting the balance of power in Congress.

The question of Texas annexation to America was resolved in the presidential election of 1844. James K. Polk won the election on the platform that Texas would be annexed into the union. In 1845, a joint resolution passed Congress to this effect. This resolution paved the way for war. At issue, was the western boundary of Texas. The Texans claimed that the boundary was at the Rio Grande River and the Mexicans claimed that it was 150 miles further north at the Nueces River. The significance of the Rio Grande River was that it ran aimlessly northwest instead of straight north as did the former. This included several thousand square miles of territory, which included parts of New Mexico and Colorado.

With the pressure from the advocates of Manifest Destiny, President Polk tried to resolve the dispute by offering to purchase the rest of New Mexico for $5 million and California for $25 million or even more. The Mexican nationalist viewed such an offer with indignation. They threatened their president, José Joaquín Herrera, with rebellion if he negotiated such a treaty. Eventually, General Mariano Paredes overthrew the Herrera government and established himself as the leader. This set the stage for the war with the United States.

The United States Congress was reluctant to go to war with the Mexicans unless they were attacked first. While the issue of war was being discussed, hostility between General Zachary Taylor's army and the Mexicans broke out on May 6, 1846, over the dispute of the boundary between the Nueces and Rio Grande Rivers. This gave President Polk the ammunition he needed to persuade Congress to declare war against Mexico.

America declared war on Mexico on May 9, 1846, and the war ended on February 2, 1848, with the signing of the *Treaty of Guadalupe Hidalgo*, which ceded more than half of the northern territory of Mexico to the United States, which including Texas, New Mexico, California, Arizona, and part of Colorado. In return for this territory, the United States agreed to pay Mexico $18,250,000: $15,000,000 in cash payment for the land and to assume

$3,250,000 in claims that the U.S. citizens had against the Mexican government.

The next issue to be settled was the question of citizenship for those Mexicans residing in the conquered land. At time of the signing of the treaty, there were estimated to be between 70,000 and 100,000 Mexican citizens living in the southwest area.[48] The question of citizenship posed serious psychological problems for the Americans. The issue centered over the fact that two-thirds of the Mexicans were nonwhites and non-Protestants. Granting nonwhite citizenship conflicted with the racial doctrine on which this country was founded up to this period of time (i.e., only whites could become citizens).

The issue of importance to our study is what decision did the United States made as to how it was going to treat the Mexicans, who were not a homogeneous racial group. The conclusion of the war came at a time when the discussion of white nationalism, Manifest Destiny, and expansion were in vogue. Before the war, the expansionists had advocated annexing Mexico as a part of the United States. The nationalists rejected this movement because the Mexican populations were not pure white. They were of the opinion that nonwhites could not be assimilated into the American society like other white groups. The pro and con arguments for the westward expansion can be found in the literature on the "free soil" movement and need not be repeated here.[49]

The issue of citizenship was of major concerns to the creoles. As mentioned previously, Mexico consisted of four different classes of people: mestizos, creoles, Indians, and Africans. For centuries, the Mexicans had no law prohibiting mixed marriages, whereas the United States had specific laws prohibiting such marriages. Some of these laws remained in effect until the late 1960s.[50] The nationalists were opposed to annexing Mexico because it would force them to accept their nonwhite populations, which would have been against the American tradition of being a true white society.

The issue as to how the Mexicans were to be treated was resolved in Article IX of this Treaty. It stated that those Mexicans who decided to remain in the United States territory were to enjoy "all the rights of citizens of the United States, according to the principles of the Constitution; and in the mean time, shall be maintained and protected in the free enjoyment of their liberty and property secured in the free exercise of their religion without . . . restrictions." In essence, the government told the Mexicans that they were going to be treated as a white man. Such rights are very important in comparing the Mexican Americans' rate of social upward mobility with that of African Americans. Although the Mexicans were granted citizenship rights in 1848, eight years later the government told African Americans, in the *Dred Scott* decision of 1857, that they had no rights that the white man was bound to respect. This policy remained in effect for the latter group up to and after the 1964 Civil Rights Act.

By granting the Mexicans full citizenship at the onset, the Mexicans were spared the humiliation of being saddled with the disability of race. The factor that constrained their upward mobility was not their race but their lack of the necessary human capital to compete on an equal footing in a competitive society. As far as America was concerned, the Mexican was a white man and was free to compete on an equal footing with whites. This fact was pointed out in the *Rodriguez* case in 1972.[51]

From the end of the Mexican American War up to the first quarter of the twentieth century, Mexico was plagued with the internal dissensions and revolutions. These revolutions placed them into—what Thomas Hobbes called—the natural state of war. In such a state, Hobbes argued there is no room for growth and development. After the war, the Mexicans did not undergo any land reform before the 1950s. As argued, land reform is necessary for the masses to grow and develop socioeconomically. However, Mexico did experience a period of stability under the dictatorship of Porfirio Díaz. The country experienced an expansion in its manufacturing and mining. Its national income rose "from 20 million pesos to 100 million during the 34 years"[52] of Diaz' rule. This improvement in economic status made Mexico eligible to borrow money at 4 percent interest. However, this prosperity was enjoyed by the ruling class. The masses still remained impoverished. During the first quarter of the twentieth century, approximately 75 percent of them experienced a reduction in their low levels of living. These conditions prompted them to start immigrating to the U.S.

In short, what this chapter has attempted to demonstrate was that the lower socioeconomic status of the Mexicans today can be traced back to the structural conditions in their homeland from the colonial period up to their migration to America. These conditions constrained their socioeconomic growth and development. The next chapter will consist of an examination of their experience in the United States.

Notes

1. "Spain," Microsoft® Encarta® Online Encyclopedia 2003. Also see David R. Ringrose, *Spain, Europe, and the "Spanish miracle," 1700-1900 (*Cambridge, MA : Press Syndicate of the University of Cambridge, 1996).

2. Michael C. Meyer and William L. Sherman, *The Course Mexican History* (New York: Oxford University Press, 1995), p. 195.

3. Michael Marcus, *The Jew in the Medieval World: A Sourcebook, 315-1791* (New York: JPS, 1938), pp. 51-55.

4. Meyer and Sherman, p. 103.

5. For a discussion of the impact of the diseases on the natives see, Eduardo Guerra, "Bosquejo Histórico de la Comarca Lagunera 1739-193," *Ciclo de Conferencias* (Torreón: Comité Americano de "Amigos de la Paz," 1939, mimeo.); Esteban L. Portillo, *Catecismo Geográfico, Político e Histórico del Estado de Coahuila de Zaragoza* (Saltillo: Tipografía del gobierno en palacio, 1897), pp. 103-114.

6. Meyer and Sherman, pp. 214-215.

7. John Hodge, Donald K. Struckmann, and Lynn Dorland Trost, *Cultural Bases of Racism and Group Oppression* (Berkeley: Two Riders Press, P.O. Box 4129), pp. 124-127.

8. *Dred Scott v. Sandford,* 60 U.S. 393; 15 L. Ed. 691 (1856).

9. *Loving v. Virgina*, 388 U. S. 1; Ct. 1817; 18 L. Ed. 2d 1010 (1967).

10. George M. McBride, *The Land Systems of Mexico* (New York: American Geographical Society Research Series No. 12, 1927), p. 51.

11. Eyler Simpson, *The Ejido: Mexico's Way Out* (Chapel Hill: The University of North Carolina Press, 1937), p. 9.

12. D. A. Brading, *Haciendas and Ranchos in the Mexican Bajío León 1700-1860* (New York: Cambridge University Press, 1978), pp. 7-8.

13. Frank Tannenbaum, *Mexican Agrarian Revolution* (Washington, D.C.: Brooking Institution, reprinted in 1968), p. 109.

14. McBridge, p. 60.

15. Ibid., p. 53.

16. Ibid., p. 60.

17. Ibid., p. 49

18. Meyer and Sherman, p.169.

19. D. A. Brading, *Haciendas and Ranchos in the Mexican Bajío León 1700-1860* (New York: Cambridge University Press, 1978), p. xvi.

20. Thomas E. Cotner, *Essays in Mexican History* (Austin: the Institute of American Studies, The University of Texas, 1958), p. 19.

21. Catner, p.19.

22. McBride, p. 25.

23. Meyer and Sherman, p. 461.

24. McBride, p. 82.

25. For a discussion of the rancheros, see Frans J. Schryer, *The Rancheros of Pisaflres: The History of a Peasant Bourgeoisie in Twentieth-Century Mexico* (London: University of Toronto Press, 1980).

26. McBride, p. 85.

27. This was a dynasty that began in 1521 and lasted up to 1821.

28. Enrique Krauze, *Mexico Biography of Power: A History of Modern Mexico,* 1810-1995), p. 94.

29. Ibid., p. 91.

30. Lucas Alamán, *The Historia de México, 5* vols. (Mexico, 1990), vol. 2, p. 71.

31 Lemoine, *Morelos su vida revolucionarica a través de sus escrito y de otros testimonios de la época Mexico, 1991,* p. 181.

32. See Carlos Navarro y Rodrigo, "Vida de Agustin de Iturbide," in *Memorias de Agustín de Iturbide* (Madrid, 1919); Mario Mena, *El Dragón de fierro: Biografía de Agustín de Iturbide* (Mexico, 1969); Silvio Zavala and José Bravo Ugarte, "Un nuevo Iturbide," in Historia Mexicana (Mexico), vol. 2, no. 6, Oct-Dec. 1952, pp. 267-276.

33. Rodrigo, "Agustín Iturbide," in *Historia Mexicana*, pp. 237-38.

34. Kruaze, p. 124.

35 Alamán, *Historia*, vol. 5. p. 609.

36. Kruaze, p. 127.

37. Ibid., p. 127.

38. Meyer, p. 324.

39. Charles H. Harris, III, *A Mexican Family Empire: The Latifundio of the Sánchez Navarro Family, 1765-1867* (Austin: University of Texas Press, 1975), p. 6.

40. John Locke, *Second Treatise of Government*, Sec. 50.

41. Meyer and Sherman, p.178.

42. Ibid., p. 271.

43. "Coahuila y Tejas–Index, *Sons of Dewitt Colony of Texas, 1997-2002.*

44. Kruaze, pp. 99-105.

45. *Coahuila y Tejas-Index* (www.bamu.edu/dewitt/dewett/htm)

46. Meyer and Sherman, p. 336.

47. Ibid., p. 340.

48. David G. Gutiérrez, *Walls and Mirrors* (Berkeley: University of California Press, 1995), p. 1.

49. See George M. Fredrickson, *The Black Image in the White Mind: The Debate on Afro-American Character and Destiny, 1817-1914* (Middletown, Conn.: Wesleyan University Press, 1971), Chapter 5.

50. *Loving v. Virginia, 388 U.S.* 1 (1967).

51. *San Antonio School District V. Rodriguez, 411 U.S. 1 (1973).*

52 Clarence Senior, *Land Reform and Democracy* (Westport, Conn.: Greenwood Press, 1958), p. 13.

CHAPTER 14
Mexican Americans and the Mexican Immigration from the 1920s to the Present

The experience of the Mexicans' immigration to the United States is similar to that of the Irish Catholic, Puerto Ricans, and African Americans' migration. All three groups, to repeat, emigrated/migrated from an agrarian background where they did not have the necessary human capital to offset the effect of group discrimination. As we have seen in Chapter 8, the Irish Catholics were able to overcome their deprived position after the federal government adopted a set of affirmative measures to safeguard their right to acquire and possess property. African Americans and the nonwhite Puerto Ricans did not receive such protection from the New Deal Era up to the adoption of affirmative action measures.

The Mexicans started immigrating to the U.S. in the 1920s, seeking employment as a result of the economic turmoil created by a series of revolutions and soon revoked between the period of 1910 and 1920. The first revolution in the twentieth century was commenced in 1910 when Francisco I. Madero overthrew the Porfirio Díaz's regime. As mentioned in the last chapter, Diaz's dictatorship brought about thirty years of stability in which Mexico's economy had begun to grow for the first time since Mexico Independence. But Madero's revolution disrupted this growth and reignited the spirit of revolution that has plagued this country since its independence in 1821. His revolt was followed by a series of other revolts which lasted up to 1929.[1] Politically, these revolts can be characterized in the Hobbesian definition of a country that has been thrown into the natural state of war. In such state, to repeat, there is very little room for growth and development.

As a result of these revolts, the economic conditions of the peons turned for the worse. They represented more than 90 percent of the lower class. The vast majority of them lived in the rural areas. Power and wealth were concentrated in the hands of the upper class which constituted 1.4 percent of the population.

There was a small middle class (some 20 percent) that was not sufficient to starve off a revolt. According to the 1910 Census, Mexico had a population of 12,698,330. Out of this number, the ownership of property was controlled by 49,542 members of the upper class that lived in the urban area. The rest of the property was owned by 133,464 who lived in the rule area.[2]

A combination of the disproportionate distribution of land ownership and high unemployment provided the basis for revolts. Out of necessity, the lower class peons were forced to seek employment in the United States. As demonstrated throughout this book, there has always been a magnet that draws immigrants to the American shores. The magnet that drew the Mexicans to the United States in the 1920s was the need for farm workers.

The Mexican immigrants were constrained by the requirements of the Immigration Act of 1970 which required all immigrants over the age of fifteen (1) to be educated and to have a skill, (2) proof of literacy, and (3) an eight dollar head tax—which very few Mexicans had. These provisions automatically eliminated 90 percent of the farm workers from being eligible for legal immigration. Whenever there is a restriction on any commodity, a lucrative black market is automatically created for smugglers. The smuggling of Mexican farm workers to perform agricultural work was no exception.

The smugglers were called *coyotes* because of their skills to avoid authorities. The smugglers were unscrupulous. They raped and assaulted the immigrants. The *coyotes* recruited them by promising lucrative wages. When they arrived in the United States, these workers were often economically exploited because they had no system of protection. Unlike the British West Indians, they had no consul who could intercede on their behalf by filing a diplomatic complaint with the State Department. In order to file such a complaint, they must have legal status.

The immigration of the Mexicans to America was a response to the short labor supply created by World War I. Many southern farm workers, both African Americans and whites, had migrated North to work in the factories to support the war effort. Many northern white males had gone off to war. During the war, the United States became the granary and arsenal for the world. As mentioned in Chapter 6, the War Department issued a directive, "fight or work." In order to feel the vacuum of labor shortage in the Southwest, workers had to be recruited from Mexico.

Between the period between 1850 and 1900, the Mexicans could freely migrate back and forth across the border with ease. There was no policing of the borders. But, in 1924, the United States adopted its first formal immigration quota laws where restrictions were placed on immigrants coming to America. These laws favored northern Europeans and disfavored people from southern

Europe. However, these laws did not apply to Canada, Mexico, or Central and South America. But the immigration laws of the 1920s, began to affect the Mexican immigrants. The freedom to move back and forth across the borders was curtailed by these laws. Mexicans now had to produce documentation to the legality of their immigration. Producing such a document became a burden both financially and paper wise. Immigrating from a debt-slavery system, many peons could not afford the $8 a head tax. Consequently, they started devising ways to by pass the border patrol. This practice led to illegal immigration. *taxation*

Illegal immigration remained unchecked during the period of economic expansion in America during and after World War I. During the 1930s, when the Great Depression set in, many workers became unemployed. Soup and welfare lines were formed to aid them. These lines became increasingly swollen, and officials began to seek ways to relieve this pressure. One attempt they made to resolve this problem was to send the Mexicans back to Mexico. The system of repatriation and deportation was initiated. Some Mexicans who were American citizens were also deported in the hysteria of this movement. It virtually limited immigration from Mexico to a trickle during the 1930s. It did not pick up again until the labor shortage of the 1940s. This was created as a result of two factors: the war and the economic expansion. The war absorbed many males into the military and the rest were absorbed by the military-industrial *MP* complex that was created to support the war. This absorption created a shortage of labor in the agricultural industry which could only be filled by turning to Mexico.

When the United States turned to Mexico for labor for the second time, the Mexican authorities stepped in to seek a system of protection for their citizens. They wanted to avoid the mistreatment that the United States accorded their workers during the 1930s (i.e., deportation and repatriation). To avoid such mistreatment, the Mexican government insisted on a formal agreement between the two governments. In 1942, they sign the Bracero agreement.[3] *protection*

The Bracero agreement served two purposes. First, it represented Mexico's contribution to the war effort. Second, it was designed to protect the Mexican workers from mistreatment by their employers. This agreement stipulated the method of recruitment, the means of transportation, and protection against discrimination. In addition, the issue of adequate healthcare, wages, housing, working conditions, and food were also stipulated in the agreement.

The Bracero Agreement and Program

The Bracero program was intended to be temporary because the Mexican government did not want this program to be a prominent drain on its human resources. It also hoped that the Mexican workers would acquire skills which they could bring back to Mexico to help bolster their economy.

The Bracero program was similar to that of the *patroni* system that the Italians used to facilitate their immigration. It recruited workers from various sectors of Mexico and transported them to those areas where the United States had requested them. The employers who requested them were the growers in the southwestern states: Texas, California, and Colorado.

Since the economic conditions in Mexico were in a State of constant deterioration, the unemployment rate was very high. As the result, thousands of workers crowded the recruitment centers seeking a permit to join the Bracero program. Whenever there is a shortage of resources and a high demand for the same, corruption automatically sets in. To accommodate these demands, a bribery system was set up which the Mexican called the *mordida*. It became a common practice to bribe the officials to get a permit to emigrate to the United States. However, the bribery system could not accommodate all of the workers. Consequently, many resorted to illegal immigration (i.e., immigrating without official papers). These individuals could easily find jobs as agricultural workers.

One of the first impacts that the Bracero program had up on the American economy was that it depressed the wages in the agriculture industry. The Bracero agreement stipulated that the Mexican workers were to be paid a minimum of fifty cents an hour. Many growers viewed the minimum as the maximum. Because fifty cents an hour was considerably more than the Mexicans were receiving under the debt slavery system in Mexico, they were willing to work for less than fifty cents.

The Mexican workers drove down the wages so low that American agricultural workers refused to work for such low wages. This resulted in the Mexican displacing many domestic American workers in the agriculture industry. Another factor that helped the Mexican workers to displace domestic workers was the composition of the Mexican migrant workers. Most of them were males. In contrast, most of the domestic farm workers were migrant families. This meant that the growers had to provide adequate housing for them, whereas the Mexican workers were all men could be placed in barrack housing. This inevitably cut the cost of the upkeeps of workers for the growers. Subsequently, the Mexicans became preferred workers for agriculture work.

The major political significance of the Bracero program in relation to the employment of domestic workers is that it was indirectly a form of subsidies for the agricultural industry by the federal government. By supporting the Bracero program, the government was driving down the prices of wages which meant less money that the growers had to dole out for labor.

Although the Bracero agreement had stipulated which prohibited discrimination against the Mexican workers, this agreement proved to be a covenant without a sword. The growers ignored the agreement and the government refused to develop a mechanism for enforcement. As a result, discrimination against the Mexicans was so widespread in Texas that the Mexican government forbid the use of their citizens in the fields of Texas. The Texas growers circumvented this restriction by using what became known as "wetbacks" (a definition of this term follows) instead of workers from the Bracero system.[4]

The conclusion of World War II brought an end to the labor shortage. However, the Bracero system continued recruit workers. In fact, more workers were recruited after the war than they were during the war. For example, the highest number recruited during the war was in 1944, which was 62,170 workers. Four years after the war ended, more than 143,435 workers were recruited.[5] The highest number recruited during the twenty-year period was 143,447 in the year of 1960. In 1960, the year in which the program ended, there were 6,127 workers recruited.

The term *wetback* is used to describe Mexican immigrants without official papers. The origin of this turn can be traced back to Texas when the borders began to close. These workers were called wetbacks because they swam across the Rio Grande river into either El Paso or Brownsville. But this term is also used to describe those Mexicans who crossed the borders on dry land. Over period of time, the term has been broadened to describe all Mexicans without official papers. Culturally, it has become a symbol to demean and stereotype all Mexicans.

The numbers of the legal Mexican immigrants into the United States cannot be adequately counted. By the mere fact that they are illegal makes an accurate account impossible. But the number apprehended by authorities can be counted accurately because they have been apprehended. The number apprehended is closely related to the economic conditions in the United States and Mexico. The highest number apprehended was 1,575,168 in 1954. This was the period when there was a recession in the United States and the authority initiated "operation wetback."[6] After this year, the number apprehended began to decrease and only started picking up again in 1975 where more than 600,000 were apprehended and returned to Mexico.[7]

Avoidance of the Disability of Race

As we have seen in the previous chapter, the U.S. government did not saddle the Mexicans with the disability of race. Unlike African Americans, whom the government told them that they were unfit to associate with the white race, the Mexicans were granted full rights and privileges as white citizens, as we have seen in the *Treaty of Guadalupe Hidalgo*. In the field of education, the government did not relegate them to segregate an inferior schools as it did African Americans. They had the freedom to attend the same schools as whites. But, the factors which constrained their growth and development can be reduced to two—their lower socioeconomic status, and the fact that they had not lerned to speak English before immigration.

From 1848 up to the 1960s, the United States had a policy of forced assimilation. In order to become a full citizen, immigrants were required to learn to speak English. This posed a serious problem for the Mexicans. They immigrated from a debt-slavery and impoverished environment where education was reserved for the selected few. Therefore, the literacy rate among them was very low. Unlike legal immigrants, which the immigration laws restricted their immigration to the literate and skilled, the Bracero program recruited the literate and illiterate alike. Again, the legal immigrants had an advantage over the Mexicans. If they could not speak English when they arrived, they could attend night school to learn English. But the Mexicans were farm workers where night schools were far removed from their place of employment. Besides, the long hours required for farm workers precluded any ambition to attend night school to learn English. Consequently, learning English became a major obstacle for their social upward mobility.

In addition to farm workers, Mexicans were also recruited by business to depress minimum wages. This was an attempt by businesses to counteract the pressure placed on the government by unions to raise minimum wages. By recruiting illegal Mexican workers, businesses were able to set the wages below the minimum. If these workers remained in the United States, their children by law had to attend school. When they entered school, they spoke Spanish. Their teachers were Anglo-Saxon who spoke only English. Many states passed laws prohibiting the use of Spanish for instruction. Consequently, the teachers' task was to force and encourage the Mexicans to learn English. One method of encouragement was to punish students for speaking Spanish on campus or in the classroom. It was not until the 1970s when states began to recognize that the Mexican students' major problem in their low academic achievement was related to not understanding instruction in English. California was the first state to officially recognize that bilingual education was necessary for instructing Mexican students in K–12. Consequently, many school districts started offering bilingual education. It was then and only then that the children of migrant workers started to become educated.

Another factor which retarded the Mexicans' educational attainments was their low socioeconomic status. In order to make ends meet, all members of the family who were of age had to seek employment. Instead of encouraging their children to finish high school, they would force them to dropout of school to seek a job in order to earn money to help the family make ends meet. Consequently, a high school education became a luxury for them instead of a value or a symbol of achievement as it was for the rest of American citizens. The need to have the whole family employed to make ends meet can account for the current high dropout rate found among the Mexican students.

Although the Mexicans were allowed to attend school with whites, they did not necessarily receive the same quality of education. Students with Spanish surnames were too often corralled into special classrooms that were known as the "Mexican" room. This was a sophisticated way of placing them on a slow track or special education. On the other hand, when the Mexicans attended school with middle-class whites, this automatically posed a problem for Mexican students. It is extremely hard to teach lower-class students alongside middle-class students. The former students, by operation, would be so far behind that it would make education impossible. By simply placing lower-class students in classrooms with other students of their age and grade, will not guarantee them a quality education. The teacher has to constantly slow down to address the needs of lower-class students. This is one of the major shortcomings of busing for school integration in an attempt to achieve a quality education. African Americans and Spanish students have been bused from their intercity schools of Los Angeles out to the suburbs in the valley just to be placed on low-ability tracks, which they were already in their neighborhood schools. Busing within itself does not guarantee a quality education. Such education can be obtained only by placing students in a program where the curriculum is designed to provide a quality education.

Therefore, the educational upward mobility of the Mexicans was very slow until the adoption of bilingual programs and the various outreach programs that were created for African Americans in an attempt to suppress the violence that was taking place in the 1960s. Because these outreach programs offered benefits, the Mexicans, for the first time, stop claiming the status of white and started claiming minority status for the purpose of receiving government benefits. These benefits significantly improved their educational attainment.

Social Assimilation

Culturally, the Mexicans' freedom to interact with the dominant white society was not foreclosed like African Americans'. Long before the civil rights movement of the 1960s, the Mexicans could easily assimilate into the white society once they achieved middle-class status. They did not have to discard their Spanish accents to be accepted. This is evidenced in the movies and the media. Their interracial marriage with whites was not subjected to public ridicule as was the case with African Americans. For example, the interracial marriage on the "I Love Lucy" Show was widely accepted by the dominant society. At the same time, the only African American show that was acceptable to whites was the "Amos and Andy Show," which demeaned the image of African Americans.

The Mexicans could avoid the negative stereotype of being associated with the term Mexican by changing their names from Alberto to Al. This was one of the practices that the Jews used to overcome discrimination and to avoid anti-Semitism (i.e., changing their name from Goldberg to Golden).

The greatest advantage that the Mexicans enjoyed, which was explicitly denied to African Americans by federal law, was the freedom to take advantage of the *bonanza giveaway* in the FHA housing program. As we have seen in our discussion of Levittown, a white couple could move into a brand new house at a cost of $7,990 with no money down for $50 per month. In twenty years, the value of this house had skyrocketed to more than $160,000. This money provided the family with the means to send their children to college. In other words, it facilitated the family's capacity to activate the principle of intergenerational mobility. Because the Mexicans were considered white by the federal government, they also were able to take advantage of the *bonanza giveaways* and eventually catapult their children upon to the middle-class plateau.

A wider range of employment opportunities were available for the Mexicans than for African Americans. They could pursue those skilled jobs that the federal government told African Americans were white men's jobs. Since the government had characterized the Mexicans as white, they did not have to overcome the racial barriers. Also, the Mexicans could move up the career ladder through self-initiative and hard work. They could become managers and supervisors of companies. This opportunity was completely foreclosed to African Americans before the adoption of the civil rights laws of 1964 and the implementation of affirmative action.

The major factors which constrained the rate of the Mexicans' upward mobility were their lower socioeconomic status and their lack of citizenship. This was especially true in California where the state provided free tuition for college up to the 1980s. Because a large number of Mexicans did not have legal status, they could not take advantage of the free education as was the case with African Americans. For example, long before the adoption of affirmative action, African Americans constituted more than 20 percent of the student populations at California State University, Los Angeles in the 1960s. When California State University at Dominguez Hills opened its doors in the latter part of the 1960s, African American students constituted more than 60 percent of the student population. Their high rate of enrollment at these two institutions was not a function of affirmative action but equal education opportunities. At the same time, the Mexican student enrollment at both of these institutions remained low until the government stepped in and started offering financial aid under the Equal Opportunity Program, which it adopted for African Americans as a means to prevent them from rioting. This marked the beginning when the Mexicans started disavowing their status as whites and started claiming minority status in order to take advantage of those benefits earmarked for those racial groups that the government had saddled with the disability of race.

The Distribution of Mexicans

According to the 2000 Census, the largest concentration of the Mexican populations can be found in seven metropolitan areas: Los Angeles (46 percent), Chicago (26 percent), Houston (37.4 percent), San Antonio (58.7 percent), Dallas (35.6 percent), and Phoenix (34.1 percent), El Paso (76,6 percent), (see Table 27).

Table 27

Ten Largest Places in Total Population and in Hispanic Population, 2000
(For information on confidentiality protection, nonsampling error, and definitions, see www.census.gov/prod/cen2000/doc/sf1.pdf)

	Total population		Hispanic population		Percent Hispanic of Total
	Number	Rank	Number	Rank	Population
New York, NY.	8,008,278	1	2,160,554	1	27.0
Los Angeles, CA	3,694,820	2	1,719,073	2	46.5
Chicago, IL	2,896,016	3	753,644	3	26.0
Houston, TX	1,953,631	4	730,865	4	37.4
Philadelphia, PA.	1,517,550	5	128,928	24	8.5
Phoenix, AZ	1,321,045	6	449,972	6	34.1
San Diego, CA.	1,223,400	7	310,752	9	25.4
Dallas, TX	1,188,580	8	422,587	8	35.6
San Antonio, TX.	1,144,646	9	671,394	5	58.7
Detroit, MI	951,270	10	47,167	72	5.0
El Paso, TX	563,662	23	431,875	7	76.6
San Jose, CA.	894,943	11	269,989	10	30.2

SOURCE: U.S. Census Bureau, Census 2000 Summary File 1.

There are ten places where the Mexicans are in the majority: East Los Angeles (96.8 percent), Laredo, Texas (94.1 percent), Brownsville, Texas (91.3 percent), McAllen, Texas (80.3 percent), Hialeah, Fl (90.3), El Paso, Texas (76.6 percent), Santa Ana, California (76.1 percent), El Monte, California (72.4 percent), Oxnard, California (66.2 percent), and Miami, FL (65.8 percent) (see Table 28).

Table 28

Ten Places of 100,000 or More Population With the Highest Percent Hispanic, 2000

(For information on confidentiality protection, nonsampling error, and definitions, see www.census.gov/prod/cen2000/doc/sf1.pdf)

Place and State	Total Population	Hispanic Population	Percentage Hispanic of Total Population
East Los Angeles, CA*........	124,283	120,307	96.8
Laredo, TX	176,576	166,216	94.1
Brownsville, TX	139,722	127,535	91.3
Hialeah, FL	226,419	204,543	90.3
McAllen, TX	106,414	85,427	80.3
El Paso, TX	563,662	431,875	76.6
Santa Ana, CA	337,977	257,097	76.1
El Monte, CA	115,965	83,945	72.4
Oxnard, CA.	170,358	112,807	66.2
Miami, FL ..`..............`	362,470	238,351	65.8

*East Los Angeles, California is a census designated place and is not legally incorporated.

SOURCE: U.S. Census Bureau, Census 2000 Summary File 1.

The largest concentration of Mexicans in where they make up the highest percentage of the total population can be found in the following cities: Los Angeles, 46.5 percent; Chicago, 26 percent; Houston, 37.4 percent; San Antonio, 58.7 percent; Phoenix, 34 percent. (See Table 27 for the total population of the cities.)

Assimilation and Upward Mobility

According to the 1970 census, there were 4,532,435 Mexicans living in America. In 2000, this number had increased to 20,640,711.[8] The rate of the increase in population growth has become a concern of social scientists in general and sociologists in particular. The first to address the Hispanics' assimilation were the sociologists. They were concerned with the rate of the Hispanics' assimilation in comparison to that of the European immigrants who had immigrated early.

A recent study by Jeffrey Grogger and Stephen Trejo argued that the Mexicans are not assimilating into American mainstream at the same rate of European groups because they are less committed to assimilation than latter groups.[9] But a new study by James Smith tend to refute their arguments. His research shows that the children and grandchildren of Hispanics are moving up the social economic ladder as quickly as the European immigrants did.[10] In fact, he argues that they are moving up the social economic ladder faster than the European immigrants did.

The major flaw in both of these analyses is that the writers selected dependent variables as their basic units of analysis (i.e., education and income indexes). By doing so, they overlooked the independent variables that protect and broaden groups' opportunities to pursue a wide range of educational and economic opportunities. Any attempt, it must be noted, to compare the rate of education of groups over period of time must examine the impact that the child labor laws have had on constraining the educational development among each group. Around the turn of the twentieth century, one-third of the work force in factories consisted of children. This was a function of the labor shortage of adult males during this period and the puritanical ideas that idleness among children produce evil. In an attempt to reduce this evil, parents and employers cooperated to place children in the work force in which they had to work in the factories ten to twelve hours a day. Through political pressure by reformers, Congress passed a series of child labor laws that were struck down by the U.S. Supreme Court. Their success in regulating child labor laws came during the New Deal era. At the time, one million children were employed in the factories while six million adult males were unemployed. The general consensus of the factory owners was: Why pay a male one dollar a day when you can pay a child ten cents.

The law put the final nail into the child labor coffin was the National Industrial Act of 1933. This law established the minimum age of ten for workers in the factories. Many industrial states enacted compulsory education for children under the age of ten as a mean to control juvenile delinquency. This law did not apply to agricultural workers where a large percentage of Mexicans worked; therefore, education in the agricultural states remained significantly farther behind than the industrial states. This difference can partially explain why the level of education among the Hispanics prior to the 1970 was lower than the national average.

In studying the rate of assimilation of the Hispanics, Smith found that those Mexicans who immigrated to America between the period of 1905 and 1919 had a fifth grade education. However, there was a progressive increase in their educational attainments where their sons completed the ninth grade and their grandsons completed high school. Smith used this as evidence that the Hispanics were assimilating faster than the European immigrants did early. What he was overlooking were the environmental factors that constrained and promoted educational attainment among the Hispanics. First, the Hispanics' behavior toward schools was affected by the compulsory laws which mandated that children under the age of sixteen must attend school. Such laws did not exist for the twentieth century European immigrants. Secondly, Smith overlooked the influence that President Johnson's "Great Society" program had upon expanding education opportunities for Hispanics. There were numerous programs adopted to keep Hispanics in school. These programs were not available for the European immigrants.

After the adoption of the affirmative action programs, the Mexicans switched from the status of white to that of minority for the purpose of receiving financial aid that was established for African Americans in an attempt to curb the rioting during this period. By switching from the status of white to that of minority, the Mexicans were able to make a quantum leap in their social economic status comparison to their previous experience. The variables that made this difference were the various government's financial aid programs in education. As we have seen in Chapter 9, the European immigrants of the late nineteenth century did not show a marked increase in acquiring a college degree until the adoption of the G.I. Bill, which was a form of affirmative action. Therefore, the rate of the Hispanics assimilation in terms of education attainments is determined by the financial assistance that they received from the government. Without such assistance, groups will not be able to attend college, particularly the lower class immigrants of the 1980s and 1990s. This statement does not mean to ignore the principle of intergenerational mobility among the Mexican middle class. As mentioned, education for middle-class populations, regardless of class and ethnicity, is largely obligatory.

The Hispanics' economic success can be view as a function of the government public policy *insidious racism*. This is a policy that the dominant society adopted in an attempt to avoid its responsibility of addressing the conditions brought upon African Americans as a result of its racial policies. Instead of addressing these conditions, social scientists have attempted to shift the blame for these conditions on the backs of African Americans themselves. They find it painful to address these conditions, because they will inadvertently remind them that America has not atone for its sins for enslaving them. Therefore, to avoid addressing the race issue, America has redefined the term minority to include all nonwhites as minority regardless whether they have been saddled with the disability of race by the government. As a result of the American policy of insidious racism, the Hispanics have been able to make a quantum leap in their socioeconomic status between the period of 1980 and 2000 in comparison to the European groups that immigrated prior to the 1940s.

Starting with the Reagan administration, the federal government launched a protracted war on civil rights in general and the socioeconomic status of African Americans in particular. (This topic will be discussed in the Summary and Conclusion.) Instead of supporting African Americans in their quest for the equality of opportunities in the fields of education and employment, the Reagan administration directed the Justice Department to side with the opponents of civil rights in filing complaints of reverse discrimination.

One of the strategies that the Reagan administration undertook to block the advancement of African Americans was to substitute Hispanics, who the government has not undertaken a public policy to saddle them with the disability of race, as minority groups. From this point onward, the Hispanics began to make quantum leaps in their socioeconomic status.

In the field of education, the Hispanics were not affected by the policy of racial discrimination as was the case with African Americans. For example, in Texas where African Americans fought many cases of racial discrimination in education, the middle class Mexican students could enroll in the dominant white universities. It must be noted here, as we have seen in Chapter 9, the only students who attended college prior to the adoption of the G.I. Bill were the middle and upper class. Therefore, the only factor that blocked the Mexicans from attending college during this period was the lack of financial support. In K–12, the Hispanics did experience discrimination in education. But such discrimination was based more on their economic status than their ethnicity. The school boards in Texas adopted a policy of de facto segregation, i.e., forcing students to attend school within that neighborhood. This policy was supported by the federal housing policy adopted in the 1950s, as we have seen in Chapter 9.

Another factor that constrained the educational attainment of Mexicans was the language. As mentioned previously, many states had adopted a policy that English was to be the official language spoken on campus. This posed a serious problem for the Mexicans. Immigrating from a debt-slavery environment, the literacy rate among the Mexicans was very low. There immigration to America was not affected by the restrictions placed on immigration by the

Immigration Act of 1917. As we have seen, this law restricted immigration to literate and skilled persons. The combination of the Bracero program and the practice of the Mexicans immigrating without official papers contributed to their low level of education attainments prior to the 1980s. These programs allowed them to bypass the legal restrictions placed on immigration.

The Mexicans without official papers could not file complaints of discrimination because they did not have the status of citizenship. Prior to the 1970s, the Hispanics were primarily used as agricultural workers in the southwest states and California. After the 1970s, industries started to implore them in low-level jobs in an attempt to suppress the label cost. At this time, there was a fight over minimum wages by the Democrats and Republicans. The Democrats fought for an increase in minimum wages and the Republicans fought for a differential in the minimum wages for teenagers. Because the Democrats controlled the majority of those in both houses of Congress, they were able to prevail in raising the minimum wages. To counteract this strategy, the industries started employing the Hispanics without official papers. Because this group was not citizens, the industries found that they could exploit them economically without their filing a complaint with authorities. Furthermore, the low wages that a company paid the Mexicans were significantly higher than the ones in which they received in their homeland. Consequently, Mexican immigrants would work hard for low wages to earn money to send back home to support their families and loved ones. Prior to the September 11 attack on the World Trade Center, a study commissioned by the Inter-American Development Bank found that $12 billion is sent to the Latin Americans countries each year. Over one-half it is sent to Mexico.[11]

The fact that Mexican immigrants are forced to seek low-level employment coupled with their low rate of literacy can account for the low level of education in comparison to the other Latino immigrants. As Table 29 indicates, the Mexicans have the lowest education attainments among the five Latino groups. The Latino groups with the highest number of students with a high school degree or higher are the ones in the "Others Hispanic Origin" category, followed by the Cubans. This difference can be accounted for by the restrictions that the Immigration laws placed on legal immigration. These laws apply to every group except the Cubans, who are refugees. Typically, refugees consist of the upper class of immigrants that are trying to escape the oppressed conditions in their homeland.

Because the Latino groups are allowed to switch from the status of white to minority, the Mexicans were able to take advantage of the minority programs established for African Americans. These programs provided education assistance and financial aid to attend college. Without this financial assistance, the

Mexicans would not have achieved the level of educational attainments as the data indicate in the 2000 Census. Their experience would have been similar to that of the late nineteenth century immigrants that wanted to attend college, but could not do so because the lack of financial means. As we have seen in Chapter 9, the G.I. Bill provided them with this means.

Table 29
Hispanics' Educational Attainment

	His-panic Total	Mex-ican	Puerto Rican	Cuban	Cen-tral and South Ameri-can	Other His-panic
Persons of 25 years Old and over.	16,425	10,020	1,636	1,008	2,634	1,127
High school graduate or higher	56.1	49.7	63.9	70.3	64.0	71.1
Bachelors degree or higher . .	10.9	7.1	11.1	24.8	18.0	15.0

SOURCE: U.S. Bureau of Labor Statistics, *Employment and Earnings*, January 2000.

Because the Census Bureau did not make a distinction between Mexican Americans and Mexican immigrants, it is hard to adequately access the level of social upward mobility for the Mexicans. If we use their percentage in the managerial and professional category, we can see in Table 29 that the Mexicans have the lowest occupation achievement than any group in this cohort, 10.9 percent compared to 27.5 percent for the cohort. Attempts have been made to compare the social economic status of Mexicans with that of African Americans. Such tasks are extremely hard to accomplish because the geographical background of each group has to be taken into account. African Americans are situated throughout America, whereas the Mexicans are concentrated in the southwest and western states.

If education is used as an index to measure the Mexican rate of assimilation, their success has to be measured in terms of their financial means to acquire an education. This raises the question as to the obligation of the government to adopt special measures to help them to secure educational advancement. Unlike African Americans, the U.S. government has not saddled them with the disability of race. The question will always be what justification does the government have to adopt special measurements to secure educational advancements for immigrants when the cost of attending college is affecting middle-class white Americans?

Increasing funds for Hispanics to attend college raises the question of the obligation that the U.S. government has in providing them with special measures to increase the education when the government itself has not undertaken a policy to saddle them with the disability of race. Unlike the Asians who are largely in the middle class, Mexican families do not have the necessary funds to spend on their children's education. This problem is compounded by the continuous influx of those immigrants crossing the borders without official papers. This problem does not exist for immigrants from the other Latino's countries that immigrate with official papers. By law, these groups are in the middle class where the principle of intergenerational mobility is in operation.

In short, the problem of the Mexicans and Mexican Americans is more of a class problem than one of racial or ethnic discrimination. They are the only immigrants that can immigrate in large numbers without official papers. Without such papers, they are not able to take advantage of the many opportunities that are offered to legal immigrants. Their illegal immigration has been condoned by the federal government as a result of the business and agricultural industries seeking cheap labor. The reason for the government classifying all Spanish-speaking populations as minority is beyond the scope of this study. Suffice to say that such classification has grave political repercussions for those minority groups that the government has saddled with the disability of race, as we shall see in the the Summary and Conclusion, is a form of insidious racism.

Notes

1.   Enrique Krauze, "Historical Chronology," in *Mexico Biography of Power: a History of Modern Mexico, 1810-1996* (New York: HarperCollins Publishers, 1997), p. xx.

2.   Clearance Senior, *Land Reform and Democracy* (West Port, Conn.: Greenwood Press, 1974), p. 15.

3.   For a detailed analysis of this program see Richard B. Craig, *The Bracero Program* (Austin and London: University of Texas Press, 1971).

4.   See Julian A. Samora, Los Mojados: *The Wetback Story* (Notre Dame: University of Notre Dame Press, 1971).

5.   Julian Samora and Patricia Vandal Simon, *A History of the Mexican-American People* (Notre Dame: University of Notre Dame Press, 1977), 144.

6.   Ibid.

7.   Ibid.

8. Hispanic population, 2000, Table 1.

9. Jeffrey Grogger and Stephen Trojo, *Falling Behind or Moving Up?* (San Francisco: Public Institute of California, 2002).

10. James Smith, "Assimilation across the Latino Generations," *in The American Economic Review,* (May 2003): 315-319.

11. Chris Kraul, "Latino Immigrants Sending Less Money Home Economy: Remittances from workers in the U.S. to the families they left behind have fallen as unemployment and cutbacks have risen," *Los Angeles Times*, December 17, 2001; "Mexican Immigrants Sending More Money Home Latin America: But some observers question the accuracy of figures showing a big leap in cash remittances in 2001," *Los Angeles Times*, September 24, 2001.

Summary and Conclusions

The overall thrust of this book has been directed toward offering a scientific explanation for the age-old question as to why African Americans have been unable to escape the slums like other groups. To achieve this goal, it was necessary to develop a systematic comparative macro-analysis that was capable of identifying those independent variables that constrain and promote groups' social mobility. This conceptual framework allows us to state the following propositions concerning groups' socioeconomic behavior. Group upward mobility and inequality are a function of government policies that operated to promote or constrain such behavior. Those groups that were able to escape the slums in America did so as a result of the government providing them with a system of protection to secure adequate advancement. On the other hand, the reason some groups did not escape the slums was that the government has historically refused to offer them the same system of protection as it did for other groups. This is particularly true for African Americans. In fact, the government has undertaken special measures to constrain their upward mobility.

Based on the data presented in this book, we can state unequivocally that no group in America has been able to make it to the middle-class plateau without some forms of government assistance. They were either in the middle class before they arrived or the government stepped in and provided them with some forms of assistance. This assistance has come in various forms, but we have referred to it throughout this book as a set of bootstraps, and have argued that in order for a group to make it to the middle-class plateau it needs two things: *a pair of boots (human capital)* and *a set of bootstraps (a system of protection)*. One without the other will not enable groups to elevate themselves onto the middle-class plateau, as was demonstrated in Chapter 3 on the Irish-Catholics' experience. Those groups that did not have the necessary human capital to compete in a competitive society when they first made contact with the American polity remained impoverished until the government stepped in and offered them some forms of assistance.

It also was demonstrated that race within itself does not constrain group upward mobility. This is evidenced by the relative success of the British West Indians–who are African descendants the same as African Americans–and the Asians–who are nonwhite. On the other hand, we have seen that the Irish-Catholics–who are white–remained impoverished for five generations because they did not have the necessary human capital to take advantage of the economic opportunities that the government offered immigrant groups at the time of their immigration. Again, we saw that there is a differentiation in the social status of the Latino groups, the newcomers. Mexicans, for example, are on a lower socioeconomic status than the rest of the Latino populations. They immigrated from an impoverished environment where there were less mechanization and industrialization in comparison to other Latino countries. They immigrated without the necessary human capital to compete in a competitive society. As we have seen, the immigration laws restrict official immigration to the literate, skilled, and well-off individuals. But many Mexicans were able to bypass these restrictions by crossing the border without official papers. Their immigration was assisted by the agricultural and manufacturing industries that were seeking cheap labor.

Throughout this book, we have presented sound theories–and compelling evidence to support them–to refute many of the traditional arguments that have been advanced to explain group upward mobility such as "strong family structures," "Protestant work ethic," "hard work," and so on. We found these arguments to be dependent variables. Statistical data can easily be marshalled forward to make a strong case for them. But once subjected to systematic scrutiny, these arguments tend to fall apart. Take, for example, the strong family structure argument. The Jews that immigrated in the late nineteenth century had a reputation for having strong family structures and values. Yet, they were unable to escape the slums until after World War II when the government intervened and provided them with a system of protection in their quest to secure adequate advancement in education, employment, and housing. Housing is often used as a social index to measure a group's ability to escape the slums. As discussed in Chapter 9, the Jews and other European immigrants could not escape the slums before this period, even if they wanted to, because they did not have anywhere to go. It was only after the government stepped in and started subsidizing housing in the suburbs that they found a place to escape. In fact, very few of the immigrants of the nineteenth century, prior to the adoption of the immigration law of 1917, were themselves able to escape the slums; their children did.

The Adoption of Civil Rights Laws

Since the close of the Civil War, African Americans have fought against a policy of *invidious discrimination* (i.e., those laws that explicitly denied them the same rights to life, liberty, and the pursuit of happiness that were accorded to other groups). After 100 years of fighting, they were able to achieve this goal by convincing Congress to adopt various civil rights measures during and after the 1960s. In a political sense, African Americans were petitioning the government to adopt positive laws to create a level playing field so that they could secure adequate advancement like other groups. When Congress adopted the civil rights laws of the 1960s, African Americans viewed them as a remedy to eradicate this country's legacy of racism (i.e., the politics of exclusion).

Under the civil rights laws, many programs were adopted and implemented. The one that caused the most controversial is affirmative action. President Johnson conceived the program, but it was President Nixon who placed teeth in the program with his Philadelphia Plan. These programs opened up doors for African Americans in education, employment, and business. Unlike the President Johnson programs, the Nixon programs operated to connect African Americans to the mainstream of society's income redistribution system. It is necessary, to repeat, for a group to be connected to this mainstream in order to be able to take advantage of a wide range of social and economic opportunities that society has to offer. Without such connection, government can provide a wide range of opportunities; but, if African Americans do not have the necessary human capital, they will not be able to take advantage of these opportunities.

The Politics of Confusion

Before the wrinkles in the civil rights programs could be ironed out, African Americans found themselves broadsided by new forms of racism with which they were not familiar. Because of the extent of these forms of racism, only two will be covered in this chapter: *the politics of confusion and insidious racism.*

The politics of confusion is to be understood here in the same manner as the Chinese philosopher Confucius stated it. It consists of the critics' success in launching a protracted anti-civil rights propaganda campaign against affirmative action and other civil rights measures. These critics were academicians. Their aim was to cast doubt on the need and legitimacy of the affirmative action programs. They anchored their argument on the false presupposition that these programs constituted racial discrimination in reverse. One of their strategies was to argue that African Americans can better secure adequate socioeconomic advancement if they would only place their rights to do so on the good-will of their adversaries and competitors. This argument is antithetical to the liberal democratic theory. To paraphrase the renowned Justice John Marshall, we have a government of laws and not of men.[1] Nevertheless, the critics marshalled forward data purporting to support their argument that African Americans were already moving into the middle class before the adoption of civil rights, and there was no need for these policies. In fact, they argued that these programs cause African Americans more harm than good.

The first writers to advance such arguments were Ben J. Wattenberg and Richard Scammon in 1973.[2] They were followed by Nathan Glazer in 1975 in his book, entitled *Affirmative Discrimination*.[3] Between the period of 1975 and 2000, critics were able to recruit many more writers, including African Americans, to advance similar arguments. These arguments were presented in various forms, but they drew the same conclusion (i.e., African Americans could better secure socioeconomic advancement if they were to institute their rights to do so among the goodwill of their competitors and adversaries). As we have seen, the European immigrants did not secure such advancement until their right to do so was placed on a principle of law (i.e., the collective bargaining laws and other measures adopted after WWII).

Among the writers of the politics of confusion, the book published by Stephen and Abigail Thernstrom, entitled *America in Black and White: One Nation, Indivisible*,[4] stands out more than the others. In 1997, they published this 708-page book, in which they just rehashed the antithetical democratic theories advanced in the 1970s by Wattenberg and Scammon, and Glazer. As demonstrated in Chapters 8 and 9, white groups did not secure such advancement until their rights to do so were instituted upon a principle of law. In fact, some of them remained impoverished for five generations, as demonstrated in Chapters 8 and 9.

The Thernstroms selected the period between the 1940s and 1960 to extract statistical data from the literature to make their case. In conducting research, analysts must keep in mind the Eastonian criteria for systematic research: that is, theories must be supportive by data and data must be tutored by theory. Otherwise, research may prove to be trivial. Again, analysts must also keep in mind that theories could be internally consistent, but if they do not cover the subject that analysts are trying to understand, they may be, what Amitai Etzioni termed, "manifestly irrelevant."[5]

The Thernstroms' book, although they produced a voluminous amount of data, fits neatly within Etzioni's theory for being "manifestly irrelevant" so far as offering a scientific explanation for the cause of African Americans' inequality. They selected mainly dependent variables and ignored independent ones. They placed a lot of emphasis upon African Americans' economic progress between the period of the 1940s and 1960s. To support their argument, they cited numerous statistical incidences. What this data does not take into account are those environmental factors which precipitated a change in African Americans' socioeconomic status. Specifically, the Thernstroms overlooked the relationship between the great changes in the economic growth and development that took place in America during this period, and the racial laws that operated to foreclose African Americans' freedom to take advantage of those social economic opportunities that were common to life.

During the period in which the Thernstroms studied, this country shifted from *a laissez-faire* to a *mixed economy* where the government became involved in doling out government largess. This involvement brought about great economic changes. Essentially, it was the Keynesian economic theory which required the government to pump billions of dollars into the economy to stimulate it. Millions and millions of jobs were created during this period, which inadvertently broadened job opportunities for African Americans. However, many of the laws that operated to foreclose their freedom to compete on a level playing field were not removed. The two laws that had the greatest impact on constraining their economic growth and development were the Davis-Bacon Act, which set aside high-paying in government-subsidized jobs, as the "white man's job," and the restrictions that the FHA housing policy placed on African Americans' freedom to take advantage of the *bonanza giveaways*. As we have demonstrated, these laws were not removed until the latter part of the 1960s (i.e., the passage of the 1968 Fair Housing Act and the implementation of the Nixon Administration Philadelphia plan).

The underlying factor that supported the discriminatory laws was the cultural-value choice which defines the social status of whites (i.e., they must be better than African Americans). This cultural-value choice is not simply a goal value that the white man ought to strive to achieve; it was, and still is, obligatory for him to achieve his status as a white man. The only way that he can achieve this status is to tilt the playing field in his favor and to create artificial barriers that will operate to foreclose African Americans' freedom to compete with him on an equal footing.

From their extreme manifestations, many of the racial conflicts since the passage of the civil rights laws can be characterized as an attempt by the dominant society to maintain their social status for being better than African Americans. In order to achieve such status, they have to undertake special legal measures to foreclose African Americans' freedom to pursue those occupations that require the use of the mind. This proposition can, in part, explain the controversy over affirmative action. This policy operates to protect African

Americans' freedom to pursue those jobs that require the use of the mind which, inadvertently, protects their freedom to connect themselves to the mainstream of society's income redistribution system, which is the prerequisite for group upward mobility.

The Thernstroms and other writers have marshalled forward ample data to support their argument that African Americans have made remarkable progress as a result of the change in whites' negative attitudes toward race. This change in attitude was brought about not by the good nature of whites but by the change in laws that supported these negative attitudes. Negative attitudes, to hypothesize, are short lived if they are not supported by law. For instance, the number of race hatred incidences has decreased dramatically since the passage of various hate crime laws. Under these laws, individuals can be prosecuted for hate crimes. Prior to the adoption of these laws, these crimes were interpreted as a function of the freedom of expression that was beyond the reach of Congress to address.

In short, the progress that the Thernstroms, and other writers of the politics of confusion, have asserted that African Americans made before the adoption of civil rights laws and affirmative action is simply a function of the economic expansion that took place in this country. This expansion created a labor shortage which African Americans filled–not out of a sense of fairness–but out of necessity.

The Politics of Invidious and Insidious Racism

The term racism, as it was defined in Chapter 1, is the politics of exclusion. Traditionally, this form of racism is thought of as *invidious racism,* which consists of the adoption of public policies with an evil eye. These policies specifically state that an entire racial group is to be denied their basic rights to life, liberty, and the pursuit of happiness that are accorded to other groups. The sole purpose of this denial is to oppress this group's socioeconomic advancements. This form of racism is to be found in the various Jim Crow laws such as racial segregation in public accommodations, schools, and employment as well as setting aside high-paying jobs as "the white man's job" as the government did with the Davis-Bacon Act. This is the form of racism that African Americans fought against from the end of the Civil War up to the mid 1960s. After 100 years of fighting, they were able to convince Congress to adopt various civil rights measures during and after the 1960s to safeguard them from this form of racism. As soon as these laws were implemented, they were, as mentioned previously, broadsided by *insidious racism.*

Insidious racism, it must be noted, differs markedly from *invidious racism*. Whereas the latter is overtly done with an evil eye, the former is done covertly by conspiring to adopt positive laws designed to deny African Americans their freedom to compete on an equal playing field for their fair share of those community's material possessions necessary for their preservation. One of major tactics that the proponents of insidious racism have used was to conduct propaganda campaigns to dupe the courts and legislators to adopt policies that will operate to truncate the support for affirmative action measures. In its totality, insidious racism is a form of the politics of exclusion.

The politics of insidious racism takes on many of the elements of the politics of confusion, such as advocating that African Americans can better secure adequate advancement with their civil and human rights instituted among the goodwill of their competitors and adversaries. They have been successful in duping the courts to accept their argument that Titles VI and VII of the Civil Rights Act of 1964 were designed to protect individuals against discrimination but not groups. In their totality, these titles protect a racial group's human rights–but not civil rights. The latter rights are absolute; in sofar as they can be distributed to an entire race. But Titles VI and VII are concerned with the authoritative allocation of a limited number of government benefits and resources where no individual can claim an equal protection right to them. Yet, the critics have duped the courts into accepting the position that non-African Americans have an equal protection right to a government benefit based on merit *if and only if* a company has adopted an affirmative action program.[6] In the absence of such a program, no such equal protection rights exist.

The next strategy that the critics used to institute the politics of insidious racism was to expand the definition of minority to include all ethnic groups. First, they attempted to include those white groups that immigrated during the latter part of the nineteenth century. They argued that these groups, too, have been the victims of racial discrimination. Because of its political and economic ramifications, the courts did not accept their argument. However, it did accept the argument that other racial minority groups could be included in the protected class even though the government had not saddled them when the disability of race. At the time of the adoption of the affirmative action laws, the government had considered these groups as white. Furthermore, many of these groups were not in the United States when the affirmative action program was adopted.

The major political repercussion of including those nonwhite groups into the protected class is that it increases *the pool of applicants* for a limited amount of government benefits *without increasing the pot of these benefits*. By operation, this would truncate the advancement of African Americans who have been saddled with the disability of race. It will also allow America to avoid the responsibility of addressing its sins for the enslavement of the African Americans. America has found it painful to address the race issue. Instead of addressing it, America has adopted a policy of placing the blame for the low socioeconomic status of African Americans on their own backs.

The practice of the politics of insidious racism has become a convenient political tool for America to avoid addressing the conditions of African Americans created by a history of racism. Whenever African American leaders begin to place pressure on the system to address these conditions, policymakers will take special care to include all other racial minority groups into the pool so that the limited resources would be spread among these groups. These groups are included regardless whether they have petitioned the government for such benefits. On the other hand, this writer has found through research and in-depth interviews, that whenever other non-African Americans petition the government for programs to secure adequate advancement for their group, policymakers would adopt programs to address the grievances only for that group. But when African Americans would make the same claim, administrators would take special care to include all minority groups into the resolution, regardless whether they have made a grievance or not.

Another tactic that proponents of the politics of insidious racism have used to truncate the advancement of African Americans has been to dupe the courts in accepting the position that all race-based programs should be subjected to the *strict scrutiny rule*. Originally, the court established this rule to serve as a system of protection to safeguard racial groups from the tyranny of the majoritarian rule. But the critics have been successful in getting the court to adopt the position that the strict scrutiny rule has a two-edged sword effect. Under this ruling, it is falsely assumed that a policy of racial inclusion has the same disparity impact upon the majority as a policy of racial exclusion has had upon African Americans. Such definition is based on the false presupposition that all race-inclusive programs will operate to foreclose the freedom of all the non-African Americans from obtaining benefits at a particular company. For example, when a large company such as the Los Angeles Fire Department gives an examination for 20 openings, it typically has more than 16,000 applicants applying for these positions. If the department were to adopt an affirmative action program which requires the hiring of four well-qualified African Americans out of these 20 positions, the strict scrutiny rule would automatically give the rest of the 15,980 non-African American applicants equal protection rights to those four positions despite the fact that it is logically impossible for all of these individuals to obtain these positions. What give these individuals an equal protection right to these positions is that they can allege that the company used race, notwithstanding the fact that the four applicants might have been more qualified than they.

Another form of insidious racism has been the courts' allowing other protected class groups to challenge those affirmative action programs designed to secure adequate advancement for African Americans. The courts have upheld challenges brought by a white female in Texas (*Texas v. Hopwood*) and a Hispanic in Maryland (*Podberesky v. Kirwan*). Both of these individuals challenged affirmative action on the bases that the institution used race as a factor. In the absence of affirmative action, it must be noted, these individuals would not have had a prayer in obtaining the benefits that they successfully claimed affirmative action deprived them of. There are numerous other such cases that fit within this situation, which need not be cited here. Suffice to say, the two-edged sword use of the strict scrutiny rule allows non-African American applicants to acquire a government benefit that he/she could not otherwise have obtained.

The recent politics of insidious racism that will have a profound effect upon African Americans is the policy that the U.S. Bureau of the Census adopted to include all Latin Americans into the category of minorities. As we have seen in the last two chapters, the U.S. Bureau of the Census has reported that the Hispanics are the fastest growing minorities in America. As we have pointed out, there are two major flaws with this policy. First, many Latin American immigrants are white. Secondly, the American government has not adopted a public policy that operated to saddle them with the disability of race. Third, except for the Mexicans, immigrants from Latin America immigrated through the legal channels where the immigration laws restricted their immigration to those individuals who are literate and skilled. Therefore, they are not impoverished. Placing them in the affirmative action category will operate to reduce the amount of resources set aside to address the legacy of racism against African Americans.

African Americans' Progress as Entrepreneurs

Other than the various forms of racism (i.e., the politics of exclusion and insidious discrimination), the factor that is hampering African Americans' growth and development is their lack of a meaningful class of entrepreneurship among them. The political significance of this class is that it broadens job opportunities for a group. This factor can account for the low unemployment rate among the Asians that immigrated after the 1960s. These groups immigrated with entrepreneurial skills. Instead of seeking jobs from the existing institutions, many of them created jobs for themselves by establishing their own businesses.

The primary reason for African Americans' low performance in business has historically been because they migrated from an agrarian background where they did not have the freedom to interact in an entrepreneurial environment. The only way, as has been hypothesized, that individuals can acquire entrepreneurail skills is to have the freedom to interact in such an environment. There are four groups that fall into this category: the Irish-Catholics, African Americans, Puerto Ricans, and, to a certain extent, Mexicans. What can account for African Americans' level of success in business, discussed previously, is affirmative action. This policy protected their freedom to interact in an entrepreneurial environment long enough to acquire the necessary capital (both human and physical) to succeed in business.

As a result of affirmative action, African American-owned businesses grew approximately 46 percent between the period of 1987 and 1992. This policy protected their freedom to interact in an entrepreneurial environment.

This writer has found that the independent variable that can best explain individuals' success in business cannot be obtained by statistical analysis alone. In addition to statistics, it is necessary for researchers to leave their ivy towers, go out on the streets, and conduct in-depth interviews with small entrepreneurs to ascertain how they were able to start their businesses. Utilizing this approach, coupled with statistical analysis, this writer has found that the independent variable that can best explain individuals' success in entrepreneurship is their acquiring these skills before they attempted to start their businesses.

The major political impact that affirmative action has had in increasing entrepreneurship among African Americans is that it removed the government support from the concept that these types of jobs were set aside as "the white men's jobs." Removing such support does not within itself account for African Americans' success in business. The impact of the resistance to the implementation of affirmative action also has to be taken into account. At first, many companies went out and hired any African Americans, regardless of their qualifications, and placed them in window dressing positions with a high salary, just to meet the affirmative action guidelines.

The practice of hiring African Americans for window dressing positions was truncated after the courts started giving legitimacy to the reverse discrimination arguments. The positive impact of the reverse discrimination arguments was that it forced companies to start recruiting those African Americans whose qualifications equal those of whites. When the emotions of the reverse discrimination arguments receded, companies found that African Americans' performance in business equaled to and, in some instances, excelled that of whites because they felt that they had something to prove. The fact that African Americans could perform equally in businesses is not as important as their freedom to acquire entrepreneurial skills.

The increase in African American-owned businesses during this period cannot be accounted for by skills alone. There were many other factors that came into play during this period, namely the corporate downsizing and acquisitions. A combination of these two factors resulted in many employees being laid off. Through in-depth interviews, this writer found that a large percentage of African Americans entrepreneurs were victims of this layoff. This lay off, it must be noted, was not necessarily race-based; it applied across the board. African Americans have always been laid off during periods of austerity. What made a difference with their layoffs during this period, compared to pre-affirmative action, was that they had acquired the necessary entrepreneurial skills to create jobs for themselves by starting their own businesses.

Since affirmative action had protected their freedom to be connected to the mainstream of society's income redistribution system, African Americans were in a position to take advantage of the benefits of downsizing. During this process, many companies paid their employees servant packages which included money ranging from $100,000 to $500,000. Some African Americans used this money to start their own businesses. This servant package solved the problem that has historically plagued African Americans in starting a business (i.e., the lack of startup capital).

Determining the aged-old question as to which is the most important variable to run a successful business is similar to the metaphysical one of which comes first: the chicken or the egg. Based on in-depth interviews, this writer has found that acquiring entrepreneurial skills come first. If a person has the skills to run a successful business, he also has the skills to raise the necessary funds to start up the business.

As a result of affirmative action, there have been many African Americans who have become millionaires after establishing their own businesses. This group does not include the athletes and entertainers, although many millionaires can be found among this group. Mathematically, there are a limited number of individuals who can possibly enter these fields, even if there was no evidence of racial bias. The millionaires that this writer is referring to here are those that came from the rank-and-file of the working class. As a result of affirmative action, they were hired at those companies that offered stock options to their employees which many took advantage of these opportunities along with other employees. With a combination of the servant package and stock options, some African Americans walked away as millionaires.

Another area in which this writer has found that African Americans have succeeded in becoming millionaires is in multi-level marketing. One company, with which this writer is familiar, was formed in the early 1990s which marketed long distance telephone services. Within a period of five years, this company had produced fifty millionaires. Among these, thirty-five were African Americans. This company, it must be noted, was not under any affirmative action obligation to hire minorities. It simply had a level playing field for entry-level positions. It employed representatives–and not employees. The only qualification for becoming a representative was to purchase a sale kit for $500. Success in this business depended on hard work and self-initiative. Most of the African American representatives who became millionaires seem to have come from the fields of engineers and business.

In comparison to their number prior to affirmative action, African Americans have made a quantum leap in the area of entrepreneurship. This is evidenced by the number of success stories that appear in the African Americans' news organs such as *Black Enterprise, Ebony,* and *Jet* magazines and local African American newspapers. The successes listed in these organs do not give as true a picture of African Americans' success in business as the survey conducted by the U.S. Department of Commerce.

In 1996, the Department of Commerce published a survey of all non-farm businesses in the United States with receipts of $500 or more. It found that African American-owned firms, receipts increased from $19.8 billion in 1987 to $32.2 billion in 1992. This represented a 63 percent increase compared to the 67 percent for all firms.[7]

The problem of raising the necessary capital to start a business is still a major problem not only for African Americans but non-African Americans as well. As stated in Chapter 6, African Americans have cited discrimination in loans by the banks as one of the major reasons for their low rate of performance in business. But as pointed out in Chapter 5, the British West Indians, Chinese, and Japanese relied on a rotating credit system to raise the necessary capital among themselves to start a business. This pattern can also be found among the Southeast Asian refugees of the 1980s. This group uses this system extensively to raise money for business, purchase homes, and a host of other things.

The major problem with the rotating credit system is that it only works among those groups that have internalized a cooperative value system. This value system automatically will make this program inoperative for African Americans and non-African Americans alike who have internalized the American competitive and individualistic value system. There is a high probability that individuals with this value system will not adhere to the rules of the rotating credit system.

Increasing entrepreneurship among African Americans will be one of the solutions to their chronic unemployment. As stated previously, their major problem in this area have been that they migrated from an agrarian background that does not promote their acquiring the entrepreneurial skills that are needed to run business in urban areas. To overcome their problem in this area, African Americans must establish a national institute specifically dedicated to training them how to become entrepreneurs and to be able to take advantage of the economic opportunities that this rapidly changing technological society has to offer. This institute must be established in the private sector in order to safeguard it against the practice of insidious racism (i.e., critics conspiring to undermine its operations by insisting on casting a net to cover all racial minority groups with a limited amount of resources). With entrepreneurial skills, African Americans would be able to broaden their employment opportunities like the Asians and Mideastern immigrants.

African Americans and Education

As far as education is concerned, African Americans have made remarkable progress, although they have not closed the academic gap between themselves and the middle-class populations. There are many reasons for this academic gap. First, African American leaders started petitioning the government for *fish* and it gave them *scorpions*. That is, they petitioned the government for equality in educational resources (fish) as a means of improving the education of the African American child. Instead of granting them equality in resources, the government forced them to accept busing and integration (scorpions) as a means to improve their children's education.

There were two apparent negative impacts that forced busing and integration had upon the education of the African American children. First, it placed them in an environment that was not conducive to learning. Second, it stripped them of their mentors and role models for whom they could identify. These individuals are as important to educational experience of the growing child as air is to fire. They serve as mediators to mediate the complexities between the African American children's private lives and the educational institutions which are becoming increasingly complex. As Carolyn Murray and James Jackson have pointed out, non-African American teachers are conditioned to have lower expectations of African American students' ability to learn. Whenever an African American student excels academically, he is too often punished instead of rewarded for his performance like other students.[8]

As has been demonstrated elsewhere, the purpose of busing was never intended to close the academic gap between African American and white students.[9] As mentioned in Chapter 9, the schools in the suburbs were built by FHA Housing policy, which transformed public schools into private ones and, at the same time, remained supported by government funds. These schools were able to deliver a better education than private ones because of government supported. Toward the end of the 1960s, these schools had begun to lose their student populations as a result of their maturity and going away to college. Their parents remained in their homes. Consequently, this outflux of students produced a shortage of students. Since most schools are funded on the formula of average daily attendance (ADA funding), the suburban schools were threatened with the possibility of losing their funding to maintain their quality of education which was based on teacher-student ratios–that is, one teacher to less than 17 students per classroom. The loss of students meant the loss of ADA funding.

To avert the loss of ADA funding, school administrators started pushing busing. The purpose here was to bus minority students from their inner-city neighborhood schools to the suburbs to make up for their loss of students. As demonstrated elsewhere, the difference in the academic performances of African American students and non-African Americans lie more in the curriculum than any other factor.[10] The curriculum in the suburban schools is structured to fit the format of the standardized tests whereas the curriculums in the inner-city school are not. When African American students were bused to the suburbs, they were not placed in a curriculum that was designed to prepare them to do college work. In fact, research shows that they are currently being placed predominantly on low ability tracts where they are not taught the level of math and other courses needed to succeed in college. Too often, they are corralled into remedial courses such as business math.[11]

The injustice that the policy of busing had upon constraining the educational growth and development of the African American child was not racism alone, but class played a major role. The busing policy for the purpose of closing the education gap between African American students and non-African Americans overlooks the class factor. For example, eighth grade students from low-income neighborhoods cannot compete successfully with eight graders in a middle-class neighborhood because the resources in these schools are not equal. Students attending schools in low-income neighborhoods very seldom take the necessary math courses that require them to succeed in the eighth grade. This is more of a class factor than one of race. In other words, white students from the moderate, low-income neighborhood of South Gate, California, cannot be bused to the upper-middle-class white neighborhood of Brentwood, California, and still be expected to keep up. But when African American students are bused under the same circumstances, their failure to compete successfully is too often interpreted as evidence of their biological inferiority.

In short, the problem of closing the education gap between African Americans and non-African Americans cannot be resolved simply by busing and integration. The issue of inequality in the curriculum and the distribution of funds has to first be addressed. Recently, California attempted to address this problem by mandating that the classroom size in the first three years of school be limited to a faculty-student ratio of less than 22 students per classroom. But this policy is always subject to be derailed by the budgetary crises that schools experience.

How Long Will African Americans Need Some Form of Affirmative Action?

The most frequently raised question since President Johnson implemented his "Great Society Programs" has been: How long will African Americans need some form of affirmative action? The Johnson Administration started implementing various programs after his 1964 election. As discussed previously, the proponents of the politics of confusion launched their anti-civil rights campaign in the early 1970s. Many writers and commentators alike have written numerous articles and books where they advanced the argument that the government has done everything for African Americans, and it seems as though nothing can be done to improve their conditions. The underlying assumption of this statement is that 200 years of the legacy of racism can be rectified with a quick-fix approach.

The notion that there is a quick-fix approach that can solve problems created by the legacy of racism is devoid historical data. One of the major political repercussions of this legacy is that it created abject poverty among African Americans. This racial injury cannot be cured by a stroke of the pen, as President John F. Kennedy once stated. Instead, a policy is needed to usher them through a period of transformation in their socioeconomic behavior. Such a proposition raises the question as to how long will it take for them to undergo such a transformation.

There is no study in the literature, which this writer is aware of, that specifically addresses the question of the transformation of a group's socioeconomic behavior. However, an examination of historical data will give us some clues as to the time it will take for such transformation. Through such examination, we can identify two independent variables: *time factor and some form of reparation*. Both of these variables can be extracted from the Israelites' experience when they were freed from slavery in Egypt.

When the Israelites first left Egypt, they migrated into the deserts. God instructed them to go back to Egypt and asked their former masters for "lent" (reparation) in the form of gold and silver. This instruction is very important in understanding the prerequisites for the transformation of the socioeconomic behavior of freed slaves. The question here is why would God, the Almighty, would instruct the Israelites to go back to their former masters and to ask for gold and silver, when He could have provided them with all the gold and silver that they could have possibly needed. This is evidenced by the fact that He fed them for 40 years on manna. The reason for such instruction can only be extrapolated; it was intended to serve as a symbolic gesture for future masters of slaves. That is, they had an obligation to grant their emancipated slaves some kind of freedom dues.

As was demonstrated in Chapter 2, the colonial government followed this policy by granting the indentured servants freedom dues in the form of fifty acres of land or some other provisions suitable to the service needs. But when it came to African Americans, Congress passed a law to grant them freedom dues in the form of forty acres of land and a mule, but President Johnson vetoed the bill. As argued earlier, this land would have connected African Americans to the mainstream of society's income redistribution system.

Historically, individuals' freedom has only come about when there was a land reform after the dismantling of the large land holding system. Whenever a state failed to undertake land reform, poverty usually develops among a peasant population or this population will undertake some form of revolt. This was, as has been demonstrated, what happened in Mexico after it received its independence.

As far as the variable time is concerned, we have the experiences of both the Israelites and the Russian slaves from which we can extract some clues. The Israelites had forty years. The Russian slaves were given twenty years. By contrast, America gave her slaves less than ten years after the Civil War and five years under the poverty programs. From these two experiences, we can postulate that it will take a minimum of one generation of uninterrupted government support for African Americans to undergo a socioeconomic transformation. This time period will allow the principle of intergenerational mobility to kick in among them. Evidence as to whether this principle has kicked in will occur when the parents started making provisions for their children to remain on the same middle-class plateau on which they were born. This includes paying for their children's college education. This was precisely what the parents who benefitted from the New Deal programs and the G.I. Bill were doing for their children in the 1960s when President Johnson declared war on poverty.

For the question as to how long will it take African Americans to undergo a transformation in their socioeconomic behavior, this writer hypothesizes that it will take at least one generation of a policy of reparation that is free of the susceptibility of being subjected to the practice of *insidious racism.* This requires a law to be written in such a way as (1) to prevent bureaucrats from arbitrarily casting the net of this policy to include other minority groups that the government have not saddled with the disability of race, (2) increase the pool without increase the pot of funds, and (3) to keep individuals from challenging these programs under the false presupposition that they could have been awarded such benefit if it were not for this program.

The strongest evidence that we have to support the argument that some form of reparation is needed is to examine the level of government support (i.e., *bonanza giveaways,* that the European immigrants of the late nineteenth century received between the period of the 1940s to the 1960s). The government granted them billions of dollars to facilitate their socioeconomic transformation and at the same time maintained a *de jure* policy of racial exclusion which applied only to African Americans. If African Americans were allowed to participate in those *bonanza giveaways* during this period, the principle of intergenerational mobility would have kicked in among them in the 1960s. This would have eradicated the abject poverty that plagues them today.

Notes

1. *Marbury v. Madison,* 1 Cranch 137 (1803).
2. Ben J. Wattenberg and Richard Scammon, "Black Progress and Liberal Rhetoric," *Commentary,* vol. 56, No.4 (April 1973): pp. 33-44.
3. *Affirmative Discrimination: Ethnic Inequality and Public Policy* (Cambridge, Massachusetts: Harvard University Press, 1975).
4. Stephen and Abigail Thernstrom, *America in Black and White: One Nation, Indivisible* (New York: Simon & Schuster, 1997).
5. J. Owens Smith, *The Politics of Ethnic and Racial Inequality,* p. 13.
6. J. Owens Smith, "Why Busing Failed to Close the Academic Gap," in *Race and Ethnicity: A Study of Intracultural Socialization Patterns,* co-authored with Carl L. Jackson (Dubuque: Kendall/Hunt Publishing, 1989).
7. "Black-owned Businesses: Strongest in Services," U.S. Department of Commerce, Economic and Statistics Administration, Bureau of Census, SB/96-3.

8.   Carolyn Murray and James Jackson, "The Conditioned Failure Model," in *Race and Ethnicity: A Study of Intracultural Socialization Patterns,* ed. J. Owens Smith and Carl Jackson(Dubuque: Kendall/Hunt Publisher, 1989), pp. 319-355.

9.   Smith and Jackson, pp. 296-317.

10.   Ibid.

11.   Ibid., pp. 319-343.

Appendix

Table 30

Employment Status and Major Occupations of Foreign Males Ten Years of Age and Over in Certain Selected States, 1920

Subject	Total	English[a]	Germans	Swedes	Norwe-gians	Irish	Italians	Russian Jews
Males employed	289,292	24,065	67,457	27,665	27,568	12,612	53,708	12,559
Percent	100.0	100.0	100.0	100.0	100.0	100.0	100.0	100.0
Agricultural:Farmers	37.6	18.1	64.6	81.4	87.3	13.5	0.9	4.1
Coal Mine Operatives	31.2	41.0	8.0	3.9	0.2	18.5	50.2	33.9
Managerial, Foreman, etc.	2.5	5.6	2.8	1.3	0.5	8.3	2.8	2.8
Skilled Mechanics: Carpenters	9.2	13.8	8.1	10.3	11.3	18.5	10.2	11.5
Laborers:								
Blast Furnaces	10.0	8.0	6.0	1.4	0.03	15.8	16.4	16.2
Steam Railroad	4.1	2.0	1.6	0.5	0.04	8.6	13.4	2.8
Professional: Physicians and Surgeons	0.6	0.8	0.8	0.09	0.05	0.8	0.7	3.8
Clerical: Salesmen	6.0	10.5	8.0	0.8	0.4	15.8	5.2	25.0

SOURCE: Edwatd P. Hutchinson, *Immigrants and Their Children*, pp. 283-84.

[a]The English category encompasses all of the groups from the United Kingdom (Scots, Welsh, and English), except the Irish.

Notes: The data in this table are limited to the extent that they cover only six states (Massachusetts, New York, Pennsylvania, Michigan, Minnesota, and Wisconsin) and do not represent the total population for each group. However, these states were selected because they had the largest numbers of foreign-born employed in occupations selected.

Table 31
Occupation of Ethnic Groups by Sex and Age

	Total 100%	Males	Females	Under 14 yrs.	14-45 yrs.	Over 45 yrs.	Total 100%	Professional	Commercial	Skilled	Unskilled
African (Black)	3,786	62.2	37.8	9.1	86.8	4.1	2,921	3.0	2.6	45.6	48.8
Armenian	1,895	75.1	24.9	11.8	84.3	3.9	1,390	3.4	5.1	38.5	53.0
Bohemian & Moravian	12,958	57.3	42.8	20.7	73.9	5.4	7,985	1.3	1.2	43.6	53.9
Bulgarian, Serbian, & Montenegrin	11,548	96.2	3.8	1.9	96.2	1.9	11,025	0.1	0.3	3.7	95.9
Chinese	1,485	94.1	5.9	4.5	81.5	14.0	1,261	6.9	66.0	1.5	25.6
Croatian & Slovenian	44,272	86.5	13.5	3.8	94.1	2.1	40,125	0.1	0.1	3.7	96.1
Cuban	5,591	67.4	32.6	17.2	73.2	9.6	2,842	10.3	19.1	55.9	14.7
Dalmatian, Bosnian, & Herzegovinian	4,591	95.1	4.9	1.7	96.3	2.0	4,373	0.1	0.3	7.7	91.9
Dutch & Flemish	9,735	67.0	33.0	17.6	76.4	6.0	5,849	5.2	7.9	30.1	56.8
East Indian	271	93.0	7.0	5.5	90.5	4.0	222	9.9	52.7	5.4	32.0
English	45,079	62.1	37.9	13.5	75.3	11.2	28,249	10.8	13.5	51.3	24.4
Finnish	14,136	67.4	32.6	7.1	90.8	2.1	11,959	0.4	0.3	7.2	92.1
French	10,379	57.1	42.9	8.6	81.7	9.7	6,823	16.5	12.9	31.3	39.3
German	86,813	59.2	40.8	15.1	78.6	6.3	55,095	4.3	6.7	29.7	59.3
Greek	23,127	96.3	3.7	3.1	95.9	1.0	21,615	0.5	2.6	9.4	87.5
Hebrew	153,748	52.1	47.9	28.3	66.3	5.4	76,605	1.4	5.6	66.7	26.3
Irish	40,959	50.9	49.1	4.6	90.9	4.5	35,387	1.7	2.9	15.1	80.3
Italian(North)	46,286	78.9	21.1	8.6	87.9	3.5	36,980	1.4	2.3	19.4	76.9

Table 31 (continued)

	Total 100%	Males	Females	Under 14 yrs.	14-45 yrs.	Over 45 yrs.	Total 100%	Professional	Commercial	Skilled	Unskilled
Japanese	14,243	89.6	10.4	1.0	97.1	1.9	11,797	2.2	10.3	2.8	84.7
Korean	127	81.1	18.9	16.5	81.1	2.4	90	6.3	15.0	2.5	76.2
Lithuanian	14,257	66.1	33.9	8.9	89.5	1.6	11,568	0.2	0.2	9.2	90.4
Magyar	44,261	71.8	28.2	9.G	87.5	3.5	34,559	0.6	0.5	9.3	89.6
Mexican	141	66.0	34.0	14.9	74.5	10.6	65	23.1	35.4	24.6	16.9
Pacific Islander	13	76.9	23.1	7.7	76.9	15.4	9	33.3	0.0	66.7	0.0
Polish	95,835	69.3	30.7	9.3	88.5	2.2	77,437	0.2	0.2	7.7	91.9
Portuguese	8,729	58.4	41.6	20.9	70.7	8.4	5,815	0.5	1.1	4.8	93.6
Romanian	11,425	92.5	7.5	2.0	94.0	4.0	10,759	0.2	0.2	2.5	97.1
Russian	5,814	82.7	18.3	10.0	86.8	3.2	4,591	3.2	2.4	10.8	83.6
Ruthenian	16,257	75.7	24.3	3.6	93.9	2.5	14,899	0.1	0.0	2.7	97.2
Scandinavian	58,141	62.1	37.9	9.1	86.4	4.5	47,352	1.8	1.6	23.5	73.1
Scottish	16,463	66.1	33.9	12.9	78.8	8.3	11,207	5.7	9.9	62.8	21.6
Slovak	38,221	69.6	30.4	8.9	88.4	2.7	29,817	0.0	0.1	4.9	95.0
Spanish	5,332	83.6	16.4	7.1	84.6	8.3	4,211	5.7	19.2	44.4	30.7
Spanish American	1,585	69.7	30.3	17.0	74.4	8.6	790	23.7	37.1	21.1	18.1
Syrian	5,824	70.4	29.6	15.2	80.9	3.9	4,023	1.1	11.1	19.9	67.9
Turkish	2,033	95.7	4.3	1.9	%.0	2.1	1,914	1.5	4.4	8.3	85.8
Welsh	2,367	7.1	29.9	12.5	78.2	9.3	1,639	4.9	6.7	62.4	26.0
West Indian	1,476	58.9	41.1	14.8	76.1	9.1	900	7.6	15.0	49.4	28.0
Other Peoples	1,027	94.5	41.1	14.8	76.1	9.1	932	1.2	4.1	18.0	76.7
Total	1,100,735	69.5	30.5	12.4	83.0	4.6	812,275	1.8	3.1	21.7	73.4

SOURCE: Reports of Commission General of Immigration, 1906, Table 8, p. 28.

Table 32

Population of the Caribbean Area by National Affiliation and Race, 1936

Political Area	National Affiliation	Total	Colored	White	Others
Total		12,397,222	8,084,778	3,862,058	451,376
Bahamas	Great Britain	62,697	48,697	13,000	1,000
Barbados	Great Britain	180,055	162,055	18,000	--
Bermuda	Great Britain	29,896	17,862	11,684	350
Cuba	Republic	4,011,088	1,300,000	2,444,000	268,088
Grenada	Great Britain	78,662	62,919	15,576	157
Guadeloupe	France	267,407	213,925	52,948	534
Haiti	Republic	2,650,000	2,646,000	3,500	500
Jamaica	Great Britain	1,090,269	1,040,269	20,000	30,000
Leeward Islands	Great Britain	132,973	106,378	26,330	265
Martinique	France	234,695	187,756	46,470	469
Puerto Rico	United States	1,623,814	473,664	1,150,000	150
St. Lucia	GreatBritain	62,000	49,600	12,276	124
St. Vincent	Great Britain	47,961	44,549	2,173	1,239
Santo Domingo	Republic	1,478,121	1,444,621	30,000	3,500
Trinidad	Great Britain	425,572	265,572	15,000	145,000
Virgin Islands	United States	22,012	20,911	1,101	--

SOURCE: Ira De Reid, *The Negro Immigrant* (New York: Columbia University Press, 1936), p. 238.

Table 33

Family Income by Ethnic Origin, 1950[a]

					Origin			
	Total	English	Germans	Irish	Italians	Norwegians	Poles	Russian Jews
All persons	25,559,964	1,306,685	3,558,005	1,766,335	2,774,495	618,925	1,771,245	1,459,520
Percent	100.0	100.0	100.0	100.0	100.0	100.0	100.0	100.0
Percent of persons with income	62.4	6.4	63.0	63.1	63.2	65.3	65.4	61.5
Under $500	12.3	9.0	9.3	7.7	5.8	9.8	5.9	6.0
$500 to $999	9.4	7.5	7.6	7.6	5.6	8.0	5.4	4.5
$1,000 to $1,499	7.3	5.6	5.8	5.6	6.4	6.6	6.7	4.9
$1,500 to $1,999	6.6	5.5	5.5	5.9	7.8	6.6	6.7	4.9
$2,000 to $2,499	7.0	6.6	6.5	7.4	9.9	6.1	9.3	6.7
$2,500 to $2,999	5.3	5.0	5.6	6.5	8.2	7.0	8.8	6.0
$3,000 to $3,999	7.7	11.0	10.6	11.4	11.9	10.6	14.2	10.2
$4,000 to $4,999	3.0	5.3	5.1	5.0	4.0	5.0	4.9	5.4
$5,000 to $5,999	1.5	2.8	2.6	2.5	1.6	2.4	1.9	4.2
$6,000 and over	2.2	4.4	4.0	3.2	1.6	3.5	2.2	7.4
Median income	$2,245	$2,322	$2,245	$2,309	$2,137	$2,475	$2,775	$2,887
Not reported	6.1	5.3	4.7	5.5	5.1	3.7	4.6	5.5
Percent above $2,500	19.7	28.4	27.9	28.6	27.3	28.5	32.0	33.2

Table 33 (continued)

	Spanish	Swedes	Blacks	Puerto[c] Ricans	Japanese[b]	Chinese[b]
All persons	566,540	820,870	10,505,185	216,830	109,410	90,615
Percent	100.0	100.0	100.0	100.0	100.0	100.0
Percent of persons with income	55.2	66.0	61.3	56.8	62.7	56.7
Under $500	13.2	8.0	18.7	6.0	8.8	6.9
$500 to $999	10.9	6.5	13.1	8.7	9.0	8.1
$1,000 to $1,499	8.6	5.5	8.8	10.1	8.0	8.1
$1,500 to $1,999	6.6	5.7	7.1	11.5	8.0	8.3
$2,000 to $2,499	6.1	7.3	--	9.7	9.7	8.8
$2,500 to $2,999	3.8	6.4	--	4.6	6.0	4.7
$3,000 to $3,999	4.2	12.3	2.8	--	7.6	6.1
$4,000 to $4,999	0.9	6.3	0.4	0.4	2.3	2.3
$5,000 to $5,999	0.2	3.1	--	0.5	1.2	1.2
$6,000 and over	0.3	4.3	0.2	0.7	1.7	1.5
Median income	$1,200	$2,483	$952	$1,654	$1,839	$1,799
Not reported	5.7	4.2	7.6	--	6.9	10.4
Percent above $2,500	9.4	32.4	3.4	6.2	18.8	15.8

[a]Calculated from: U.S. Bureau of Census, U.S. Census of Population: 1950, vol. 4. Special Reports, Part 3, Chapter A, Nativity and Parentage (Washington: Government Printing Office, 1954), pp. 13-45,56-83.

[b]Calculated from: U.S. Bureau of Census, U.S. Census Population: 1950, vol. 4, Special Reports, Part 3, Chapter B, Nonwhite Population by Race (Washington: Government Printing Office, 1953), pp. 14-20, 30-40.

[c]Calculated from: U.S. Census of Population: 1950, Continental United States (Washington: Government Printing Office, 1953), chap. 2.

Table 34
Family Income by Ethnic Origin, 1970

	Total	English	Germans	Irish	Italians	Poles	Russian Jews	Swedes
					Origin			
Total famlily heads	10,375,309	590,853	949,127	423,888	1,314,594	740,112	635,270	277,584
Percent	100.0	100.0	100.0	100.0	100.0	100.0	100.0	100.0
Under $1,000	3.8	1.3	1.8	1.3	1.3	1.0	1.1	1.3
$1,000 to $1,999	5.0	2.1	3.9	2.0	1.3	1.3	1.2	2.7
$2,000 to $2,999	6.0	3.7	6.4	3.3	1.7	1.8	1.8	4.8
$3,000 to $3,999	6.4	8.9	6.5	3.9	2.2	2.3	2.1	5.1
$4,000 to $4,999	6.0	4.4	6.0	4.0	2.6	2.5	2.4	3.8
$5,000 to $5,999	6.2	4.4	6.1	4.3	3.5	3.4	2.9	5.0
$6,000 to $6,999	6.2	4.6	5.6	4.6	4.6	4.2	3.3	5.2
$7,000 to $7,999	6.3	5.2	5.8	4.9	5.8	5.3	3.8	5.4
$8,000 to $8,999	12.0	11.7	11.6	13.5	14.3	13.2	9.3	11.9
$10,000 to 14,999	22.7	28.0	24.2	29.1	33.3	32.0	25.0	26.0
$15,000 to $24,999	12.4	22.3	16.8	24.2	23.2	24.9	27.6	20.7
$25,000 or more	4.4	7.2	5.1	7.0	5.8	7.6	18.6	6.7
Median income	$11,374	$11,374	$9,352	$11,776	$11,857	$12,274	$14,281	$10,568
Income below poverty	5.4	8.1	5.1	4.5	3.8	3.8	6.2	
Percent above $10,000	39.5	57.5	46.1	60.3	62.3	64.5	71.2	53.4

Table 34 (continued)

				Origin		
	Norwegians	Spanish	Blacks	West Indians	Japanese	Chinese
Total family heads	201,125	375,255	4,729,091	29,968	80,727	27,713
Percent	100.0	100.0	100.0	100.0	100.0	100.0
Under $1,000	1.5	3.3	6.6	2.6	0.8	1.5
$1,000 to $1,999	3.4	4.0	8.1	2.4	0.8	2.0
$2,000 to $2,999	5.5	5.4	9.0	3.0	1.8	2.2
$3,000 to $3,999	6.0	6.8	9.2	3.9	1.4	2.8
$4,000 to $4,999	5.7	7.3	8.5	4.2	1.6	2.8
$5,000 to $5,999	5.3	7.7	8.2	5.1	2.6	4.5
$6,000 to $6,999	5.4	8.5	7.8	6.3	3.0	4.5
$7,000 to $7,999	5.8	8.6	7.1	6.4	4.0	4.6
$8,000 to $8,999	11.9	16.2	11.6	12.1	10.4	10.6
$10,000 to $14,999	25.7	24.0	15.9	28.0	31.4	27.8
$15,000 to $24,999	17.9	9.4	6.6	20.0	32.9	27.8
$25,000 or more	5.2	1.3	0.8	5.1	9.3	8.7
Median income	$9,826	$7,846	$6,005	$10,624	$13,775	$12,606
Income below poverty	7.6	20.6	30.3	5.1	3.2	6.4
Percent above $10,000	48.8	34.7	23.3	53.1	73.6	64.3

Calculated from: U.S. Bureau of the Census, Census of the Population: 1970, Subject Reports, Final Report PC (2)-1A, National Origin and Language (Washington: Government Printing Office, 1973), pp. 23-40,65-70.

Table 35

Employment Status and Major Occupation of the Male Population Fourteen Years Old and Over, by Ethnic Origin, 1950[a]

Subject	Total	English	Origin Germans	Irish	Italians	Poles	Russian Jews
Males employed	9,021,899	455,617	1,283,475	556,598	1,075,069	711,598	597,%3
Percent	100.0	100.0	100.0	100.0	100.0	100.0	100.0
Prof., techn.,& kindred wkrs.	6.2	11.2	7.3	9.7	6.0	6.9	15.3
Farmers & farm managers	9.7	5.7	14.8	2.8	1.1	2.3	4.9
Mgrs.,offs., & props., exc., farm	8.9	14.6	12.5	12.4	11.1	25.5	
Clerical & kindred wkrs.	11.5	17.6	12.9	12.0	15.2	13.8	23.9
Craftsmen, foremen, & kind. wkrs.	15.4	22.0	22.4	19.3	21.3	22.3	10.5
Operatives & kindred workers	20.8	17.0	16.2	16.3	28.4	31.4	12.0
Private household workers	0.5	0.1	0.1	0.1	0.05	0.5	0.02
Service wkrs., exc. priv. household	9.0	5.5	5.2	10.9	6.5	4.6	2.7
Farm laborers & foremen	4.4	0.2	0.7	0.15	0.1	0.37	0.9
Farm Laborers, exc. unpaid & foremen	3.6	1.0	1.8	0.6	0.5	0.8	2.5
Laborers, exc. farm & mine	13.0	4.5	0.7	5.4	8.3	7.3	--

Table 35 (continued)

			Origin				
	Swedes	Norwegians	Spanish[c]	Blacks[b]	Puerto Ricans	Japanese	Chinese[b]
Males employed	330,875	241,033	179,220	3,501,481	64,980	42,499	40,131
Percent	100.0	100.0	100.0	100.0	100.0	100.0	100.0
Prof., techn., & kindred wkrs.	10.3	7.5	1.8	2.2	5.1	6.4	6.3
Farmers & farm managers	13.0	22.4	2.7	13.4	0.2	15.3	1.4
Mgrs., offs., & props., exc., farm	13.3	11.4	2.9	2.1	5.3	8.6	22.2
Clerical & kindred wkrs.	14.3	11.9	7.6	4.2	9.4	9.1	11.2
Craftsmen, foremen, & kind. wkrs.	22.7	18.8	13.2	7.7	32.4	7.6	3.3
Operatives & kindred workers	14.1	12.3	23.6	21.0	0.1	9.7	16.3
Private household workers	0.09	0.09	0.1	1.0	24.6	8.7	1.8
Service wkrs., exc. priv. household	3.8	3,9	6.2	13.2	0.05	8.7	32.3
Farm laborers & foremen	0.7	1.4	2.25	10.3	2.5	2.3	0.1
Farm laborer, exc. upaid & foremen	1.7	3.3	17.5	--	7.1	14.4	1.3
Laborers, exc. farm & mine	4.8	5.7	20.7	23.3	1.6	13.5	1.9

[a]Census of Population: 1950, vol. 4, Special Reports, Part 3.
[b]Census of Population: 1950, vol. 4, Special Reports, Part 3, Chapter B.
[c]Census of Population: 1950, Continental United States

Table 36
Employment Status and Major Occupation of the Male Population Fourteen Years Old and Over, by Ethnic Origin, 1960[a]

Subject	Total	English	Germans	Origin Irish	Italians	Poles	Russian Jews
Males employed	8,627,270	599,610	1,002,960	434,682	1,272,754	784.066	652,605
Percent	100.0	100.0	100.0	100.0	100.0	100.0	100.0
Prof., techn., & kindred wkrs.	9.3	15.1	9.8	13.3	9.6	11.4	20.0
Farmers & farm managers	4.5	3.2	11.7	1.5	0.8	1.6	3.5
Mgrs., offs., & props., exc., farm	9.5	15.0	12.7	12.7	11.6	10.5	23.3
Clerical & kindred wkrs.	7.7	9.5	7.3	14.2	8.8	8.1	7.0
Salesworkers	5.8	8.5	6.6	7.8	7.0	6.6	16.0
Craftsmen, foremen, & kind. wkrs.	18.0	17.7	23.1	18.6	23.4	24.0	12.0
Operatives & kindred workers	23.1	14.8	16.1	14.6	23.8	25.3	10.0
Private household workers	0.3	--	--	--	--	--	--
Service wkrs., exc. priv. household	10.1	5.8	5.5	10.4	7.3	8.4	3.0
Farm laborers & foremen	3.9	0.6	1.5	0.4	0.2	5.2	0,5
Laborers, exc. farm & mine	12.1	3.7	4.7	4.3	6.2	2.1	--

Table 36 (continued)

Swedes			Origin			
	Norwegians	Spanish[c]	Black[s]	Puerto Ricans	Japanese	Chinese
Males employed	299,583	276,392	3,336,641	181,991	113.472	66,704
Percent	100.0	100.0	100.0	100.0	100.0	100.0
Prof. techn., & kindred wkrs.	13.1	4.2	3.0	2.7	12.6	18.3
Farmers & farm managers	9.7	1.3	6.2	0.1	12.0	0.7
Mgrs., offs., & props., exc., farm	14.8	3.6	0.9	3.1	9.5	15.5
Clerical & kindred wkrs.	7.6	5.8	4.9	7.3	7.6	7.6
Sales workers	7.2	3.4	1.2	2.7	5.8	6.0
Craftsmen, foremen, & kind. wkrs.	22.9	18.0	9.7	10.6	20.1	6.8
Operatives & kindred workers	13.7	18.0	24.3	38.8	11.5	12.5
Private household workers	5.8	0.6	--	--	--	--
Servicewkrs., exc. priv. household	4.3	6.6	0.7	0.06	4.7	22.7
Farm laborers & foremen	1.1	10.6	13.9	17.1	5.9	0.4
Laborers, exc. farm & mine	6.0	15.8	20.4	6.1	6.2	1.7

[a]Calculated from: U.S. Bureau of the Census, U.S. Census of Population: 1960. subjects, Nativity and Parentage, final Report PC (2)-A (Washington: Government Printing office, 1965), pp. 34-65, 70-80.

[b]U.S. Bureau of the Census, U.S. Census of Population: 1960. subject Reports, Nonwhite Population by Race, final Report PC (2)-C (Washington: Government Printing office, 1963), pp. 56-87.

[c]U.S. Bureau of the Census, U.S. Census of Population: 1960. subject Reports, Persons of Spanish surname. Report PC (2)-B, pp. 13-8.

[d]U.S. Bureau of the Census, U.S. Census of Population: 1960, Puerto Ricans in the United States final Report PC (2)-ID, pp. 11-34.

Table 37

Employment Status and Major Occupation of the Male Population Fourteen Years Old and Over, by Ethnic Origin, 1970[a]

				Origin			
Subject	Total	English	Germans	Irish	Italians	Poles	Russian Jews
Males employed	8,734,692	447,424	657,150	329,688	1,231,052	685,002	586,991
Percent	100.0	100.0	100.0	100.0	100.0	100.0	100.0
Prof., techn., & kindred wkrs.	11.2	19.6	14.3	17.6	12.5	15.5	25.4
Mgrs., adm., & exc. farm	9.8	16.0	13.4	15.0	13.7	11.5	23.5
Sales workers	5.5	8.6	7.4	8.4	7.5	7.2	16.0
Clerical & kindred wkrs.	7.1	9.1	7.6	12.3	9.0	8.7	7.5
Craftsmen, & kindred wkrs.	18.3	20.5	22.0	17.5	23.7	23.6	12.0
Operatives & exc. farm	13.8	9.0	10.3	7.0	11.9	16.7	5.2
Transport equip. operatives	7.0	4.2	4.6	4.9	6.2	4.5	3.5
Laborers, exc. farm	6.8	3.6	4.0	3.7	5.3	4.5	1.9
Farmers & farm managers	1.9	2.0	8.0	0.7	0.6	0.9	2.4
Farm laborers & farm foremen	2.1	0.5	1.3	0.3	0.2	0.2	0.4
Service wkrs., exc. priv. household	21.4	7.2	7.6	12.3	9.3	7.1	3.7
Private household workers	00.2	0.03	0.03	0.03	0.02	0.01	0.0

Table 37 (continued)

	Swedes	Norwegians	Hispanics	Blacks	West Indians	Japanese	Chinese
Males employed	204,424	151,127	360,098	3,933,984	27,881	84,142	33,606
Percent	100.0	100.0	100.0	100.0	100.0	100.0	100.0
Prof., techn., & kindred wkrs.	16.7	14.4	6.7	5.6	17.3	20.0	27.7
Mgrs., adm., & exc. farm	16.2	14.3	5.1	3.0	8.6	13.8	14.0
Sales workers	8.0	7.3	3.7	2.0	5.3	5.8	6.0
Clerical & kindred wkrs.	7.7	6.6	7.2	7.8	16.0	8.5	14.2
Craftsmen, & kindred wkrs.	22.0	21.5	21.9	15.2	16.7	22.2	10.5
Operatives & exc. farm	8.6	8.0	17.0	19.8	9.3	6.5	7.5
Transport equip. operatives	3.7	4.3	7.7	10.0	7.6	3.6	1.7
Laborers, exc. farm	3.5	4.0	12.0	16.0	6.0	9.0	4.2
Farmers & farm managers	6.7	11.5	0.5	0.9	0.9	4.3	0.7
Farm laborers & farm foremen	1.0	1.5	6.8	3.5	0.3	2.2	0.4
Servicewkrs., exc. priv. household	5.9	6.6	9.2	15.6	14.6	5.5	12.9
Private household workers	0.04	0.0	0.07	0.4	0.06	0.09	0.2

[a]U.S Bureau of the Census, Census of the Population: 1970, Subject Reports, Final Report PC (2)-1A.

Table 38

Highest Grade of School Completed by Persons Fourteen Years Old and Over, by Ethnic Origin, Male, 1950[a]

Percent Distribution by Years of School Completed

Origin	Total No (thousand)	Total Percent	Elementary			High School		College		Median School Yrs. Completed
			0-4 Yrs.	5-7 Yrs.	8 Yrs.	1-3 Yrs.	4 Yrs.	1-3 Yrs.	7 Yrs. or more	
Total	11,929,853	100.0	13.6	20.1	18.9	19.2	15.3	5.6	5.1	
English	612,515	100.0	3.9	12.2	21.0	20.4	21.8	9.6	9.1	10.7
Germans	1,673,760	100.0	6.5	18.8	32.2	15.5	14.7	5.5	5.5	8.7
Irish	804,425	100.0	3.8	12.4	23.4	20.6	22.5	7.8	7.8	10.0
Italians	1,364,750	100.0	2.9	12.7	20.1	29.6	23.7	5.6	4.2	10.4
Norwegians	297,325	100.0	4.1	14.6	30.8	16.1	18.2	8.4	6.6	9.0
Poles	871,580	100.0	3.6	13.3	21.8	25.4	21.8	7.0	5.9	10.2
Russian Jews	718,720	100.0	2.1	6.2	13.0	18.6	26.8	14.3	17.5	12.3
Spanish[b]	260,140	100.0	21.5	27.1	14.6	22.1	9.5	2.6	0.9	7.6
Swedes	398,590	100.0	2.5	10.1	26.7	19.2	22.9	9.3	8.2	10.6
Blacks[b]	4,717,840	100.0	26.7	29.3	12.0	15.8	7.5	2.8	1.5	6.6
Puerto Ricans[c]	99,185	100.0	15.9	24.3	19.9	17.9	9.5	3.2	2.2	8.2
Japanese[b]	57,645	100.0	4.1	4.2	13.5	13.9	36.2	11.6	7.7	12.2
Chinese[b]	53,480	100.0	15.1	15.8	11.5	14.3	14.6	9.1	9.1	8.4

[a]U.S. Bureau of the Census: 1950, vol. 4, Special Reports, Part 3, Final Report PC (2)-1A.

[b]U.S. Bureau of the Census: 1950, vol. 4, Special Reports, Part 3, Chapter B.

[c]U.S. Census of Population: 1950, Continental United States.

Table 39
Highest Grade of School Completed by Persons Fourteen Years Old and Over, by Ethnic Origin, Male 1960[a]

| | | | Percent Distribution by Years of School Completed | | | | | | | |
| | | | Elementary | | | High School | | College | | Median |
	Total No (thousand)	Total Percent	0-4 Yrs.	5-7 Yrs.	8, Yrs.	1-3 Yrs.	4 Yrs.	1-3 Yrs.	7 Yrs. or More	School Yrs. Completed
Total	12,391,165	100.0	11.1	18.8	17.3	24.3	18.9	7.5	7.0	10.0
English	848,367	100.0	2.9	10.9	17.4	22.2	23.3	11.5	11.8	11.5
Germans	1,475,457	100.0	5.8	18.4	28.5	17.4	16.0	7.3	6.7	8.9
Irish	626,142	100.0	10.8	19.3	22.5	23.4	10.7	11.7	11.0	11.3
Italians	1,505,313	100.0	2.6	11.1	17.4	29.1	25.2	7.4	17.2	10.9
Norwegians	287,051	100.0	3.6	13.6	27.6	16.7	20.4	9.4	8.7	9.9
Poles	938,061	100.0	3.2	12.5	18.7	35.1	22.1	8.7	9.8	10.9
Russian Jews	754,926	100.0	1.8	5.6	11.6	19.2	24.0	15.2	22.7	12.5
Spanish	389,074	100.0	21.1	20.7	13.7	23.8	13.6	5.1	2.1	8.6
Swedes	391,736	100.0	2.3	10.4	23.8	19.6	23.6	10.3	10.1	11.1
Blacks[b]	5,427,941	100.0	18.6	24.3	13.6	12.3	12.7	4.2	2.3	8.3
Puerto Ricans[c]	267,303	100.0	16.1	2.4	18.0	24.7	11.6	3.2	1.7	8.2
Japanese[d]	152,747	100.0	3.3	7.0	12.2	19.5	33.4	12.0	12.2	12.2
Chinese[d]	57,815	100.0	6.4	9.4	9.3	16.1	26.9	13.1	13.9	11.7

[a] U.S. Bureau of the Census: 1960, Final Report PC (2)-A, Final Report PC (2)-1A.
[b] U.S. Census of Population: 1960, Final Report, PC (2)-IB
[c] U.S. Census of Population: 1960, Final Report, PC (2)-IC
[d] U.S. Census of Population: 1960, Final Report, PC (2)-ID

Table 40

Highest Grade of School Completed by Persons Fourteen Years Old and Over, by Ethnic Origin, Male 1970[a]

Percent Distribution by Years of School Completed

	Total No (thousand)	Elementary				High School		College		Median School Yrs. Completed
		Total Percent	0-4 Yrs.	5-7 Yrs.	8 Yrs.	1-3 Yrs.	4 Yrs.	1-3 Yrs.	7 Yrs. or More	
Total	10,480,741	100.0	2.3	7.6	13.8	20.6	23.9	8.4	9.6	12.4
English	614,245	100.0	0.4	1.4	12.4	18.2	29.5	13.4	17.5	12.4
Germans	1,028,662	100.0	0.6	3.3	25.3	16.8	21.5	8.5	10.0	10.2
Irish	460,629	100.0	0.5	1.4	13.8	19.3	29.7	11.9	16.4	12.3
Italians	1,355,062	100.0	0.7	1.6	14.0	25.4	30.4	8.4	10.1	11.9
Norwegians	221,605	100.0	0.4	2.0	25.2	15.6	24.5	10.2	12.2	11.3
Polish	785,523	100.0	0.5	2.0	16.0	13.8	26.0	9.2	13.3	11.8
Russian Jews	664,142	100.0	0.5	1.0	9.3	14.7	26.3	14.9	28.6	12.8
Spanish	361,908	100.0	6.9	12.8	10.5	19.8	20.8	7.9	4.6	9.4
Swedes	297,561	100.0	0.3	1.2	19.8	17.5	28.3	11.6	13.9	12.1
Blacks	4,582,583	100.0	4.0	14.0	10.2	23.0	19.8	5.6	3.9	9.3
Chinese	31,908	100.0	3.7	3.5	5.4	10.5	26.0	16.0	27.4	12.7
Japanese	86,923	100.0	0.6	1.3	7.5	12.3	40.8	14.5	18.6	12.6
West Indians	29,990	100.0	1.4	1.9	6.0	20.1	34.0	15.0	14.8	12.4

SOURCE: U.S. Bureau of the Census, Census of the Population: 1970, Subject Reports, Final Report PC (2)-1A.12

Table 41
Class of Worker of the Native Population of Native Parentage by Ethnic Origin, 1970

Subject	Total	English	Germans	Irish	Italians	Norwegian	Poles	Russian Jews
Males employed	8,762,573	477,424	657,150	329,688	1,231,052	151,127	685,002	586,991
Percent	100.0	100.0	100.0	100.0	100.0	100.0	100.0	100.0
Private wage and salary workers	74.0	74.0	70.0	70.0	72.0	62.9	76.5	66.4
Federal government workers	6.3	4.9	3.7	6.5	4.9	5.0	4.8	4.9
State government workers	2.8	3.5	2.6	3.6	2.5	3.2	2.2	2.6
Local government workers	7.3	7.6	6.3	12.6	8.5	7.3	6.4	5.8
Self-employed workers	8.7	9.7	17.0	7.1	11.3	21.5	9.6	20.2
Unpaid family workers	0.2	0.1	0.4	0.1	0.0	0.3	0.1	0.1
Females employed	5,877,737	278,658	359,589	204,156	650,890	85,486	384,400	319,863
Percent	100.0	100.0	100.0	100.0	100.0	100.0	100.0	100.0
Private wage and salary workers	74.8	73.7	75.4	75.5	80.0	70.0	80.0	71.1
Federal government workers	5.3	3.3	3.0	3.5	2.5	3.8	2.5	3.1
State government workers	4.8	4.5	3.9	4.2	3.0	4.7	2.8	3.6
Local government workers	11.6	13.5	10.8	13.8	9.3	14.5	9.5	14.7
Self-employed workers	2.9	4.0	5.3	2.4	3.6	5.4	3.6	5.7
Unpaid family workers	0.7	1.0	1.7	0.7	0.9	1.8	1.1	1.8

Table 41 (continued)

	Mexicans	Swedes	Blacks	Indians	Japanese	Chinese
Males employed	360,098	204,428	3,933,984	27,881	84,142	33,606
Percent	100.0	100.0	100.0	100.0	100.0	100.0
Private wage and salary workers	78.8	69.3	77.0	63.6	63.0	62.9
Federal government workers	6.9	4.5	7.5	11.0	9.1	12.4
State government workers	2.4	3.2	3.0	3.9	5.1	6.3
Local government workers	6.6	6.4	8.0	16.6	5.2	5.9
Self-employed workers	5.2	2.7	4.6	4.7	17.3	11.4
Unpaid family workers	0.2	0.8	0.1	0.0	0.2	0.8
Females employed	184,714	115,806	3,193,920	23,137	56,240	20,870
Private wage and salary workers	70.0	71.5	73.5	61.8	67.0	65.5
Federal government workers	4.5	3.3	1.0	7.7	6.3	6.5
State government workers	3.6	4.7	5.6	5.9	11.2	9.1
Local government workers	8.7	14.2	11.9	22.0	7.2	11.1
Self-employed workers	2.5	4.7	1.8	2.3	5.8	4.9
Unpaid family workers	0.5	1.5	0.2	0.3	2.3	2.6

SOURCE: Calculated from: U.S. Bureau of Census, Census of the Population 1970: Subject Report, Final Report PC (2)-1A, National Origin and Language (Washington: Government Printing Office, 1973).

Table 42
Employment Status and Major Occupation of the Female Population Fourteen Years Old and Over by Ethnic Origin, 1970

Subject	Total	English	Germans	Origin Irish	Italians	Poles	Russian Jews
Females employed	5,854,600	278,658	359,589	204,156	650,893	384,400	319,863
Percent	100.0	100.0	100.0	100.0	100.0	100.0	100.0
Prof., techn., & kindred wkrs.	12.7	20.3	15.0	19.8	9.7	11.8	19.6
Mgrs., adm., & exc. farm	2.9	5.2	4.7	5.0	3.9	3.9	6.9
Sales workers	5.4	8.6	9.0	6.6	9.3	8.7	12.0
Clerical & kindred wkrs.	28.7	42.5	37.0	47.0	37.90	35.6	4.5
Craftsmen, & kindred wkrs.	1.8	4.5	2.0	1.3	2.2	2.6	1.2
Operatives & exc. farm	15.3	7.5	10.1	6.5	21.5	22.0	5.9
Transport equip. operatives	0.5	0.4	0.3	0.2	0.3	0.3	0.1
Laborers, exc. farm	1.2	0.6	0.8	0.4	0.8	1.0	0.4
Farmers & farm managers	0.2	0.2	0.7	0.07	0.05	0.1	0.1
Farm laborers & farm foremen	0.8	0.2	0.6	0.06	0.07	0.1	0.1
Service wkrs., exc. priv. household	20.1	12.1	16.0	11.1	3.6	13.8	7.6
Private household workers	10.6	0.03	3.4	1.3	0.6	1.5	8.6

Table 42 (continued)

	Origin						
	Swedes	Norwegians	Hispanics	Blacks	West Indians	Japanese	Chinese
Females employed	115,806	85,486	360,098	3,193,920	23,137	56,240	20,875
Percent	100.0	100.0	100.0	100.0	100.0	100.0	100.0
Prof., techn., & kindred wkrs.	18.7	18.2	6.7	11.1	20.6	15.3	19.6
Mgrs., adm., & exc. farm	5.5	5.3	5.1	1.6	3.8	4.7	4.2
Sales workers	8.5	5.3	3.7	1.6	3.8	4.7	4.2
Clerical & kindred wkrs.	40.4	35.7	7.2	20.4	43.8	37.1	47.7
Craftsmen & kindred wkrs.	1.7	15.7	21.9	1.4	1.6	2.3	1.2
Operatives & exc. farm	7.5	7.8	17.0	16.3	8.6	12.0	5.2
Transport equip. operatives	0.4	0.2	7.7	0.4	0.2	0.08	0.1
Laborers, exc. farm	0.6	0.7	12.0	1.5	0.6	0.9	0.8
Farmers & farm managers	0.3	0.6	0.5	0.2	0.1	0.9	0.1
Farm laborers & farm foremen	0.4	0.6	6.8	1.0	0.3	1.6	0.9
Service wkrs., exc. priv. household	13.3	17.4	9.2	25.7	13.5	14.5	11.7
Private household workers	2.8	3.5	0.07	18.0	3.2	3.5	1.5

[a] U.S Bureau of the Census, Census of the population: 1970, Subject Reports, Final Report PC (2)-1A.

Table 43
Highest Grade of School Completed by Person Fourteen Years Old and Over, by Ethnic Origin: Female, 1970

Origin	Total (thousand)	Total Percent	Elementary 0-4 Yrs.	5-7 Yrs.	8 Yrs.	High School 1-3 Yrs.	4 Yrs.	College 1-3 Yrs.	7 Yrs. or More	Median School Yrs. Completed
Total	12,141,262	100.0	1.8	5.6	12.7	14.1	22.7	29.0	5.9	--
English	728,816	100.0	0.4	1.0	5.9	12.0	18.6	36.7	9.9	12.3
Germans	1,235,590	100.0	0.5	2.9	13.1	26.1	17.3	26.5	5.3	10.3
Irish	582,670	100.0	0.4	1.2	6.5	14.3	18.3	40.3	10.0	10.3
Italians	1,404,142	100.0	0.9	1.8	9.5	16.0	24.5	37.9	3.9	11.7
Norwegians	254,435	100.0	0.3	1.2	6.5	20.4	15.5	33.3	7.6	12.2
Polish	843,642	100.0	0.6	2.2	1.0	18.9	22.4	32.5	5.8	11.3
Russian Jews	711,901	100.0	0.5	1.0	4.1	10.0	14.7	43.0	13.1	12.5
Spanish	378,579	100.0	6.5	13.2	18.5	13.6	20.5	22.3	2.1	9.0
Swedes	354,807	100.0	0.3	0.8	5.4	16.7	17.3	35.6	7.7	12.2
Blacks	5,505,598	100.0	2.7	9.4	18.2	10.8	17.2	21.9	4.5	10.0
West Indian	32,249	100.0	1.6	1.1	4.8	5.5	26.6	44.4	11.0	12.7
Chinese	25,415	100.0	3.2	2.9	2.9	4.7	8.4	36.7	20.1	12.7

SOURCE: U.S. Bureau of the Census, Census of the Population: 1970, Subject Reports, Final Report PC (2)-1A.

Selected Bibliography

Abrahams, Israel. *Jewish Life in the Middle Ages.* London: Macmillan, 1897.

Blalock, Jr., Hubert M. *Toward a Theory of Minority-Group Relations.* New York: Wiley, 1967.

Adams, John T. *The Founding of New England.* New York: Atlantic Monthly, 1963.

Allen, Walter R. "Black Family Research in the United States: A Review, Assessment and Extension." *Journal of Comparative Family Studies* 9 (Autumn 1978): 167-189.

__. "Class, Culture and Family Organization: The Effects of Class and Race on Family Structure in Urban America." *Journal of Comparative Family Studies* 10 (Autumn 1979): 301-313.

Andrew, Charles M. *The Colonial Period of American History.* New Haven: Yale University Press, 1938.

Ardener, Shirley. "The Comparative Study of Rotating Credit Associations." *Journal of the Royal Anthropological Institute* 94, pt. 2 (1964): 201-229.

Arkoff, Abe. "Need Patterns in Two Generations of Japanese Americans in Hawaii." *Journal of Social Psychology* 50 (August 1959): 75-79.

Arsensberg, Conrad. *The Irish Country-Man: An Anthropological Study.* New York: Macmillan, 1937.

Auletta, Ken. *The Underclass.* New York: Random House, 1982.

Bailey, Thomas A. *The American Pageant.* Boston: D.C. Heath and Company, 1956.

Balch, Emily Greene. *Our Slavic Fellow Citizens, Charities Publication Committee.* New York: John Wiley and Sons, 1910.

Banks, Charles. The *English Ancestry and Homes of the Pilgrims Fathers* .Baltimore: Genealogical Publishers Company, 1971.

Batten, J. Minton. *Protestant Background in History.* New York and Nashville: Abingdon-Cokesbury Press, 1946.

Becker, Gary S. *The Economics of Discrimination.* Chicago: University of Press, 1957.

__. *Human Capital.* New York: Columbia University Press, 1964.

Bienenfeld, F. R. *The Germans and the Jews.* New York: University of Chicago Press, 1960.

Blassingame, John W. The *Slave Community.* New York: Oxford University Press, 1972. Darling

Blumberg, Paul. *Inequality in An Age of Decline.* New York: Oxford University Press, 1980.

Brown, Lawrence Guy. *Immigration.* New York: Longmans, Green and Company, 1933.

Carmichael, Stokely, and Hamilton, Charles. *Black Power.* New York: Vintage Books, 1967.

Cash, Wilbur. J. *The Mind of the South.* New York: Vintage Books, 1960.

Caudhill, William. "Japanese-American Personality and Acculturation." *Genetic Psychology Monographs* 45 (February 1942): 3-102.

Chambers, Jonathon D. "Enclosures and the Rural Population: A Revision." in *The Industrial Revolution in Britain.* eds. A. M. Taylor, Boston: D.C. Heath and Company, 1958. pp. 43-63.

Chenault, Lawrence. *Puerto Rican Migrants in New York City.* New York: DuBois Columbia University Press, 1938.

Chitwood, Oliver P. *A History of Colonial America.* New York: Harper and Brothers, 1931.

Claghorn, Kate H. "The Foreign Immigrant in New York City." In United States Industrial Commission, *Reports on Immigration.* 42 vols. Washington, D.C.: Government Printing Office, 1901, 15: 442-494.

Clark, Victor S. *History of Manufacturers in the United States:* 1607-1860. New York: McGraw-Hill Co., 1929.

Clark, Helen F. "The Chinese of New York Contrasted with Their Foreign Neighbors." *Century* 53 (November 1899): 110.

Clarkson, L. A. The *Pre-Industrial Economy in England* 1500-1700. New York: Schocken Books, 1972.

Cobb, Sanford H. *The Rise of Religious Liberty in America.* New York: Research Service, 1970.

Cochran, Thomas. *The Puerto Rican Businessman.* Philadelphia: University of Pennsylvania Press, 1959.

Commons, John R. *Races and Immigrants in America.* New York: Macmillan, 1913.

Crosby, Fay J. *Relative Depravation and Working Women.* New York: Oxford,1982.

Cruse, Harold. *The Crisis of the Negro Intellectual.* New York: Morrow, 1961.

Curtis, Edmund. *A History of Ireland.* London: Methuen and Company, 1968.

Dahl, Robert, *Who Governs?* New Haven: Yale University Press, 1971,

Darling-Hammond, L. *Equality and Excellence: The Educational Status of Black Americans.* Santa Monica, Calif.: Rand, 1985.

Davie, Maurice. *World Immigration.* New York: Macmillan, 1936.

Davies, Margaret G. The *Enforcement of English Apprenticeship.* Cambridge: Harvard University Press, 1956.

Davis, Allison, Gardner, Burleigh B. and Gardner, Mary R. *Deep South.* Chicago: University of Chicago Press, 1941.

Deutsch, Martin. "Equity, Equality, and Need: What Determines Which Value Will Be Used As the Basis of Distributive Justice?" *Journal of Social Issues,* 31(2): 137-149.

Dobb, Maurice. *Studies in the Development of Capitalism.* New York: International Publishers, 1963.

Drake, St. Clair, and Clayton, Horace R. *Black Metropolis.* New York: Harper and Row, 1962.

DuBois, W. E. B. "The Freedman's Bureau." *Atlantic Monthly* 87 (1901): 354- 365.

___..*Black Reconstruction in America:* 1860-1880. Cleveland: World, 1935.

___. The *Philadelphia Negro.* New York: Benjamin Blom, 1967.

___. *The Souls of Black Folk.* New York: Fawcett World Library, 1961.

___. The *Suppression of the African Slave Trade.* Baton Rouge: Louisiana State University Press, 1965.

___. The *Negro American Family.* Cambridge, MA.: MIT Press, 1970.

Elazer, Daniel J. *Cities of the Prairie,* New York: Basic Books, 1970.

___. Embree, John F. *Suye Mura: A Japanese Village.* Chicago: University of Chicago Press, 1939.

Ernst, Robert. *Immigrant Life in New York City:* 1825-1863. New York: King's Crown Press, Columbia University, 1949.

Eulau, Heinz. *The Behavioral Persuasion in Politics.* New York: Random House, 1967.

Evans-Gordon, Major W. *The Alien Immigrant.* London: William Heinemann, 1903.

Fankelsurd, Alfred O. *The Scandinavian-American.* Minneapolis: K. C. Halter Company, 1915.

Feagin, Joe R. *Subordinating the Poor.* Englewood Cliffs, NJ.: Prentice-Hall, 1975.

Foerster, Robert F. The *Italian Emigration of Our Times.* New York: Russell and Russell, 1968.

Franklin, John H. *Reconstruction After the Civil War.* Chicago: University of Chicago Press, 1961.

___. *From Slavery to Freedom.* New York: Alfred A. Knopf, 1967.

Frazier, E. Franklin. *The Negro in the United States.* New York: Macmillan, 1967.

Geiser, Karl Frederick. *Redemptioners and Indentured Servants in the Colony and Commonwealth.* New Haven: Tuttle, Marchouse and Talyer, 1901.

Gilder, George. *Wealth and Poverty.* New York: Basic Books,1981.

Glazer, Nathan. *Affirmative Discrimination.* New York: Basic Books, 1975.

Gusset, Thomas F. *Race: The History of an Idea in America.* Dallas: SDU Press, 1963.

Grant, Madison. *The Conquest of a Continent.* New York: Charles Scribner's Sons, 1933.

Gutman Herbert. "Persistent Myths About the American Negro Family." *Journal of Interdisciplinary History* 6 (Autumn 1975): 181-210.

___. *The Black Family in Slavery and Freedom,* 1750-1925. New York: Pantheon Books, 1976.

Handlin, Oscar. *Boston's Immigrants.* Cambridge: Harvard University Press, "1959.

__. *The Newcomers.* Cambridge: Harvard University Press, 1959. *The Uprooted.* Boston: Little, Brown and Company, 1951.

Hansen, Marcus Lee. *The Atlantic Migration 1607-1860.* Cambridge: Harvard University Press, 1940.

Harrington, Michael. *Other America.* New York: Macmillan, 1962.

Hernton, Calvin. *Sex and Racism in America.* New York: Grove Press, 1965.

Higgs, Robert. *Competition and Coercion: Blacks in American Economy: 1865-1914.* Chicago: University Press, 1977.

Hill, Robert. *The Strengths of the Black Family.* New York: Emerson Hall, 1971.

__. "The Synthetic Method: Its Feasibility for Deriving the Census Undercount for States and Local Areas." In *Proceedings of Tile Conference on Census Undercount.* Washington, D.C.: Government Printing Office, 1980.

__. "The Economic Status of Blacks in America." In James D. Williams, ed. *The State of Black America.* Washington, D.C.: National Urban League, 1981.

Hirschman, Charles, and Wong, Morrison G. "Socioeconomic Gains of Asians Americans, Blacks and Hispanics: 1960-1976." *American Journal of Sociology* 190 (November 1984): 584-607.

Hirsh, Arthur H. The *Huguenots of Colonial South Carolina.* Durham: University of North Carolina Press, 1928.

Huber, Joan, and Form, W. H. *Income and Ideology.* New York: Free Press, 1973.

Hutchinson, Edward P. *Immigrants and Their Children: 1850-1950.* New York: John Wiley and Sons, 1956.

Jasso, G., and Rossi, P. H. "Distributive Justice and Earned Income," *American Sociological Review* 42 (1977): 639-651.

Jencks, Christopher. *Inequality.* New York: Basic Books, 1972.

Jernegan, Marcus W. *The American Colonies: 1492-1750.* New York: Longmans, Green and Company, 1956.

Jones, Maldwyn A. *American Immigration.* Chicago: University of Chicago Press, 1960.

Kinder, Dennis R., and Sears, Donald O., "Prejudice and Politics: Symbolic Racism vs. Racial Threats to the Good Life," *Journal of Personality and Social Psychology* 40 (1981): 414-431.

Kitano, Harry H. L. *The Evolution of a Subculture.* Englewood Cliffs, N.J.: Prentice-Hall, 1964.

Kluegel, James. R., and Smith, E. R. "Affirmative Action Attitudes: Effects of Self-Interest, Racial Affect, and Stratification Beliefs on Whites' Views." *Social Forces* 61 (1982): 797-824.

__. "Whites' Beliefs About Blacks' Opportunity." *American Sociological Review* 47 (1982): 518-532.

Knowles, Louis L., and Prewitt, Kenneth, eds. *Institutional Racism in America.* Englewood Cliffs, N.J.: Prentice-Hall, 1969.

Kulp, Daniel H. *Country Life in South China.* 2 vols. New York: Columbia University Press, 1925.

Levine, Edward M. The *Irish and Irish Politicians*. Notre Dame: University of Notre Dame Press, 1966.

Lewis, Michael. *The Culture of Inequality*. Amherst, Mass.: University of Massachusetts, 1979.

Lewis, Oscar. *La Vida*. New York: Random House, 1968.

Lieberson, Stanley. "A Societal Theory of Race and Ethnic Relations:"' *American Sociological Review* 26 (December 1961): 902-910.

Light, Ivan H. *Ethnic Enterprise in America*. Berkeley: University of California Press, 1972.

Litwack, Leon F. *North of Slavery*. Chicago: University of Chicago Press, 1961.

Long, Larry, "Poverty Status and Receipt of Welfare Among Migrants and Non-Migrants in Large Cities." *American Sociological Review* 39 (February 1974): 46-57.

___. and Heltman, Lynne R. "Migration and Income Differences Between Black and White Men in the North." *American Journal of Sociology* 80 (May 1975): 1391-1409.

Marshall, Ray, and Christian, Jr., Virgil L. "Economics of Employment Discrimination." In Ray Marshall and Virgil L. Christian, Jr., eds. *Employment of Blacks in the South*. Austin: University of Texas, 1978.

Martin, Elmer, and Martin, Joanne. *The Black Extended Family*. Chicago: University of Chicago Press, 1978.

Masters, Stanley H. *Black-White Income Differentials: Empirical Studies and Policy Implications*. New York: Academic Press, 1975.

McConahay, John. B., and Hough, Jr., J. C. "Symbolic Racism." *Journal of Social Issues* 32 (1976): 23-45.

Meeker, Edward. "Mortality Trends of Southern Blacks, 1850-1910: Some Preliminary Findings." *Explorations in Economic History* 13 (January 1976): 13-42.

___. "Freedom, Economic Opportunity and Fertility: Black Americans, 1860-1910." *Economic Inquiry* 15 (July 1977): 397-412.

Meier, August. *Negro Thought in America: 1880-1915*. Ann Arbor: University of Michigan Press, 1968.

Meier, August, and Rudwick, Elliott. *Black Detroit and the Rise of the UAW*. New York: Oxford University Press, 1979.

Meyers, Jerome. "Assimilation to the Ecological and Social Systems of a Community." *American Sociological Review* 15 (December 1950): 367-672.

Michelson, Stephen. *Incomes of Racial Minorities*. Washington, D.C.: Brookings Institution, 1968.

Miller, Herman P. *Rich Man, Poor Man*. New York: Crowell, 1964.

Mills, C. Wright, and Senior, Clarence. *The Puerto Rican Journey*. New York: Harper and Brothers, 1950.

Murray, Charles. *Losing Ground: American Social Policy: 1950-1980*. New York: Basic Books, 1984.

Myrdal, Gunnar. *An American Dilemma*. New York: Harper and Row, 1962.

Nobles, Wade. "Toward an Empirical and Theoretical Framework for Defining Black Families." *Journal of Marriage and the Family* 40 (November 1979): 679-690.

Osofsky, Gilbert. *Harlem: The Making of a Ghetto.* New York: Harper and Row, 1963.

Ottley, Roi, and Weatherby, William, eds. *The Negro in New York.* New York: Oceana Publications, 1942.

Parkin, Frank. *Class, Inequality and Political Order.* New York: Praeger, 1971.

Pettigrew, Thomas F. "Race and Class in the 1980's: An Interactive View."
*Daedalus*110 (1981): 233-256.

Philpott, Stuart B. *West Indian Migration: The Monserrat Case.* New York: Athlone Press, 1973.

Plotnick, Robert D., and Skidmore, Felicity. *Progress Against Poverty: A Review of the* 1965-1974 *Decade.* New York: Academic Press, 1975.

Pomfret, John E. *The Struggle for Land in Ireland: 1800-1923.* Princeton: Princeton University Press, 1930.

Rand, Christopher. *The Puerto Ricans.* New York: Oxford University Press, 1958.

Reich, Michael. *Racial Inequality: Political-Economic Analysis.* Princeton, N.J .: Princeton University Press, 1981.

Reid, Ira De A. *The Negro Immigrant.* New York: Columbia University Press, 1939.

Rodgers, Harrell R., Jr. "Fair Employment Laws for Minorities: An Evaluation of Federal Implementation." In Charles S. Bullock III and Charles M. Lamb, eds. *Implementation of Civil Rights Policy.* Monterey, CA: Brooks/Cole, 1984.

Rolle, Andrew F. *The American Italians: Their History and Culture.* Belmont, Calif.: Wadsworth Publishing Company, 1972.

Rudwick, Elliott M. *Race Riots at East St. Louis, July 2, 1917.* Cleveland: World, 1966.

Runcimand, Walther G. *Relative Deprivation and Social Justice.* Berkeley: University of California Press, 1966.

Sandell, S. J., and Shapiro, D. "An Exchange: Theory of Human Capital and the Earnings of Women: A Reexamination of the Evidence." *Journal of Human Resources* 13 (Winter 1978): 103-117.

Scanzoni, John. *The Black Family in Modem Society.* Boston: Allyn and Bacon, 1971.

Schiava, Giovanni. The *Italians in America Before the Civil War.* New York: Alfred A. Knopf. 1943.

Smith, J. Owens. "Affirmative Action, Reverse Discrimination and the Courts: Implications for Blacks." In Mitchell P. Rice and Woodrow Jones, Jr. eds. *Contemporary Public Policy Perspectives and Black Americans.* Westport, Conn.: Greenwood Press, 1984.

___. "The Bakke Decision: A Flagrant Denial of Human Rights." *Western Journal of Black Studies* 2 (Winter 1979): 244-255.

___. "The Politics of Income and Education Differences Between Blacks and West Indians." *The Journal of Ethnic Studies* 13 (Fall 1985) 3: 17-30.

___. and Jackson, Carl. *Race and Ethnicity: A Study of Intracultural Socialization Patterns.* Dubuque: Kendall/Hunt, 1989.

Smith, Abbot Emerson. *Colonists in Bondage*. Chapel Hill: University of North Carolina Press, 1947.

Sowell, Thomas, *Race and Economics*. New York: McKay Company, Inc., 1975.

Staples, Robert, "Towards a Sociology of the Black Family: A Decade of Theory and Research." *Journal of Marriage and the Family* (February 1971): 19-38.

Steinberg, Stephen. *The Ethnic Myth*. Boston: Beacon Press, 1981.

Sudarkasa, Niara. "Interpreting the African Heritage in Afro-American Family Organization." In Harriette P. McAdoo, ed. *Black Families*. Beverly Hills, Calif.: Sage Publications, 1981.

Thernstrom, Stephen. *The Other Bostonians*. Cambridge: Harvard University Press, 1973.

Thomas, Brinley. *International Migration and Economic Development*. Paris: UNESCO, 1961.

Thurow, Lester C. *Poverty and Discrimination*. Washington, D.C.: Brookings Institution, 1969.

Veblen, Thorstein. "The Intellectual Pre-Eminence of Jews in Modern Europe." In Leon Arozrooni, ed., *Essays in Our Changing Order*. New York: Viking Press, 1937.

Waddel, D. A. G. *The West Indies and Guians*. Englewood Cliffs, N.J.: Prentice- Hall, 1967.

Weber, Max. *Protestant Ethic and the Rise of the Spirit of Capitalism*. New York: Charles Scribner's Sons, 1958.

White, Trumbull. *Puerto Rico and Its People*. New York: Frederick S. Stokes, 1938.

Wilensky, H. L. *The Welfare State and Social Equality*. Berkeley: University of California Press, 1975.

Williamson, J. B. "Beliefs About Motivation of Poor and Attitudes Toward Poverty Policy ." *Social Problems* 21: 634-648.

Willie, Charles. *Black/Brown/White Relations*. New Brunswick, N.J.: Transaction, 1977.

___ . *The Sociology of Urban Education*. Lexington Books of D.C. Heath, 1978.

___. *Race, Ethnicity, and Socioeconomic Status: A Theoretical Analysis of their Interrelations*. Bayside, New York: General Hall, Inc., 1983.

Wilson, William J. *The Declining Significance of Race*. Chicago: University of Chicago Press, 1978.

Wirth, Louis. *The Ghetto*. Chicago: University of Chicago Press, 1929.

Wittke, Carl. *We Who Built America*. Cleveland: Case Western University Press, 1967.

Woodson, Carter G. *A Century of Negro Migration*. New York: Russell and Russell, 1969.

Woodward, C. Vann. *The Strange Career of Jim Crow*. New York: Oxford University Press, 1957.

Index